REINVENTING
AMERICA'S SCHOOLS

REINVENTING AMERICA'S SCHOOLS

∙ ∙ ∙

CREATING A 21ST CENTURY
EDUCATION SYSTEM

DAVID OSBORNE

BLOOMSBURY

NEW YORK · LONDON · OXFORD · NEW DELHI · SYDNEY

Bloomsbury USA
An imprint of Bloomsbury Publishing Plc

1385 Broadway	50 Bedford Square
New York	London
NY 10018	WC1B 3DP
USA	UK

www.bloomsbury.com

BLOOMSBURY and the Diana logo are trademarks of Bloomsbury
Publishing Plc

First published 2017

ISBN: HB: 978-1-63286-991-3
        ePub: 978-1-63286-993-7

Library of Congress Cataloging-in-Publication Data is available.

2 4 6 8 10 9 7 5 3 1

Typeset by Westchester Publishing Services
Printed and bound in the U.S.A. by Berryville Graphics Inc., Berryville,
Virginia

To find out more about our authors and books visit www.bloomsbury.com.
Here you will find extracts, author interviews, details of forthcoming events
and the option to sign up for our newsletters.

Bloomsbury books may be purchased for business or promotional use. For
information on bulk purchases please contact Macmillan Corporate and
Premium Sales Department at specialmarkets@macmillan.com.

For Christyne J. Vachon, with love and gratitude

TABLE OF CONTENTS

Education is the most powerful weapon we can use to change the world.

—NELSON MANDELA

PREFACE & ACKNOWLEDGMENTS

THE QUALITY OF OUR PUBLIC SCHOOLS will determine much about the future quality of our lives, our economy, and our society. Like most of the public sector, our school systems are experiencing profound change. Slowly but surely, they are adapting to the new realities of the Information Age.

I have been researching, writing about, and participating in this process of public sector reform for 30 years, since Ted Gaebler and I began work on our bestselling book, *Reinventing Government.* In school districts, cities, states, and other nations, centralized operations are decentralizing; accountability for following rules is giving way to accountability for delivering results; monopolies are yielding to competition; cookie-cutter services are being replaced by choices between different service providers; and hierarchical systems that employ all their workers are giving way to distributed networks that use performance contracts and other means to get services delivered by others.

In the U.S., a few cities have used these principles to pioneer an entirely new way of organizing public education. These reforms, in New Orleans, Washington, D.C., and Denver, have produced the fastest academic growth in the nation, encouraging others to emulate them. In this book I will describe these three cities' reforms in depth, because I want to communicate concretely how and why they came about, how political struggles were won, what worked, what failed, and how failures were addressed. I want you, the reader, to go beyond the usual abstractions of eduspeak to understand the concrete realities of this quiet revolution—and beyond the ideological slogans that so dominate debate of the realities.

I hope that what I have written is useful to a broad spectrum of people, from education reformers and school leaders to teachers and parents and community activists. But I also hope it is useful to the people who shape our education systems: governors, state legislators, district leaders, and school board members. I realize that not every chapter will be equally useful to all readers, and I have tried to place the more technical information—which may be valuable to those in the trenches but not to parents or other community members—in appendices. Still, there may be times when a general reader needs to skip the policy details and move on to the story. Be assured that such behavior is fine with the author.

Finally, let me be clear that this is not a book about "charter schools." It is about a new way to organize public education, in which we treat every public school—regardless of what we call it—like a charter school. In the preface to *Reinventing Government*, we quoted Marcel Proust, who wrote, "The real voyage of discovery consists not in seeking new lands, but in seeing with new eyes." After you read this book, I hope you will never again see charter schools as a minor innovation around the edges of the public system. Instead, I hope you will see them—and the "innovation schools," "renaissance schools," and "pilot schools" they have inspired—as a 21st century system emerging to supplant the old one.

As I DID this research, I benefited from the wisdom of hundreds of people involved in these reforms, who shared their stories, their thoughts, and their schools with me. Not least among them was my daughter Molly, who taught for three years at a struggling charter school in New Orleans. Hearing her stories and visiting her school, I could not escape confronting the difficult, often painful realities of educating poor minority children in the inner city— the nitty-gritty of reform, if you will. I could never float too far into the realm of abstraction.

I am deeply indebted to all of those who volunteered their time and knowledge in interviews. Some went above and beyond to help me repeatedly, and I would be remiss not to thank them by name: from New Orleans, Leslie Jacobs, Jay Altman, Paul Pastorek, Paul Vallas, Patrick Dobard, and Kevin Guitterrez; from Washington, D.C., Mary Levy, Josephine Baker, Robert Cane, Scott Pearson, Pete Weber, and Jenny Niles; from Denver, Van Schoales, Mary Seawell, Alyssa Bust-Whitehead, and Christine Nelson; and from Indianapolis, David Harris. For wise counsel in general over the years I am grateful to Doug Ross, Paul Hill, Chris Gabrieli, Bruno Manno, Mike Petrilli, Checker Finn, Andy Smarick, Neerav Kingsland, and Will Marshall. Finally, I must also thank my daughter, Anne, who put in a summer of research to help me drag the book closer to the finish line.

At the Progressive Policy Institute, where I direct a project on Reinventing America's Schools, I am eternally grateful to Will Marshall for his leadership; Sloane Hurst for her incredible talent with fundraising and events; Steven Chlapecka and Jana Plat for guiding my PPI reports through to publication; and Virat Singh, Cullen Wells, Emil Kunkin, and Taylor Miller-Freutel for their help with research and Excel graphs. I also want to thank Adam Hawf,

David Harris, Ethan Gray, and their colleagues for helping us pull off successful conferences in Denver and Indianapolis.

I am extremely grateful to our funders at the Walton Family Foundation, the Eli and Edythe Broad Foundation, and the John and Laura Arnold Foundation, without whom this book would not exist. I am also indebted to the Gates Family Foundation, Gary Community Investments, the Richard M. Fairbanks Foundation, and the Joyce Foundation for their support of PPI forums and conferences.

I want to extend a special thanks to a wonderful publisher, George Gibson, who saw the value in *Reinventing Government* 30 years ago, when he bought it for Addison-Wesley, and the value in *Reinventing America's Schools* this time around. I'm also grateful to an excellent editor, Anton Mueller, whose insight and wisdom have now guided two of my books through to publication. Many thanks also to Bloomsbury's team, particularly Sara Kitchen and Grace McNamee, for all their patient assistance.

Finally, I want to thank my wife and partner, Christyne J. Vachon, whose love, generosity, kindness, and good advice have helped immensely through a six-year process of research and writing. I will be forever grateful.

David Osborne
Gloucester, MA
May, 2017

INTRODUCTION

FOR A CENTURY, OUR PUBLIC education system was the backbone of our success as a nation. By creating one of the world's first mass education systems, free to all children, we forged the most educated workforce in the world—a key pillar of our economic strength. Our schools also helped us assimilate waves of immigrants, first from Europe, later from Latin America and Asia. Public schools offered relatively equal opportunity—if only to those with white skin—and built the world's broadest middle class. As we slowly integrated them, they supported our multiracial democracy by putting children from many different walks of life together, to learn that beneath their different accents and skin colors they were all human beings, with similar experiences and similar potential. I myself benefited enormously from attending public schools with classmates from all races and income levels; that experience shaped me in profound ways, because it taught me that most humans are good and decent, regardless of how different they look, dress, or talk.

But all institutions must change with the times, and since the 1960s, the times have changed. First, television emerged to dominate the lives of young people, undermining their desire and ability to read. Then the cultural rebellions of the 1960s and '70s brought new problems, including widespread drug use and the decline of the two-parent family. Teen pregnancy soared, the percentage of children raised by single mothers tripled, arrest rates for those under 18 shot up, and gang activity exploded. Meanwhile, immigration picked up, doubling the percentage of public school children from households that didn't speak English, from 10 to 20 percent.

At the same time, our Information Age economy radically raised the bar students needed to meet to secure jobs that would support middle-class lifestyles. And computer technologies created enormous opportunities to personalize education, so each student could learn at his or her own pace.

Held back by their traditional structures, rules, and union contracts, our public schools struggled to seize these opportunities and respond to these challenges. It's not that they declined in quality, but that they failed to respond to drastically different conditions. After all, 20th century bureaucracies were built to foster stability, not innovation. When Paul R. Mort studied the spread of successful innovations in public schools, he found that it took about fifty years, on average, for a new method to be widely implemented.

Today our traditional public schools "work" for less than half of our students. One in five families chooses something other than a traditional public school—a private school, a public charter school, or home schooling. Among those who do attend public schools, 17 percent fail to graduate on time. Even more graduate but lack the skills necessary to succeed in today's job market. Almost a quarter of those who apply to the U.S. Army fail its admission tests, more than a third of those who go on to college are not prepared for first-year college courses, and half of college students never graduate.

A large portion of middle- and high-schoolers are monumentally bored by their public schools. Only one in three rate their school culture positively. Karen Fisher, a successful writer and parent of three, offers rare insight into how much "the Internet has shifted the education game."

> *Most kids my son's age are deeply questioning the validity of formal classes past fifth grade. He and his friends learn so much more and so much faster on their own. They wait through the school day with antique teachers and an antique curriculum, then race home and learn on YouTube how to weld on their own—and everything they need to know about rehabilitating car batteries—and they start making wind generators, or whatever interests them.*
>
> *This is how natural education works: You have a problem or an inspiration, you ask someone who knows, they show you how, you do it. You fail, with no consequence except you didn't achieve what you desperately wanted to achieve. The failure spurs you to seek more information. You do, and you learn it. With the new information, you can do it better, maybe succeed. From that success, you envision the next step. And so on.*
>
> *Public school education does the exact reverse of natural education, which is why it doesn't work. The people who make policy are twenty years behind.*

Among developed nations, the United States ranks 18th or worse in high school graduation rates and in the bottom half in math, science, and reading proficiency. In 2014, the National Conference of State Legislatures launched an 18-month study of the international standing of American public schools. Two years later its report painted a dire picture:

The bad news is most state education systems are falling dangerously behind the world in a number of international comparisons and on our own National Assessment of Educational Progress, leaving the United States overwhelmingly underprepared to succeed in the 21st century economy. The U.S. workforce, widely acknowledged to be the best educated in the world half a century ago, is now among the least well-educated in the world, according to recent studies. At this pace, we will struggle to compete economically against even developing nations, and our children will struggle to find jobs in the global economy.

Since 1983, when *A Nation at Risk* delivered a similar message, we have seen wave after wave of school reforms. Unfortunately, most have been of the "more-longer-harder" variety: more required courses and tests, longer school days and hours, higher standards and harder exams. Few have reimagined how schools might function, given our new technologies.

On top of this, our leaders have tried to force change on a bureaucratic system built to resist it. Anything more than incremental change is almost impossible when school leaders can't fire failing teachers because they have tenure and school boards can't replace failing schools because employees and their unions retaliate at the polls. Caught between boards that want improvement and bureaucracies adept at containing change, urban superintendents last just three years, on average.

Three decades of reform have yielded some progress, but it has been agonizingly slow. Since 1970, 17-year-olds' scores on the National Assessment of Educational Progress (NAEP) have not budged. District reform efforts have run headlong into the limits of the old, centralized system. Principals have struggled to improve their schools when virtually all the important decisions about school design, teachers, pay, and budgets are made at district headquarters. Teachers have struggled to help their students when they have no power to change what they teach or for how long, nor how their schools work. The most successful reforms have created new schools, such as magnet programs, but they remain promising islands in a dysfunctional sea.

Our Republican leaders, from President Trump down through Congress and state legislatures, have turned to vouchers as the answer. If public schools are failing, they reason, let's help families choose private schools. In some states legislation has already passed giving half the population or more access to vouchers (or education savings accounts, as they are sometimes called). For poor, inner-city children, vouchers enhance equal opportunity. But once half the state has access to them, it won't be long before everyone else demands them. And that way lies danger.

First, vouchers offer no guarantee of academic success, because most private schools are not accountable to any public body and cannot be shut down if the students aren't learning. Experience teaches that some parents will stick with a school if it is safe and nurturing, even if test scores are abysmal, so we cannot rely on parents to abandon all failing schools. Louisiana and Indiana have made private schools that accept vouchers subject to standardized tests and public accountability, but politically, that is unlikely to fly when almost everyone is eligible for a voucher.

Second, universal vouchers will create distinctly unequal opportunity. Those who can afford it will add their own money to the voucher and buy more expensive educations for their kids, and the education market will stratify by income, like every other market. Wealthy families will pay for expensive schools, because they love their kids. Middle-class families will pay for moderately expensive schools, for the same reason. And poor and working-class families will settle for what the voucher will buy. In theory we could prohibit those who use vouchers from adding money to them, but again, that would never fly in America.

Under a universal voucher system, what little mixing of income levels we have today would vanish, and with it any hope of equal opportunity. Many children would also lose the chance to rub elbows with those from different social classes, races, and ethnic groups. That experience creates a more tolerant society, willing to embrace diversity—a huge asset in a racially and culturally diverse nation. Its absence creates the opposite.

The risk is real, because vouchers are high on the Republican Party's agenda. If we fail to create effective public school systems, voucher bills will pass in state after state, and public systems will gradually give way to private schools. That would be a tragic mistake.

To Save Public Education We Must Reinvent It

If we were creating a public education system from scratch, would we organize it as most of our public systems are now organized? Would our classrooms look just as they did before the advent of personal computers and the Internet? Would we give teachers lifetime jobs after their second or third year of teaching? Would we let schools survive if, year after year, half their students dropped out? Would we send children to school for only eight and a half months a year and six hours a day? Would we assign them to schools by neighborhood, reinforcing racial and economic segregation?

Few people would answer yes to such questions. But in real life we don't usually get to start over; instead, we have to change existing systems. And that threatens tightly held interests—such as teachers' rights to lifetime jobs—triggering enormous political conflict.

One city did get a chance to start over, however. In 2005, after the third-deadliest hurricane in U.S. history, Louisiana's leaders wiped the slate clean in New Orleans. After Katrina, they handed more than 100 of the city's public schools—all but 17—to the state's Recovery School District (RSD), created two years earlier to turn around failing schools. Over the next nine years, the RSD gradually turned them into charter schools—a new form of public school that has emerged over the last quarter century. Charters are public schools operated by independent, mostly nonprofit organizations, free of most state and district rules but held accountable for performance by written charters, which function like performance contracts. Most, but not all, are schools of choice. In 2017 the old Orleans Parish School Board, which is elected, decided to transition its last four traditional schools to charter status, and someday soon 100 percent of the city's public school students will attend charters.

The results should shake the very foundations of American education. Test scores, school performance scores, graduation and dropout rates, college-going rates, and independent studies all tell the same story: the city's RSD schools have doubled or tripled their effectiveness. The district has improved faster than any other in the state—and no doubt in the nation. On several important metrics, New Orleans is the first big city with a majority of low-income minorities to outperform its state. (For the details, see chapter 3, pp. 54–56.)

Washington, D.C., also started with a clean slate, but in a very different way. In 1996 Congress created the D.C. Public Charter School Board, which grants charters to nonprofit organizations to start schools. After 20 years of chartering, the board has performance contracts with 65 nonprofit organizations to operate about 120 schools, and 46 percent of the city's public school students attend them. Families choose the charter school they prefer. The board closes or replaces those in which kids are falling behind, while encouraging the best to expand or open new schools.

The competition from charters helped spur D.C.'s mayor to take control of the school district and initiate some of the most profound reforms any traditional district has embraced. Yet D.C.'s charter sector still has higher test scores, higher attendance, higher graduation and college enrollment rates, and more demand than the city's traditional public schools. The difference is particularly dramatic with African American and low-income students, despite the fact that charters have received significantly less money each year—some $6,000 to $7,000 less per pupil—than district schools. (For the details, see chapter 7, pp. 113–128).

Leaders in other struggling urban districts have paid close attention to such reforms, and they are spreading. A decade ago the elected school board in Denver, frustrated by the traditional bureaucracy, decided to embrace charter schools. The board gave most charters space in district buildings and encouraged the successful ones to replicate as fast as possible. Then they began turning district schools into "innovation schools," with many of the autonomies that help charters succeed. When these efforts began, Denver had the lowest academic growth of any of Colorado's 20 largest cities. By 2012 it had the highest. (For the details, see chapter 9, pp. 161–6.)

New Jersey followed New Orleans's lead in Camden, where it took over the failing school district in 2013. Memphis and Indianapolis have embraced charters but also followed Denver's lead with innovation schools. Massachusetts and the Springfield Public Schools have created an Empowerment Zone Partnership, with its own board, whose ten schools are treated much like charters. Three other states have copied Louisiana and created their own recovery districts. And 30 large districts belong to a network of "portfolio districts"—so called because they manage a portfolio of traditional and charter schools—which share what they have learned about what works and what doesn't.

Most of the debate in this field is stuck on the tired issue of whether charter schools perform any better than traditional public schools. The evidence on that question, from dozens of careful studies, is clear: on average, charters outperform traditional public schools. The studies favored by charter critics come from Stanford University's Center for Research on Educational Outcomes (CREDO). But even they show that, on average, students who spend four or more years in charter schools gain an additional two months of learning in reading and more than two months in math *every year*, compared to similar students in traditional public schools. Urban students gain five months in math and three and a half in reading. And charter parents are happier with their schools. On five key characteristics—teacher quality, school discipline, expectations for student achievement, safety, and development of character—13 percentage points more charter school parents were "very satisfied" with their schools than traditional school parents in 2016.

But when it comes to charter schools, "average" has little meaning, because the 43 states and the District of Columbia with charters all have different laws and practices. Any good idea can be done poorly, and some states have proven it with their charter laws and practices. One has to look beyond the averages to see the truth: In states where charter authorizers close or replace failing schools—a central feature of the charter model—charters vastly outperform traditional public schools, with students gaining as much as an extra year of learning every year. But in states where failing charters are allowed to remain open, they are, on average, no better than other public schools.

What matters is not whether we call them charter schools or district schools or "innovation schools" or "pilot schools," but the rules that govern their operation.

Do they have the autonomy they need to design a school model that works for the children they must educate? Are they free to hire the best teachers and fire the worst? Do they experience competition that drives them to continuously improve? Does the district give families a choice of different kinds of schools, designed to educate different kinds of learners? Do schools experience enough accountability—including the threat of closure if they fail—to create a sense of urgency among their employees? And when they close, are they replaced by better schools?

If the answer to these questions is yes, the system will be self-renewing. Its schools will constantly improve and evolve—as we will see in New Orleans, Washington, D.C., and Denver.

When Economies and Societies Evolve, Institutions Must Change

All public institutions evolve to fit their times. During the agricultural era, the dominant model of education in America was the one-room schoolhouse, in which older students did some of the teaching of younger students and the teacher was more a coach than a lecturer.

Some schools were created by public organizations, some by private organizations or individuals, and some were hybrids. There were Latin grammar schools; "dame" schools run by women in their homes; boarding schools; religious schools; and subscription schools, where parents chipped in to establish a school. Some schools received public funds, but even if they did, some among them also charged tuition. Prior to the creation of public high schools, some states chartered "academies" to offer secondary education: private organizations that received public funds. All schools were voluntary, and children often attended seasonally, when they were not needed on the farm.

In 1843 Horace Mann, then Massachusetts's first secretary of education, visited Prussia to study its new education system. After the Prussians' defeat by Napoleon, they had created a compulsory eight-year school system, focused on reading, writing, and arithmetic and structured into grades, subjects, and classes. Upon his return Mann wrote about the Prussian system in his seventh annual report, which was published not only in Massachusetts but in other states and in England. By 1852 he had convinced the Massachusetts legislature to adopt the Prussian system, and later other states followed suit.

Mann and his followers called their new public schools "common schools," because they would educate children from most walks of life in common. As one history summarizes it: "Common schools were funded by local property taxes, charged no tuition, were open to all white children, were governed by local school committees, and were subject to a modest amount of state regulation. They arose through two decades of debate prior to the Civil War in the Northeast and Midwest—and, later in the 19th century, in the South and West."

As late as 1890, 71 percent of Americans lived in rural areas, where one-room schools predominated. But over the next decade many cities tripled in size, as manufacturing boomed and immigrant labor poured in. A 19th century education system could not cope with the cities' new needs, so reformers gradually developed a new model: large districts with one-size-fits-all schools. The progressive reformers were enamored of the industrial corporations that were growing so rapidly and creating so many jobs. In 1889, U.S. Commissioner of Education William Harris spoke for them when he wrote, "Our schools are, in a sense, factories in which the raw materials (children) are to be shaped and fashioned in order to meet the various demands of life. The specifications for manufacturing come from the demands of the 20th century civilization, and it is the business of the school to build its pupils according to the specifications laid down."

The education historian David Tyack summarized the drive to emulate corporate bureaucracies in his classic book, *The One Best System*:

> *The division of labor in the factory, the punctuality of the railroad, the chain of command and coordination in modern businesses—these aroused a sense of wonder and excitement in men and women seeking to systematize the schools. They sought to replace confused and erratic means of control with careful allocation of powers and functions within hierarchical organizations; to establish networks of communication that would convey information and directives and would provide data for planning for the future; to substitute impersonal rules for informal, individual adjudication of disputes; to regularize procedures so that they would apply uniformly to all in certain categories; and to set objective standards for admission to and performance in each role, whether superintendent or third-grader. Efficiency, rationality, continuity, precision, impartiality became watchwords of the consolidators. In short, they tried to create a more bureaucratic system.*

At the time, political machines controlled many urban school boards, many of them large, with more than 20 members. They functioned more like legislatures than boards, with subcommittees that made administrative decisions for the schools. Some even had ward boards, which hired and fired teachers and principals. To stop the machines from firing teachers of the opposite party and hiring their own party members—or otherwise discriminating against those out of political favor—reformers invented teacher tenure, strict pay scales determined by longevity, and protections for seniority. "Take the schools out of politics!" was their battle cry.

The progressives also sought to standardize public education, to fashion all primary and secondary schools from similar molds. In 1892 the National Education Association (not yet a union) created a "Committee of Ten," chaired by Harvard University President Charles Eliot, to recommend improvements in high school curriculum. Eliot's committee concluded "that every subject which is taught at all in a secondary school should be taught in the same way and to the same extent to every pupil so long as he pursues it." By 1925, 34 state departments of education had managed to standardize their schools, using legislation and regulations. Accreditation agencies added muscle to the drive for uniformity.

All the while, schools grew in size and the entire system grew increasingly bureaucratic. "In the 1890s there was, on average, one staff member in state departments of education for every 100,000 pupils; in 1974 there was one for about every 2,000," according to David Tyack and Larry Cuban. "Regulations ballooned: in California the state education code took about 200 pages in 1900, in 1985 more than 2,600." By the 1960s, New York City schools employed more administrators than the entire French education system. Then many public systems unionized, and the detailed labor contracts unions negotiated intensified the rigidity.

By this time, however, the schools' customers were changing in important ways. African Americans had begun leaving the South for northern cities during World War II, and in the 1950s whites began moving to the suburbs. In 1950, Tyack tells us, roughly 90 percent of public school students in our 14 largest cities were white. By the 1970s, only half were.

On top of racial changes, a cultural revolution brought discipline problems and widespread drug use. Gallup began surveying the public about education in 1969, and for the first 20 years discipline usually ranked as the top problem listed, followed closely by drug use. Public confidence in the education system began to wane.

By 1974, when Tyack published *The One Best System*, he had concluded that our centralized bureaucracies needed updating.

> *To succeed in improving the schooling of the dispossessed, educators are increasingly realizing that they need to share power over educational decision-making with representatives of urban communities they serve, that they need to find ways to teach that match the learning*

styles of the many ethnic groups, that they need to develop many alter-
natives within the system and to correct the many dysfunctions of the
vast bureaucracies created by the administrative progressives. Old
reforms need to be reformed anew, for today many lack confidence in
the familiar patterns of power and authority that developed at the turn-
of-the-century. Substantial segments of the society no longer believe
in centralism as an effective response to human needs.

From there, the pace of change only accelerated. By 2014 a majority of public school students were minorities. The emergence of a global marketplace and the shift from an industrial economy to the Information Age created a growing gulf between those with skills and those without, driving incomes down for many. By 1989, a third of public school students were low-income (qualifying for subsidized meals). In 2013, for the first time, a majority were.

Gradually, leaders in places like New Orleans, Washington, D.C, Denver, and Indianapolis concluded that if they wanted more than incremental improvement, they had to change their operating systems. Their old systems were a century old, constructed for a different era. Slowly they have begun creating 21st century systems, in which the central administration steers the system but contracts with others to operate schools. The steering body, usually an elected school board and appointed superintendent but sometimes a mayor or appointed board and superintendent, awards charters to schools that meet emerging student needs. If the schools work, it expands them and replicates them. If they fail, it replaces them with better schools. Every year, it replaces the worst performers, replicates the best, and develops new models to meet new needs.

The result is continuous improvement. We have inherited 20th century systems whose centralized control and vast web of rules repel innovation and frustrate innovators. In their place, we are building 21st century systems that not only reward improvement but demand it. They leave behind the old model's insistence on one organization, one best way to run a school, and one correct curriculum. In its place they create an ever-evolving network of schools designed for the Information Age, with many providers, many different teaching methods, and many choices for parents and their children.

Since both parents and teachers can choose among many different kinds of schools, they are less likely to insist on the one best way—whether phonics or whole language, new math or old math. Elected school boards are politically free to create a more diverse set of schools, to meet the needs of an increasingly diverse body of students. The regimentation of pedagogy—which is profoundly unfair to children who don't learn in the one best way—finally ends.

School boards in these 21st century systems also find it easier to create new kinds of schools when new needs and opportunities emerge. For example, traditional districts have been slow to create schools that use information technology in a meaningful way, because it requires a different configuration of personnel—something teachers and their unions find threatening. In the charter sector, however, schools have embraced technology, because school leaders feel an urgency to improve student achievement and are free to change their mix of personnel.

Equally important, a 21st century system gives school boards—elected or appointed—far more control over quality, because they can choose among competing operators, negotiate specific performance standards, and replace failing schools. Traditional districts do little of that.

More than any other single reform, this model breaks the political stranglehold interest groups have over elected school boards. Most school board members want to do what's best for the children, but too often that creates problems for the adults in the system, who all vote. And when the children's interests collide with the adults', the children usually lose. This is why elected boards find it so hard to replace failing schools. Closing schools is political suicide, because employees, parents, and community members often protest, and the protesters all vote. Turnout in school board elections is often under 10 percent, so their votes usually carry the day. Hence board members who rock the boat know they are risking defeat.

In 21st century systems, where school boards contract with independent organizations to operate schools, the battle of self-interest is quite different. School operators still push for their own interests, but they no longer act as a unified block. For every school that opposes a particular change, another school supports it. Every time a school is closed for poor performance, other operators line up to take its place. Hence elected leaders are no longer so captive of adult interests; they have some freedom to do what is best for the children. And the principals and teachers feel enormous urgency to improve student learning—otherwise, their school might be replaced. For the first time, virtually every adult's priority is student achievement.

The new formula—school autonomy, accountability for performance, diversity of school designs, parental choice, and competition between schools—is simply more effective than the centralized, bureaucratic approach we inherited from the 20th century. Separating steering from rowing makes all the difference. School boards and superintendents get to focus their energy on steering: on setting policy and direction and ensuring that schools deliver the results desired. Meanwhile, those doing the rowing—operating schools—have the freedom from bureaucratic constraints they need to maximize school performance.

We will learn more about these new systems as our story unfolds. But for now, the chart below shows some of the basic differences between 20th and 21st century systems. The two graphics on the next page describe how each system is organized. (Both are simplified. In reality, even traditional districts often contract with private organizations to run "alternative" schools, for students who are hardest to reach. And in 21st century systems, some charter networks operate multiple schools, under one charter. But the graphics capture the essence of the two approaches.)

20th Century School Systems	21st Century School Systems
District is one organizational unit; all school employees are district employees.	District has a small central staff but contracts with separate organizations to operate schools. Teachers work for schools, not the district.
District steers the system and operates the schools.	District steers the system, but independent organizations operate the schools.
District controls schools through centralized rules and budgets.	District controls schools through accountability for results.
Most decisions about who to hire, pay, how to spend money, and how to design schools are made at district headquarters.	Hiring, budget, pay, and design decisions are made at schools.
Schools live on regardless of results; there are no consequences for student achievement levels (except for consequences in students' lives).	Schools in which students are falling behind are replaced; those in which students excel are expanded or replicated.
Most students are assigned to schools closest to their homes.	Most families choose their public schools.
Schools educate all students who are assigned to them.	Schools compete for students and funding follows student choices.

I believe the new approach will become the dominant model in the 21st century, just as centralized bureaucracies became the dominant model in the 20th century. It is happening in cities first because they are the most desperate for change. But the lessons they learn and the results they produce will gradually migrate out to the suburbs and rural areas. Reforms will take different forms, depending upon local conditions, but the underlying principles will be the same.

20th Century Model

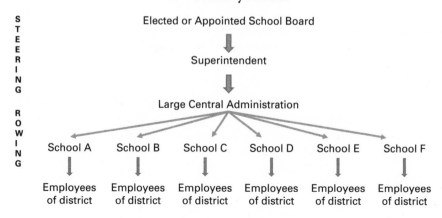

21st Century Model

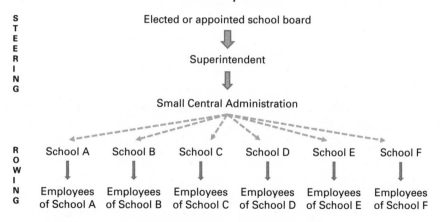

Dashed line = Contract Relationship
Solid line = Employee Relationship

Misconceptions Regarding Charter Schools

Nationally, more than 70 percent of K–12 teachers in traditional public schools belong to unions or associations similar to unions, but only about 10 percent of those in charter schools do. (And half of union members in charters belong only because their state charter laws require it, in Maryland, Kansas, Iowa, and Alaska). Most charter school leaders believe that industrial unionism, with its labor vs. management paradigm, is a poor fit for education. They prefer to view teachers as professionals, giving many of them decision-making roles.

Hence, the more teachers there are in charter schools, the fewer there will be in unions. Union leaders understand this. Though a legendary teachers union president, Al Shanker, played a key role in launching the charter movement, his successors now view the expansion of charter schools as a direct threat. They have fought charter expansion in every state where they are active.

Surveys show that roughly half of Americans don't know what charter schools are, so union-promulgated falsehoods have fallen on fertile ground. (For specific polling data, see chapter 14, p. 291). Very briefly, let me address some of the most common misconceptions.

Charter Schools Are Public Schools

Critics often speak as though charter schools are not public schools. This is nonsense, but it resonates, because people have fixed ideas about what constitutes a public school. In reality, charters are a new form of public school, which now educate more than three million students. They are organized differently from 20th century systems, but they are accountable to public bodies, they are publicly funded, and they are free and equally accessible to all students. (In a few states private universities and nonprofit organizations can authorize charters, but this has turned out to be a mistake.)

Most school districts use private companies to build and renovate their facilities and provide their furniture, textbooks, computers, and software. Many contract with private companies to provide student meals and transportation. In many cities, nonprofit organizations operate "alternative" public schools—for former dropouts, teenagers who have committed crimes, and others who have trouble in normal schools. No one thinks of such activities as "privatization," because they are so accustomed to them. But the minute public entities contract out traditional educational programs, opponents yell "privatization!" Saying it does not make it so, however. The people who want to privatize education are voucher advocates, not charter supporters.

Chartering Is Not "Corporate Reform"

Critics love to call charter leaders and funders "corporate reformers." But in the course of my research, I've met hundreds of charter school leaders, and I have yet to meet one who could be described as "corporate." As you will see when you encounter them in this book, they are passionate do-gooders trying to change the world, the equivalent of Peace Corps and VISTA volunteers in my generation. Their schools do receive some funding from foundations created by corporate leaders such as Bill Gates and Sam Walton, but so do traditional districts and teachers unions.

Nor do 21st century systems create "free markets" in education, as vouchers would. Instead, they create "social markets," which combine the creativity and accountability of market systems with the social goals of quality education and equal opportunity for every child.

Most Charter Schools Are Not-For-Profit Organizations

Critics like to charge that charters are out to make profits at the expense of children, but less than 13 percent of charters are operated by for-profit organizations. Where authorizers do their jobs well, as in New Orleans, Washington, D.C., and Denver, most for-profit operators have closed. There are none left in New Orleans or Denver, and only three non-profit charter school boards contract with for-profit operators in D.C. If a school is serious about educating inner-city kids, there is little profit to be made.

We have long used the nonprofit sector to address public needs. Many of our hospitals, universities, human service providers, low-income housing organizations, and early-childhood education providers are non-profits. In the 21st century, K–12 education is migrating to this "third sector" as well.

Our Public Education Systems Fund Students, Not Schools

Critics constantly accuse charters of draining money from public schools. Since charters *are* public schools, that is impossible. They do drain funding from traditional school districts, however—because parents have pulled their children out of district schools and placed them in charter schools. When a school no longer educates a child—because the child has moved away, or chosen to attend a school in another district, or left for a charter school— most of the money leaves as well. Many district and union leaders talk as if the money belonged to them, but it is taxpayers' money, which they spend to provide a quality education for every child.

In some states, districts get to keep some of the money for several years after a child departs for a charter. In most others, charters receive less money per child than traditional schools. (At last count, in 2014, charters averaged only 72 percent of the money per student that districts received, nationally.) In either case, when parents send their kids to charters, their local districts often end up receiving more money per child, not less.

The districts and unions complain that they have fixed costs, like heating and electricity, and when a child departs their fixed costs remain the same.

But that's true of every business and nonprofit in America, and we don't subsidize them or limit their competition. We expect them to figure out how to cut their costs, attract more customers, or rent out their empty space. When you switch doctors, does your old doctor expect you to keep paying her for a few years? When you move, does your old city or town get to keep some of your money for property taxes?

Charter critics bring to mind the American automakers of the early 1980s, when the Japanese took so many customers away because Ford, Chrysler, and General Motors made lousy cars. The auto companies wanted the government to limit their competition by capping the number of imported cars, which would have saddled us with low quality for decades to come. What forced Ford and the rest to improve was competition—and competition from charters has had exactly the same effect on our school districts.

Unlike Traditional Public Schools, Charters Are Legally Prohibited from "Cherry-Picking" the Students They Want

Critics argue that charters cherry-pick their students, then dump those they don't want on traditional schools. In truth, charters serve higher percentages of poor and minority students than district schools. And cherry-picking goes on far more frequently in traditional district schools—particularly selective magnet schools—than in charters. By law, if a charter school cannot take all who apply, it must hold a lottery; it cannot choose its students. Sometimes charters "counsel out" students they don't want, because they can't provide a good fit—just as traditional public schools do. And occasionally a charter school tries to duck students with disabilities who will be expensive to educate. But that's why a charter *system* is so much more powerful than just having a charter sector in your city. Where one authorizer is actively steering, as in New Orleans, D.C., and Denver, it prohibits such behavior—and punishes the school when it discovers it.

Conclusion

Twenty-first century systems will not solve *all* of our problems. If we want a world-class education system, we must also support low-income children from birth, so they arrive at school ready to learn. We must combat poverty in many different ways, not just in our schools. And we must give special help to children whose emotional problems make learning difficult.

But creating 21st century school systems is a good place to start. Once school boards and superintendents no longer have the responsibility to row—once they are free of the burden of operating schools—they can move on to address these other problems. They cannot solve them alone, but as we will see, they can partner with other sectors to attack some of the most intractable.

Let us turn to our emerging 21st century systems to see what is possible.

PART I

NEW ORLEANS: KATRINA WIPES THE SLATE CLEAN

CHAPTER I

THE REVOLUTION

ON SEPTEMBER 8, 1900, THE deadliest hurricane in U.S. history hit Galveston, Texas, a bustling port town of 39,000 built on a barrier island in the Gulf of Mexico. The nation's second-busiest port and Texas's second-largest city, Galveston stood only nine feet above sea level at its highest point. When a 15-foot storm surge buried the island, so many people disappeared and so many unidentifiable bodies turned up that no one could calculate the death toll; estimates suggest 6,000 in the city, 4,000 to 6,000 on the mainland.

To rebuild their city, the town's leaders asked the governor and state legislature to impose a new form of governance: five commissioners who would play both executive and legislative roles. One commissioner would act as mayor, coordinating, while the others each ran one portion of city government, such as public safety or public works.

The new model worked so well that progressive reformers such as Woodrow Wilson seized on it as a way to wrest power from corrupt mayors and their spoils systems. Within 20 years more than 500 cities were using "the Galveston Plan." Over time, it evolved into the council-manager form of government, in which an elected council hires a city manager as executive—still the dominant municipal model for cities with fewer than 250,000 people.

A century later, the third-deadliest storm in U.S. history hit Louisiana, killing 1,800. And just as the Great Galveston Hurricane wiped the slate clean for reform, so did Katrina. In its wake, the most important experiment in U.S. public education began in New Orleans.

Two years before, the governor and state legislature had created a Recovery School District (RSD) to take over the worst public schools in the state. After the storm, they handed it all but 17 of New Orleans schools. Gradually, over the next nine years, the RSD turned them all into charters. Soon, every public school student in the city will attend a charter school.

By 2014, when the state switched standardized tests, the percentage of students testing at grade level or above had jumped from 35 to 62 percent. Schools in the RSD had improved almost four times as fast as state averages.

Before Katrina, 62 percent of students in New Orleans attended schools rated "failing" by the state. Though the state raised the bar, by 2016 only 6 percent attended failing schools. Graduation and college-going rates now exceed the state average.

New Orleans has improved its schools faster than any other city in the United States. Indeed, some experts believe it has improved faster than any city in American history. This improvement would be impressive enough on its own, but it is occurring in a district in which 82 percent of the students are African American and 85 percent are poor.

THIS REVOLUTION OCCURRED in large part thanks to the efforts of one extraordinary and unlikely heroine. Leslie Jacobs was born into New Orleans's small Jewish community in 1959. Her father, the first in his family to attend college, had founded an independent insurance agency. Intense, dark-haired, and attractive, Jacobs is a woman perpetually in a hurry. At 21 she married and graduated from Cornell University; at 23 she had her first child.

In the mid-1980s, with two children and a full-time job in the family insurance business, she says she "was looking for something else to do." She heard of a Partners in Education program that recruited businesses to help schools, so she and her brother volunteered. They were assigned an elementary school that drew from a public housing development and had the highest rate of expulsions in the city. Leslie worked long hours with the school, won multiple awards, and wound up chairing the citywide Partners in Education Committee. By 1992, she and her brother had built the family firm into one of the largest insurance agencies in the South. Seized with "passion and naïveté"—her words—she ran for a seat on the Orleans Parish School Board. In a district with a majority of African Americans, she went door to door, often in public housing projects. And she won.

"Leslie Jacobs is a force of nature, multiplied by ten," says former state superintendent Paul Pastorek.

It is hard to describe how bad the New Orleans schools were at the time. In crumbling buildings, teachers napped during class, students roamed the halls at will, occasionally with knives and guns, and fights were common. Some principals' jobs went to the mistresses of top district officials, to those wired into the power structure, or to those who bribed the right administrator. If someone failed as a principal, they were kicked upstairs, into the central office. The district's books were such a mess that it could not get a clean audit finding.

Orleans Parish battled it out with St. Helena Parish for the title of worst school district in Louisiana—itself ranked in the bottom five states on national exams. Experts considered it one of the worst large districts in the nation. A

2004 study showed that one in four adults in the city had not completed high school and four in ten were unable to read beyond an elementary school level.

Not surprisingly, New Orleanians who could afford it sent their children to private schools. "There were three school systems in New Orleans," remembers Jay Altman, a founder of the city's first charter school: "private schools, academically selective public magnet schools, and everyone else. And the gap between the first two categories and the third was enormous."

Jacobs dates her radicalization to an evening in 1995, when the teachers union asked her and others to judge high school students' college essays, as part of a scholarship program. "I was president of an insurance brokerage firm, and I could not hire any of these kids for an entry-level position as a receptionist," Jacobs remembers. "Their essays had a failure of noun-verb agreement, of sentence structure, paragraphing, punctuation, much less the ability to convey something persuasively—even why they wanted to go to college. I looked at their transcripts, and they all had straight A's. It was the most depressing night."

Jacobs asked the central office to do a data run on how tenth-graders did on their first attempt at the Graduate Exit Exam (GEE). "We had schools where 100 percent of the kids failed the GEE the first attempt, irrespective of their grades," she says. "Our A students couldn't read, couldn't write, couldn't pass their first attempt at a graduation exam that at that time was at a seventh-grade level."

Jacobs hired facilitators to lead a board retreat. Since race is always an issue in New Orleans, she chose one black and one white facilitator. She gave her colleagues the essays and asked them, "How can we wake up in the morning and look at ourselves in the face? We are just lying to these children."

She proposed that they each pick a school in their district to "reconstitute"— close them down and restart from scratch, with a new principal and new teachers. She suggested they begin with Booker T. Washington High School, where the district spent more money than in any other school but one in three students was absent every day and less than one in ten graduated.

The majority stonewalled. "I've never worked so hard on something," Jacobs says with a sigh, "and accomplished so little."

But it is not in Leslie Jacobs's nature to give up. Wearing her insurance executive hat, she had worked with a Republican senator, Mike Foster, to reform the Louisiana workers compensation system, then served on the board of a new Louisiana Workers Compensation Corporation. When Foster ran for governor in 1996, she sent him a check. To everyone's surprise, he won.

"I was probably the only one in New Orleans who sent him a check, so when he won I became a very popular girl," she says. She chaired his education transition team, where she advocated making school accountability a priority.

Foster was not exactly a progressive reformer: He had promised to abolish the state board of education, give Goals 2000 money back to the federal government, and focus the schools on character education.

But Jacobs's passion is matched by her tenacity, and it was not long before the new governor succumbed. During the transition, she says, "I remember sitting to his left at one meeting. I took a pen in my hand, and I said, 'Governor, this pen is your magic wand. Exactly what law do you want to pass to teach character education, when we can't teach kids to read?'" Foster finally relented, told her to recommend what she wanted—as long as it didn't involve a constitutional amendment.

What she wanted was an accountability system: statewide standardized tests; school performance scores, based on test scores, attendance rates, and graduation rates; help for schools with low scores, in the form of money and consultants ("distinguished educators"); and forced reconstitution of schools rated failing for four years in a row. "The risk-reward ratio was fundamentally wrong," she says. "In the face of massive failure, there was no penalty for inaction. I wanted the pain of doing nothing to be more severe than the risk of doing something. That was the whole paradigm for me."

The transition team recommended appointees to the state Board of Elementary and Secondary Education, known as BESE (like the cow). Foster appointed them in January 1996, but two months later he called Jacobs at 6:15 one morning and told her one of the members was not working out, and she needed to "fix it." So she resigned from the Orleans Parish School Board and joined BESE, where she pushed through the accountability system.

The new tests were given every year from third through eighth grades, and high school students took Graduate Exit Exams. (GEEs have since been replaced by end-of-year tests in English, math, science, and history.) Students had to achieve at least a "basic" (grade-level) score in English language arts or math and an "approaching basic" score in the other subject to move from fourth to fifth grade and eighth to ninth. (Summer school was available for those who failed.) To graduate, high school students had to pass the GEE. Today they have to pass one end-of-year English exam, one math exam, and a biology or American history exam. (Alternate assessments are available for students with disabilities.)

In 2000, only one in four public school students in New Orleans scored basic or above on the new tests. For the next five years, scores improved at about the same pace as the rest of the state, as schools revamped their curricula, teachers learned to teach to the test, and students became accustomed to the tests—the normal pattern in any system that adopts standardized testing. But the city's school board continued to trip over itself. Between 1997 and 2005, it hired eight superintendents, six of them on an interim basis. While racial politics, patronage, and corruption flourished, enrollment fell by 25 percent between 1995 and 2005—and private school enrollment grew.

In the fall of 2002, the board hired Anthony Amato, a Hispanic reformer who had produced impressive results with poor kids as a superintendent in New York City and Hartford, Connecticut. When he won by one vote over a black candidate, African Americans in the audience disrupted the meeting and one protester had to be physically removed by security forces.

Amato recounted an incident from early in his term to *New Orleans Magazine*. Apparently a student told him one day that a teacher had offered to give him an A for $500. "My head blew, my heart blew apart, tears came to my eyes," Amato told the magazine. "That was the level of corruption that was rampant at the time."

On another occasion, the school board chairwoman invited Amato to lunch. When he arrived, she was sitting with a man from the district's health insurance provider. As they ate, the man asked if the board couldn't just extend the current contract rather than putting it out to bid again. Amato stood up and excused himself.

In 2003, a private investigator discovered that the district, which employed about 8,000, gave paychecks to nearly 4,000 people and health insurance to 2,000 who did not deserve them. When Amato announced that employees would have to show an ID before picking up their paychecks, 1,500 were left uncollected. Even bus drivers were stealing, using their district credit cards to buy fuel and then sell it to truck drivers.

Amato invited the FBI to station agents at district headquarters, to investigate the agency's operations. In 2004, 11 people were indicted for criminal financial mismanagement. That same year Amato stepped into a snake pit he did not even know was there: He tried to hire an attorney for the district, to replace Congressman Bill Jefferson's former law firm, which the district paid more than $1 million a year. Jefferson, who with his siblings ran the city's black political machine, had sold his firm but had reportedly negotiated a clause giving him an ongoing cut of billings to the district. At a private meeting, in violation of the state's open meeting statute, the school board voted to fire Amato. Jacobs and her legislative allies quickly intervened, but Amato knew his days were numbered. Weary of death threats, bodyguards, and his bulletproof vest, he resigned when a new board elected the next fall gave no sign of wanting to renew his contract.

By then the district was paying teachers late for lack of cash. When the federal government threatened to take away its Title 1 money if the state did not intervene, the state superintendent appointed a receiver to take control of district finances.

In the end, at least 24 district leaders were indicted. The chairwoman of the board went to federal prison, convicted of taking $140,000 in bribes in return for supporting an educational software program peddled by Bill Jefferson's brother, Mose. Mose Jefferson died in prison in 2010, of cancer; Bill Jefferson, convicted on eleven counts of bribery and corruption, received a 13-year sentence in federal prison.

JACOBS'S SECOND EPIPHANY came in 2003, when the valedictorian at New Orleans's Fortier High failed the GEE exam, despite making five attempts. "When she failed and couldn't walk across that stage and get her diploma, there was no civil rights protest, there was no religious protest, business protest, civic leadership protest—there was a deafening silence," Jacobs remembers.

> That principal was interviewed and said he didn't understand what the big fuss was about, and he wasn't fired. That was in my mind the emblem of a city that had given up all hope in its schools. I knew then that the only way to mobilize people was to prove that it could work, that we could successfully educate "these kids"—poor, inner-city kids—to much higher levels. Folks needed to believe success was possible.

She decided it was time to create a special school district to take over failed schools, a new idea in education reform circles. Her inspiration came from bankruptcy law.

> When a business is bankrupt, a judge will make the decisions about what drastic changes he will allow so the business can remain a viable entity. In essence, a business gets to start over, and that's what we meant the Recovery School District to be. We would take the failing school, strip it of the district's policies—which in New Orleans could easily stack up to be two feet high—strip away any contracts, including the collective bargaining agreement, and take the building, the students, and the money out of the district.

Unfortunately, her brainchild required a constitutional amendment, which Governor Foster had ruled off-limits. Foster once again relented in the face of her arguments, but a constitutional amendment required a two-thirds vote in the legislature, then a simple majority on a statewide ballot. The governor and his staff convinced the legislature, and Jacobs led the statewide campaign: "I raised the money, did the ad campaign, went to editorial boards all across the state. I was told it would never pass in New Orleans, so I did a mailer to black households in the city."

The Orleans Parish School Board, city council, and teachers union all came out against the amendment. "But I had served an African American district," Jacobs says. "I had walked the district; I answered my phone. I knew parents wanted good schools for their kids; I had no doubt about it." The amendment passed by close to 60 percent—both statewide and in the city.

The new district had a lot of New Orleans schools to choose from: 54 of the state's 73 failing schools were in the city. In its first two years, the Recovery School District (RSD) took control of five schools, turning them over to charter operators.

On August 29, 2005, Katrina roared in and the levees gave way. Jacobs and her family escaped to a roadside motel in Lafayette, Louisiana. "I remember going with an *Education Week* reporter back to the city in November, and it was like the twilight zone," she says. "There was not a light on in the city. It was like a smart bomb had gone off. There were no birds; there were no dogs. There was no sound. Everything was brown, white, and gray. There was also no local revenue."

New Orleans Public Schools was already broke when Katrina hit; the board was searching for a $50 million line of credit so it could meet payroll. On September 15 it put all employees on unpaid disaster leave. Soon afterward it announced it was not reopening any schools that academic year. Jacobs met with State Superintendent Cecil Picard, who lived in Lafayette, and insisted that BESE do something. Her solution: a bill to require that the new Recovery School District take over all New Orleans schools that had performance scores below the statewide average. The RSD would reopen them all as charter schools, she said.

Most state legislators were so fed up with the Orleans Parish School Board (OPSB) they were willing to jettison local democratic control if that's what it took to turn the schools around. Democratic Governor Kathleen Blanco, a former teacher, had relied on New Orleans voters, African Americans, and teachers unions to get elected. Still, she sponsored the bill—even managed to quash an amendment to require collective bargaining in the RSD. Most legislators from New Orleans opposed her. "Governor Blanco," Jacobs says simply, "has not gotten the credit she deserves."

In November, with the stroke of her pen, Blanco swept more than 100 empty schools into the RSD. With no plans to reopen schools and no money to rehire anyone, the OPSB voted in December to permanently lay off its 7,500 employees.

Louisiana's senior senator, Democrat Mary Landrieu, had secured a $1 million federal earmark for the University of New Orleans a few years before, to help it turn a group of public schools near its campus into charters. After many months of discussions, the OPSB had declined the offer—leaving the senator livid. After the hurricane she learned that the U.S. Department of Education had almost $30 million of unspent charter startup money, and she convinced Secretary Margaret Spellings to make most of it available for new charters in New Orleans. OPSB leaders decided to grab some of it by chartering seven schools that had not flooded.

Jacobs was sleeping two or three hours a night, struggling to get an insurance office up and running in Baton Rouge, trying to fix the office that had been flooded just outside New Orleans, and buying homes in Baton Rouge for her employees. In the midst of all that, she began building a support network for the new charters. She dipped into her own funds to help bankroll Sarah Usdin, a former teacher and Louisiana director of Teach For America (TFA), to create New Schools for New Orleans (NSNO), a nonprofit designed to provide whatever help the charters needed.

Usdin convinced an alternative certification organization called The New Teacher Project, where she had worked after TFA, to recruit and train 100 teachers a year for New Orleans. Then she and Jacobs took Governor Blanco to New York to convince New Leaders for New Schools, which trains principals, to help the city. TFA, which recruits bright graduates of top-notch universities to spend at least two years teaching in high-poverty schools, brought about 70 teachers a year into the New Orleans region before Katrina. Its leaders were not planning on sending any more, because the city was in such shambles. But Usdin convinced them to triple the size of their operation, and by 2011 they were bringing in 215 to 250 a year. With foundation money, New Schools for New Orleans incubated ten charter schools, providing coaching and funding for their first 18 months and training their principals.

All of these organizations—and their foundation funders—have been instrumental in helping charters succeed. "New Schools for New Orleans, Teach For America, and The New Teacher Project (TNTP) are like anchor tenants in a mall," Jacobs says. "They attract a lot of other tenants, a lot of talent."

When charter applications began to roll into the RSD, its temporary leader, Deputy State Superintendent Robin Jarvis, asked the National Association of Charter School Authorizers to vet them, to ensure quality control. To her and Jacobs's chagrin, the association recommended only six of 44 applicants in the first round. So Jarvis swallowed hard and only chartered six schools. That meant the RSD somehow had to open its own schools—three of them that spring of 2006, more in the fall—with no fund balance to draw on, no principals lined up, and no teachers.

"Basically, we became the dog that caught the bus," Jacobs remembers. We had "nothing: no schools, no buildings, no cafeteria workers, no buses."

A report from an organization called Rethinking Schools captured what happened next:

> When 17 RSD schools opened in mid-September 2006, students were confronted with all-out chaos. Textbooks had not arrived; buildings were not furnished with desks, let alone computers; and meals were frozen. And some schools had the undeniable feel of holding prisons; discipline replaced academics and security guards literally outnumbered teachers. As more and more children returned to the city, these schools struggled to accept them, because the charter schools would not. In January 2007, when newspapers reported that over 300 children had been waitlisted, even for RSD schools, the Recovery District rushed two additional schools into operation. Class size in some buildings ballooned to nearly 40:1. One English teacher reported having 53 students in one class.

"It was an absolute disaster," remembers Paul Pastorek, a New Orleans attorney who had served with Jacobs on BESE.

> I told Leslie during that winter, I said, "I think this experiment is going to fail, because we don't have the infrastructure to be able to do this job." A lawsuit was filed on the failure of the RSD to allow access to schools—you know, you can't put kids on a waiting list. There was tremendous pushback on charter schools at the time, and so they used this issue as a basis to attack the charter schools. We didn't have space, we didn't have money, we didn't have people, we were in an environment post-Katrina that was still very tenuous—real chaos in the city, still real danger from crime.

To top it off, State Superintendent Cecil Picard was dying of Lou Gehrig's disease, unable even to come into the office. In February 2007, he succumbed. "Mary Landrieu called me the day after Cecil died," Pastorek says. "Mary said, 'I want to put Paul Vallas into Cecil's place as state superintendent, because the state superintendent runs the RSD.'" Vallas had run school districts in Chicago and Philadelphia, where he managed a portfolio of some 40 contracted schools, 56 charter schools, and more than 200 district-run schools. He had learned the value of handing authority over budget and personnel to the schools but holding them accountable for results, and he had advised Mayor Ray Nagin's Bring Back New Orleans Commission to do exactly that.

Given his experience, Pastorek thought Vallas would be better suited to running the RSD than to acting as state superintendent. "So the next thing you know," Pastorek says, "I got a call from Governor Blanco, who said, 'Why don't you run the state department and you can appoint Paul Vallas?' I just laughed. I'll never forget this. It's Mardi Gras day. I'm at the driving range. I had just bought a house on a golf course—the first time I'd ever done that. I'd played a lot as a kid, never played much as an adult. I'm looking forward now to playing golf every day. And the governor calls and says, 'Why don't you take this job?' I said, 'You've got to be kidding me.'"

But Blanco persisted, and a week later Pastorek gave in. His former colleagues on BESE appointed him, and he immediately hired Vallas.

As residents migrated back into the city, the overriding challenge was to get enough buildings open. "We didn't have one building ready in March [2007] for 10,000 new students the next fall," Pastorek says. "And we didn't have one person in the office working on construction. So Paul worked on the academics, I worked on the facilities."

"I had no cash flow, no line of credit, no working capital, no capital program, but we started building new school buildings before anyone else started. We loaned the capital side huge amounts of money, which made our operating budget anemic." Then he worked out a deal with FEMA that allowed him to incur contracts and invoice FEMA on an expedited basis when the bills came through.

Five feet six, with a thick head of dark hair and an intense impatience with politics, Pastorek is a quiet, thoughtful man. He quickly earned a reputation as someone who did not suffer fools gladly. All that summer he pushed to get modular buildings constructed, showing up at construction sites, holding conference calls, screaming at those who hadn't met their deadlines. A month before school was to start, it became clear that none of the electrical transformers for ten school campuses would be ready for opening day. "You couldn't get electricity into those schools," he told me, shaking his head. The only solution was generators.

> We got a generator the size of an 18-wheeler truck for each one of those schools—cables all over the ground. Had to find 'em around the country, bring 'em in, hook 'em up, get power to 'em before school started. It was unbelievable; it cost us about $2 million. I said, "I'll take responsibility for the $2 million, but I'm gonna sue somebody."

Ten days before school was to open he had a seven A.M. conference call with the architects, project managers, and his own staff, to go through the punch lists, make sure everything was complete. He decided to visit a few school sites and call in from one. "And sure as shootin', there was a whole bunch of stuff that wasn't done. Everybody said, 'Yes, we got it done.' And I said, 'Well, goddammit, I'm standing here looking at this, and there is no ramp and there is no rail!' They panicked. I said, 'Why don't you get your goddamn ass down here so we can look together at these ramps and rails that aren't here.'"

The Friday before Labor Day, with schools due to open on Tuesday, the new campuses still weren't ready.

> *They had to pour all this pavement—parking lots and stuff—over the weekend so you could actually get onto the campuses. On one campus, the concrete pour was supposed to start at 4:30 in the morning. I was very mistrustful of them getting it done, and we had no other chances. So I got there at four o'clock, and there wasn't anybody out there at all. They should have been forming and putting metal down, and rebar, and all this kind of stuff. I'm an old construction lawyer, so I knew what they should have been doing. So I started callin' people and raisin' hell.*

The first day of school 30 percent of the kids didn't show up.

> *Then we got a call that lines were forming at our central office. All these people are sweatin' and waitin' in line 'cause their kids didn't get scheduled. It turned out it was only about 300 kids out of 10,000, but they were hot and grumpy, so we sent someone out to get a bucket of ice and some water, and Vallas and I walked around and handed out water bottles as they yelled at us, and 300 parents registered kids at the last minute.*

PAUL VALLAS IS in many ways the opposite of Paul Pastorek: tall and rangy, constantly in motion. He loves to talk, ideas spilling out one after the other in a headlong rush. Whereas Pastorek cares intensely about details, Vallas throws old arrangements up in the air, paints a vision of where they might land, and lets others pick up the pieces. "He's a turnaround guy," says his former RSD chief of staff, Rayne Martin. "He goes in and starts banging everything around, to shake up the status quo. He's got an idea a minute."

"I remember when the Saints won the Super Bowl," adds one of his former deputies at the RSD, Kevin Guitterrez. "I was celebrating, and about 15 minutes after the game ended my cell phone rang. It was Paul Vallas, who wanted to talk about some new ideas he had come up with for the RSD. I said, 'Do you know what I'm doing, Paul? We just won the Super Bowl. Let's talk about this some other time.'"

"My game plan was to create a system of either charter or charter-like schools—traditional schools with charter-like autonomy," Vallas told me.

"Rather than try to restore what was there, we would select school providers—and they didn't have to be charters, they could be old schools—based on the quality of their application. And then give all the schools the independence and autonomy they would need so that the structure of the schools—how they hired, the length of the school day, length of year, the operational plans—would really be designed to benefit kids." The central office would play a support role, providing the buildings, the materials, and the accountability.

"All the schools would be up for renewal every five years, including traditional schools"—and if they were not performing, they would be closed down. "You would be prequalifying or incubating new school providers, or identifying top performing schools that were ready to take on other schools or expand their clusters, so you would turn the weak performing schools over to the strong performing schools."

While BESE accepted every charter application its screeners (from the National Association of Charter School Authorizers) approved, Vallas and his staff also worked hard to make the schools the RSD operated succeed. They lengthened the school day and year, created alternative programs for dropouts and discipline problems, pushed "data-driven instruction," introduced performance incentives for teachers, and provided laptops, smart boards, and other technology. They treated the RSD-run schools as much like charters as possible, though teachers who survived three years automatically got tenure, under state law.

It was an uphill battle. When Vallas first arrived, in the spring of 2007, less than half the kids were showing up for school. More than 90 percent of the RSD's students lived in poverty, the vast majority being raised by single parents or grandparents. "So you take deep poverty and then you compound that by the aftermath of the hurricane, by the physical, psychological, emotional damage inflicted by the hurricane," he told the *New York Times*. "It's like the straw that breaks the camel's back."

After a couple of years, it became obvious that charters were outperforming RSD-run schools, especially at the high school level. Motivated parents were flocking to the charters; the RSD-operated high schools became dumping grounds for those paying less attention and for students dropping in and out of school. Their average entrant was four years below grade level, and every year almost half their students were new. So Vallas and Pastorek embraced the obvious solution: turn all RSD schools in the city into charters.

Partnering with New Schools for New Orleans, the RSD landed a federal Investing in Innovation grant for $28 million, to replace failing schools with high-performing charters. As the city's strongest charters took over failing RSD-run schools, a transition began from mostly single charters to charter management organizations, each with a handful of schools.

But it meant the RSD had to lay off staff every year, as more RSD-run schools became charters. Rayne Martin, Vallas's former chief of staff, remembers laying off 50 people in one day, which triggered "very high emotions." She had to keep Vallas out of it, because "he would have given people their jobs back."

"Paul Vallas was our Gorbachev," Jacobs says. "He came in and was willing to give up his power and control. He could have created a mini school district; instead, he wound down the RSD-run schools, which was very hard to do. Every year he had to lay off people, downsize his budget, because he ran fewer schools. He deserves phenomenal credit for that."

THE OTHER KEY player was Senator Landrieu. As a rule-bound bureaucracy, FEMA refused to fund anything but strict replacement of what had been there before the storm: a clock for a clock, a desk for a desk. Yet New Orleans' schools had been woefully outdated, completely unprepared for the Information Age. Senator Landrieu fought for two years to convince the Bush administration to agree instead to provide a lump sum payment of more than $1.84 billion to rebuild all the city's schools. Finally she had to push a change in the law through Congress, but she prevailed.

The FEMA money, along with Community Development Block Grant funds, allowed the RSD and OPSB to finance their $2 billion master plan, which should reconstruct or renovate every public school in New Orleans by the early 2020s, while reducing the number of permanent school facilities from 127 before Katrina to 87 today. "The FEMA lump sum made the master plan possible," Landrieu says, "and the master plan made the transformation of New Orleans' schools possible, because charters finally had access to reliable capital funding for their facilities."

CHAPTER 2

THE SCHOOLS

THE FIRST CHARTER SCHOOL IN NEW Orleans opened in 1998, founded by Tony Recasner, a young African American psychologist who had grown up in the city, and Jay Altman, a young white educator who had grown up in rural Northern California. Altman landed in New Orleans in 1988, a few years after finishing college, and fell in love with the city. After waiting on tables and tending bar, he got a job teaching at Isidore Newman, a private prep school. "I thought, 'Oh my God, why doesn't everyone get this kind of education?'" he remembers.

To help make that happen, he and his future wife launched Summerbridge, a summer program to help inner-city fifth- and sixth-graders get into private middle schools or selective magnet schools—because the alternatives were so dismal. "That's when it really hit me that there were three school systems in New Orleans," he says. "I had several parent conferences in a row where parents broke down crying. To get into the selective public schools you had to score a sixty in English and math, and their kids had one or more scores below that."

Desperate, a group of parents began talking about starting their own school. Altman and his wife agreed to help, and the parents began recruiting others. Altman knocked on the door of the St. Augustine Church rectory, in Tremé, the neighborhood later made famous by the HBO series. When the priest answered, Altman explained that they were looking for a school building and had noticed that the church had one. The priest thought about it, then said he didn't see any insurmountable obstacles. So in 1992 they opened James Lewis Extension—an extension of an existing public school—with 100 students. Parents helped renovate the building and served as crossing guards, custodians, after-school monitors, cafeteria workers, and office manager. After a year, they recruited Recasner, who was teaching at Loyola University, to serve as principal.

We created "a safe, intimate environment," Altman says, but "it was a struggle." We spent "far too much of our time meeting the constant time-consuming demands of the district bureaucracy, the political demands of an elected school board, the constraints of the collective bargaining agreement, and the demands of a state and federal education bureaucracy."

> *Trying to make better schools within the broken system at that time was a bit like farming on concrete. It doesn't matter how much fertilizer you put down, how much you water the plants, how good your seeds are—things just don't grow well on concrete. A few exceptional leaders of open admissions schools slowly tore up their own patches of concrete and began to turn their schools around within the existing system, but it was rare.*

Three years after Louisiana passed its charter school law, in 1995, he and Recasner converted the school into New Orleans Charter Middle School. For admission, they used a lottery, with numbered ping-pong balls, and a television station broadcast the event.

> *We were accepting 120 sixth-graders, and we had more than three applicants for every seat. On lottery night the cafeteria was packed. We explained to folks that the first 120 balls that came out would be admitted and that after that the 121st ball would be number one on the wait list, the 122nd would be number two on the waitlist, and so on. In many ways it was the most affirming night of the year. People would yell out and hug each other when their ball was called; one mother fell on her knees and said, "Thank you, Jesus! Thank you, Jesus!" Someone ran out into the parking lot and danced a jig.*
>
> *But then, as we got closer to the 120th ball, the tension became too great. People were praying, some had their eyes filling up with tears. And when we got past 120 and past 130 and past any hope of ever getting in off the wait list, people still stayed. They stayed until their number was called, because they wanted to make sure their ping-pong ball had been in the machine. It was deeply unfair. A child's chances for a decent education shouldn't depend on a lottery.*

The teachers union attacked them for "experimenting on our kids," but Altman and Recasner's charter became the highest-performing nonselective school in the city. The typical sixth-grader arrived two to four years behind grade level, but more than 80 percent of the graduates moved on to selective public magnet high schools or private prep schools. Their charter wasn't doing anything revolutionary, Altman says—just demanding quality from every student and staff member. "People would say, 'What's your model?' and we would say, 'Good school.'"

In late 2003 the brand new Recovery School District asked them to take over Green Middle School, with the entire student body intact. Altman was leaving for London to help start up a network of "academies," the British version of charter schools. He doubted they could do a turnaround—take the entire student body of a dysfunctional school—and make it work. "I said, 'No, don't, it'll kill you. But Tony said, 'I grew up in that area; I want to help.'"

The turnaround school had been open for two weeks when Katrina hit. Their first building was destroyed, but Green suffered minimal damage, so Recasner reopened it in January 2006, taking all comers. In March 2007 he opened Arthur Ashe Middle School, with 42 students, using the original charter from their first school. The following year he named their organization FirstLine Schools—a reference to the city's tradition of jazz funerals, in which family members make up the "first line" and musicians make up the "second line."

The schools were structured, with clear and consistent discipline, because Recasner and Altman believed that "structure liberates" poor kids to learn. But they were also filled with the joy of learning. FirstLine tore up the concrete and planted gardens at its schools, where kids learned how to grow food, cook it, and eat a healthy diet. (FirstLine joined the national Edible Schoolyard project, which delivers kitchen and garden classes and nutrition education events at its schools.)

Altman arrived back from England in 2008, as the first two schools were expanding. Recasner, Leslie Jacobs, and Sarah Usdin all told him the city's most pressing need was organizations that could turn around entire schools. That is far, far more difficult than starting a new school a grade at a time, because leaders have to change the behavior of students who have become accustomed to chaos in the classrooms and hallways. But Altman had been involved in three turnarounds in the U.K., so he now knew it was possible.

"Tony said, 'I'm exhausted, why don't you take over FirstLine and use it as the vehicle to do turnarounds," Altman remembers. Recasner stayed for two years but handed off CEO duties to Altman. In 2010, he left to run Agenda for Children, which advocates for and provides services for Louisiana children, from childcare to health care to foster care.

In 2009 FirstLine landed a federal School Improvement Grant, as well as some foundation money, to spend a year planning its first turnaround, a failing RSD K–8 school. The next spring the RSD also asked FirstLine to take over management of a charter school whose bookkeeper had embezzled $600,000. Busy planning the turnaround, Altman and Recasner declined, but the RSD pushed them to reconsider. When the staff and parents at the school voted for the takeover, they finally agreed.

By then, Altman was looking for ways to squeeze more learning out of the same dollars. In 2010–11 he began to explore the potential of educational software to help with math and reading. (In the education world this is known as "personalized" or "blended" learning—the latter term because it blends the impact of teaching and software.) They created a design team, led by two of their school leaders, that researched different models. They ran small pilots with different software and got feedback from teachers. Then in May they invited their entire staff to test the options and collected feedback, which informed their final design. Getting teacher input yielded many improvements, says Sabrina Pence, who was principal of Arthur Ashe Charter School at the time. One school that didn't solicit input encountered much more resistance from teachers.

Altman raised about $200,000 to outfit computer labs in two schools and buy software. Children in kindergarten through second grade spent an hour a day in the computer lab, which could handle 60 at a time. Those in third through eighth grades spent an hour and a half a day, divided between math and reading. The software was for practice; teachers still handled instruction. During computer lab, a teacher in the back of the room pulled out kids who were struggling, one by one, to help them, and two aides wandered the room to help those who had questions or computer problems and to keep everyone on task.

When I visited, in 2013, every child I asked said they liked working in the computer lab more than sitting in regular classes. But an aide told me that out of two classes, totaling sixty kids, three or four children didn't have the attention span required. Pence explained that some programs were extremely engaging, others less so. Math software had a big impact on their test scores, while reading software did not. If kids didn't like to read, doing so on a screen didn't seem to help.

To boost motivation, they used competition between grade levels and classes. "We found [blended learning] didn't work unless we said, here's a goal, and there are consequences—some nice rewards, and some otherwise," Pence told me. "We try to put as many positive pieces in, but it also works to say to some kids, 'You have detention, and you will complete your work in detention, and until you're finished, you'll be in detention.' We usually implement that in late November and early December. Without that, we saw varied levels of effort from the kids."

The software programs provided a steady stream of data about which children were struggling, so teachers could help them catch up. "This really allowed us to accelerate quickly," Pence said. "I can meet you where you are, fix your specific issue, and then move on to the next kid who needs help." After a

year of stagnation in math scores at Ashe, she said, blended learning produced a nine-point gain in the percentage of students at basic or above in the
first year, followed by a 17-point gain the next.

It also allowed the school to shift resources to some pressing needs. "When
you have two groups in one space all day long, and you add up the minutes
that that frees up for adults," Pence said, it means you need fewer teachers.
"We've been able to add in full-time nurses, full-time social workers, that we
wouldn't have had before that."

By 2012–13 Arthur Ashe had earned a school performance score of B,
despite the fact that 96 percent of its students were low income. (The state
scores mostly reflect test scores, not student growth, so very few schools full
of poor kids ever score above a C. For more on how the measurement system
works, see appendix A.) FirstLine's three other K–8 schools earned B's and
C's. But Altman felt it was time to move beyond the "no excuses," highly structured, test-driven model that had gotten them that far. "What got us this far, as
a turnaround, is not what is going to get us to the next level," he reasoned. "It
doesn't address the full breadth of education we want to provide. So we made
some big changes." They brought in more athletics, more extracurricular programs after school, more art and music, more Edible Schoolyard experiences,
and more exposure to possible careers, and they continued to refine their use
of blended learning. Their goal was to develop students in "mind, body, and
spirit."

Veteran Principals Liberated by Chartering

Jay Altman is typical of some charter leaders in New Orleans: He is white, he
grew up elsewhere, and he found his calling—turning around New Orleans
schools—at a fairly young age. But just as many leaders are veteran New
Orleans educators who struggled in traditional schools and were liberated by
the shift to charters.

Rene Lewis-Carter was born in Algiers, a quiet neighborhood across the
river from the rest of New Orleans. Like many middle-class African Americans, her parents and many of her aunts and uncles were teachers. "I did not
want to teach," she told me when I visited her school in 2011, "because I saw my
parents teach and then go off to a second job at night. I was a child whose parents were always off working. My life was school, there was no outside life, and
I did not like school. I just wanted to hurry up and get out of high school. I
went to summer school every year, so I finished at 15, went to Our Lady of Holy
Cross College." She graduated at 19.

She landed a job as a flight attendant at Southwest Airlines and spent two years there, loving the travel. "But eventually, somewhere along the way, there was this nudging in me that teaching was exactly what I wanted to do. I felt that I needed to honor my parents, and honor all those who had gone before, and do a much better job than they had done in the past."

After a stint next door in Jefferson Parish and a master's degree with a thesis on at-risk kids, she became a high school teacher in New Orleans. Young, attractive, intelligent, and passionate about helping kids, she was quickly recognized as a talent. Soon she was the district's special education coordinator. Then someone said, "You should apply for an assistant principal position at Carter Woodson Middle School." A new principal, Mary Laurie, had been hired to turn around the school, where two students had recently shot each other in the schoolyard. "I had the opportunity to work with my mentor, and one of the greatest leaders in this district, especially about culture and climate, Miss Mary Laurie," Lewis-Carter told me back in 2011.

They began at Woodson by bringing the faculty and staff together to paint the graffiti-covered walls. And together they transformed the school, using extra money the district was pouring into failing middle schools. Soon district leaders recruited Lewis-Carter to run her own school, back in Algiers.

As Katrina approached, she and her husband evacuated to Houston. Just before the storm a group of community leaders in Algiers had begun working on a proposal to secure charters for all 13 schools in the area. No levees failed in Algiers, so when federal money became available to open charters, the fledgling Algiers Charter School Association jumped at the chance. Lewis-Carter, now unemployed, was excited by the idea. "I've always wanted to be at the cutting edge of what was going on," she told me. "The thought of autonomy intrigued me; the thought of being able to control a budget intrigued me."

So along with more than 30 other principals who were out of work, she applied for one of five positions. "I was determined," she said, laughing. "No one is going to out-interview me, because I *know* how to run a school."

Within two weeks, she was opening Martin Behrman Elementary, a brand new charter. She hired veteran teachers who "had endured the Katrina experience and understood what the children had gone through." More than half of her students were still homeless, living in shelters or trailers or with relatives or neighbors. Her first task, she felt, was to make them all feel safe. "For weeks, we listened to their stories," she said—horrible tales of escaping public housing developments on mattresses, then enduring the heat at the Superdome.

Lewis-Carter doted on her students, who were almost all African American. "The Behrman Way," as she called it, meant going above and beyond to provide whatever her children needed. If they needed haircuts, one of her third-grade paraprofessionals was a barber. If someone needed an Easter dress, the teachers could tap a petty-cash fund to buy her one. The idea was to "take the burden off of the children so they will be free to learn."

The other key, she said, was "creating a culture and climate of success—being sure children have the opportunity to experience success daily.

> *Teachers are required to make sure the children leave here feeling good about something every day. The children here think that they're very bright. I find that when you set high expectations and give them support, they rise to those expectations. The children think they have the best uniforms, the best building. Our marching band—they believe that they're the best. We march in eight parades. That's how I treat them.*

In April of 2006 the students had to take state exams. "Our scores were dismal," Lewis-Carter admitted. "My stomach ached. How can we possibly do this? But I swore that it would never happen again." From that moment on, she focused intensely on data, assessing students regularly, strategizing with teachers about what would work best, testing different approaches, and investing heavily in professional development for teachers. Like the rest of the Algiers charters, she implemented the Teacher Advancement Program, a national initiative in which schools use mentor and master teachers to coach others and help them improve.

The next year, 98 percent of her fourth-graders passed (scored basic or above on) the English Language Arts (ELA) test, which is required to move to fifth grade, and 96 percent passed math. By 2011, 100 percent passed ELA. In 2014, on a more sophisticated test that was partially aligned with Common Core State Standards, 80 percent or more of her fourth-graders passed all four tests: ELA, math, science, and social science. These were scores that rivaled the city's selective schools. In 2015 the state named Lewis-Carter middle school principal of the year.

She did not mince words when explaining her success: "If something does not work for my children here at Behrman, be it a teacher, be it a textbook, I can get rid of it. I got to handpick teachers. I'd never been able to do that before." And those teachers "understood that things were different, that if they did not perform, they didn't have to be here the very next day. Everyone understood the sense of urgency." In a school of 52 teachers and aides, Lewis-Carter told me, she fired seven in her first five years.

"I met some great and wonderful people in New Orleans Public Schools, who helped to shape and form my career, and I will be eternally grateful to them. However, a change was needed. Schools were failing, children were failing. We have had the opportunity to see children thrive and communities thrive, with the charter schools."

Would she ever go back to the old way? I asked. Never, she insisted.

> *I have colleagues in Jefferson Parish, and they come here all the time, and they say, "But you don't have the problems we have." No I don't, because for the first time I can tell a teacher, "You know what, your teaching stinks," and I'm not going to be served with a grievance. I don't want to go back. With rules and regulations and tenure and unions, it becomes about the adults—those are adult agendas.*

Whole-School Restarts at ReNEW Schools

When Paul Vallas decided to start handing RSD-run schools to charters with their entire student bodies intact, few besides Jay Altman's FirstLine Schools were willing to take them. So Vallas turned to one of his own staff members.

Gary Robichaux is a modest, unassuming man, whose blond hair and blue eyes make him look younger than his 50-odd years. In 2001, after a dozen years of teaching in suburban St. Charles Parish, the Louisiana Department of Education named him a "distinguished educator" and sent him as a consultant and instructional coach into the second-worst-performing school in the state, a New Orleans middle school. It was a shock, for both Robichaux and the students. "I couldn't believe the literacy level of the kids," he remembers. "They were left so far behind, and completely ignored. And a lot of kids were not used to having Caucasian people in the building. Someone with blue eyes—they were just mesmerized by that. A lot of these kids were not exposed to anything but life in the housing development and the school next door."

The RSD took over the school and asked the Knowledge Is Power Program (KIPP), now the largest charter management organization in the country and one of the most effective, to run it. KIPP hired Robichaux to launch a K–8 school, one grade at a time. Three weeks after it opened, Katrina hit. His home flooded, Robichaux ended up in Florida. "A student called me from the Astrodome and said, could he go to the KIPP school in Houston?" he remembers. "I talked to a bunch of our teachers, and we flew to Houston, because we didn't have anything else to do." They found Mike Feinberg, one of KIPP's founders, walking around the Astrodome with a KIPP T-shirt on, looking for KIPP students. At least two dozen of them were sleeping on the cots that covered the Astrodome's floor. "He found us a building in 10 days, we started recruiting kids, and pretty soon we had 450 to 500 kids."

They called the school New Orleans West. Seventy percent of the staff were first-year Teach For America volunteers who had evacuated. They did so well that the RSD gave them a K–8 building in the French Quarter the next fall. Because the need was acute and Robichaux's Houston school had performed well, Feinberg let him open all nine grades simultaneously. "We were the only two KIPP schools in the nation to start nine grades at a time," Robichaux says. "But we outperformed the KIPP school in New Orleans that started a grade at a time."

Robichaux wanted to replicate his school quickly, but KIPP's leaders preferred a slower expansion. When Paul Vallas heard this, in 2007, he hired Robichaux to oversee his 24 RSD-run K–8 schools. The RSD was part of the state department of education, however, and Robichaux chafed at the bureaucracy. Then, three years after Katrina, teachers in the RSD began to earn tenure. "I went to Paul and said, 'We don't have a level playing ground. The charters don't have tenure, but our schools do. They can move teachers out; they have more resources, and they have more flexibility. So I asked him to let me take the two worst schools each year and turn them into charters."

Robichaux called his organization ReNEW Schools, and both New Schools for New Orleans and the New School Venture Fund supported it financially. He started with two K–8 schools where less than 20 percent of the kids were scoring at grade level. "We had a tough population of kids," he says. "I had kids the first year that I chased around the school—they were just out of control.

> *The first thing you need to fix is the culture. In one middle school there were several fights every day, before we took it over. After we took over, we had a couple fights a week, at first. The second year, a couple of fights a semester. I don't think we have any fights there anymore. We have a tough leader there. He's consistent—he doesn't scream at the kids; he's into tough love. He sets limits, and he follows through on them. That was the key, the calmness, and the focus on academics.*

ReNEW assigned a leader for kindergarten through second grade, one for third through fifth, and a third for sixth through eighth. "The way you run grades kindergarten through two is very different from the way you run grades six through eight," Robichaux says. "And each leader can concentrate on just 200 kids and 10 teachers."

Because poor kids are often behind already when they start kindergarten, ReNEW created pre-kindergarten programs, including one classroom for three-year-olds. And because poor kids lose so much ground over a long summer break, ReNEW schools ran from mid-July to mid-June, with two-week breaks in the fall, at Christmas, at Mardi Gras, and in the spring. ReNEW gave benchmark tests constantly—as most successful charters in the city did—to see where kids needed remediation.

In 2011 ReNEW also started an intensive therapeutic program for kids who were so emotionally disturbed they presented a danger to themselves and others. Some of the kids had had a family member murdered or jailed; others had suffered physical and emotional abuse, or chronic neglect, or a lifetime of bouncing between homes and guardians. Robichaux suspects that many had mothers who had abused drugs or alcohol when they were pregnant. By 2014 there were two teachers, three paraprofessionals, one full-time counselor, and a psychiatrist—for 16 kids. RSD per-pupil funding covered $350,000 per year, and the school raised another $150,000 through grants. In addition to small-group instruction, students received individual and group therapy and participated in a variety of activities, including field trips and therapeutic time with pets. The goal was to transition them back to regular classrooms. By 2014, three students had made the full transition, though they still received some special services. Violence had plummeted: before the program, each student had received the maximum ten days a year of suspensions for unacceptable behavior, but in 2013–14, only one student was suspended, for two days. The average student was achieving a year and a half of reading improvement every year.

When I visited in December 2013, the first two ReNEW schools were in their fourth year. They had turned around completely; behavior had become an afterthought. Now the rewards and sanctions were focused on academics: If a child's grade point average was below a certain level, he might not get recess. If it was above a certain level, he might be invited to a dinner to celebrate high achievers. "We also focus on the high-performing kids being leaders— having them help us lead discussions in class," science teacher Erin Brady told me. "This is a new thing we are now ready for—academic conversations led by students."

By 2014 ReNEW had four schools that went from prekindergarten through eighth grade. Before ReNEW took over, its first two restart schools had school performance scores of 23 and 27 on the state's new scale—equivalent to low F's. By 2013–14 they were up to 75, a C, and 60, a D. "All of our schools have grown 30 to 40 points," Robichaux told me. "The state wants you to grow five points a year; we average over ten. We want all of our schools to be A or B schools. We want to stop expanding for the next few years, perfect everything, and get 'em all to A or B." By 2015–16, despite the transition to much more demanding exams in 2015, all four schools earned C grades, scoring between 72 and 75.

The Discipline Dilemma

Many of the successful charter schools full of low-income kids used strict discipline to keep control of classrooms, so students could learn without constant disruptions. There were exceptions, such as the Algiers Charter Schools Association (ACSA) schools run by Rene Lewis-Carter and Mary Laurie, but many handed out suspensions regularly. Critics often accused them of being far too strict. But without firm control, schools struggled. In her book *Hope Against Hope*, Sarah Carr described in detail how KIPP's first high school lost the battle for discipline—and therefore student learning—during its first year. (It has since become the first school in the RSD to earn an A from the state, in 2016.)

As I mentioned in the preface, my daughter Molly taught at a struggling K–8 charter school in the ACSA. There I saw what happens when school leaders fail to enforce discipline effectively. Some adults screamed at kids when they disrupted class or fought—often telling them they were "no good"—but rarely imposed consequences. Discipline policies spelled out the consequences for a first infraction, a second, and a third: detention, suspension, and so on. But the dean in charge of discipline rarely imposed them. Instead, he would send kids who had been kicked out back to class ten minutes later, completely undermining the teachers' authority. Teachers lost precious time and sometimes lost control of their classrooms. Morale plummeted, and the school had trouble retaining good teachers.

The charter network that took the most heat for its strict discipline was Collegiate Academies, a local organization that operated three charter high schools. In November 2013 a group of students walked out of two of their schools to protest being "disciplined for anything and everything." The next month students and community members held a rally and tried to present a set of demands to the board of Collegiate. The following spring a group of families filed a civil rights complaint, alleging a "harsh and punitive" culture. Collegiate officials denied the accusations and said most of those involved in the protests were community members and alumni, not students or parents. One of the outsiders who organized the complaint was a long-time critic of the district, who had sought a charter and been turned down. The director of the Louisiana Association of Public Charter Schools, Caroline Roemer Shirley, described the suit as a "PR stunt" by "a certain set of folks who are angry that they are not the decision-makers." Still, Collegiate provides a useful window into the controversy over strict discipline in charter schools, which has become a national issue. It also illustrates the evolution of discipline policies in New Orleans.

*   *   *

BEN MARCOVITZ WAS 28 when he founded Collegiate's first high school, Sci Academy. A graduate of Yale, he had taught school in New Orleans and Boston, earned a master's in education at Harvard, and served briefly as assistant director of a similar charter high school in New Orleans.

In 2008 he opened the doors to 83 freshmen in temporary trailers, with no playing fields or gym. The average enrollee was reading at a fourth-grade level, which meant Marcovitz and his staff had to throw out their entire curriculum and start over. Five years later, when I visited, the average enrollee was still reading at a fourth- to fifth-grade level, and one in five was at a second-grade level or below. The campus had moved, but it was still in temporary, prefabricated buildings that sat on a bleak parking lot ten miles east of downtown.

Marcovitz and his teachers began each year with home visits. Every morning as students got off their buses, they greeted each one with a firm handshake. Freshmen were required to walk on one side of the halls, silently, for the first three weeks. They immediately heard a lot about discipline: These are our expectations, our structure, our rules, our consequences, and this is why it's important. Each student was assigned to a same-sex "advisory" group, ideally led by the same teacher for four years, where much of the talk focused on values. Teachers were available by phone during the week until 9:30 P.M. for anything students needed.

Students very quickly "get a message that this school is unlike other schools that I've been in," Marcovitz said. By having kids walk on separate sides of the aisle, the school minimizes hallway confrontations that might waste the precious time students have for learning. And by reining in negative behavior quickly, they create a safe environment. Students arrive at high school expecting it to be a "physically and emotionally scary place," Marcovitz told Sarah Carr. "We try to overturn that assumption very quickly by showing them the adults are extremely in charge."

Things loosened up a bit as students got older, but the schools used one-day suspensions heavily, usually for the rest of the day after an incident. They typically had the highest self-reported suspension rates in the city. In 2012–13, the year before the protests, 69, 61, and 58 percent of students were suspended at least once at Collegiate's three schools. But the strategy appeared to work: When I walked the halls, it was obvious that the students were focused on learning, not disrupting things. Other observers consistently reported the same thing.

The school had "culture deans" for each grade level, and they chose one value for each grade to concentrate on each year. "The first week of advisory in ninth grade, we focus on excellence—we talk about it, define it, spend all our time on it," one administrator told me. "Our senior class is working on values like self-advocacy and initiative." At first, some kids were cynical about the whole values thing, she said, but as time wore on, "they become a language they use."

Two hours of homework was the norm, and the school worked hard to build motivation. During the first week of ninth grade everyone visited a college; by the middle of junior year they had toured at least 20, in seven states. Every morning every student got a feedback slip, with merits (Scibucks) and demerits for behavior, as well as feedback on their participation in every class.

After the walkout Collegiate surveyed parents and found that 93 percent of them were satisfied with their children's education. No one was forced to go to its schools, yet they remained popular choices for families. Still, Marcovitz took the criticisms to heart. He set a goal of zero out-of-school suspensions in 2014–15 and began exploring restorative justice strategies, which ask students to talk through problems with others, take responsibility for their behavior, and make amends for any damage they have inflicted on others. Members of the Micah Project at a local Catholic church took Collegiate's leaders to other cities to see well-run restorative justice programs, and Collegiate then implemented its own—as many schools in New Orleans are now doing.

In 2014–15, Collegiate's three schools expelled only ten students between them, and they suspended only 2 percent of students. Instead, disruptive students were usually sent to an in-school "Positive Redirection Center," to write out their reflections about the incident and continue with their schoolwork. But that didn't happen until three teachers had reported a problem on the same day. This use of "in-school" suspension has become common in New Orleans.

Collegiate Schools are obviously not for everyone. Of the 83 in Sci Academy's first class, only 52 stayed on to graduate. Half of the rest left for other schools in the city, for a variety of reasons, while the others left the city, were held back a year, or were expelled, according to Collegiate. But the schools have expanded their extracurricular and sports programs, to hold on to more students, and their retention rates have risen.

It's hard to argue with Collegiate's results. Although 92 percent of its students are low income (qualifying for subsidized meals), in 2012 Sci Academy was the highest-scoring nonselective high school in the city. It earned a grade of B in 2014–15 and 2015–16, despite the shift to more challenging tests aligned with Common Core standards. In 2015, 53 percent of its students scored a 20 or above on the ACT (American College Testing) exam, the highest of any nonselective school in New Orleans. And in 2012, 100 percent of the first graduating class—including all special education students—went on to college, all but 3 percent to four-year colleges. In the second graduating class, 92 percent enrolled in four-year colleges and 8 percent in two-year colleges. By 2016, the combined number was 80 percent, still well above the state or national average.

For some students, Sci Academy has performed near miracles. Consider Troy Simon, an African American student who lived with his family in an abandoned building for six months and at 14 made money tap dancing for tourists in the French Quarter. He wrote the following column for the local newspaper after the civil rights complaint was filed in 2014:

> Lately, Sci Academy and other New Orleans public charter schools have been the center of some controversy over their disciplinary policies. As a recent alumnus, I can confidently say that my time as a student at Sci Academy was one of the most academically challenging and rewarding experiences I have ever had, and that, without Sci Academy, I never would have made it to college.
>
> Before I attended high school, I struggled with illiteracy. I was embarrassed, and so I turned to mischief to hide my difficulty reading. I refused to do my work in class and deflected my teachers' questions whenever they would call on me. Other times I started fights or pretended to sleep until the bell rung. I had mixed feelings about school, because I thought that my teachers had marked me as a failure.
>
> When I got to Sci Academy, I initially disagreed with the level of discipline and structure that the school expected. I did not understand why we were required to shake hands with our principal and teaching staff every morning, why we were told to walk through the hallways along lines of tape on the floor, and why we received demerits when our homework was incomplete. I did not understand why the school needed a rigid disciplinary system. My teachers told me that the system increased efficiency and responsibility to maximize learning, but I didn't believe them.
>
> After spending some time at Sci Academy, I transferred back to my former Recovery School District high school. This was a mistake. By then I was a different student; I went to class regularly and participated in discussions. I asked questions and tried to articulate my answers, but I wasn't receiving the same kind of education I had at Sci.
>
> Class discussions were rare, and we did not talk in depth about topics I found interesting, such as the Romantic and Modernist periods, as we had at Sci. Instead, when we did talk, it was hardly ever about the classwork. In the hallways, students slid on swivel chairs, ran up and down the stairwells jostling each other and got to class late without being penalized. When teachers tried to get our attention and actually teach, students talked, texted or pretended to sleep. Most of my classmates dropped out.

I realized that Sci Academy was a better fit for me, so I transferred back . . . It didn't take long for Sci Academy to learn that I had been illiterate. I told them my story and how much education meant to me. So they assigned extra homework, study sessions and one-on-one tutoring. The teaching staff was patient with me and talked me through problems I didn't understand. They always made sure I knew the material as well as possible.

It became clear why Sci Academy had a challenging educational and strict disciplinary system—to help students like me who came from low-performing schools and needed extra attention. The system really did help students learn, despite what some in the press have claimed.

Troy Simon graduated in 2012 and went on to Bard College, where he studied American literature and graduated in 2016. In 2014 he was invited to speak at a White House conference on expanding higher education opportunities for low-income Americans, where he met the president and first lady. After Bard, he enrolled at Yale Divinity School. He also wants to pursue a joint degree in nursing or social work, so he can "help the mentally ill and physically wounded—I think that is my place."

None of this would have happened without Sci Academy, he believes. "Sci Academy was willing to push me till the glass ceiling broke," he told me.

Sci wanted to help me reach my potential in the best way possible, and that was pushing me. The school didn't have silos; teachers collaborated with each other—"This student needs help with this." I saw that they were a team, and they were willing to put all that energy into a student. I saw that they were exhausted at the end of the day, but they were very serious about my education, they really cared.

Simon's sister now attends Collegiate, and he loves the schools' shift to restorative justice. Suspending a student helps no one, he says. Instead, students need counselors, to talk through their situations. "So I think the approach Sci is taking now is absolutely wonderful."

Phase 2: Building a More Sophisticated Model

As these examples illustrate, many schools in New Orleans have evolved over the years. Because failing schools are replaced and new schools open to meet emerging needs, the entire system also evolves.

The experiment began with a few selective former magnet schools, a lot of "no excuses" schools (with strict discipline, long school days and years, and an intense focus on academics), some quite conventional schools, and a few outliers—a bilingual school, a Montessori elementary, and so on. Tony Amato returned to run the International High School, a charter, and in 2011 launched an International Baccalaureate program. He also hosted Bard Early College, which later invited selected New Orleans juniors and seniors to spend half their days taking college courses, for credit. In 2011 the New Orleans Military and Maritime Academy also opened, and by 2014–15 it had earned a grade of A from the state.

Early on, there were few options for those who had serious emotional problems, who had dropped out or been expelled, or who were returning from the criminal justice system. The trauma of Katrina had impacted many, but the epidemic of gun violence among young people in New Orleans was almost worse. In 2012, 35 children under the age of 21 were murdered. A survey of more than 1,000 youths aged 11 to 15, taken from 2012 to 2015, found that 38 percent had witnessed domestic violence, 40 percent had witnessed a shooting, stabbing, or beating, 54 percent had experienced the murder of someone close to them, and nearly 20 percent had experienced post-traumatic stress—four times the national rate.

In 2011, FirstLine created the NET at Clark High School, a year-round program for former dropouts and over-age students ages 15 to 21. Soon it spun off as a separate charter high school, with 160 students and intensive use of restorative justice to deal with conflicts. For every five students in 2015–16, one was involved with the judicial system, one was homeless, and one was either pregnant or already a parent.

The next year others founded Crescent Leadership Academy, to educate seventh- through twelfth-graders who had been expelled from other schools. Some 15 to 25 percent of its students were homeless at any given time, and in its first four years, 14 of its students were murdered. Staff included counselors and social workers, and they were available to students at any hour.

Also in 2012, ReNEW Schools launched Accelerated High School, for dropouts and over-age students age 16 to 21. There were no sports; the entire focus was academics—catching up and getting a high school diploma. The school's 300 students took only two courses at a time, for six weeks, then took the state's end-of-course test. Once they had reached a sixth-grade reading level, they spent 75 percent of their time using educational software; they could even take laptops home. The rest of the time they worked in small groups with a teacher. "We speed it up, catch kids up," Gary Robichaux told me. "In a traditional high school kids do six Carnegie units a year; our average is eight or nine."

Louisiana had two types of high school diplomas, career prep and college prep. Accelerated aimed for college prep diplomas, which were more demanding, because its leaders felt they would better prepare students for a two-year college. In 2014 100 kids graduated, and fewer than 15 percent dropped out each year, according to Robichaux. "We work with the kids to get into technical schools, to get careers," he says. "Most of our kids choose that or the military."

For students with dyslexia and other reading disabilities, Cypress Academy, an elementary school, opened in a synagogue between Uptown and the Garden District. For Vietnamese and Latino immigrants, Foundation Preparatory Elementary opened in East New Orleans, with Spanish and Vietnamese speakers on its staff.

When it became clear that blended learning worked at FirstLine, other networks quickly joined in. Leslie Jacobs pulled together a group of local funders and began making grants to schools, and by the fall of 2013, KIPP, ReNEW, and Collegiate Academies were all in the pilot stage. In 2014 New Schools for New Orleans landed a big grant from Next Generation Learning Challenges, which matched the $3 million raised locally. NSNO and Jacobs's organization, Educate Now!, have awarded $300,000 whole-school implementation grants to eight schools and smaller exploration and pilot grants to many others. They also fund fellowships for teachers who want to lead efforts in their schools, and they facilitate a personalized learning community focused on blended learning, through which teachers and leaders meet regularly to share what they have learned.

MOST CHARTER HIGH schools discovered at some point that many of their graduates floundered in college. Most were poor, and most were the first in their families to attend college. Hence many high schools hired people to help them make it *through* college. At KIPP Renaissance High School, for instance, a KIPP Through College team tracks graduates' grade point averages, how many hours a week they're working, how much they owe, how many credit hours they've earned, their career goals, and other indicators, to see if they need help. Every graduate has a monthly check-in with an advisor, in person or over the phone. The advisors intervene with financial aid offices, read important student papers and provide feedback, help the students find resources they need, even help with school transfers if necessary. If a student drops out, the monthly check-ins continue. "No matter how many times our plan has to adjust, we adjust," KIPP's lead alumni advisor in New Orleans told the *Times Picayune*. "But we keep moving forward. This summer I got six of my unenrolled students back in school."

Most New Orleans schools have few white students: in 2016–17, only 8 percent of all public school students in the city were white. But by 2012, people were beginning to propose charters that would be deliberately integrated. In 2011 Matt Candler, then CEO of New Schools for New Orleans, had left to create 4.0 Schools, an "early-stage education incubator," to help people start new and creative schools. Bricolage Academy, an elementary school that aims for racial and income diversity and uses project-based learning to stimulate critical thinking, opened in 2013 as one of 4.0's first projects. Homer A. Plessy Community School opened the same year, with roughly the same objective and an arts-focused, hands-on curriculum. "We just want to be a different kind of choice," Plessy's principal, Joan Reilly, told National Public Radio in 2014. "We want to be the school that takes the creators and the dreamers and channel it into something that's awesome. It's not the traditional sit-in-your-desk and have someone give you the knowledge all day. It's more of the let's get on the floor, let's get messy, let's learn by doing." Orleans Parish School Board has authorized another "diverse-by-design" school, Élan Academy, to open in 2017.

What About Those Who Don't Want College?

Schools in New Orleans don't improve just "because the people running them are better," says Jay Altman. "Rather, it is because teachers and school leaders have more autonomy to be adaptive in this new system—they can improve more quickly, they can more easily make the thousands of small changes and decisions that need to be made every week and every year to better meet the needs of students and parents and teachers. The new system allows schools to evolve more quickly, and demands it."

Consider the challenge of helping students who don't want to go to college. Like their counterparts around the country, most New Orleans charters have focused obsessively on getting kids into college. But that misses a lot of young people, with serious consequences. A study by Tulane University's Cowen Institute for Public Education Initiatives found that 14.5 percent of New Orleans youths ages 16 to 24—some 6,820 young people—were neither in school nor employed in 2014.

"The majority of jobs created in this country over the next decade will require more than a high school degree but less than a four-year college degree," Leslie Jacobs pointed out in an op-ed. "Locally, our region will need 17,000 skilled workers over the next three years, and many of these will be in the fields of science, technology, engineering and math (STEM)." She described jobs paying between $30,000 and $64,000 a year—for nurses, medical technicians, carpenters, and others—going begging, "unfilled due to an unprepared and untrained workforce."

In typical fashion, Jacobs and charter leaders began to respond. Jacobs's organization, Educate Now!, convened a dozen different groups, from the RSD and OPSB to Baptist Community Ministries and the city of New Orleans, to create YouthForce NOLA. By 2017 they had raised $13 million of the $15 million they had budgeted for the first five years, to provide paid summer internships to high school students and to give grants and technical assistance to high schools to develop career-tech programs. Four high schools had such programs when the 2016–17 school year began.

One of the first was at FirstLine. In 2011 Jay Altman had agreed to take over Joseph S. Clark Preparatory High School, the lowest-performing non-alternative high school in the state, with its student body intact. The year before it had a school performance score of 22.8 out of a possible 200. By 2014–15, under FirstLine, that was up to 62.4 (on a new scale of zero to 150), and its four-year graduation rate reached 69 percent, up from 33 percent in 2010. But the state still rated it a D.

In August 2014 FirstLine launched "NOLA Tech," a program in which students enrolled in both Clark and Delgado Community College and pursued industry-based credentials in areas such as health care, digital media, construction, and manufacturing. They could earn dual credit and get summer internships. By the first spring, 19 students were on track to earn industry credentials, 81 had applied for the program for 2015–16, and the school was struggling to accommodate the demand. But by then, competition between high schools in the city had increased dramatically, and Clark was struggling to attract enough students overall to be financially viable. Altman turned to the Clark Community Council, a small group made up mostly of Clark alumni, which had formed when they were considering whether they wanted FirstLine to take over. Together they decided to turn Clark into a small career-tech school, mainly for juniors and seniors in high school.

But when they floated the idea with the larger community, the reaction was almost unanimous: Why not do this on a bigger scale? They set up a working group in partnership with YouthNOLA, the RSD, and OPSB, and the group decided to create a career-tech center serving all the city's high schools, probably in a new location. They hope to have it open by 2019 or 2020, offering a range of programs and equipment that no single high school can afford.

Taking over Clark, Altman says, forced him to think about the kids who were not destined for college. Then, Clark's failure to attract enough students led to the invention of an entirely new school model. The system *demanded* a response—and produced one.

In August 2017, it happened again: Jonathan Johnson opened Rooted Charter School, the city's first high school completely devoted to career-tech education. A four-year veteran of KIPP Central City Academy, Johnson had already spent a year refining his model with 14 juniors and seniors as a pilot within the larger Algiers Technology Academy. "We want our students to compete for the same high-tech jobs as college graduates," he says.

Rooted students will spend half the school day on general education, using a comprehensive digital curriculum called Edgenuity, to work at their own pace, while teachers provide support. The other half they will spend working on projects designed by Rooted's teachers and industry partners. "By junior year," the school's website explains, "a Rooted student will spend up to half of the school day interning with a partner or completing college/technical school courses." They will have the opportunity to earn advanced industry credentials. "This will position any student for acceptance to a post-secondary program and/or job offer for entry-level employment with one of our partners."

CHAPTER 3

THE RESULTS

HAVE THE REFORMS IN NEW ORLEANS paid off? Has all the controversy and hard work been worth it?

In a word, yes.

Before Katrina, 60 percent of New Orleans students attended a school with a performance score in the bottom 10 percent of the state. A decade later, only 13 percent did.

Before Katrina, roughly half of public school students in New Orleans dropped out, and fewer than one in five went on to college. In 2015, 76 percent graduated from high school within five years, a point above the state average. (Five-year rates for 2016 were not yet available at press time.) In 2016, 64 percent of graduates entered college, six points higher than the state average.

The fastest progress took place in the RSD schools. Because the Orleans Parish School Board (OPSB) was only allowed to keep schools that scored above the state average, the failing schools were all in the RSD. In the spring of 2007, only 23 percent of students in those schools tested at or above grade level. Seven years later, *57 percent did*. (The state adopted a new standardized test in 2015, so scores are no longer comparable to those of the previous decade.) As figure 3-1 shows, RSD students in New Orleans improved *almost four times faster than the state average*.

In 2014–15, New Orleans high-schoolers performed at the state average, ranked 31st out of 69 parishes. Of all Louisiana high schools where three quarters or more of the students were low income, New Orleans had the top five performers.

Despite a huge increase in the percentage of students taking the now mandatory ACT college readiness exam, scores in New Orleans have increased faster than in any other district in Louisiana. They have risen from an average of 17 in 2004–5—ranking 61st out of 68 parishes—to 18.8 in 2014–15, ranking 35th. (The state average for public school students was 19.4 in 2015.)

Stanford University's Center for Research on Education Outcomes (CREDO) studied charter school results between 2005–6 and 2011–12. Charter students in New Orleans gained nearly half a year of additional learning in math and

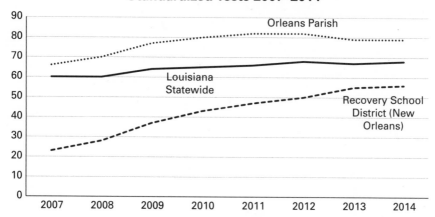

Percent of Students at Basic (Grade Level) or Above on Standardized Tests 2007–2014*

Figure 3-1 Source: Louisiana Department of Education.

*The 2014 exams were more difficult because they were more closely aligned with the Common Core standards, which explains why progress leveled off in the Recovery School District and the state and Orleans Parish scores fell. In 2015 Louisiana switched to the PARCC (Partnership for Assessment of Readiness for College and Careers) exams, which are based on Common Core standards.

a third of a year in reading, every year, compared to demographically similar students, with similar past test scores, in the city's non-chartered public schools.

Little of this appears to be the result of demographic changes. In 2013–14, 84 percent of public school students qualified for a free or reduced-price lunch, compared to 77 percent before Katrina. And census data tells us that poverty among residents younger than 18 rose from 33 percent in 2007 to 39 percent in 2013, approaching pre-storm levels.

If anything, today's students may be *more* disadvantaged than those before Katrina, because they lived through the hurricane and a subsequent spike in violent crime.

Some improvement in test scores could reflect a small increase between 2004 and 2016 in the percentage of white students in New Orleans public schools, from 3 to 8 percent. But African Americans still make up 82 percent, down from 93 percent before the storm. And they have made the greatest gains relative to their counterparts statewide, no doubt because the RSD schools, which have improved the most, were more than 95 percent black during the post-Katrina years.

If one counts only African Americans, New Orleans had the lowest test scores in the state before Katrina, eight percentage points below the state

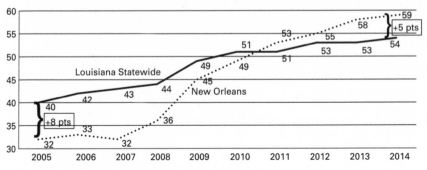

Percentage of African American Students Scoring Basic (Grade Level) or Above, All Standardized Tests, 2005–2014

Figure 3-2 Source: Louisiana Department of Education

average. By 2014 its scores exceeded the state average by five points, as figure 3-2 shows. On the new Partnership for Assessment of Readiness for College and Careers (PARCC) tests in 2015, which covered third through eighth grade, black students in New Orleans again outperformed their counterparts across the state—as well as in six other states (and Washington, D.C.) that used PARCC. (The one exception was Massachusetts, the nation's highest-scoring state on many tests.) ACT scores of the city's black students, which averaged 17.8 in 2015, were about a point higher than the national average for black students, 16.9. Black males in New Orleans graduated from high school at higher rates than their counterparts in both the state and nation.

Test scores, school performance scores, graduation and dropout data, ACT scores, and independent studies all reveal the same pattern: RSD schools in New Orleans have doubled or tripled their effectiveness since Katrina. But standardized test scores don't necessarily translate into success in the real world. More important indicators are high school graduation rates—and what happens *after* graduation. It's too early to say how many from New Orleans will graduate from college, but college *attendance* rates have sky-rocketed. Indeed, this has been the most dramatic indicator of improvement. The city's high school graduation and college-going rates now match or exceed state averages—an unprecedented feat for a large city with a majority of poor minority residents.

Winning the Political Battle

It is one thing to deliver results. It is quite another to win the hearts and minds of a majority of voters.

Race is a wound that festers beneath the surface of virtually every issue in New Orleans. African Americans were enslaved, then kept poor and powerless for a century through Jim Crow laws. When the first public schools opened, in the 1840s, free blacks were banned and Louisiana made it a crime to teach a slave to read. In 1900, local officials limited black education to five years. When federal courts finally forced integration, whites abandoned the public schools en masse.

Before Katrina, two thirds of the city's residents were black. After the civil rights movement gave African Americans their constitutional rights to vote, they won more and more elective offices. For several decades they ran city government and the public schools, and public sector jobs became a significant path to the middle class. In the land of Huey Long and Edwin Edwards corruption was the norm, so it was no surprise that African Americans continued the tradition. In the schools, sadly, their children paid the price.

By the time Katrina hit, the black community still harbored deep distrust of the white power structure. When the school district laid off its 7,500 employees—three quarters of them black—it triggered enormous anger. When charters and the RSD began reopening schools in 2006, they hired veteran teachers and principals from the district. But the available data suggest that less than half of the 7,500 former OPSB employees landed jobs with OPSB, the RSD, or charters. The public school population had fallen dramatically, after all, and 30 percent of OPSB teachers who applied to the RSD failed its basic skills test.

To make matters worse, blacks had to watch white reformers at the state board and the RSD take over the schools and white charter operators and teachers flood the city. By 2015 African Americans still made up only 51 percent of school leaders and roughly half the teaching force, down from 71 percent of teachers before the storm. To some, it didn't matter that most of the newcomers were idealistic liberals bent on helping poor black children. "Teach For America was the biggest slap in the face," Caroline Roemer Shirley, who runs the Louisiana Association of Public Charter Schools, told me in 2011. "'I don't have a job here, and you gave it to a 22-year-old that's never been in the classroom?' There's a lot of hostility about that."

In 2007 whites won a majority on the city council, and in 2008 they did the same on the Orleans Parish School Board. Many black activists suspected a white conspiracy to keep blacks from returning to the city, so whites could take over. In 2010 one activist said publicly that charters "are being given access to [school] buildings like it's cargo, like it's a slave ship."

Leslie Jacobs was accustomed to charges of racism. When she pioneered the standardized LEAP (Louisiana Education Assessment Program) tests, which students must pass to advance from fourth to fifth grade and from eighth to ninth, a black woman spat in her face and accused her of trying to send all black boys to prison. Behind her back, people called her "the white devil."

On polls, Jacobs says, a quarter to a third of African Americans have consistently expressed anger about the school reforms. "They want the schools returned to the OPSB, they resent charter schools, they're not supportive of the RSD, and they're angry," she says. "It's the same group of people who feel that their power has been taken from them, and what happened post-Katrina is a white conspiracy against them."

Having spent 30 years trying to improve schools in which almost all students were African American, Jacobs is philosophical about the attacks. "A lot of that stuff came my way, and I don't internalize it and I don't remember it," she says. "On OPSB, African American activists often berated all the whites on the board, called us a lot of names, and the president of the board did nothing to stop it. I just figured, they don't know me, they're angry, and I may be a symbol, but it's not me they're really angry at."

The most vocal opposition came from those who lost power or jobs. They pulled out all the usual arguments against charters: They're really private schools; they don't take their fair share of kids with disabilities; they get their test scores up by pushing out the toughest kids; and they get more money than other public schools.

None of those arguments stand up to the light of day. As I argued in the introduction, the fact that a private, nonprofit organization performs the teaching does not make a school private. Charter schools in New Orleans are funded with public money, granted charters and held accountable by publicly elected and appointed boards, and with the exception of a handful of selective schools—most of them former magnets in the traditional district—they offer equal access to all. There were a few for-profit charter operators early on, but they have all failed or closed down.

The charge about special education was long true of OPSB's charters, several of which were selective. But by 2012–13, 11.1 percent of students in RSD charters received special education, higher than the citywide average of 9.9 percent. According to a 2013 CREDO study, special education students in charter schools gained 65 days a year of additional learning in reading and 43 in math, compared to their counterparts in non-charters.

As for money, FEMA funds helped the city rebuild its devastated schools. But by 2010 RSD schools received slightly less than the Louisiana average in state and local *operating* funds and slightly more in federal funds, because they served so many poor children who were eligible for Title 1 money. Some of the charters raise extra money from foundations, but any public school is free to do that. Nationwide, traditional districts raise as much foundation money as charters do.

Teachers unions and their allies have spent years pointing out how many RSD charters are labeled D or F by the state's accountability system. But as those numbers dwindle, they never add that most charters are making significant progress toward higher grades, those that don't are shut down, and the schools they replaced were much, much worse.

Michael Deshotels, a former Louisiana teachers union president, voiced another common critique: "Those charter schools that showed impressive gains got much of it by carefully screening applicants and pushing out students who did not perform according to expectations. In addition, many under-performing students are counseled into transferring to other public schools that become dumping grounds."

There are always a few bad actors in any system, charter or traditional. A few charters in New Orleans have been disciplined or closed for counseling out difficult students. But by 2014, the RSD had closed its last dumping-ground schools and replaced them with higher-performing charters. And in 2012 it adopted a new, computerized enrollment system, called OneApp, that makes it very hard for schools to screen out applicants. Finally, it is a mathematical impossibility that all the charters showing impressive gains in New Orleans could be doing so by handpicking the best students; there are simply too many showing such gains. Anyone who has spent time in them knows that's not their secret.

Douglas Harris, an economist at Tulane University, created a research center to investigate education reform in New Orleans. He and his team have looked into every possible explanation for the improvements, and in the process have proven that they are just what they appear: the result of profound reforms. For instance, they examined whether demographic changes in the city could have contributed to the improved test scores. They concluded that, at most, demographics accounted for only 10 percent of the difference between progress in New Orleans and in other districts hit by the storm. But because New Orleans students experienced more trauma and disruption than those in the other districts, they added, "The factors pushing student outcomes down were at least as large as the population changes pushing them up."

Did the reforms come at the expense of any group of students? No: "All major subgroups of students—African American, low-income, special education, and English Language Learners (ELL)—were at least as well-off after the reforms, in terms of achievement." Nor did reforms increase the segregation of African American students.

Critics have accused charters of increasing the "churn rate" in the city's schools, forcing students to switch often among the constantly evolving mix of schools. But a 2016 study by Harris and his colleagues proved that students changed schools less often after Katrina than before, even in the early years, from 2008 to 2011.

Harris and his colleagues compared the performance of New Orleans students to those in other school districts hit by Hurricanes Katrina and Rita (which followed soon after), which they felt were fairer comparisons than with the state as a whole. This way, the data would account for the trauma and disruption kids experienced and the contribution made by schools they attended while displaced. Before the storm the other districts performed better than New Orleans, and both were improving at a gentle pace. But, Harris reports:

> *The performance of New Orleans students shot upward after the reforms. In contrast, the comparison group largely continued its prior trajectory. Between 2005 and 2012, the performance gap between New Orleans and the comparison group closed and eventually reversed, indicating a positive effect of the reforms of about 0.4 standard deviations.*

The black-white achievement gap in the United States is about one standard deviation, so New Orleans had eliminated 40 percent of that gap by 2012, the last year of data the study examined. "We are not aware of any other districts that have made such large improvements in such a short time," Harris concluded.

TODAY A SOLID majority of New Orleanians supports the reforms, because they are working. The Cowen Institute for Public Education Initiatives does a poll every year. In 2009, only 31 percent of public school parents said the schools had improved since Katrina. Two years later 66 percent believed the schools had improved.

The broader public is even more supportive. In April 2016, 63 percent of voters surveyed in New Orleans agreed with the statement: "Public charter schools have improved public education in New Orleans." Among African Americans, 57 percent agreed. Three quarters of those surveyed supported public school choice (72 percent of African Americans), and 62 percent thought it had had a positive impact on the quality of education (52 percent of African Americans).

Elsewhere in the state, support for radical reform is even deeper. In a March 2012 poll by Louisiana State University's Public Policy Research Lab, 86 percent of Louisianans agreed that the public schools needed "fundamental change" or a "total overhaul," and 70 percent supported charter schools.

The political struggle over charters came to a head in the fall of 2011, when eight of eleven seats on the state board of education were contested. Leaders of two teachers unions, two associations of superintendents and school executives, the Louisiana Retired Teachers Association, the Louisiana School Boards Association, and several other organizations announced a new Coalition for Louisiana Public Education and campaigned against the reformers. On election day, they lost all but one seat. Reformers who had only a six-to-five majority during Pastorek's years emerged with a nine-to-two majority on many votes. They have maintained a healthy majority ever since for John White, who succeeded Paul Vallas at the RSD in 2011 and Pastorek as state superintendent about six months later.

Why the New Orleans Model Works

No one is claiming that New Orleans schools are perfect. Their most ardent supporters acknowledge that with only 60 percent testing "proficient" in 2016, the city still has a long way to go. Yet the progress has been unprecedented. What can other states and school districts learn from the city's startling turnaround? Based on my research in New Orleans and several decades of research on other examples of bureaucratic transformation in the public sector, I believe its success rests on seven fundamental pillars that distinguish it from traditional districts:

- Control: Decentralizing operational decision making to the school level
- Choice: Creating different kinds of schools for different children and giving families choices
- Consequences: Creating accountability for performance
- Culture: Giving school leaders the freedom to mold school cultures
- Capacity: Building talent pipelines of teachers and school leaders
- Contestability: Ensuring that no school has a right to continue if its students are falling too far behind
- Clarity of purpose and role: Separating steering (setting policy and direction) from rowing (operating schools), so system leaders and school leaders can each focus on clear missions and the former are no longer politically captive of their employees

Let us examine these principles one by one.

Decentralizing Operational Control to the School Level

Most charters in New Orleans are either independent or part of a charter network that has only a few schools. Even KIPP, the largest with ten schools, lets its principals make most of the decisions, as long as they are faithful to a handful of philosophical tenets. So school leaders—not superintendents— make the key operational decisions in New Orleans.

Ask any charter principal why the new model works, and you will hear the same story: We can hire good teachers, fire mediocre ones, and spend our money in whatever way works best for our kids. In traditional districts, most hiring, budget, and curriculum decisions are made at central headquarters, and it is virtually impossible to fire a teacher who has tenure.

Mary Laurie, Rene Lewis-Carter's mentor, was also a principal in New Orleans before and after Katrina. In 2013 she received the first Enduring Impact Award, for a lifetime of achievement, from the Orleans Public Education Network. When I talked with her, she made it clear she did not tolerate mediocre teachers:

> I have no mercy, because my job is to make sure these children are educated. That's why we're here. I don't believe anyone should be guaranteed a job. When we interview someone, we always say, "Come to Walker unannounced and see what it's like, the kids who come through our doors. I expect you're going to educate them. They're going to come to you at a sixth- or seventh-grade level. Don't sign on to this job if you cannot deliver."

Doris Hicks, who runs Dr. M. L. King Jr. Charter School, which offers prekindergarten through high school, is another longtime African American principal in the city. When she first heard about charter schools, she didn't like the idea. "I thought charter was synonymous with magnet, so our kids wouldn't be able to come here if we were a charter," she remembers. "But I tell you, I would not trade it for the world." If New Orleans decided to go back, "I would have a fit. All the charter operators would. This is truly education reform. You've got to have an effective teacher in every class, and we're able to do that."

Sabrina Pence, who is white, is chief academic officer at Jay Altman's First-Line Schools. She was principal of Arthur Ashe when it pioneered blended learning, and she says that would have been next to impossible in a traditional district. "I was a principal in a district school, and I only controlled a small amount of my budget," she told me. "I got $14,000, for paper and supplies. If there is one reason I love being in a charter school, that's it. At the end of the day, it's prioritizing your resources around your strategy."

Kathleen Riedlinger, also white, was a traditional principal for 25 years, in a selective magnet school, before it was chartered by OPSB. "Before, I had teachers with tenure, and teachers unions, and collective bargaining, and teachers' rights," she says. "I had to learn to play the game to get the best teachers

I could get. I would develop relationships in HR, try to work the system, to make sure I could get the people I needed. No matter how veteran I became, no matter how much I tried, occasionally I got it right, and occasionally I didn't."

In 25 years she was able to remove just three teachers, by going through a long and arduous process to prove they were incompetent. But, as she says, "There's a big difference between being excellent and being incompetent," and she had to tolerate many teachers who fell between those extremes. "For 25 years my main leadership strategy was 'Would you please?' Because when you have a strong union, that's what you have. I learned how to 'would you please' pretty well. I could 'would you please' as well as anybody in the school district. But I always thought it would be pretty nice to have a little more oomph than 'would you please.'"

While controlling hiring and school budgets are the two greatest advantages, freedom from school districts' other rules is also important. Even seemingly insignificant rules can have a profound effect. At the RSD school where he taught, one charter principal told me, "We couldn't keep kids after school for detention, because an RSD rule said all kids had to go home in a yellow bus." That one rule undermined the school's ability to enforce discipline. At the charter "we can do that, plus have Saturday school."

Creating Different Schools for Different Kids and Letting Families Choose

As chapter 2 described, there are many kinds of schools in New Orleans. There are "no excuses" schools, with a laserlike focus on getting poor, minority children into college. There are selective schools for high achievers. There are schools with a special focus on science and mathematics, technology, creative arts, and language immersion. There is a Montessori school, where children are free to pursue their own interests and each class contains a three-year age span. There are many schools that use blended learning and some that embrace project-based learning. There are two high schools that offer the demanding International Baccalaureate program, one military and maritime high school, and three alternative high schools for kids who are far behind, over-age, or have dropped out or been expelled. Several charter networks have created special programs for students with emotional and behavioral problems. Four schools have career and technical education programs, and a fifth dedicated entirely to that pursuit just opened.

In a system that provides different kinds of schools for different children, it makes no sense to force a student to attend any particular school. Hence no one in New Orleans is assigned; every family chooses. With the exception of a handful of selective OPSB schools, two international schools that have language requirements, and the New Orleans Center for the Creative Arts, which requires auditions, all schools are open to all children. (Siblings get preference, and in K–8 schools half the seats are reserved for kids from fairly wide zones around the schools.) All RSD and OPSB schools are required to provide transportation for their students.

With choice, a culture has grown up in which parents move their children if they are not happy. By 2014, some 86 percent attended a school other than the one closest to their home. On a 2011 survey, 90 percent of parents agreed that it was important to be able to choose their child's school. Parents named academics the most important factor in their choices—though a 2015 analysis showed that location and extracurricular activities, such as sports, also play an important role. Those factors being equal, however, parents clearly prefer schools with higher performance scores.

To make the choice process easier, the RSD in 2012 launched a computerized enrollment system, "OneApp," and the OPSB joined a year later. Families list up to eight choices, in order, and a computer program matches students with available seats. Ninety percent of the public schools in the city participate, plus many preschool programs and all private schools accepting state vouchers. (Most OPSB charters say their charters do not require them to participate, but the board will force them to participate when it renews their charters. The four selective schools will be allowed to remain selective, but will participate in OneApp.) For the 2014-15 school year, 71 percent of students got their first choice and 80 percent got one of their top three choices. The following year 75 percent got one of their top three choices.

The RSD set up four centers around the city to help parents trying to decide which schools to list. And private employers such as hotel chains and Tulane University have hired a nonprofit called EdNavigator to provide advisors for their employees, to help them navigate the system and deal with any problems they or their children encounter at school. Employers see it as an investment to reduce employee turnover, and many parents see it as a lifeline.

Creating Consequences for Performance

When families choose, public dollars follow their choices, so school operators are in direct competition for funds: The more students they attract, the more funds they have.

"It's very competitive," Mary Laurie told me. "From a business perspective, all monies come back to your enrollment numbers. So we have to let them know we have a good art program. We have to let them know we have dual enrollment at no cost, in five universities."

But the consequence that motivates principals, teachers, and charter boards even more than losing students and funds is the threat of closure if students are not learning enough. Everyone knows their job is on the line if students aren't learning, so they usually pull together and do what it takes, no matter how difficult.

Nolan Grady taught math for more than 40 years at O. Perry Walker High School. "You as an individual teacher, you can't be stagnant, not in this day of charters," he told me. "You have to constantly reflect, review, and improve. You don't have the job security you had with the old system. That's a hard pill, but it's a reality. It makes you work harder."

Elected school boards rarely close failing schools—in any district—unless they are in fiscal crisis and have no choice. As I discussed in the introduction, closing a school is often political suicide. But in a charter system closures are much easier, because only one school usually protests. Other school operators welcome the opportunity to compete to run a school in the vacated building. In New Orleans, parents, alumni, and staff at a few schools have protested closures, particularly at the high school level, where communities are often very invested in their local high school. But in most cases there has been little resistance. The boards that oversee each charter school or network have at times recognized when schools were failing and voluntarily surrendered their charters or brought in another operator.

"I think it would have been harder *not* to close failing schools right now," Kevin Guitterrez, then with the RSD, told me in 2011. "Because the naysayers think everything is done for the charters, so if we gave a school a pass, it would have created a really negative scenario. Most closures happened without a murmur. Nobody came to the table and yelled and screamed."

By 2017–18 New Orleans had about 80 charters, and at least 22 had closed or changed hands. In two cases, charter boards fired their operators and hired new ones. In three others, charter boards decided to close the school. OPSB took over a charter that had financial problems, and the state board closed a K–12 charter that had a series of irregularities, including charges of attempting to bribe a state official. But the state board closed most of the others for academic failure, usually handing the buildings to stronger operators.

Closing failing schools accomplishes two things. First, it keeps all adults in a charter school on their toes. In a traditional school, teachers may know the students are failing, but turning that around—particularly with low-income students—is difficult and inconvenient. The status quo is far more comfortable, and most teachers have lifetime tenure. So why make heroic efforts? Why put in the extra time? In such an environment, it takes extraordinary leadership to convince enough teachers to embrace real change.

In a charter that may close, in contrast, the adults tend to work together to turn things around. My daughter witnessed firsthand what schools did when closure loomed as a possibility. Her school had a 2012 performance score of 63.3, an F. To survive it would need to get a 75 the following year. (This translated to a 50 on the revamped scale the state put in place in 2013.) So the Algiers Charter School Association sent in a new school leader to handle operations, freeing the principal to focus on improving academics. (Many charters have learned this lesson and created two positions, operational leader and instructional leader; some in New Orleans even have three.) The school hired full-time aides for the fourth- and eighth-grade classes, whose students had to pass standardized tests to move to the next grade. The principal revamped the school's 90-minute "Response to Intervention" classes, making them smaller and assigning the students according to where they most needed remediation. And in the final weeks before the tests, he pulled disruptive students out of their classrooms and put them all together, with one teacher, so the other students could prepare undisturbed.

Everyone in the school pitched in on what they understood was a life-or-death effort. And when test scores came in, 55 percent of the students were at grade level or above. On the new scale, the school had earned a score of 70.9, jumping all the way from an F to a C. It was named a "Top Gains School," one of those that made the most progress with struggling students. Unfortunately, school leaders did not solve the leadership and discipline problems that had made it an F school in the first place, and it has since returned to that status. Informed observers expect it to be closed or replaced next time its charter comes up for renewal.

Which brings us to the second thing closure accomplishes: improving the mix of schools by weeding out the worst ones. This is far more effective than trying to turn the worst ones around. The Obama administration spent $7 billion to turn around schools performing in the bottom 5 percent of their state, through School Improvement Grants. The results were disappointing. A 2015 study of 50 cities by the Center on Reinventing Public Education found that roughly 40 percent of schools in the bottom 5 percent remained there for three years in a row. But New Orleans, according to the study, was an exception: "None of the schools that performed in the bottom 5 percent in the first year of our data (for reading and math) stayed at that level for three consecutive years." Those schools disappeared from the data altogether: They "likely either closed or were reconstituted in some way."

The only other exception was Memphis—no doubt because Tennessee had copied the RSD and its strategy of handing failing schools to charters, as we will see in chapter 11.

Closure works best when failing schools are *replaced* by stronger schools, which has been the norm in New Orleans. Douglas Harris's group at Tulane University studied the impact of closures. In New Orleans, students in failed elementary schools had gained significant ground two years after their school was closed or taken over by a charter: more than 0.3 standard deviations, or about a third of the black-white achievement gap. High-schoolers gained almost as much. "The positive effects of closure and takeover in New Orleans explain 25 percent to 40 percent of the total effect of the New Orleans post-Katrina school reforms on student achievement," the researchers concluded. (On top of that, imagine the benefits for future students, who never have to attend the failing school.) In contrast, when East Baton Rouge closed failing schools, students just ended up in other failing schools, and they lost ground.

This is one reason why an all-charter system is so powerful: Those doing the steering can replace low performers with schools run by high performers. Not only are individual schools motivated to improve, but the city's mix gets better every year. In New Orleans the bar continues to rise, as the state gradually toughens its grading system. (See appendix A for an explanation of that system.) And schools asking for the second renewal of their charter must do more than avoid failing; they must earn at least a C.

Jay Altman puts it well: "If we can keep an accountability system and say, 'Here's the bar, and it's set high, and if you can't meet it, someone else is going to run your school,' New Orleans could become the only city in the country where every kid goes to a good school."

Changing School Cultures

Children tend to meet the expectations of adults in their lives, and for too long in New Orleans, those expectations were set woefully low. Charter schools have reset them. Most aim from day one at college as the goal for every student. They put college banners in the hallways and classrooms, name each homeroom after the teacher's college, and call each class by the year it will graduate from college. They also put tremendous stress on a series of school values. Signs about the values cover the walls, many with brief sayings from famous people.

Motivation is the key to learning. A motivated student can learn almost anything; an unmotivated student will learn almost nothing. Too often, the adults in public schools assume their students arrive with motivation; little effort goes into creating it. But that assumption is false in high-poverty communities, where many students see no reason to graduate from high school. Hence, charter leaders often view motivating students as their first task. "It's huge," says Gary Robichaux. "We won't hire someone who thinks our kids don't want to learn—that's their job, to create that motivation. Traditional teachers colleges don't train their teachers to do that, but in high-poverty schools, it's everything."

When ReNEW took over its first schools, Robichaux and his staff brought students in for an extra week before school. "The very first week of August, we brought in sixth- to eighth-graders only, and we worked on culture for the whole week," Robichaux says.

> We did some diagnostic testing, and we worked with them on our rules and policies, why we want this to be a good school, what that looks like, and how we want you to go to college. It's a motivation session, a rah-rah week.
>
> After Thanksgiving break, we took a day for culture. After Christmas break, the same. After Mardi Gras, again. We revisit what we want the culture to look like. We show all the kids their data on reading— "You're in eighth grade, reading at a third-grade level, we've got to fix this." We show them the data, try to motivate them.

"We do big field trips at the end of the year" to reward the kids, Robichaux adds. The first year sixth- and seventh-graders went to Bryce and Zion national parks and the Grand Canyon; eighth-graders went to Washington, D.C., to see colleges and the federal government; and third- through fifth-graders went to Sea World and slept by the shark tank.

Successful charters explain what the consequences will be for certain behaviors and then impose them consistently. Very soon, the children learn there is a new sheriff in town, and their behavior changes. My daughter had a friend who taught at a school ReNEW took over. Her first year, before the takeover, discipline was a major headache. The next year, she said, was like the difference between night and day. Teaching became much, much easier. An academic study published in 2016 validated such anecdotes by proving that New Orleans schools that produced higher test scores also had a positive impact on students' behavior.

Culture change involves teachers as well as students, of course. In New Orleans, most schools have embraced the use of data to manage instruction, and traditional teachers have had to learn an entirely different way of operating. Schools test their students at least every seven weeks, then help teachers use the data to tailor instruction to students' needs. Many teachers have coaches or mentors who visit their classrooms regularly and give them feedback. They spend hours every week on professional development—not on courses that may bear only tangentially on their classroom experience, as in a typical public school, but on refining how they actually work with students. Many charters also give performance bonuses—typically up to $5,000—to teachers whose students make significant annual gains.

Building a Talent Pipeline

Creating excellent public schools in a poor community is not easy. According to Leslie Jacobs, the RSD's biggest problem has been finding effective school leaders. It has used New Leaders, an organization that develops school principals, to bring people in, and New Schools for New Orleans has incubated new charters, mentoring their principals for a year or two to help them get started. Yet neither of those measures has guaranteed success.

Almost everyone in the charter school world agrees that school leaders are a critical element of success. "The right leader is everything," says Gary Robichaux. "Even with good systems, the school will fail if the leader is not strong, not motivating, not good at discipline." But it's not always easy to tell who that will be in advance. "We've made mistakes," Robichaux admits. "We tried hard to have veteran local people from within the schools, and in most cases they didn't work out—though we have two doing excellent jobs." More often, he says, it's been younger teachers, with six to eight years of experience, who have taken on the leadership challenge and pushed the schools further, faster. "I think they're not set in their ways. A lot of them have worked in excellent schools, so they've seen that model, they've experienced it. I think it's a reference for excellence that some veteran people that have been in the systems for a long time don't have."

Fortunately, reformers have had much better fortune importing talented teachers, through TFA and TNTP (called TeachNOLA in the city). Both programs are selective, accepting only the brightest candidates, and studies have consistently shown that their teachers outperform graduates of the state teachers colleges. TFA teachers often come from the top 10 percent of their classes at outstanding universities, and it makes a difference. For instance, Troy Simon learned to read because two first-year TFA teachers recognized that he was illiterate, took him aside, and worked with him one on one. By 2011, more than 30 percent of the city's teachers came from TFA and TeachNOLA.

Some criticize TFA because most of its teachers are white. They may be excellent teachers, these critics point out, but their ability to understand the lives of their students is inevitably limited. In addition, black children benefit from having black role models. Kira Orange Jones, TFA's leader in New Orleans, is African American, and she has worked hard to recruit more minorities, in part by recruiting more at local universities. In 2011 only about 5 percent of TFA's corps in the city was African American. By 2016, that number was up to 23 percent, and 41 percent of TFA teachers were people of color. Overall, 82 percent of public school students in the city were African American in 2016–17, but only half of the teachers were, according to the state Department of Education. Roughly 46 percent of teachers were white, the rest Hispanic, Asian, or Native American.

Others criticize TFA teachers because they only commit to teach for two years. But a national survey showed that 60 percent of TFAers teach longer than two years, 28 percent for at least five years. And in New Orleans, TFAers often move on to become effective school leaders. TFA claims that 80 percent of its New Orleans alumni pursue education careers, as teachers, school leaders, or education policy leaders. "Today, TFA corps members and alumni comprise a full 20 percent of the New Orleans teaching force," the organization says, "and over 50 alumni serve as leaders at the school or school systems level."

Teacher burnout is a problem, as it is in all inner-city schools. The work is extremely challenging and often frustrating. But charters in New Orleans are addressing it by bringing in blended learning, to lighten their teachers' loads. And if the system produces the fastest academic improvement in the country, how big a problem could teacher turnover be? Luring highly talented people to spend two to five years teaching seems to produce better results than hiring mediocre people who spend an entire career in the classroom.

Talent pipelines have been instrumental in New Orleans's success. But if other cities seek to emulate them, they should understand that they would dry up if the city did not offer innovative schools where the best and the brightest wanted to work.

Separating Steering and Rowing to Encourage Contestability

What truly sets New Orleans apart is the governance system. The RSD's job—and soon the OPSB's as well—is simply to steer: to set direction, solve system-wide problems, enforce compliance with the few rules that govern the schools, and replace failing schools.

In a typical system, the district employs all principals, administrators, teachers, aides, nurses, custodians, and lunchroom workers—sometimes even bus drivers. As I have noted, the school board often becomes politically captive of its employees, many of whom belong to unions and almost all of whom vote in school board elections, which have notoriously low turnouts.

Before Katrina, everyone who worked in the New Orleans Public Schools would probably have agreed that the schools' foremost purpose was to educate children. But other, more pressing, purposes kept interfering—all related to the needs of adults. Board members needed patronage positions, so they could win votes by finding people jobs. They also needed campaign contributions from vendors, who needed contracts. The teachers union needed better pay and benefits for teachers. And teachers needed job security.

Today, doing what's best for children is foremost. The districts' core purpose is student achievement. If schools put adult interests first and student achievement suffers, they are replaced. Teachers are kept on if they can educate kids and let go if they can't. Principals are kept on if their schools educate kids and let go if they don't. The needs of administrators, teachers, unions, and school bus operators do not override the needs of children.

In sum, no one has a right to operate or work at a school for life. Such rights are *contestable*: the steering body has the power—and the political independence—to award the school building to a competitor with a superior track record.

Separating Steering and Rowing to Create Clarity of Purpose and Role

In a traditional system, the board and administration get sucked into rowing. Because their organization operates schools, they spend their time and energy worrying about hiring teachers, assigning them to schools, negotiating union contracts, making sure the buses run on time, dealing with broken water mains or vacation schedules or even scandals in the schools. They often run from crisis to crisis, losing sight of their core purpose.

And few principals in traditional schools have the autonomy necessary to define clear missions, hire their own people, and get the job done. Most have little control over their budgets or personnel and no mission other than operating a traditional, cookie-cutter school. Too often their real purpose becomes self-preservation, which means not rocking the boat. They are governed by "the rule of the ringing telephone"—if they minimize complaints to the school board and superintendent, by minimizing change, everyone will do fine.

Everyone except the kids, that is.

Success is rare when a large school district tries to steer and row at the same time. "Any attempt to combine governing with 'doing,' on a large scale, paralyzes the decision-making capacity," management sage Peter Drucker wrote long ago. Successful organizations separate top management from operations, he taught, so top management can "concentrate on decision making and direction." Operations are run by separate staffs, "each with its own mission and goals, and with its own sphere of action and autonomy." That is precisely the model the RSD has created: It steers, but it uses independent organizations, each driven by a clear mission and goals, to operate schools.

In this new paradigm, district administrators become skillful buyers of educational programs. They learn how to measure and evaluate schools. Both the RSD and OPSB conduct on-site reviews of each school every year, plus a high stakes review when their charters come up for renewal. Both authorizers shift their supply to meet the needs of their students—replacing schools that fail, replicating schools that succeed, and opening new schools to meet new needs. They work together to address systemwide issues, like special education and equal access to quality schools.

This wasn't always the case. Since both districts in New Orleans initially operated schools themselves, their leaders were sucked into rowing and neglected some important steering functions. For instance, until 2012 the city had no central admissions process to ensure that every child got into an appropriate school. Instead, parents had to apply for spots in multiple schools and hope. Those who didn't apply took what they could get among the worst schools. Parents who moved to New Orleans midyear had to go from school to school to find places for their children.

By abdicating this role, the RSD and OPSB allowed certain inequities to develop. A few aggressive charters worked hard to get good students—holding early lotteries, for instance—while counseling out families they didn't want and expelling difficult students. Parents of children with disabilities often had trouble finding a good fit.

"You can't wear both hats well," says Patrick Dobard, who became RSD superintendent in 2012 and served for five years. In the early years "it was difficult to manage, because on the one hand, we were trying to find our way to be a good authorizer for charter schools, while at the same time managing a network of schools that we directly ran." Since they decided to get out of the business of operating schools, however, Dobard and his staff have done a much better job of steering. They have addressed a long list of systemwide problems in a few short years—and pushed OPSB to join in creating solutions. "It was easier in the sense that our focus became solely on being a quality authorizer, versus directly managing schools," Dobard says.

The first step was OneApp, which gives all families an equal shot at schools and makes it difficult for schools to "cream" the best students and avoid the worst. Participating schools are required to accept students midyear and fill seats left empty by departing students, if parents choose them.

The RSD and OPSB also adopted new policies governing expulsions and transfers, to ensure that charters did not expel or counsel out difficult or expensive students. In 2013 the RSD developed a citywide student code of conduct and created one central review team to carry out expulsion hearings, and the OPSB signed on. The new policy banned expulsions for lesser offenses, like "willful disobedience" or not wearing school uniforms, and instituted discipline conferences prior to any expulsions. In the new system's first year, 2013–14, the central hearing examiners overturned 200 of 485 expulsions. By the following year, the city's expulsion rate had fallen below the state average.

The RSD also launched a Youth Opportunities Center for chronically absent students, designed to connect families with social services before getting the courts involved. It also serves students in the judicial system or returning from prison. And in 2015 the RSD opened a therapeutic day program for children with severe mental health and behavior problems, in partnership with OPSB and Tulane Medical school.

Thanks to FEMA money, by 2021 every school building in the city should be new or newly renovated. But school districts are notorious for avoiding expenditures on maintenance and letting their buildings fall into disrepair. To prevent that happening again, the RSD and OPSB put an initiative on the December 2014 ballot to create a new fund dedicated to maintenance of school facilities, which passed with 59 percent of the vote. Most of the money goes directly to the schools, and the RSD uses its contracts and leases with school operators to require them to spend it on maintaining their facilities. If they don't, says Dobard, their charters might not be renewed.

In the early years, one of the new system's biggest challenges was special education. Charters had a disincentive to take on kids with severe learning disabilities, because they received no extra funding to cover the costs. Not surprisingly, some parents complained that charters were not interested in serving their children, and the Southern Poverty Law Center sued on their behalf.

The OneApp system helped a great deal, because it meant participating schools could not avoid enrolling kids with special needs. In 2013 the RSD changed its differentiated funding formula, to give schools more money for students who were more expensive to educate. The money already followed the children to their schools, but under the new formula there were five funding tiers for special education students, and those with severe disabilities brought up to three times as much money as easier-to-educate students.

Dobard and his staff then pulled together school operators, the OPSB, the Southern Policy Law Center, and other advocates to design a series of other solutions. "This was the first time we were able to coalesce around a specific policy area, where we were able to bring in a majority of the schools and activists around the city" to work together, Dobard says. In 2014 they developed a "cooperative endeavor agreement" between the RSD and OPSB, which included a citywide "exceptional needs fund" to help schools with the most expensive students. The U.S. Department of Education awarded New Schools for New Orleans and six partners a three-year grant to improve special education training for teachers and school leaders, and NSNO committed $3.4 million over three years to help charter schools implement new special education programs.

With all this funding, charters quickly began creating special centers for kids with severe needs. Collegiate Academies even created post–high school "Opportunity Academies" at two of its high schools, to give those with moderate to severe disabilities up to four more years of school. Designed to help them transition to adult life, the academies focus on job and life skills and help students become more independent.

In 2015 the RSD helped shape state legislation allowing OPSB to adopt a special funding formula for its charter schools. The two districts designed a new formula, which kept five tiers for special education but also allocated extra funding for English-language learners, over-age students, and a bit for gifted and talented students. It took effect in July 2016.

Test scores of special education students have surged. In 2005, only 11 percent tested at or above grade level; by 2013, 44 percent did, exceeding the state average by a point. (On the tougher PARCC tests in 2015, 39 percent were proficient, two points behind the state average for students with disabilities.) In 2003, only 10 percent graduated on time; by 2014, 60 percent did—17 points higher than the state average. In five years, the RSD and OPSB turned a special-education system that failed too many children into one that Dobard believes is in the top 20 percent in the state.

With all this progress, the plaintiffs settled their lawsuit in 2015, requiring nothing beyond what had already been done. Together with the judge and the defendant, the Southern Poverty Law Center wrote a letter to the editor of the New Orleans *Times-Picayune*, praising the RSD for its efforts to create equal opportunity for all.

Altogether, the RSD has taken the lead on addressing at least five citywide problems since 2012: enrollment, expulsion, truancy, differentiated funding for those with special needs, and special education. That would have been impossible had it still been preoccupied with operating schools.

"I'm often asked, 'What's the key to your success?'" Dobard says. "My answer is the nimbleness of our policy making. Traditional districts are like luxury cruise ships: If they want to change direction, it's going to take a long time. New Orleans is like a bunch of swift boats: When we need to change directions, we're able to change nimbly, and quickly."

The Future

Leslie Jacobs, Paul Vallas, Paul Pastorek, John White, Patrick Dobard, and their allies did not set out to remake American education. They were pragmatists who seized on whatever they thought would work. In the process, however, they developed a better way to run a public school system.

The New Orleans model is significant for three reasons, State Superintendent John White argues:

I think the most obvious is the fact that a public-private partnership came together to dramatically—at scale—improve the lives of the most abjectly impoverished group of students in this country. That is of its own value, obviously. But I think there is a longer-term piece to this, which is that it showed that there can be dramatic intervention enacted by government that can come to a resolution. I think there has been a cynicism about government's ability to get out of these quagmires, but Louisiana proved it can work. Third, the RSD ushered a system that was once the most hidebound, through a decade-long process, into what is now the most progressive. It's not even close: This is the most progressive school system in the country.

It is hardly perfect, of course. Putting the RSD within the Louisiana Department of Education was a big mistake, because the state's bureaucratic civil service, procurement, and financial rules often hamstring RSD leaders. There is no start-up money in the state system for charters; most of that has come from foundations and federal grants. And the RSD and BESE still use a cookie-cutter version of school accountability, holding almost all charters to the same academic standards. (See appendix A, "Measuring School Performance in New Orleans, D.C., and Denver".) The only exceptions are "alternative schools," where cookie-cutter standards obviously won't work and BESE has created an alternative set of standards.

The original charter idea was to have different standards for *most* schools. A charter is supposed to be a performance contract, which lays out the school's goals, how progress will be measured, and what level performance must reach for the charter to be renewed. BESE considers its standards minimums that should apply to all, but even those minimums discourage the creation of certain necessary schools. As Jay Altman points out, for instance, "The accountability system doesn't help if you want a vocational-technical focus." And if a school focuses on music or art or dual-language immersion, shouldn't it be held accountable for how well it accomplishes that mission?

Fortunately, New Orleans will have an opportunity to revisit all of that, because all the RSD charters will return to OPSB by July 1, 2018, or 2019. The new board will be free to handle accountability and start-up funding as it pleases.

In 2015, a Democrat who opposes charter schools, John Bel Edwards, was elected governor of Louisiana. He had pledged to remove John White as state superintendent of education, although he lacked the votes on the state board, which hires and fires the superintendent. (The governor appoints three members; the other eight are elected from regions.) Leslie Jacobs realized that the legislative environment for charters might get worse under Edwards, and

White would eventually leave. She had led a citywide process in 2010 to design a structure for the return of the RSD schools to local control, but she had ended up tabling it. Now she decided it might be time.

Late that fall she invited about 30 stakeholders in New Orleans—RSD and OPSB leaders, charter school leaders, charter board members, leaders of important local organizations, elected officials, and business leaders—to discuss what local control might look like. In a series of meetings, they quickly agreed on the fundamentals: a return of RSD schools to the OPSB as charters, with strict protections for school autonomy, parental choice, and accountability. Leaders in the reform community agreed there might never be a better time to get a bill passed embodying those fundamental principles. A broad coalition supported the idea, and State Senator Karen Carter Peterson, the African American chair of Louisiana's Democratic Party, introduced a bill. She represented New Orleans; she had sponsored the creation of the RSD, in 2003; and now she sponsored the return of RSD schools to OPSB.

With the mayor and most state legislators from New Orleans in support, the bill passed easily. The RSD charters will return to OPSB by July 1, 2018, if majorities on OPSB and BESE agree that the local board is ready, or a year later, if not. An advisory committee with 13 voting members will evaluate OPSB's readiness and recommend moving ahead or postponing a year; a delay will only be considered if a majority of committee members vote for it. (The bill does not impact five charter schools authorized by the state board that are not part of the RSD or OPSB.)

The legislation is the first in the nation to codify how a 21st century school system should operate. It reserves 98 percent of the funding for the schools, only 2 percent for district administration. It prohibits the school board from limiting charter autonomy in all the important areas, including school programming, curriculum, scheduling, hiring and firing, employment terms and conditions, budgeting, and purchasing. All charters must participate in the OneApp enrollment system, however. The board has the power to manage that system, reserving no more than half the seats in grades K–8 for students residing in a geographic zone (though exceptions are grandfathered in). It can add or reduce seats in response to demand and student needs, and it will control the differentiated student funding formula and the expulsion system. It can also levy taxes, if voters approve, to meet other needs, such as early childhood education, mental health services, and the like.

To ensure a diversity of providers and prevent any one from gaining too much political power, the board may limit the percentage of enrollment any operator may provide. To prevent local politics from interfering with authorizing decisions, it will take a two-thirds vote of the board to override the superintendent's decisions about charter approval, extension, renewal, and revocation. And to minimize cheating, charter schools up for renewal must arrange independent monitoring of state tests by a third party approved by the board.

After Peterson's bill passed, the OPSB board unanimously approved the superintendent's unification plan. The November 2016 board elections produced a board on which all seven members had endorsed the reformers' principles, published in a statement, "Forward New Orleans for Public Schools." Four pro-charter reformers ran unopposed: With few jobs and contracts to distribute, seats on the board were apparently less attractive than in the past. And all three challengers who were anti-charter and wanted the legislature to rewrite Peterson's bill lost.

In December 2016, Superintendent Henderson Lewis announced his intention to convert OPSB's remaining five direct-run schools to charters. The new board supported him, and the conversions will probably occur by July 2018. New Orleans will become the first large city in the country to convert all its schools to charters. "The public clearly supports the new model of public school governance," Jacobs says. "The governance debate in this city is over."

The return of schools to the OPSB is not without risks. Will the OPSB staff prove competent to run a 21st century system? Will there be enough funding to address some of the systemwide challenges effectively, such as mental health and early childhood education? Will the elected board become reluctant, over time, to replace mediocre schools with better schools, because they prefer not to rock the boat and stir up opposition? (As a defense against this possibility, it will take five of seven votes to overrule the superintendent's decisions.) Will OPSB continue to open new, innovative schools? Will they whittle away at charter autonomy, despite the law's constraints? If they do, charter schools can seek authorization from the state board instead. And if state board members feel OPSB is doing a poor job, they can authorize new charters in New Orleans.

One thing is certain: OPSB's ability to steer well will be critical. Personally, I expect they will continue to break new ground, just as the RSD has over the years. For instance, new board member Ben Kleban, who founded one of the city's charter networks, has advocated policies to promote racially and economically integrated schools. Today, he says, nearly all middle-class families, black or white, enroll their children in the same 10 percent of schools— mostly the former magnets that still have selective admissions. He has advocated allowing some schools to add admissions criteria based on income levels for a portion of their seats, to guarantee economic integration. "Low-income and low-performing children should benefit from learning alongside high-income and high-performing children," he believes, "making every child more prepared for life beyond school."

Several dozen schools in Denver already do this, and as we shall see, it works. New Orleans is poorer than Denver; 83 percent of New Orleans's students are "economically disadvantaged." So initially there will be room for fewer "diverse by design" schools. Still, the four schools that participate in OneApp and reflect the city's socioeconomic and racial mix are among the most sought after in the city, often being chosen by three times as many families as they can accept. Over time, growing their number would be a perfectly logical next step for OPSB.

Will the New Orleans Model Spread?

It took a hurricane, a flood, and a state takeover to make all this possible, a skeptic might argue. Such conditions will never be duplicated elsewhere, so the model will never be replicated.

Yet as we saw, Katrina was not the first hurricane to clear the path for revolutionary reform. Before the 1900 hurricane Galveston had a fairly typical city government. Americans have always been suspicious of centralized political power, and in the 1800s they purposefully spread it out among independently elected boards and commissions (one for parks, another for public works, a third for public health, and so on), large city councils (sometimes bicameral), and multiple other elected officials (auditors, treasurers, judges, solicitors). To get anything accomplished, political parties developed ward-based machines through which party bosses could pull the strings—but with machines came the corruption and spoils systems that frustrated so many citizens.

As in the case of New Orleans's schools, Galveston's business and professional elite had struggled for a decade to reform their government, with limited success. After the hurricane, they were convinced the city could not rebuild without a radical change in governance. So they asked the governor and state legislature to impose a five-member commission appointed by the governor, which would hold all executive and legislative power. Opponents protested the loss of democratic governance, so bill sponsors allowed a friendly amendment: two of the five commissioners would be elected. In 1903 a court ruled the plan unconstitutional, so the legislature made every commissioner elected, and all incumbents were quickly returned to office.

With state aid, the new commission balanced the books, paid off the city's debts, secured a credit rating, and floated bonds to pave streets, improve storm drains, and repair schools and municipal buildings. The city and county undertook two enormous public works projects: a massive, 3.5-mile-long, 17-foot-high sea wall and an effort to raise the city by ten feet. The latter took seven years: laborers lifted 2,000 buildings with jacks (including a church that weighed 3,000 tons), dredged 16.3 million cubic yards of sand out of the harbor, and pumped it into the city.

Long before these engineering feats proved their worth in subsequent hurricanes, word of Galveston's success spread. A 1906 report in *McClure's* was so popular the magazine reprinted 12 million copies. Houston adopted the "Galveston Plan" for commission government in 1905; two years later Dallas, Ft. Worth, El Paso, and Des Moines, Iowa, followed suit. Most of these cities added another set of progressive reforms—the initiative, referendum, and recall—as a necessary check on the commissioners' centralized power. Des Moines's included nonpartisan elections, in an attempt to remove politics from city administration, and a merit-based civil service system, to limit patronage hiring. All five reforms quickly became associated with commission government.

The new model had enormous appeal, for it seemed a businesslike approach to management, while giving progressives the means to wrest power from corrupt urban machines. It also fixed responsibility for departmental performance squarely on each elected commissioner. There was no more finger pointing among weak mayors, divided councils, and boards and commissions.

By 1915 almost 600 cities had adopted the new model. By then, however, even its supporters had begun to acknowledge two flaws: Elected legislators did not always make the best managers, nor did they always pull their departments in the same direction. So progressive leaders tweaked the model, inventing a "commission-manager" plan, under which an elected commission hired a professional as city manager and he hired the department heads. (At the time women could not even vote, so it was always a "he.") This was the true business model, they said: The commission was the city's board of directors, and it hired a chief executive officer to run the corporation. This refinement, known as the "council-manager" form of government, spread to thousands of cities, large and small, affluent and poor.

The Galveston Plan spread because it worked. Similarly, the New Orleans model is capable of producing better results almost anywhere, because it harnesses the power of decentralization, choice, competition, contestability, clarity of purpose, accountability for results, and culture change. For cities facing 21st century challenges, it is simply a more effective form of governance.

Will it spread as widely as the Galveston Plan? Some reformers think so. "Just as Teach For America was the proof point on teachers and KIPP was the proof point on schools, we deeply believe we can be a proof point on this," Sarah Usdin told me back in 2011. "We can be the city that demonstrates that we don't have to have these massive disparities. We really believe we can be the proof point for the nation that you can do this at scale in a whole city."

PART II

A Tale of Two Systems: Education Reform in Washington, D.C.

CHAPTER 4

THE BIRTH OF CHARTER SCHOOLS IN D.C.

WASHINGTON, D.C., OFFERS A RARE real-world laboratory: two public school systems of roughly equal size, occupying the same geography, with different governance models. The older of the two, D.C. Public Schools (DCPS), uses the unified governance model that emerged more than a century ago, in which the district operates all but one of its more than 110 schools and employs their staff, with central control and most policies applied equally to most schools. Since 2007, when Michelle Rhee became chancellor, DCPS leaders have pursued the most aggressive, sustained reform effort of any unified urban district in America.

Competing with DCPS is a model designed and built largely in this 21st century. In 1996, Congress passed a bill creating the DC Public Charter School Board to authorize charters, while also allowing the traditional school board to authorize them. The Charter Board owns or operates none of its schools; instead, it contracts with 65 independent organizations—all of them nonprofits—to operate 118 schools (as of 2016–17). Like DCPS, the Charter Board is a leader in its field, considered by experts one of the best charter authorizers in the nation.

After a contentious first decade, a remarkable amount of collaboration has emerged between these two sectors, as we will see. But ultimately, they are in direct competition. And the results of this competition have profound implications for the future of public education. If a traditional district led by the nation's most aggressive reformers—a district making real progress—still cannot keep up with the charter sector, it suggests that the charter governance model is superior.

CONGRESS PASSED LEGISLATION creating D.C.'s Public Charter School Board 18 months after the Republicans took control of both houses in the 1994 election. With D.C.'s local government facing a projected $700 million deficit, the Republicans put an appointed Control Board in place to run it, and that board commissioned a review of the school district.

The review labeled DCPS "educationally and managerially bankrupt." The district was remarkably similar to New Orleans Public Schools: Half of all students dropped out, only 9 percent of ninth-graders in public high schools went on to graduate from college within five years, and almost two thirds of teachers reported that violent student behavior interfered with their teaching. "The longer students stay in the District's public school system," the report declared, "the less likely they are to succeed educationally."

Board of Education members, who often used their positions as stepping-stones to higher office, routinely engaged in patronage hiring. "Whenever a new superintendent was hired, it was understood that he or she would have to do political favors for board members whose political aspirations and path had been calculated far in advance," wrote Kevin Chavous, who chaired the City Council's Education Committee in the 1990s. Board members "got involved with every nitty-gritty detail," steering contracts to supporters and jobs to friends and relatives.

A 1992 investigation had found a payroll full of "ghosts"—people drawing paychecks who had no responsibilities. Auditors were unable to track millions of dollars. Two of every three schools had faulty roofs, heating or air conditioning problems, and inadequate plumbing, according to the General Accounting Office. Nepotism was common, and Mayor Marion Barry steered contracts to supporters, even when it meant paying 25 percent more.

In 1996, the Financial Control Board stripped the elected school board of its authority over DCPS and handed the reins to an appointed board of trustees.

Meanwhile, House Speaker New Gingrich had asked moderate Republican Steve Gunderson, from Wisconsin, to come up with an education reform bill for D.C. Gingrich talked publicly about using D.C. as a "laboratory" for conservative reforms—particularly for a voucher program—which hardly endeared him to the city's leaders. Gunderson's young staff person, Ted Rebarber, had concluded that all public schools should be charter schools, or something like them. He wrote a memo for Gunderson advocating that approach. The congressman "was a little taken aback," Rebarber says. "But to his credit, he was willing to look at it."

The key turning point came when Gunderson and Rebarber met with Al Shanker, president of the American Federation of Teachers, with which the Washington Teachers Union was affiliated. Gunderson asked Shanker what he thought of charter schools, unaware that he was a key originator of the idea. "Shanker said, 'Every school should be a charter school,'" Rebarber recalls. "Gunderson almost fell out of his chair, and he talked about it for days after the meeting. He told me, 'Wow, we could really do something big, if that's what Al Shanker thinks.'"

Rebarber had studied a dozen state charter bills that had already passed, and he picked out the best aspects of each one. He and Jim Ford, staff director for the City Council's Education Committee, wrote a strong bill, which created two charter authorizers, the D.C. Board of Education and a new Public Charter School Board (PCSB). It allowed the city council to create a third—which it has never done—and required that D.C. spend the same amount per child in charters as in district schools.

After a long stalemate with Democrats over a voucher program Gingrich insisted on, the speaker finally dropped the voucher language and the bill passed with bipartisan support. It called for five-year charters, but charter leaders in other states were learning how hard it was to get long-term mortgage loans with only five-year guarantees of survival. So Congress passed an amendment extending charter terms to 15 years, with a serious review every five years.

The original law also lacked funding for buildings for charter schools. When local activists decided they needed to change that, they had only one Republican among their ranks: Malcolm "Mike" Peabody, who had been the civil rights officer for New York and Massachusetts state governments in the 1960s and whose brother Endicott Peabody had served as governor of Massachusetts. After a long stint at the federal Department of Housing and Urban Development, Mike Peabody had founded Friends of Choice in Urban Schools (FOCUS) to push for a charter bill.

Peabody convinced Gingrich, who asked the House Appropriations subcommittee that dealt with D.C. to amend the bill to require facilities funding. Peabody then convinced City Councilman Kevin Chavous to base the funding formula for charter facilities on a rolling average of what DCPS had spent on facilities for the previous five years.

Let a Hundred Flowers Blossom

Jack McCarthy remembers the moment he got hooked on charter schools. He was at a real estate investment firm in Boston, in 1993, when Massachusetts passed the nation's fifth charter school law. He was also treasurer for a nonprofit organization that decided to create a charter school. He helped them find a building in downtown Boston, secure financing from the Massachusetts Government Land Bank, and raise money for the down payment. The moment of truth came on lottery night, when the school's directors pulled names out of a hat to see which of the many applicants got in.

Sixteen hundred people were there: parents, kids, babies, even pets. It was midnight before the last name was pulled. McCarthy thought everyone would cheer at that point, he remembers. But "just the opposite: people started crying. It was so incredibly moving. I'm in the back of the room and I'm crying too, and I said to the guy who was working with me on that campaign, Lex Towle, 'I had no idea how important this idea of education was, how much it meant to people. If we ever get the chance to do this again, we've got to do this.'"

Soon afterward, a trustee from a foundation that had helped with the down payment visited from Washington. The D.C. charter bill was about to pass, and she ended up recruiting McCarthy to come help get things going. Once there, he and Towle founded the AppleTree Institute, to help people write charter applications and to create an incubator space for new schools. They discovered that the Environmental Protection Agency was about to leave the Waterside Mall, near the Navy Yard—"a dumpy mall in a part of the city that was going to be renovated," McCarthy says.

> We found this obscure act called the Public Facilities and Cooperative Use Act of 1976 that provided, when the federal government had surplus space, that they would make it available for a dollar a square foot, or something of that nature, to qualified non-profits. We literally walked into the GSA and said, "I understand you have some space at Waterside Mall. Under the Public Facilities and Cooperative Use Act, we'd like to lease 36,000 square feet." The guy looked at me, said, "Okay."

They also discovered that the city was about to lose millions of federal Community Development Block Grant dollars it hadn't managed to spend, so they talked their way into $680,000 of it, to renovate their space.

One of those who came to AppleTree for help was Irasema Salcido, a slight, intense assistant principal at a district high school. Salcido's family had moved to California from Mexico when she was 15; she was the only one of five siblings who had graduated from high school. After seven more years—holding full-time jobs the entire time—she had graduated from college. Her new husband, a law student at Harvard, urged her to attend Harvard's Graduate School of Education. That turned out to be the hardest year of her life, "because I was not prepared," she says. "That's when I realized, if I'm going to do something, I have to do something in secondary education, so kids can be prepared and go to college."

She aspired to become a DCPS principal, but when Congress passed the charter bill, she decided to open a charter high school. "I benefited from the American dream," she says, "working hard, going to college, and I saw the difference education made in my life. Imagine having that direct impact on the lives of students. I went to my husband—I was pregnant with my fifth child—and he said, 'Hey, if you want to do it, go for it.'"

She named the school after one of her heroes, César Chávez. Being in D.C., she thought, why not focus it on public policy?

"But what was hard was I opened and realized that a lot of our kids were not prepared. It was a constant struggle to make sure the kids would come to school, would do their homework." By the end of the first year, only 40 of her 100 ninth-graders were ready for tenth grade. So she told the other 60 they would have to repeat ninth grade. "That was the most difficult decision. But I thought to myself, I don't want to keep making the same mistake. If they're not prepared, they're not prepared."

"I was afraid they were going to close me down," she admits, "that too many kids would leave." She lost about 20, but for those who stayed on, repeating the year made a huge difference.

She had made writing a 15–20 page thesis a requirement for graduation, because it was a good test of whether kids were ready for college. But when the first class reached senior year, she and her staff had long discussions about whether the students were capable of doing it. "I finally said, 'Stop! We can't lower our standards. If we do, what are we doing different?'"

"Now it is a given," she says. "It's expected—no one questions that."

In ninth grade, students at the two César Chávez high schools stop classes two weeks before the end of the year and, in seminars, examine problems in their communities: homelessness, gentrification, dropouts, crime. They research an issue, interview residents, write an op-ed, and if they have the opportunity, present their findings to the city council. In tenth grade they do the same thing, but with international topics. In 11th grade they do three-week fellowships with public policy organizations. "That is the experience they most remember and appreciate," Salcido says, "because I think a lot of our kids have not had the opportunity to be exposed, and don't necessarily have parents who have jobs. Being able to go to a place, to be accountable for the work, to be treated like professionals, I think that was a foreign world to our kids. That's where a lot of our kids blossomed."

Senior year, in their thesis class, they do research, pick a topic, and dive into it. All 130 seniors write a thesis and present it, with PowerPoint, in front of a panel of volunteers from the public policy world. The three judged best present at a symposium at Georgetown University.

SEEING HOW FAR behind the ninth-graders were at César Chávez and another high school AppleTree incubated, McCarthy and Towle realized they needed to start earlier—before kindergarten. So in 2001 they founded a private preschool, funded by donors. They started with 36 kids, most of whom lived in public housing, in a church basement in southwest Washington. "It seemed like the natural thing to do," says McCarthy. "Our theory of change was that we wanted to develop a model that would close the achievement gap before kids entered kindergarten."

After four years of research and development—to pioneer an effective preschool curriculum and pedagogy—they received a federal grant and applied for a charter. Today AppleTree operates six of its own charter preschools and partners with four other charter networks to run five more. Widely considered the premier preschool provider in the city, it gives the curriculum it developed, Every Child Ready, to other schools free of charge.

As these two examples suggest, the charter law unleashed an astonishing variety of schools. Because DCPS had eliminated its funding for adult-education schools during the 1996 fiscal crisis, one of the first schools authorized, Carlos Rosario Public Charter School, was a former DCPS school that taught adult immigrants English and workforce skills. The charter law said nothing one way or the other about adult schools. So when Rosario applied, the charter board went to the city council's Kevin Chavous and asked if the council could approve the charter. Chavous agreed and pushed legislation through to establish a funding formula for adult schools, and they have since flourished in D.C.—a rarity in the charter world.

Leaders from the Latin American Youth Center felt that Latino kids had few quality options in the city. There was only one bilingual language immersion school at the time, but parents had to camp out in line for a week to get their children in, says Cristina Encinas. She had taught at a Montessori school in Florida, and she was "completely sold on it." So she and her colleagues founded the Latin American Montessori Bilingual Public Charter School, which now educates 350 children, from three-year-olds to fifth-graders, on two campuses.

Over time, others created four more bilingual elementaries, in Chinese, Spanish, French, and Hebrew. An African American woman opened Roots Public Charter School, an elementary school with an Afrocentric curriculum. Two young men launched the nation's first public boarding school, for sixth- through twelfth-graders. "Expeditionary learning" schools used project-based learning, especially in the world outside school buildings, to engage their students. A new high school in the city's poorest ward, named for former Supreme Court Justice Thurgood Marshall, focused on the law. Maya Angelou Public Charter School, a year-round alternative school for teenagers who had been incarcerated, included paid vocational work in its curriculum and had overnight residences for those who needed them. Several schools opened for those ages 16 to 24 who had dropped out or were far behind in school. Another served students with severe emotional problems, intellectual disabilities, and autism. KIPP opened one school after another, until it had 16 in the city.

The Battle with DCPS Begins

Initially, the new D.C. board of trustees created by the Control Board was sympathetic to charters. Mike Peabody knew the chair, and they worked out a process to give charters preference for empty DCPS buildings. Charters got control of almost a dozen buildings over the course of a year, according to Peabody, because General Julius Becton, then superintendent of DCPS, was supportive. But when Becton resigned the cooperation ended, and the first big battle between charters and the city began.

Josephine Baker served as chair of the Charter Board from its inception in 1996 to 2002. When its first executive director, Nelson Smith, resigned in 2001, the board spent a long, fruitless year searching for a replacement. Finally its members turned to their chairwoman and asked her to step in. You're already doing the work, they told her.

Baker had enormous credibility. She had taught elementary school in DCPS for 25 years, then had become a professor of education at George Washington University. A strong African American woman, she fought hard to force DCPS, the Control Board, and the mayor to give charters their rightful share of school funding and buildings and their rightful place at the decision-making table. "I started off in '97 with boxing gloves on," she told me. "I became known as the push-back person. Then I became a little more selective about what I did. Some things you could just massage, and some you really had to put your gloves on."

When the battles over empty DCPS buildings began, Baker started showing up at meetings the deputy mayor held on facilities. "I would say, 'Show me where the charters are in this equation,'" she remembers, "and they weren't there. 'So that means we need to put them in there.' This went on for months."

Peabody went back to the House Appropriations subcommittee and asked its chair to pass legislation giving charters legal preference to use any empty DCPS building. Local elected officials in D.C. deeply resented such intrusions, and Mayor Tony Williams "went berserk," in Peabody's words. Peabody met with him and made a deal: Williams would create a process to hand out empty schools, and FOCUS would have its bill withdrawn. Unfortunately, Williams didn't follow through. He and his successor, Adrian Fenty, each leased a few empty buildings to charters, but as Williams later told me, community pressure to support DCPS made it politically difficult.

In D.C.'s expensive real estate market, the scarcity of suitable buildings became the charters' Achilles' heel. A 2012 study reported that "many charter schools lack cafeterias, gyms, and outdoor athletic facilities." They had to cram their students into far smaller spaces than DCPS schools enjoyed. To give but one example, Latin American Montessori Bilingual—an outstanding school—moved six times in search of decent facilities.

The second big fight occurred because the law allowed both district and private schools to convert to charter status if two thirds of their faculty and parents signed a petition to do so. When several DCPS schools expressed interest in converting, Superintendent Arlene Ackerman, who served from May 1998 to July 2000, did everything in her power to block them. At one school, Hearst Elementary, she offered enough concessions to convince the leaders to call off the conversion. Soon afterward, she transferred the principal and two of the most popular teachers; other teachers were "threatened with transfers if they discussed these personnel actions," says Josephine Baker, then chair of the Charter Board. "Parents were so upset that eighty-five percent of them signed a petition protesting the transfers." Two parents and one of the transferred teachers founded Capital City Public Charter School.

Only one school, Paul Junior High, persevered through actual conversion to become a charter. The teachers union supported the conversion, but some of its members organized a student walkout in protest. They also sought an injunction to stop the conversion, which the court denied. Ackerman even tried to take away Paul's building, in violation of a DCPS policy that allowed converted schools to remain in their district-owned buildings. When she finally backed down, neighborhood activists sued DCPS in protest, and it took a court decision to establish the principle that schools converting to charter status could keep their buildings.

"DCPS's central office was not going to make it easy and thereby possibly open the floodgates for other neighborhood schools to leave the city's school district," says Baker. And it succeeded: After witnessing such resistance, no other DCPS school tried to convert.

Meanwhile, the city failed to provide nurses in charter schools and the police department refused to provide crossing guards and school resource officers.

Despite the resistance, the new law did protect the Public Charter School Board from control by hostile politicians. The U.S. secretary of education nominated possible members of the board, who were then chosen from the list by the mayor. (In 2010 the city council passed a law removing this role from the secretary, and Congress did not object, so the mayor now appoints board members alone, with the consent of the council.) This political insulation turned out to be indispensable in the early years, because it allowed the board to make decisions based on the merits rather than participate in political horse trading.

The charter movement got one other early break. Soon after the Control Board went out of existence, the teachers union was distracted by a scandal. In 2001, a union member tipped off the American Federation of Teachers that its Washington local was overcharging members for dues. An AFT audit discovered that the local president, her assistant, and her treasurer had overcharged members for six years—stealing $5 million and using it for everything from flat-screen televisions and luxury clothing to Cadillacs and political contributions. The president and her associates went to prison, and the AFT put the local in receivership for two years. "The union's dysfunction and implosion in the beginning of the sector's evolution gave the burgeoning charter school sector an opening to blossom," Baker wrote in her history of chartering in D.C.

CONTROVERSY ERUPTED AGAIN in 2008 when the Roman Catholic diocese of Washington decided to convert eight schools it could no longer afford into charters. The American Civil Liberties Union and Americans for Separation of Church and State objected, fearing public funding would be used for religious instruction. Some parents resisted as well, and the archbishop gave them the opportunity to raise money to keep their schools private, but only one succeeded.

By then Tom Nida, a local banker, was chair of the Charter Board. Just before its hearing on the conversions, Nida got a call from Mayor Fenty's deputy mayor for education, who asked him not to approve them, because the new students would cost the city too much money. "I told him, 'Go straight to hell,'" Nida remembers. "We were going to make our decision based on the merits of the case, and I was not going to take any outside influence." Most of the students would end up in public schools if the board turned down the request anyway, he pointed out.

As for the worries about publicly financed religion, "The reality was, in the entire system of seven schools that came over, there was a total of two nuns. Most of the teachers were not even Catholic, and most of the kids weren't. They just wanted a safe, affordable school, because the neighborhood school was awful, and they couldn't get into a charter." Politically free to vote based on the interests of the children, the board approved the conversions. Though it later closed one of the seven schools for low performance, the other six, known as the Center City Public Charter Schools, have thrived.

Inheriting Board of Education Charter Schools

Almost by definition, some charter schools fail. Educating poor, inner-city children takes enormous commitment, creativity, and persistence, and not all who try it succeed. Gradually, the Charter Board began to weed out the failures.

In 2006, it inherited 18 charters from the city's Board of Education (BOE), several of them quite weak. Back in 1997 and '98 the BOE had rushed its first charters into place—with predictable consequences. By 2006 it had been forced to close seven schools, some after scandals or financial troubles. When a school sued to block closure and the BOE had no funds to fight the suit, FOCUS found two top lawyers who took the case pro bono. Their victory established a precedent that charters could be closed without judicial review.

In 2006, thanks to a tip from a DCPS staff member, the Board of Education discovered that the director of its charter oversight office was stealing hundreds of thousands of dollars and directing no-bid contracts to her friends. The board fired her, and she was convicted and sent to prison. Embarrassed, board members voted to stop authorizing charters. When Adrian Fenty became mayor two months later, he convinced the City Council to give him control of the district and to transfer all surviving BOE charters to the Public Charter School Board.

"There were some doozies," remembers Baker. "We had one we had to close in January"—Howard Road Academy, an elementary school with two separate buildings, in one of the city's poorest wards. "They ran out of money."

"Quietly," Tom Nida remembers, "we reached out to a number of schools that we thought had the horsepower to pull off a takeover, and we asked them to put together, if they were interested, a proposal to do just that.

> We went and hired a church in the neighborhood, a big fellowship hall. We had a first meeting where we, in public, determined that we needed to terminate the charter. That can cause some really angry parents, as you might imagine. There were a couple of folks that were just commandeering the microphone—they were just nonstop. I found it necessary and appropriate to come out from behind this long table, which we had as the dais, and personally confront the people at the mike by getting upfront and close.

Nida is a large man, well over six feet tall and broad shouldered. "We're going to have some order in this room so we can make some decisions, and I expect everybody in this room to act like adults," he told them, "because right now, you're acting like a bunch of bratty kids, so stop." Taken aback, the angry parents quieted down, and the board voted. "Now, before you get all up in arms," Nida said, "we're going to have another meeting here next week, same time, same place.

> *There are going to be four existing high-performing charter schools that are going to be making their proposals to not only us but all of you. We're going to pick one to take over this failing school now terminated, but you will have the opportunity as parents to hear all four presentations. You are free to pick any one of the four you would like your kids to go to. Of course, you're free to pick anything else you want, too. You're not bound by our decision.*

During Baker's near-decade as executive director, the Charter Board closed an average of two schools a year, mostly when they had financial problems. But all schools encountering financial problems were also struggling academically. The two were linked, because charters were funded based on their number of students. Schools that could not attract enough students often ran short of money.

Closures were expensive: School debts had to be paid off, students needed help finding appropriate new schools, and sometimes lawsuits had to be fought. The Charter Board received only half a percent of its charters' public funding, compared to 3 percent for authorizers in several states. Every year it had to raise extra funds from philanthropists or the city to make ends meet. Josephine Baker told me, "If you do school closure well, in a way that takes care of the needs of children, and the businesspeople who have supported them"—vendors, banks, leaseholders—"it takes money. Our staff had angst: 'If we close three schools this year, how's that going to work? How do we pay for it? And how do we handle the workload?'"

After they inherited the BOE charters, members of the Charter Board began to feel the need for more rigor in holding schools accountable for student learning. "Our first objective, frankly, was to get adequate quantity, to have critical mass so we were likely to survive as an entity," says Nida. "Once we got that, then all right, now we're going to start shifting our focus to improving the quality, not just the quantity."

"When I came on the board we were only closing schools for financial reasons," adds Skip McKoy, who joined in 2008 and became chair in 2013. "That's one of the two criteria in the reform act. The other is not meeting goals" set out in schools' charters. "But so many of the goals were apple pie and fluff. And the schools weren't doing the measuring against those goals, and the PCSB was not requiring them to do it. So it was hard to close a school for academic reasons."

In 2008, the board decided to create a Performance Management Framework, a common yardstick for most charter schools, so it could compare them and would have more ammunition to close the laggards. It was already measuring their annual academic gains, but it wanted to make decisions on the basis of more than tests scores, says Baker. She raised money from the Gates and Dell foundations, and Gates funded the Boston Consulting Group to do some of the technical work. Creating a viable yardstick for such diverse schools ended up being a far greater challenge than anyone anticipated, however—and led to an entirely new phase in the sector's development.

CHAPTER 5

MICHELLE RHEE BRINGS IN HER BROOM

IN THE LATE 1960S, D.C. PUBLIC Schools had 150,000 students. When the charter bill passed, in 1996, it was down to 78,648. By 2007, it had less than 53,000, and many of its buildings were half full. The board had been timid about closing schools, because closures always drew protests. But with charters growing rapidly and many parents moving to Maryland or Virginia in search of better schools, DCPS was bleeding both students and dollars.

By 2007, when Adrian Fenty was elected mayor, there had been few signs of improvement and two major corruption scandals. That year, DCPS tied for the worst reading scores among the 11 big cities tested under the National Assessment of Educational Progress (NAEP). Yet it spent more per child than almost every other big city.

Charters now educated almost 20,000 children—27 percent of all public school students in D.C.—and they were outperforming DCPS. This competition "forced the traditional school system to change or die," says Josephine Baker. Charters were not the only factor, but they helped create a climate in which city councilors were ready to vote for change. They also weakened the teachers union, reducing its membership by 25 percent. (No charters in D.C. have unionized, though unions are allowed by law.) And by creating successful schools in the poorest neighborhoods, charters removed the excuse DCPS had relied on for years—that kids from poor, dysfunctional families were just too difficult to educate.

During his campaign in 2006, Fenty said nothing about taking control of the schools. Then, after he won a decisive victory in the Democratic primary, which historically has determined the eventual winner, he announced that he wanted to take control of DCPS schools from the Board of Education. In a changed political environment, his bill passed the city council nine votes to two.

Fenty surprised everyone by hiring Michelle Rhee, a reformer who had founded The New Teacher Project, as chancellor of DCPS. Rhee began perhaps the most publicized reform effort in the country. She convinced the city council to convert her central office staff to at-will employees, then began laying people off. She concluded that the district needed only about 70 of the 144 schools it was operating, so she closed 23 in her first year and a few more thereafter.

D.C. was not New Orleans, however: There had been no hurricane to scatter those who had benefited from the old system. When she laid off hundreds of teachers, thousands rallied at protests organized by the AFL-CIO, the American Federation of Teachers, and the Washington Teachers Union. THIS IS NOT RHEEZISTAN! their signs declared. Rhee refused to back down. "I attended hundreds of meetings in that time period and everywhere I went it was the same," she told the journalist Richard Whitmire, who wrote a book about her tenure as chancellor. "I was called every name in the book, things were thrown at me, people picketed my office. It was intense."

Rhee also began firing principals and assistant principals. By the time she left, in 2010, only half the principals who had been there when she arrived were still in place. She worked hard to negotiate a contract that would allow her to fire teachers, but the union refused. Only 8 percent of her eighth-graders were proficient in math and only 12 percent in reading, yet 95 percent of teachers received ratings of "satisfactory" or better. So she created a new system to evaluate teachers, called IMPACT, that used student improvement on test scores and observations by principals and master teachers as the most important rating factors. (The ratings are "highly effective," "effective," "developing" (added later), "minimally effective," and "ineffective.") Those rated "ineffective" would be subject to immediate termination; those rated "minimally effective" would have one year to improve or lose their jobs. At the time, Whitmire noted, "No schools superintendent anywhere in the country was dismissing more than a handful of teachers for ineffectiveness."

In her negotiations with the union, Rhee offered a tempting carrot: huge pay increases and performance bonuses, financed in the early years by $64 million from the Eli and Edythe Broad Foundation, the Laura and John Arnold Foundation, and the Robertson and Walton family foundations. She offered a contract under which each teacher could choose between the status quo and a new track that stripped away tenure protections but offered big pay boosts based on performance. Yet union leaders stonewalled her.

Finally, Rhee began firing teachers *without* the union's approval, based on their IMPACT ratings. That changed the game. "It made the rank and file realize they did not have the protections they thought they had," Rhee explained. "It made them feel, 'My God, this woman is willing to go further than anyone else. She's not playing around.' They thought, 'If this is going to be reality, then we might as well get some money, too.'"

The continued inroads made by charters also created leverage. The president of the teachers union told his members they had to accept change. Charters had taken 35 percent of their jobs already, he pointed out. Did they want to go for 100 percent?

In 2010, the union ignored Rhee's offer of two tracks and agreed to performance pay for all teachers. According to Rhee, the new contract raised average teacher salaries from $67,000 to $81,000, allowed them to earn annual bonuses of up to $25,000, ended the practice of forcing unwanted teachers on principals, and created new policies desired by teachers to deal with student discipline and professional development.

Within months, Rhee handed out $45 million in pay increases to 650 educators who had been rated "highly effective." She also fired 165 teachers rated "ineffective" and put another 737 rated "minimally effective" on notice. Overall, she fired about 400 teachers for performance during her three and a half years as chancellor. Roughly half the district's teachers departed, through terminations, layoffs, resignations, or retirements.

With significantly higher pay to offer, Rhee aggressively recruited new principals and teachers. DCPS had been "reconstituting" schools since the early 1990s—closing the old school and hiring a new principal with freedom to hire all or mostly new staff. Though it hadn't been very effective, Rhee doubled down on the strategy. She even reopened some of the schools one grade per year, as most successful charters do. She recruited high-performing principals, some from the charter sector, and gave them renovated buildings when she could. Existing teachers rated lower than "effective" lost their jobs if the new principal did not want them. Those rated "effective" or higher who were not hired could retire with a boost to their pension, take a $25,000 buyout, or remain on salary for a year, assigned to another job temporarily while they looked for a permanent position in the district. If they failed to secure one, they were out of a job—although they could always reapply. In three and a half years, Rhee reconstituted 18 schools.

Meanwhile, Rhee increased foreign-language and advanced placement courses and International Baccalaureate programs. Using funds provided by a universal preschool bill City Council Chairman Vincent Gray had pushed through in 2008, she created more than a thousand new preschool seats in district schools. And, beginning in 2008, the city began to spend $300 to $400 million a year to renovate schools.

Rhee also began adopting several key charter practices. She diversified her schools, using foundation funds to launch 13 "catalyst schools." These included "world cultures" schools that promoted foreign languages and a global perspective; "STEM" schools focused on science, technology, engineering, and math; and schools with an intensive arts focus. She contracted with charter schools to operate four failing district schools. And although she tightened the reins on most principals, she empowered 16—in "autonomous schools" and a new DC Collaborative for Change—to make more of the key decisions about budgeting, staffing, curriculum, and professional development.

By the time she left, the 50-year enrollment decline had ended, thanks to the new preschool enrollments. Scores on standardized tests were moving up, but a cheating scandal involving the 2008 and 2009 tests undermined confidence in the numbers. Although scores also improved on the 2009 and 2011 National Assessment of Educational Progress, most of the progress was in math, not reading. Low-income students (those eligible for subsidized meals) made almost no progress in reading, while their progress in math was dwarfed by that of nonpoor students. And DCPS schools still lagged behind the charters, which continued to take students away.

The Political Backlash

In Washington, race is a powerful underlying reality, and Rhee, a Korean American, had fired hundreds of African Americans. She seemed to revel in it: she posed for the cover of *Time* with a broom, and she volunteered to fire someone on camera for the documentary *Waiting for Superman*. Many black residents were angry, and the teachers union was furious.

When Adrian Fenty ran for reelection in 2010, both groups vented their fury. By election day, according to Whitmire, only 25 percent of African American women in the district viewed Rhee positively. "The disdain for Rhee's reforms was about jobs," he wrote. "In the midst of a recession and gentrification pressures, seeing DCPS employees fired struck many voters as black removal and no explanation could have convinced them otherwise."

Fenty's opponent, Vincent Gray, had supported mayoral control of the schools, along with most other aspects of reform. But he could not stand the gusto with which Rhee fired black employees. Still, he explained to the union that he supported most aspects of reform and would continue them, then asked them not to endorse him. But he was Fenty's opponent, and they could not resist.

Fenty and the *Washington Post* wrongly portrayed Gray as a man who would turn back the clock on reform. Gray tried to reassure those who supported district reform, while also courting the pro-charter vote. Fenty had alienated many D.C. leaders and activists—including charter leaders—because they found him unavailable and unresponsive. He had largely ignored charters, and twice he had tried to cap charter facilities funding well below the agreed-upon formula. On the city council, Gray had come to the charters' rescue.

On primary day, Fenty lost by ten percentage points. He won 53 of 58 majority-white census tracts, but Gray won 108 of 118 majority-black tracts. Fenty blamed his loss on his school reforms but said he would do it all again if he could.

Then came the biggest surprise, at least to those who thought they had stopped reform in its tracks: Gray appointed Rhee's deputy, Kaya Henderson, as chancellor. "We cannot and will not revert to the days of incrementalism in our schools," he announced.

Insiders understood how close Henderson and Rhee were. Henderson had helped Rhee craft all her reform initiatives, particularly IMPACT and the new union contract. They had worked together long before Rhee arrived in D.C., and Henderson publicly called Rhee her "best friend." But there are three differences between the two women that matter a great deal in Washington. First, Henderson is African American. Second, she had lived in D.C. for almost 15 years when Gray appointed her chancellor. Third, Henderson's style is different from Rhee's: She reaches out to the community, listens, and adjusts her plans based on what she hears. And, as she told me, "We don't do press releases around firing teachers anymore."

Henderson continued all of Rhee's reforms, although she slowed the pace of school closings and reconstitutions and modified IMPACT. In 2012, she proposed 20 more school closures due to overcapacity. But she had learned from Rhee's experience: "I spent a year talking about why we needed to close schools, making the case for what I could provide on the other side if we closed schools," she says.

> I told them, "We could have a library in every building if we weren't spending so much money supporting such small schools." Then I put out a proposal publicly, and I asked people to give feedback and tell us what was wrong, what was right, what was otherwise. My philosophy is, when you have a hard problem to solve, you involve the community in solving it with you. That way, it's our problem, and our solution. And you don't get to point at Kaya Henderson at the end and say, "I don't like your school closing proposal," because we did this together.

After months of community meetings, Henderson pared the list to 15, based on the input she had received. When the schools closed in 2013, other big cities were doing the same, but with more conflict. In Chicago, she points out, teachers struck, and in Philadelphia they took over the district headquarters. "And we had no protest, no nothing. It was calm. It was quiet."

Henderson continued using IMPACT to terminate about 100 teachers a year, and she implemented a separate IMPACT system for principals. But she modified the system for teachers, shifting value-added measures based on student test scores from 50 percent of a teacher's score to 35 percent, allowing teachers facing dismissal to appeal directly to her if they felt their evaluation was unfair, and adding a fifth category, "developing," to the ratings. She also hired school-based coaches to help teachers improve between evaluations.

IMPACT gives teachers five detailed evaluations per year, typically five to seven pages each. Until 2016–17 three were by the principal and two by "master educators" from the teacher's academic specialty, who did evaluations and mentored teachers full-time for a few years. Previously, "It was very rare that a teacher would get observed by their administrator, and certainly never by someone from outside the school," says Jason Kamras, a former DCPS and national teacher of the year who, as chief of human capital, helped design IMPACT.

Only about 15 percent of teachers teach math, reading, or English language arts in grades covered by PARCC, D.C.'s standardized test. So a majority of teachers are scored on the basis of learning goals and assessments suggested by teachers and agreed to by their principals. However, these are given only 15 percent of the weight in their evaluation formulas. (The 15 percent who teach PARCC subjects are judged based on both value-added scores, given 35 percent of the weight, and their learning goals and assessments, given 15 percent of the weight.)

Teachers rated "highly effective" receive bonuses of up to $25,000, and those with consecutive ratings of "highly effective" are also eligible for salary increases of up to $28,832. If they work in schools where at least 50 percent of students are eligible for free or reduced-price lunch, they get additional bonuses. Teachers can earn $100,000 after just five years and reach the top of the salary schedule within nine years—almost three times as fast as in the average district. By 2014–15, 765 teachers were earning $100,000 or more, and an outstanding teacher could earn $131,540 a year, according to DCPS—far more than teachers in other cities. Those rated "ineffective" once, "minimally effective" two years in a row, or "developing" three years in a row lose their jobs.

A study published in late 2013 by professors from Stanford and the University of Virginia suggested that IMPACT was working. James Wycoff and Thomas Dee found that it helped drive the lowest-performing teachers out of DCPS (both through dismissal and voluntary departure), helped retain the high performers, and incentivized those in the middle to improve. A subsequent study Wycoff and Dee did with two other researchers found that the departure of low-rated teachers from high-poverty schools yielded significant improvement in student test scores.

Henderson also continued Rhee's practice of firing principals at failing schools, recruiting promising candidates to replace them, and firing the replacements if their schools didn't show improvement within two years. Along with retirements, this produced a 25 percent annual turnover in principals. Critics harped on this instability, but Henderson was unapologetic. Effective leadership is the single toughest thing to find in inner-city schools, according to many seasoned experts. "Given how much leadership matters, if we're going to fail, we have to fail fast and move forward," Henderson told me.

> We can't allow a leader who's not going to be successful to just sit there. What it takes to be a leader in an urban district that is in the midst of reform is very different. You might have been a successful leader in another place, and you might not be able to lead successfully here. You might not be the right fit for a particular kind of school, and we might need to move you to a school that is a better fit. I think we've gotten much better at finding the right people to lead our kinds of schools.

The district has also worked hard to develop its own principals. "Early on, most of the new principals we were hiring were from other school districts," Henderson said. "So they had a set of values and culture and ways of doing things that worked for those other school districts. Sometimes they worked here; sometimes they didn't. So I think we realized you've got to grow your own leadership."

The district has "tripled the size of the principal recruitment and selection team and completely revamped our selection process," says Kamras. To provide the best possible guidance and oversight, Henderson handpicked her instructional superintendents and cut the number of principals each one supervised from 25 to about 10. She increased professional development for principals. And she launched a fellowship that identifies rising stars, puts them through an 18-month program run by Georgetown University's Business School and other partners, and gives them experience working for successful leaders in DCPS. The fellowship is graduating a dozen new school leaders a year and has trained nearly half of the principals hired in recent years—and, according to Henderson, they have outperformed the district's other principals.

District leaders are also trying to make the principal's job less demanding. "This year we're taking a page out of the charter sector by piloting a director of operations in ten schools," Kamras told me in 2014. This allows the principal to focus on academics while the director runs the business operations. It was successful enough that 60 schools, more than half the district, had adopted the model by 2016–17. Traditional public schools, Kamras pointed out, often have 30 people reporting directly to the principal—far too many. "No other industry has that," he said. "It's very bizarre."

After years of investing in the hiring and development of effective principals, Henderson and Kamras shifted the responsibility for all evaluations to the principals. Beginning in 2016–17, they added student survey results to the evaluation formula. They also shifted the money for master educators and professional development to funding for coaches, teacher leaders, and assistant principals, who each coach small teams of teachers, meeting with them weekly to examine student assessment data and figure out how to improve. The new approach was developed by a task force that included teachers and principals.

Henderson's highest priority was the development of a more demanding and varied curriculum, aligned with the Common Core standards and including enrichment through art, music, physical education, and Spanish for all students. Until she changed matters, every school was free to set its own curriculum. "What we chose to say was that autonomy might be nice, but we want to set a standard for the district where every kid—whether you're in Ward Three or Ward Eight—is getting a particular caliber of instruction," she explained. "The curriculum is the anchor of that."

Henderson made a priority of turning around the 40 lowest-scoring schools, by recruiting high-performing teachers and principals, awarding grants ranging from $10,000 to $450,000, and reconstituting nine more schools. In partnership with the National Academy Foundation, she also launched seven career academies at six high schools. Working with university and industry partners who offered students internships, they focused on engineering, the hospitality business, and information technology, and they provided industry-recognized certifications. Finally, Henderson and her principals lengthened the school day at 41 schools and the school year (by 20 days) at 11.

Much of this agenda was expensive: the teacher salary increases and bonuses, the extended hours, the new schools, and the renovated buildings. According to a decade-long research project on per-pupil revenue for K–12 students in 50 large cities, by 2011 DCPS was the most expensive large district in the country.

CHAPTER 6

THE CHARTER BOARD GETS SERIOUS ABOUT QUALITY

BY 2010, NATIONAL CHARTER leaders were shining a spotlight on school quality, putting a new priority on closing failing schools. The D.C. Public Charter School Board decided to do the same. But that fall, when its staff unveiled a proposed Performance Management Framework (PMF)—designed to compare most charters' performance on an apples to apples basis, using test scores, graduation rates, and the like—a revolt broke out. "If you had a model that was aimed at taking highly disadvantaged kids and making a lot of growth, it would have punished you, but if you had taken in affluent white kids and sort of been nice to them for two years, you'd be okay," says Jack McCarthy, president of AppleTree Institute.

Charter leaders also argued that some of the benchmarks were not appropriate for all schools: For instance, should the same third grade literacy standard be applied to normal schools and bilingual immersion schools? They felt the framework rested too much on inputs, such as whether schools had student and staff handbooks and a school leader succession plan, rather than on student outcomes. In general, they felt it was too bureaucratic. "The PMF subjects our schools to burdensome rules and regulations," their letter to the board said, "and equally burdensome reporting requirements and on-site monitoring."

The charter leaders requested a meeting with the board. Brian Jones, then board chairman, talked with Josephine Baker about it. "Her response was to say, 'Look, I was once a second-grade teacher, and what we're hearing from the schools is exactly what my second-graders would say when I would give them a bad grade,'" Jones recalls. "'Of course they didn't want a bad grade, so they would complain about the fairness of the test.'"

Jones discussed it with a few school leaders he respected and decided to hold the meeting. It was an evening session, and the PCSB staff expected eight or ten people to show up. Instead, 50 did. "There were not actually pitchforks there," laughs Clara Hess, who had just been hired by the Charter Board to deal with the PMF, "but people were definitely exercised and agitated."

"We were trying to make our argument," McCarthy remembers, "and we were being shut down in a public meeting. I kind of lost it. I said, 'Look, under the School Reform Act, we don't have to sign this thing, okay? This is something that's a cooperative agreement. We won't sign this PMF if this is the way this is going, and there's nothing you can do about it.'"

The board voted to hit the pause button. "The thing I was most concerned with was, as we rolled out the PMF, to have a big hiccup, and then the whole accountability effort gets set back," Jones says. The board put together working groups, made up of board members and staff and charter leaders, to deal with the issues. It also decided to create separate frameworks for preschool charters, elementary and middle schools, high schools, adult education charters, and alternative schools, because each kind differed from the rest.

This was the first public rift between the board and its executive director, but other issues had been brewing. After 15 years of fighting for charter rights, Baker had learned not to trust the mayor or DCPS. When the Bill and Melinda Gates Foundation approached her about negotiating a compact with DCPS, to increase collaboration, she had little interest. Brian Jones saw it as an opportunity to get DCPS and the mayor's office to commit to some things that would benefit charters.

Jones was also interested in recruiting successful charter operators from elsewhere, but Baker disagreed. After watching KIPP struggle mightily with its first replication and other charter groups fail because they grew too fast, she had grown skeptical about replicating successful charters.

Jones and Baker sat down and discussed their differences. After more than 40 years in public education, Baker had earned a well-deserved reputation as the godmother of charter schools in D.C. Now, given her differences with the board, she decided it was time to retire.

The board conducted a national search to replace her and hired Scott Pearson, a former business executive who had helped found a group of charter high schools in the San Francisco area, then had run President Obama's charter support office in the Department of Education. Pearson was in tune with national efforts to improve charter quality by weeding out low performers. Using the recently completed PMF, he divided schools into three performance tiers, based on their scores, so everyone could see where they stood. By law, the Charter Board can close a school for poor performance only if it is failing to meet the goals laid out in its charter—not for being in tier 3 for several years. To resolve that problem, Pearson pushed charters to include a score on the PMF as one of their goals. If a charter is rated tier 3 for two years running, they usually close it. Sometimes they act after one year, and they have even closed schools in the lower part of tier 2. (See appendix A for more on the PMFs.)

Every five years the Charter Board staff puts schools through a serious review. In addition to the PMF, they rate schools on a 100-point financial and audit review framework. They look at schools' academic performance, financial performance, and compliance with legal requirements. If a school is performing well in all three categories and achieving the goals in its charter, staff encourage it to expand or to replicate itself so it can serve more students. "If they aren't meeting their goals at 15 years they close, no questions asked," Pearson says. "If they aren't meeting their goals at five or ten years, depending on the degree to which they've missed their goals, we either close the school right away or put them on a strict improvement plan under which they close if they don't meet the plan targets in future years."

If a school is performing well in some areas but not in another, they put it on notice and monitor it until the problem is resolved. Those succeeding with some grade levels but not others may find their charter partially revoked: say, for middle school but not for elementary.

Pearson and his staff have used the PMFs to close an average of five schools a year. Overall, about a third of all charter schools opened in D.C. were closed over the first 20 years—a total of 46 through 2016. Pearson has continued a practice begun by Baker of looking for thriving charters willing to take over those that are failing, as long as the board of the failing school approves.

Josh Kern founded Thurgood Marshall Academy, an outstanding charter high school, and after ten years left to create TenSquare, a consulting firm that works with charters. He is critical of the Charter Board for issuing too many rules and requiring too much compliance reporting. But, he adds, "One of the great things that Scott has done is he has clearly communicated to schools in a way that school boards and school leaders feel an urgency that they may not have felt before. That has allowed for interventions to occur that wouldn't have occurred before. There has to be urgency—that is the most important thing you can do" as an authorizer.

Pearson and his staff have also recruited strong charter networks from elsewhere. To make D.C. more attractive, they created a more streamlined approval process for successful, experienced operators than for those with less than three years of experience in operating a charter. The board has also continued to be quite careful about who gets a charter in the first place. In Pearson's first four years, it approved only 13 of 41 applications by inexperienced operators.

All this effort appears to be paying off. The percentage of charter students enrolled in tier 1 schools has risen over time, while the percentage in tier 3 has fallen.

A Hundred Flowers Still Blossom

Meanwhile, Washington's extraordinary level of innovation in school models continues. In 2006, Briya Public Charter School opened, providing "English, computer skills, parenting, and civics training to parents while preparing their children ages 0–5 for future school success," according to its website. It is perhaps the only school in the nation that serves both infants and adults. With four campuses and almost 600 students, Briya "engages the whole family in learning."

Creative Minds International opened in 2012, offering a project- and arts-based curriculum as well as foreign-language classes in Spanish and Mandarin Chinese to elementary students, beginning with preschool. The next year, Ingenuity Prep opened in a very poor neighborhood, with most teaching done in small groups of eight pupils and liberal use of computers. Also in 2013, Sela Public Charter School opened the city's first English–Hebrew language immersion elementary school, and 60 percent of its students were African American. Five other bilingual elementary charters worked together to create a bilingual middle school, which is growing into a high school.

In recent years, the Charter Board has approved five highly acclaimed school operators from other states: Democracy Prep, a successful charter operator from Harlem; BASIS Charter Schools, whose high-academic-expectations model has been astonishingly successful in Arizona and now in D.C.; Harmony Public Schools, an award-winning network of STEM charter schools that boasts a 100 percent college acceptance record in Texas; Rocketship Education, the Silicon Valley network that uses educational software as a core part of its curriculum in elementary schools; and Goodwill Excel Centers, which operates career-tech schools that help adults get high school diplomas in Indiana, Tennessee, and Texas. The board has also opened a fourth Montessori school, a school specializing in children with disabilities, and its second weekday boarding school, beginning in fifth grade—this one for children in foster care or at risk of placement.

The National Alliance of Public Charter Schools has published two reports on the health of the charter school movement, in 2014 and 2016. In both, it rated D.C.'s charter sector the nation's healthiest.

Attacking Systemwide Problems

Pearson and the board have also attacked some of the systemwide problems in the charter sector, just as the RSD and OPSB have in New Orleans. For instance, most administrators and principals I interviewed in DCPS were convinced that some charters screened out particularly difficult students. To prevent that, the Charter Board helped launch a computerized assignment system like OneApp in New Orleans, called "My School D.C." In addition, Pearson and his staff have prohibited anything that might dissuade a family from applying, such as requiring that applicants submit essays and transcripts or reveal whether they have a disability. They screen charters' marketing material to remove anything that might discourage applicants. Staff even telephone charters posing as parents, to detect any efforts to screen out challenging students. If they find such efforts, Pearson says, they bring the school before the board and give it a warning.

Critics also charge that charters drive out troublesome students, who then land at DCPS schools. "The day after the enrollment audit"—which secures charter funding based on the number of children enrolled—"three or four kids came into the ten [DCPS] schools that I manage," Eugene Pinkard told me. Pinkard, who had run both a charter and a DCPS school, was an instructional superintendent at the time.

To expose such tactics, Pearson and his staff came up with the idea of annual "equity reports" for each school. The deputy mayor for education, D.C.'s Office of the State Superintendent of Education (OSSE), and DCPS embraced the idea. The reports show midyear entries and withdrawals. For special education students, low-income students, and each of six racial or ethnic groups, they also show enrollment, attendance rates, disciplinary actions such as suspensions, and academic proficiency. If a school has particularly low rates of special education students or high rates of withdrawals, suspensions, or expulsions, Charter Board staff sit down with school leaders to discuss the issue and how they might improve. Since this data was first published, in 2013, midyear withdrawals have fallen from 5.5 to 4.9 percent. Charters have expanded their special education enrollment to 15.4 percent of their students, slightly higher than DCPS. Suspension rates have declined each year, to just above DCPS rates, and expulsions declined from 186 in 2012–13 to 81 in 2015–16.

Pearson also convinced the city council to double the board's budget, to 1 percent of charter schools' public funding, which has done away with the need to scramble for extra appropriations or philanthropic support.

Sadly, financial scandals have occurred among charters, including some in which schools have paid exorbitant management fees to for-profit firms owned by their founders. The Charter Board revoked two charters for this reason during Pearson's first four years—turning the schools over to another charter group and DCPS. It is a sad truth: Wherever public money is involved, someone will try to steal it. Both the Charter Board and DCPS have endured their share of financial scandals, and both are working to tighten up their financial oversight. In 2016, Pearson finally convinced the city council to let his staff examine the books of any organization that contracts with a charter school and receives 10 percent or more of its income. This added transparency should help reduce corruption.

An Ecosystem of Support

Charter schools would not be as successful as they are in Washington without the support of many other organizations. FOCUS has long served as their principal advocacy group, while also providing technical assistance to existing schools and training to those who want to start schools. It published a 600-page guidebook on school design and the charter application process; it provides data analysis for schools; and it has put performance data on all D.C. public schools on its website, broken down by ward, race, and other categories. As an advocate, FOCUS funded a study proving that charters receive less operating money than DCPS schools, in clear violation of the federal charter law. The city then created a commission to research the same question, which also found a disparity. When the mayor and council did not act, FOCUS funded a lawsuit against the city, which was still pending as this book went to press.

Another critical organization was the New Schools Venture Fund, which raised philanthropic money to invest in charter schools. D.C. was one of four cities the fund made a priority. Starting in 2008 it raised close to $50 million to invest in charters and support organizations in the city, including FOCUS, the Public Charter School Board, and many other organizations mentioned below. The fund's staff provided hands-on support as well as money, published reports on successful innovations so they would spread, and brought organizations they funded together to learn from one another. In 2016, the D.C. office spun off as a separate entity, Education Forward DC, with the goal of doubling "the number of underserved students who are college and career-ready in the next five years."

Often in the charter world, the boards of charter schools are the weakest link. "Every school that stumbled badly and failed—either fell on their own sword or were terminated—the root cause, when you dug down deep enough, was always poor governance," says Tom Nida. "Many of the early schools had boards comprised of FOFOF—friends and family of founders. They were top-heavy with people that had some neighborhood or education interest but had very little business or finance savvy. They were making incredibly silly decisions"—and sometimes "micromanaging."

Carrie Irvin is an education reformer who took eight years off to stay home with her children. During those years she wound up chairing the board of their private preschool. By the time she was ready to go back to work, she had learned that a good board is critical to success. She began talking with others about the idea of strengthening charter school boards. "Everyone we talked to said, 'Thank goodness, you hit the nail on the head,'" she remembers. "This is the soft underbelly of the charter movement. These boards are hapless or worse—micromanaging or disengaged."

The New Schools Venture Fund had reached the same conclusion. Someone put Irvin and her fellow founder in touch with them, and soon Charter Board Partners had its first grant, in 2010.

Their original plan, Irvin says, was to recruit "high-caliber talent" for boards. But "about six months in we realized it wasn't just the right people—these people really didn't know what they were doing, they were all reinventing the wheel." So they developed six standards for effective governance and created a program of training, coaching, and tools for boards. They bring board members together to talk about school governance and learn from one another. And they recruit potential board members, get to know their skills, their perspectives, their personalities, and what they want to contribute, and match them with schools. Sometimes they help boards replace members with more effective people, or remove board chairs or school leaders who need to go. By 2015 they were working with 25 schools and had recruited about 250 board members.

Kristin Ehrgood focused on another weak link in the chain: schools' connections with parents. Like so many reform leaders, Ehrgood is an alumnus of Teach For America, who went on to run the organization in New Jersey for a time and then served on the TFA board in D.C. In 2006 she and her husband founded the Flamboyan Foundation, and in 2008 they brought it to D.C. Like Carrie Irvin, Ehrgood talked with a variety of people to figure out the most pressing needs in the city. She kept hearing the words "family engagement."

So she and her staff read all the research, which says that family engagement is critical to student achievement. They also did focus groups and built partnerships with 11 D.C. schools, both charter and traditional. They discovered that different kinds of engagement have different effects. Involvement in a PTA or parent-teacher night is relatively unimportant. Instead, the keys are "a parent holding high expectations and setting goals for their individual child, monitoring progress and holding them accountable, and supporting learning at home," as one Flamboyan paper put it. One study found that "teachers who reached out to parents through initiating face-to-face meetings, making phone calls, and sending information home about how to support student learning had higher student test scores than teachers who did not conduct this outreach."

Ehrgood decided that her foundation needed to help teachers engage families in ways that made a difference. During focus groups, Flamboyan found "across-the-board distrust" between parents and schools in D.C., resulting from parents' past experiences with schools. So they decided to train teachers to do home visits, to build relationships. "The first questions are, 'What are your hopes and dreams for your child?' and 'Tell me about your child,'" Ehrgood says. "Parents are blown away that these are the questions; it validates that the parent is the expert on the child, and it puts the relationship on an equal footing."

Teachers also ask, "What are your expectations of me as your child's teacher? How do you like to be communicated with—texts, emails, or phone calls? And tell me about your own school experiences—what you liked, what you didn't." The teacher is allowed to leave the family with one expectation, such as trying to get their child to school every day, or making sure they do their homework.

By 2017, Flamboyan had partnerships with 40 D.C. schools, both charter and traditional, and had trained teachers at 153 schools in the city. Most of these schools had their teachers do paid home visits—almost 13,000 a year. The foundation also funded Teach For America to develop a family engagement curriculum for teachers and New Leaders for New Schools—the New York–based group that trains principals—to develop a curriculum for principals.

The charter ecosystem is home to many more organizations:

- Groups that help both sectors recruit and train good teachers, such as Teach For America, TNTP, and the Urban Teaching Center
- The Achievement Network, which helps both sectors improve their teaching by using diagnostic tests every six to seven weeks, then analyzing the data and handcrafting responses to help students who are falling behind or moving far ahead
- Reading Partners and the Literacy Lab, which provide volunteer tutors for children reading below grade level in elementary school
- Ed Ops, which provides back-office services for charters, such as accounting and budgeting
- Building Hope, which provides financing and space to new charters
- TenSquare, which coaches and consults with charter leaders and helps with charter school turnarounds
- The D.C. Special Education Cooperative, which pools charters' resources to provide training, technical assistance, and other services for schools and special education teachers, to improve education for students with disabilities

- And many organizations dedicated to increasing access to college for
  D.C. graduates from both sectors

Josh Kern of TenSquare points out that these organizations play part of the
role a central office plays for traditional school districts. "There are vendors
that are readily available to charter schools that can provide true expertise in
all these different areas," he says. "All these things require a level of expertise
that it's not reasonable to expect especially single-campus charter schools to
know. Charter schools are now outsourcing all of it to experts."

Collaboration Between the Sectors

One of the reigning myths about charter schools is that they were created to
be laboratories from which traditional schools could learn, but they have
shown little interest in sharing their innovations. In D.C., nothing could be
further from the truth. District leaders have recruited talent from and learned
a great deal from charters, and vice versa. Principals and teachers move
between the sectors, and some district principals even take their teachers to
charters to see new strategies in action. "D.C. operates like a small town—just
about everybody knows everybody," Justin Jones, then with the Achievement
Network, told me. "There's a lot of collaboration, and we try to help facilitate
that." Through A-Net, new innovations developed by both charters and district schools have spread.

E. L. Haynes Public Charter School, founded in 2004 by Jennifer Niles
(named deputy mayor for education in 2015), has also worked diligently to
spread best practices. Niles's vision was not to replicate her highly successful
school, which begins with three-year-olds and goes through high school.
Instead, she wanted to launch innovations that would spread to other schools,
in both sectors. For instance, she and her staff spurred creation of the D.C.
Common Core Collaborative, through which 120 teachers from 22 schools—
half charters and half DCPS—worked together in grade-level groups to prepare
for the transition to new standards.

In partnership with KIPP, she also founded the Capital Teaching Residency, which has trained 400 people to teach in high-need charters by working
with a high-performing mentor teacher at E. L. Haynes or KIPP, full-time, for
a year. After their residency year, they commit to at least two more years of
teaching at E. L. Haynes, KIPP, or another charter school in D.C. Kaya Henderson gives the Capital Teaching Residency credit for inspiring her to pilot a
similar residency program at DCPS, in partnership with the Urban Teacher
Center.

Perhaps E. L. Haynes's most famous innovation is LearnZillion, now spun off into a private company that claims its lessons and videos are used by a third of the nation's teachers. It began when the school's principal, Eric Westendorf, watched a sixth-grade math teacher explain how to divide whole numbers by fractions. Her explanation was so simple and compelling that he wanted to share it with other teachers at the school, via video. Some of the teachers were already using Khan Academy's online videos, but they found that sometimes students misunderstood them. So Westendorf and several teachers created a homemade website with videos of powerful lessons. It proved popular, so they expanded it, then spun it off and recruited stellar teachers to help them develop more content. Students and teachers can use its more than 5,000 videos, all linked to Common Core standards, for free.

"Our model of impact is not replication, it's this stuff," Niles told me before she left E. L. Haynes. "We want to be one pre-K to 12th grade school, but we can do these projects to strengthen education cross-sector for all kids."

The Charter Board, DCPS, and the Office of the State Superintendent of Education also collaborate regularly. Together they created My School DC and the equity reports. In 2014 the charters invited DCPS schools to join their annual Ed Fest, where they show off their wares to interested parents. More recently, DCPS has agreed to take over two schools whose charters have been revoked, and a DCPS Academy for Construction and Design at Cardoza High School—told by DCPS to find a new home—has merged with a charter school. Once Niles became deputy mayor for education, she created a cross-sector task force to spur further collaboration and solve other problems.

In September 2016, Kaya Henderson resigned, to spend more time with her family after nine exhausting years with DCPS. The mayor hired Antwan Wilson to replace her. Wilson had spent almost a decade as a principal and then assistant superintendent in Denver, followed by two years as superintendent in Oakland, California. Wilson's experience in Denver, which has embraced charters as an integral piece of district strategy, suggests that collaboration between DCPS and the charter sector will only intensify.

CHAPTER 7

COMPARING THE CHARTER AND TRADITIONAL SECTORS

SINCE MICHELLE RHEE LAUNCHED her reforms in 2007, DCPS has improved faster than any of the other 20 large districts that take the National Assessment of Educational Progress (NAEP) tests. DCPS leaders deserve enormous credit for this. But charter schools in D.C. still perform better, and in the city's low-income wards it is no contest: Charters far outdistance district schools.

In making comparisons, we have to be careful to understand the context. Since 2007, D.C. has grown more affluent and whiter, so test scores have naturally improved. In 2006–7, somewhere between 82 and 85 percent of public school students were African American; by 2015–16, that figure was down to 70 percent. White enrollment had grown from about 5 percent to 9.7 percent, while Hispanic enrollment had grown from 10.5 to 17 percent.

The two sectors have slightly different demographics. In 2015–16, DCPS had more white students (13 versus 5 percent), who were mostly middle-class or above in income, and fewer black students (64 versus 76 percent). DCPS had about the same percentage of students with disabilities and a slightly higher percentage of English-language learners (9 versus 7.3 percent). The racial balances matter because there is a huge gap between the academic performance of white students and others in D.C. On the 2014 standardized tests, for instance, 92 percent of whites scored proficient or advanced in reading, compared to 50 percent of Hispanics and 44 percent of blacks.

Another difference is financial: Charters get significantly less money per student than DCPS schools. By law, operating expenditures are supposed to be equal, but the lawsuit filed by several charters and the D.C. Association of Chartered Public Schools claims that charters have received, on average, $1,600 to $2,600 less in annual per-pupil operating funds. The law does not require equal expenditures for facilities or pensions, and here everyone agrees that DCPS schools get more money. Although various experts come up with different figures, and they change from year to year, the total difference in operating plus facilities funding has probably been $6,000 to 7,000 per student in recent years.

The financial and racial differences suggest that DCPS schools should easily outperform charters, but other factors work in the opposite direction. Charter students' families actively choose their schools, whereas only half of DCPS families do. Many believe this gives charters an advantage. Most experts agree that while overall poverty levels are similar, DCPS schools in the poorest wards have more students who are "in crisis" than charters, because those families are unlikely to apply for charters.

Though it is hardly perfect, D.C.'s closest approximation to a measure of "low income" is students who are "at risk of academic failure": those whose families are on welfare (TANF) or food stamps (SNAP), those who are homeless or in foster care, and high school students who are at least a year overage for their grade. Almost half of all D.C. public school students fit this category.

In 2015–16, 47.6 percent of DCPS students were "at risk," while 43.8 percent of charter students were. But, unlike charters, DCPS's distribution is bimodal: some DCPS schools have mostly middle-class students or above, while others have mostly at-risk students. In 2014–15—not counting alternative schools—some two dozen DCPS schools had more than 75 percent "at risk" students, while only one charter school did. These 24 schools, in the poorest wards, struggled with concentrated poverty and high student turnover.

Charters also expel more students than DCPS, though the numbers are way down since the Charter Board began to address the issue in 2012—to two for every 1,000 students, which is within national norms. Nor do charters have to accept students midway through the school year or "backfill" seats after students leave, though some do. Most DCPS schools accept students midyear, and most backfill empty seats when they can—although some selective high schools won't take students after ninth or tenth grade.

Many DCPS principals, including some who have also run charters, say they receive challenging kids who have left or been expelled from charters. A 2015 mobility study by the Office of the State Superintendent of Education (OSSE) revealed that about 600 students left charter schools for DCPS schools during the course of the school year, while less than 50 moved in the opposite direction. (Most of these had *not* been expelled.) But even more students—about 700—left one DCPS school for another. DCPS schools that received these students often struggled, because they inherited some of the toughest kids.

The city is encouraging schools to retain students by restructuring the funding system, so that money follows each child, even at midyear. This way, all schools will have a financial incentive to keep students and to accept students midyear.

A Close Look at the Data

It is difficult to say how all these realities balance out. DCPS has more extremely challenging students but also more middle-class and white students; charters can refuse to accept kids midyear or backfill seats, but they get far less money per child. Fortunately, two studies from Stanford University's Center for Research on Education Outcomes (CREDO) try to compensate for student demographics (but not for the other factors).

From 2007–8 through 2010–11, CREDO found, charter students gained an average of 72 more days of learning per year in reading than demographically similar DCPS students who had similar past test scores. In math, the difference was 101 days—well over half an academic year. A more recent CREDO study, published in 2015, found the same trends, while also showing that by a student's fourth year in a charter, the impact was more than double this amount. According to Jeffrey Noel, OSSE's former measurement expert, no one has seriously questioned CREDO's conclusions.

Another independent study, which compared students' actual progress on test scores to their expected progress, given their income levels and race, came to similar conclusions. Among middle schools, for instance, only seven of 27 DCPS schools produced higher proficiency levels than predicted in math and only six of 27 did so in reading. At the same time, 24 of 33 charters produced higher proficiency than predicted in math, while 25 did so in reading.

The most important measures by which to compare charter and DCPS schools are not test scores but long-term outcomes, such as high school and college graduation and future employment. Unfortunately, there is no data on employment, and any data on college completion is, by its nature, at least seven years old, because it measures rates of college graduation within six years of enrollment. Before 2007, only an estimated 9 percent of D.C. public school ninth-graders—charter and DCPS—graduated from college within five years of high school completion, compared to 23 percent nationwide. We lack good data on college cohorts since then, though college persistence rates are improving, according to OSSE.

Data on high school graduation exists, but its meaning is less than clear, because several hundred students leave charters for DCPS high schools each year, and no one has studied how many of them later graduate and how many drop out. On top of that, few charters accept new students after ninth grade, as most DCPS high schools do. That said, charters graduated 73 percent of their students within four years in 2016, while DCPS schools graduated 69 percent. The five-year graduation rate in 2015, the last year for which data is available, was 76 percent for charters and 63 percent for DCPS. Among black and low-income students, charters outperformed DCPS by about ten percentage points on the four-year rate in 2015. Given that almost seven of every ten black males who drop out of high school will be imprisoned by their mid-thirties, this is an important difference.

Charters clearly outperform DCPS high schools when it comes to college acceptance. DCPS has no data available on college acceptance rates. Phone calls to each DCPS high school in the spring of 2015 revealed why: With two exceptions, both high-performing schools, the schools either had no idea how many of their students had been accepted to college or simply ignored repeated messages. In contrast, every charter high school had an answer, because the Charter Board not only publishes the number as part of its Performance Management Framework but also requires proof in the form of actual college acceptance letters. In 2016, 97.2 percent of charter graduates were accepted to college.

Not all students who are accepted enroll, however. The most recent data available about actual enrollment is from 2012. Based on incomplete data from OSSE, college enrollment from all public high schools increased from 47 percent in 2006 to 57 percent in 2012. Charter schools improved from 44 percent to 63 percent during those years, while DCPS fell somewhere short of 55 percent.

Attendance data is problematic as well, because different schools may define "unexcused" absences differently. For what it's worth, DCPS reported average attendance of 89.7 percent in 2015–16, while charters reported 92.2 percent.

Data on parental demand also favors charters. In recent years, charters have grown by 2,000 to 3,000 students per year, while DCPS schools have grown by less than 1,000, on average. In 2016–17, charter enrollment grew by almost 7 percent, while DCPS enrollment barely changed. (These are net gains, after losses.) And more than 8,640 students were on waiting lists for charter schools in 2016, while only 7,790 were on waiting lists for DCPS schools.

Finally we come back to test scores, which get the most attention. Test score data is important, but it has many limits: Cheating scandals have occurred in both sectors, the tests have changed in recent years, and tests are an imperfect proxy for outcomes. They should never be used as the sole measure of school quality.

With that caveat, let us examine the results of three standardized tests: the DC CAS (Comprehensive Assessment System), which began in 2006; PARCC, which took its place in 2015; and NAEP, the national assessment. The first two have had high stakes attached; hence there were incentives to cheat and to teach to the test. OSSE has tightened test protocols and monitoring, so although cheating goes on in any high-stakes testing, OSSE officials believe it is now rare and quickly detected. NAEP, which comes with no stakes attached, is therefore considered by most a more reliable gauge.

On the DC CAS test, charter students consistently performed better and improved faster, with a particular advantage in the poorest wards. DCPS schools moved from composite (math and reading) scores of 31 percent proficient or advanced in 2006 to 49 percent in 2014, an increase of 18 points. Charters moved from 36 to 57 percent, an advance of 21 points. In Wards 5, 7, and 8, which are D.C.'s poorest, with the highest concentrations of African Americans, charters performed dramatically better than DCPS, as the graphs on the following pages show.

The same trends continued on the PARCC exams. In 2016, charter schools outperformed DCPS schools in nearly every grade level and subject. In the two poorest wards, charters had nearly three times the percentage of students "meeting" or "exceeding" expectations (the new definition of proficiency) as DCPS schools. Among African Americans and at-risk students, the ratio was almost two to one. Among Hispanics, charters edged DCPS by only a few points. In high school, five charters outperformed all nonselective DCPS schools. (Charters in D.C. are not allowed to be selective.) All six schools that earned "Bold Performance Awards," for proficiency rates at least 20 percentage points higher than schools with similar demographics, were charters.

DCPS leaders prefer to use NAEP data. After years of abysmally low scores, D.C. has shown significant improvement. In 2013 and 2015, the two sectors combined improved faster than any state, though two recent analyses found that a quarter to a third of the last decade's increase can be attributed to changing demographics. DCPS has also made great progress on its own, moving from a tie for last among 11 urban districts tested in 2007 to tenth and 11th in fourth grade reading and math out of 21 urban districts tested in 2015. Eighth-graders ranked 14th in reading and 15th in math in 2015.

But DCPS's greatest progress has come among middle- and upper-income students and in elementary schools. Low-income eighth-graders still ranked 21st out of 21 districts in reading in 2015 and 20th in math, ahead of only Detroit. Low-income fourth-graders tied for 15th and 14th, respectively.

Charters have performed far better among African American and low-income students, where they are concentrated. (For Hispanic students, sample sizes are too small to generalize with any confidence.)

Figures 7-7 through 7-14 show the last decade's NAEP results for all students and for African American students, comparing both sectors to the national averages in cities with 250,000 or more residents. Two underlying realities explain these results. First is the huge gap between white and other students. White students in DCPS score higher than whites in any of the 20 other NAEP/TUDA districts. But they also score 55 to 65 points higher than black students in DCPS. Given that ten points is considered about a year's worth of learning, that is a huge gap. To put it differently, 75 percent or more of whites in DCPS score "proficient" or above on NAEP, while only 8 to 18 percent of blacks do. The gaps have not narrowed over the past decade.

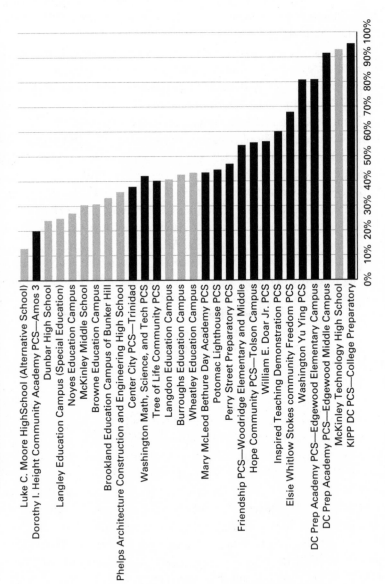

Figure 7-1 Source: Friends of Choice in Urban Schools.

Ward 5 Percent Proficient and Above in Reading on the 2014 DC CAS

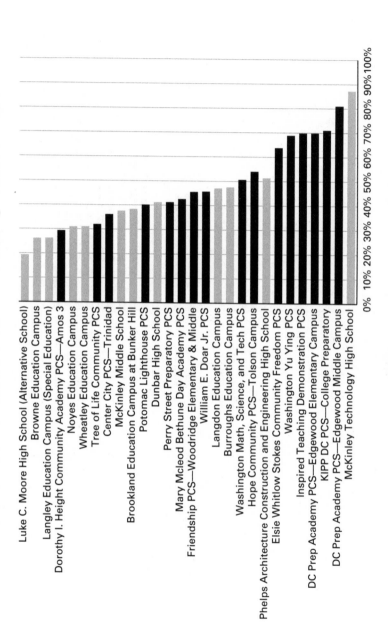

Figure 7-2 Source: Friends of Choice in Urban Schools.

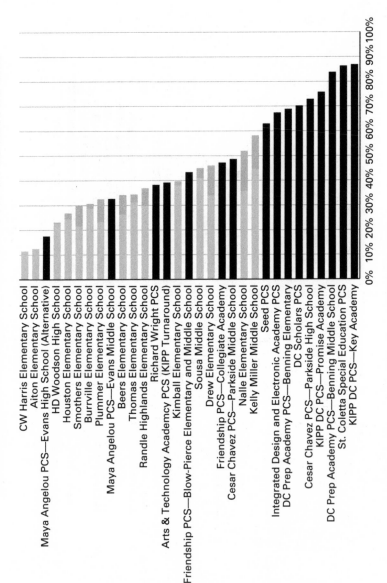

Figure 7-3 Source: Friends of Choice in Urban Schools.

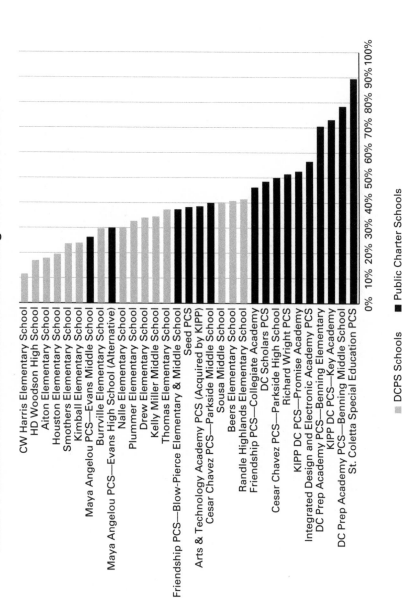

Ward 7 Percent Proficient and Above in Reading on the 2014 DC CAS

CW Harris Elementary School
HD Woodson High School
Aiton Elementary School
Houston Elementary School
Smothers Elementary School
Kimball Elementary School
Maya Angelou PCS—Evans Middle School
Burrville Elementary School
Maya Angelou PCS—Evans High School (Alternative)
Nalle Elementary School
Plummer Elementary School
Drew Elementary School
Kelly Miller Middle School
Thomas Elementary School
Friendship PCS—Blow-Pierce Elementary & Middle School
Seed PCS
Arts & Technology Academy PCS (Acquired by KIPP)
Cesar Chavez PCS—Parkside Middle School
Sousa Middle School
Beers Elementary School
Randle Highlands Elementary School
Friendship PCS—Collegiate Academy
DC Scholars PCS
Cesar Chavez PCS—Parkside High School
Richard Wright PCS
KIPP DC PCS—Promise Academy
Integrated Design and Electronic Academy PCS
DC Prep Academy PCS—Benning Elementary
KIPP DC PCS—Key Academy
DC Prep Academy PCS—Benning Middle School
St. Coletta Special Education PCS

0% 10% 20% 30% 40% 50% 60% 70% 80% 90% 100%

■ DCPS Schools   ■ Public Charter Schools

Figure 7-4 Source: Friends of Choice in Urban Schools.

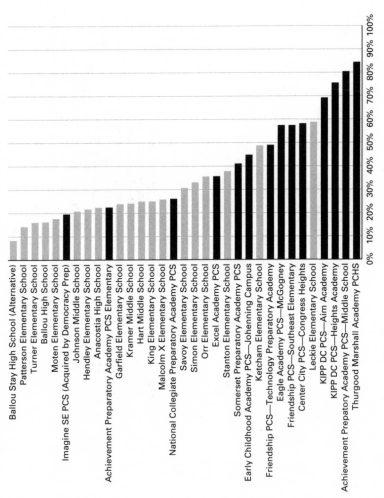

Figure 7-5 Source: Friends of Choice in Urban Schools.

Ward 8 Percent Proficient and Above in Reading on the 2014 DC CAS

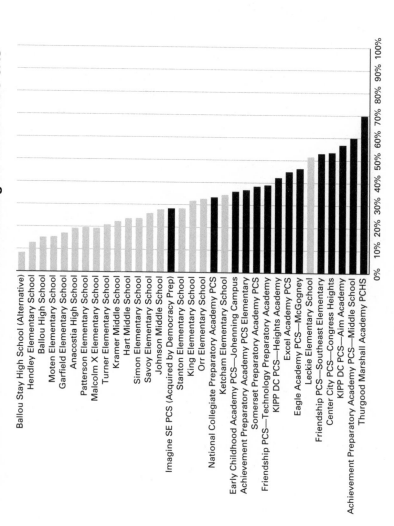

Figure 7-6 Source: Friends of Choice in Urban Schools.

This is probably the case for two reasons. First, NAEP exams are less tied to a particular curriculum than DC CAS or PARCC tests. Middle-class students' home environments generally make them better prepared than poor students for such exams. Second, low-income black students in DCPS schools are struggling, particularly after elementary school. Consider Ward 8: in its three DCPS middle schools, only 8 percent of students met PARCC expectations for reading in 2016; at its two DCPS high schools, Ballou and Anacostia, only 6 percent met expectations.

Which brings us to the second underlying reality: DCPS has done well with elementary students, but with adolescents, who pose far greater challenges, charters produce much better results. As the graphs show, both sectors have been roughly equal and have made similar progress over the years with fourth-grade scores, though DCPS had a huge increase between 2013 and 2015 in fourth-grade reading, the largest in the history of the test, and wound up five points ahead of charters. But when students hit middle school, DCPS's performance plummets, in part because so many white students peel off to private schools. Indeed, a 2014 *Washington Post* poll found that only 24 percent of D.C. residents would choose to send their children to a DCPS middle school.

In other words, DCPS has done a good job with those who are easiest to educate: white, middle-class, and elementary school students. When all is said and done—when all test scores have been compared, along with attendance, graduation rates, college enrollment, parental demand for each type of school, and independent studies—the charter model is clearly superior.

Why Charters Outperform DCPS Schools

DCPS leaders have implemented aggressive reforms, raised salaries dramatically, imported many charter practices, and produced significant improvement in student performance. Yet charters continue to outpace them. Why?

If you talk with enough DCPS principals, the reason becomes clear: The constraints under which they operate limit their use of the most powerful levers that drive charters, such as school-level autonomy, parental choice, and the threat of closure. Charters excel not because their people are somehow better than those in DCPS. As in New Orleans, they excel because their governance framework creates an environment in which the extraordinary measures necessary to educate poor minority children are not only easier to implement, they are indispensable if schools are to survive.

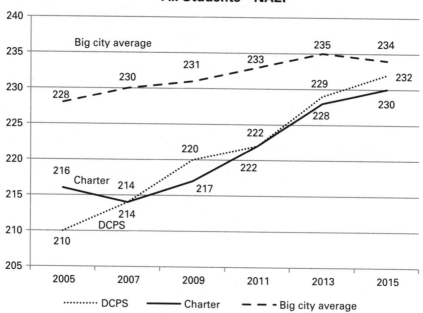

Figure 7-7: DCPS, Charters & Big City Average 4th Grade Math All Students—NAEP

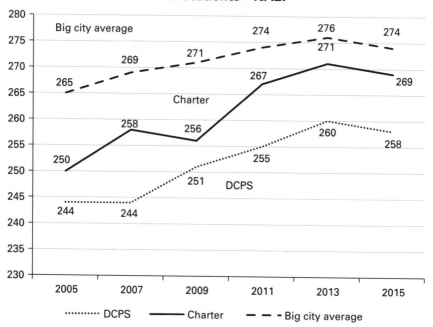

Figure 7-8: DCPS, Charters & Big City Average 8th Grade Math All Students—NAEP

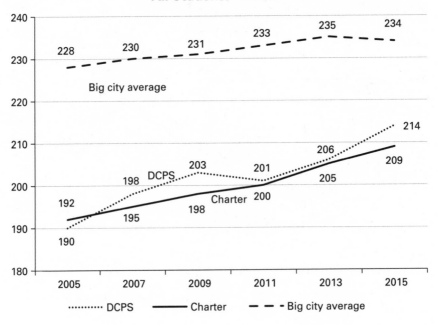

Figure 7-9: DCPS, Charters & Big City Average 4th Grade Reading All Students—NAEP

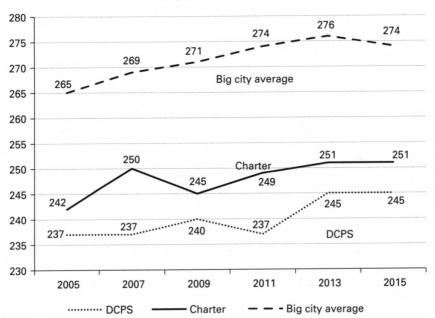

Figure 7-10: DCPS, Charters & Big City Average 8th Grade Reading All Students—NAEP

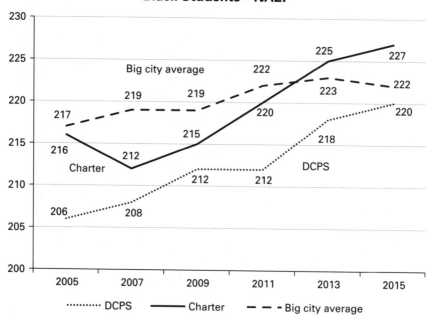

Figure 7-11: DCPS, Charters & Big City Average 4th Grade Math Black Students—NAEP

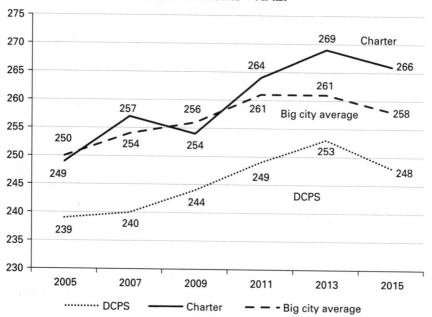

Figure 7-12: DCPS, Charters & Big City Average 8th Grade Math Black Students—NAEP

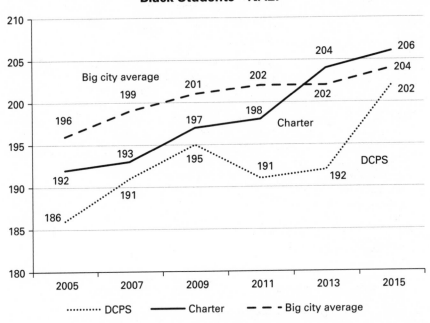

Figure 7-13: DCPS, Charters & Big City Average 4th Grade Reading Black Students—NAEP

.... DCPS   —— Charter   — — Big city average

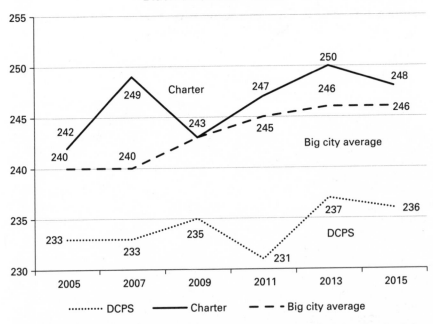

Figure 7-14: DCPS, Charters & Big City Average 8th Grade Reading Black Students—NAEP

.... DCPS   —— Charter   — — Big city average

Source of data: For DCPS, NAEP Data Explorer, National Center for Education Statistics, http://nces.ed.gov/nationsreportcard/naepdata/; for charters, Public Charter School Board. Graphs prepared by Mary Levy. "Big city average" refers to the average of all urban districts with 250,000 residents or more on NAEP, not just the 21 TUDA districts.

School-Level Autonomy

For starters, charters have significantly more autonomy than DCPS schools. Being empowered helps motivate their leaders and staff, while removing the usual excuse used by low-performing schools: "We're trying hard, but the central office ties our hands."

There is a common human tendency to assume that there is one best way to run a school, which leads to uniform policies. Charters were invented in part to counter this, because, in reality, different children learn differently and flourish in different environments. To tailor their efforts to their students' learning styles, behavior, and backgrounds, schools need a fair amount of autonomy.

Charters in D.C. are protected from the one-best-way impulse by law, although city council members often propose standardized solutions for all schools. "We never go more than a week or ten days without a new battle," Robert Cane, former executive director of FOCUS, told me. "You'll get a council member who thinks children should be in uniform, so introduces a bill saying every child should be in uniform. We have to go tell them that violates the law."

District schools not only lack such protection, their leaders have often shared the one-best-way view. In 2014–15, for example, the City Council appropriated $80 million in new money for "at-risk" kids. It was intended to go straight to the schools so principals could decide how to use it, and that's what happened with charters. But Kaya Henderson decided she knew better than her principals, dedicating the money instead to specific initiatives. "We know what will help our neediest students—a longer school day, engaging content, parent engagement, social and emotional supports—and we want to ensure that our at-risk students receive these services," she wrote to the council. Henderson also required that all high schools offer at least eight advanced placement courses—even in high-poverty schools, where none of the students passed AP tests.

In addition, DCPS's union contracts limit principals' ability to lengthen their school day or demand more from their teachers in other ways. "At charter schools, they have the freedom to alter schedules as they need," says Justin Jones, who worked with many charter and district schools at the Achievement Network. For example, many charters set aside a full day after every periodic student assessment for teachers to examine the data and figure out what to do to improve learning. Though some are beginning to emulate them, "many district schools don't have that option."

More than half of the charters use a 200-day school year, with a much shorter summer break and two-week breaks spread throughout the year, to avoid the dreaded "summer slide." Most DCPS principals have not had the option of going beyond 180 days, though DCPS has recently implemented 200-day schedules in 11 high-poverty schools.

DCPS principals can now use IMPACT to fire ineffective staff, a huge improvement, but the process takes much longer than in charters and is more labor intensive. And some principals complain that staff members are learning to game the IMPACT system. The district also has rules about who can be hired. These rules sometimes frustrate principals; for instance, they might find a strong candidate with the right experience who lacks a required degree.

Most DCPS schools have to use services provided by the central office— unlike charters, which can purchase them when and where they get the best value. And everyone in DCPS is frustrated with the procurement system, which makes it impossible to buy goods and services as soon as schools need them, as charters can. Henderson herself cited the example of a school that was using software to help teach math and got 40 new students in the middle of the year. "If you want to procure 40 laptops in DCPS, you can't call up and get a laptop tomorrow," she told me. "The procurement and budget stuff precludes you from all that. And you'll be tested on those kids who, for two or three months, were working without the appropriate materials."

Nor do DCPS principals have as much flexibility with their staffing and budgets as charters do. DCPS staffing patterns are set at district headquarters. "Each year, we have some positions that we cannot move off the budget, even though something else might be more important to us at the school," says Natalie Gordon, a successful charter principal Henderson recruited to turn around Jefferson Middle School, then promoted to instructional superintendent. Gordon cites the example of librarians, who cost close to $100,000 each. She might need a school counselor more than a librarian, because the humanities teachers can handle the library. "But, in order for me to get that librarian off my budget, I have to petition. If I have a strong enough case, they may say yes. If my case is not in line with the chancellor's priorities, or if my case is not well worded, or if my instructional superintendent doesn't really get my vision somehow, then that petition is not going to be approved." Principals considered weaker by central headquarters staff often have their petitions denied, she says.

One of Henderson's priorities was funding Spanish, art, music, and physical education classes in every school. Principals were seldom allowed to use any of that money for something else, such as extra reading instructors. "As a principal, I'm like, 'Hello! Those kids can't read!'" says Gordon. "I'm not going to put my kids in art when they can't read, so how do we do both? Those are the kinds of fights that we have that we didn't have to have in the charter world, and that's frustrating."

Though he was a successful DCPS principal at two different schools,

Patrick Pope chose to leave and now runs a charter school. During his DCPS career he experienced a move toward greater centralized control, he says. He lacked "the autonomy to put staff and resources where they needed to be. They will say the word 'autonomy,' but the model is, you can have autonomy when you get to a certain level of student performance measures."

Discipline policy offers yet another example. Charters are free to establish their own methods, but the district imposes standard policies. For instance, it discourages expulsions so strongly that they almost never occur. DCPS schools can transfer students or give them long-term suspensions, which send them to an alternative school for up to 90 days. But that process is time consuming, says Rachel Skerritt, former principal of Eastern High School. "It's an extremely laborious process; I feel like a part-time lawyer when I go [in front of a judge]. It's a huge time away from your building and it's considered to be used only for really serious offenses." Sometimes the slow pace of decisions endangers students—for instance, when two kids need to be separated by transferring one to another high school. "When things are urgent and you know what this means for the safety of your building, it can be really challenging," Skerritt says.

The central office has also required that schools participate in many initiatives, from reading programs to behavior management programs to professional development. Particularly for the 40 lowest-performing schools, which are kept on tighter leashes, this is the greatest burden, says Carolyn Albert-Garvey, principal at Maury Elementary. "I think the district is doing a great job in selecting high-quality programs—the leadership is very thoughtful about what's been proven," she says. "But it's the quantity. Have they really sat down with each school leader to figure out what the priority is, and where they should start?"

Natalie Gordon calls it "the DCPS monster."

> It's very challenging to manage all the very many initiatives that are taking place in the district. If I get an update that says, "Oh, you need to choose a point of contact for testing, you need to choose a point of contact for the keyboarding initiative, you need to choose a point of contact for blah, blah, blah," where am I going to find these people who are going to teach and also do all this other work? That, to me, is the biggest challenge.

Accountability for Performance

After autonomy, the second big lever the Charter Board uses to drive quality is accountability for performance. Under the traditional rules of public education, says former mayor Vincent Gray, D.C. schools experienced "tremendous decline. There was complacency that set in, and there was a view that whatever you did was kind of okay." But charters and competition changed all that. "I honestly think that one of the principal reasons for the improvements we're seeing is the feeling that if you don't get better, you're going to go out of business." Thanks in part to this pressure, charter schools do things that never occur to most traditional school leaders—like sending staff to kids' homes to collect them when they don't show up on rainy days, or hiring staff members to help their graduates get through college.

The competition from charters has clearly been good for DCPS, creating the sense of urgency leaders need to push through big changes. And to its credit, DCPS has adopted its own versions of accountability, though it has not gone quite as far as charters have. Thanks to Michelle Rhee's insistence on IMPACT, weak teachers can be fired now, after a year of documentation, and outstanding teachers can be paid more. Rhee closed about 25 schools because their buildings were underutilized and reconstituted another 18 due to low performance; by mid-2015 Henderson had closed 15 and reconstituted another nine. When either happens, teachers rated less than "effective" lose their jobs.

These new realities are highly motivating. But experience and data both suggest that when *everyone* in a school building knows their jobs are at risk, the effect is greater. The motivation is not just individual; it affects everyone. If staff members believe in their leaders, they tend to pull together to do what's necessary. CREDO studies show that in cities and states where authorizers consistently close low-performing charters, charter students far outpace their district counterparts on standardized tests. Where they don't close schools—even though charters can easily fire weak teachers—charters often underperform their district counterparts. By weeding out the worst schools, authorizers not only bring up the average, they motivate everyone working in the surviving schools. DCPS benefits from some of this dynamic—far more than most districts—but probably not as much as charters do.

Parental Choice

The third significant lever driving charters is parental choice. All charters in D.C. are schools of choice, whereas most DCPS schools are neighborhood schools. Families that choose tend to be more committed, their children more engaged. Half of DCPS students do choose, but their choices are limited: if a DCPS school is in high demand, the chances are slim for those outside the neighborhood.

Charters also receive a set dollar amount for every child, so if they attract more families, they get more money, and if they lose students, they lose money—and may even have to close. This keeps those without waiting lists very attuned to what parents want. Undersubscribed schools in DCPS sometimes close as well, but not always. Indeed, by 2015–16, 18 open schools filled fewer than 70 percent of their seats. So DCPS schools experience some of the same pressure to remain attractive to parents, but probably less than charters.

Being schools of choice, charters do not have to appeal to everyone. They can specialize, creating bilingual schools, residential schools, schools intended for over-age students, schools intended for students in foster care. Cristina Encinas, principal of Latin American Montessori Bilingual Public Charter School, reminds us that "equity is not everybody having a shoe, but having a shoe that fits."

This handcrafting makes it easier for charters to build school cultures that produce success, even with students who arrive with neither motivation nor middle-class values and habits. As in New Orleans, charters work hard to create that motivation—setting college as the goal, using systems of rewards and sanctions, taking end-of-the-year trips to reward students who put in the effort required for success. And they resist actions that will undermine their hard-won cultures, such as accepting too many transfer students.

DCPS has also worked hard to create specialized schools: by 2016–17 it had nine bilingual immersion schools, four Montessori preschools, two adult education schools, ten elementaries with an arts focus, a handful of STEM schools, career-tech programs within 15 high schools, seven schools that participated in the International Baccalaureate program, 18 schools that embraced blended learning, and a new all-male high school. Students at all of its high schools could apply for tuition-free dual enrollment at Georgetown University and the University of D.C. Community College, and those at some schools could also apply to George Washington University or Howard University.

Overall, D.C. probably has more diversity of school models, for its size, than any other city. Still, the majority of DCPS principals know they have to meet the needs of all types of students and their parents. "Every charter school only has to satisfy their constituency," Henderson told me. "And, if you don't like them, you can choose something else. We have to satisfy every constituency." Hence, there is pressure to standardize school offerings and methods— pressure augmented by standardized curriculum and staffing requirements.

Entrepreneurial Drive

A fourth reason charters excel is their entrepreneurial drive. Educating poor children in the inner city is so challenging that it often requires leaders to reinvent the educational process—the basic school design. Those who open charters are often driven by such visions. Consider Irasema Salcido, who knew from her own experience how important it was to prepare minority children to succeed in college. She designed a high school built around public policy, with Saturday school, student presentations to the city council, fellowships at public policy organizations, and a thesis required to graduate. Her vision has grown into two high schools and two middle schools.

Or consider Aaron Cuny and Will Stoetzer, who decided to create a charter school, beginning with age three and slowly growing to 12th grade, in a poor section of town with the largest gap between the number of kids and the availability of quality schools. It's called Ingenuity Prep, and three quarters of its students are classified "at-risk" by the city, the highest percentage of any charter elementary school. "We want to be the proof point that shows that when the adults get it right, a very high at-risk population of kids can achieve at high levels," says Cuny. To do so, they designed a school with a longer year, longer days, and all instruction delivered in groups of eight kids and one teacher. How do they manage that, financially? By using four levels of teachers: master teachers, lead teachers, associate teachers, and resident teachers. They also amplify their efforts with fairly intensive use of educational software.

When visionaries like Irasema Salcido or Aaron Cuny succeed, they often replicate their schools. The charter sector creates four or five new schools every year. One of its new high schools in 2016, Washington Leadership Academy, won $10 million from the Super School Project, funded by the philanthropist Laurene Powell Jobs to reimagine high school. The school combines online, project-based, and service learning with emerging technologies such as virtual reality.

To its credit, DCPS also creates new schools, but less often. And it rarely replicates successful schools. Entrepreneurial behavior is far more likely in a charter system than in a large bureaucracy.

Political Freedom

The final driver of success for charters is the political freedom to do what is best for the children, including closing failing schools, even when it conflicts with adult interests. Both the Charter Board and the DCPS chancellor are appointed by the mayor, not elected. Indeed, both offer proof that direct election of school boards is a bad idea—particularly in big cities, where patronage politics and posturing to reach higher office are so common. Most developed democracies do just fine without elected school boards, and it is worth noting that on international exams, the U.S. lags behind many of them.

D.C.'s experience suggests that we need a balance between local democratic control and insulation from political pressures. The Charter Board began with enormous insulation, because its members were selected by the mayor from nominations made by the U.S. secretary of education. Initially, this was critical in establishing the board's political independence. With the secretary no longer involved, the mayor now appoints members to staggered terms, and the city council confirms the appointments. This creates a degree of democratic control, but far less vulnerability to political pressures from interest groups than direct election of board members. So far, no mayor has tried to dictate to the board, which has been free to make decisions that reflect the interests of children. When the Charter Board closes schools, Scott Pearson says, he gets calls from city council members, but because his board is insulated, he can ignore them. In the future, if a mayor does seek to dictate to the board, staggered terms will limit how quickly he or she can control a majority of seats.

Because the chancellor is also appointed by the mayor, the more important difference between the two systems is DCPS's potential for political captivity by its thousands of employees. When the Charter Board considers closing schools, it gets pressure only from those school communities. But when DCPS contemplates closing schools, it gets pressure from across the system, including employees, their unions, parents, and neighborhood activists. Since most of those people vote, the mayor feels that pressure—indeed, it cost Adrian Fenty his job in 2010. You can be sure the current mayor remembers what happened to Fenty and will act to avoid that fate herself. If new Chancellor Antwan Wilson were to anger the employees and community, as Rhee did, a typical mayor would rein him in.

In sum, the charter sector outperforms DCPS because it has more autonomy, more accountability, more choice, more ability to handcraft schools that meet the needs of diverse students, more entrepreneurial drive, and more freedom to do what is best for the children. DCPS is now far stronger than most urban districts on all these counts, but on none can it go as far as the charter sector.

DCPS is like a race-car driver piloting a Model T, when its competitor drives a 21st century model. The Model T still works pretty well for most middle-class students—particularly after the district rebuilt the engine and transmission in recent years. But for those with greater needs, a Model T will not suffice. To succeed with poor, inner-city youths, schools need academic designs shaped to the specific needs of their students, extraordinary leadership, and 100 percent commitment from their staffs. DCPS is racing to provide all of this, but a Model T will only go so fast.

Where to from Here?

Many good things are happening in D.C. schools. Families are no longer leaving D.C. in droves when their children approach school age. Indeed, public school enrollment climbed 25 percent between 2006–7 and 2016–17. Having the nation's most robust preschool program—with free, full-day preschool available to all three- and four-year-olds—has helped.

But the schools still have a long way to go. On the 2016 PARCC exams, only 28 percent in charters and 24 percent in DCPS schools met or exceeded "college- and career-ready" standards. If the mayor and city council want to go the whole distance, what should they do?

If New Orleans is any guide, they should gradually turn their worst schools over to charter operators, and they should open new, innovative charters. If they do, dumping-ground schools and dropout factories will gradually disappear, replaced by more effective schools.

That will happen slowly even if city leaders don't act, as the charter sector continues to expand and DCPS continues to close schools. But there are several plausible ways the city could speed it up. The most logical would be for DCPS to turn over failing schools to the Charter Board, which would hand them to strong charter operators. In a political world, however, the most logical choice is often the least likely. Given the rivalry between the two systems and the protests that would greet this strategy, it is extremely unlikely.

DCPS could also contract with charter networks to operate more of its failing schools. It has done this in the past, with mixed results, and Kaya Henderson told me she wanted to do more of it, using the lessons learned from that experience. The new DCPS chancellor, who spent almost a decade in Denver, could borrow from lessons learned there and create an innovation zone with an independent, nonprofit board, to authorize these schools (see chapter 9).

The city council could even create a second authorizer specifically to take on the failing DCPS schools. This way those schools' employees would no longer be district employees, so it would be easier to close the schools if they failed. The authorizer would also be less susceptible to pressure from DCPS if it opened schools that competed directly with district schools.

If D.C.'s leaders want to go all the way, they could even take the advice of Andy Smarick, author of *The Urban School System of the Future*, and let the new body authorize all DCPS schools, so they are accountable to a neutral, outside board. That way, decisions about closure, replacement, expansion, and replication would not be made by the district, with its natural loyalty to schools it owns and people it employs. DCPS would operate schools, but authorizing decisions would be made by a neutral party that could put children's interests first—the same situation faced by charter operators.

Even if D.C.'s leaders went that far, however, they would still have two school systems, and solving citywide problems would require that they work together. To succeed over time, someone would need the power to steer the entire system. In D.C., that should be the mayor, who would have leverage because she would appoint both authorizing boards. To ensure that these two bodies cooperated, the city council could give the mayor the power to enforce policies that both sectors had to follow, relating to empty school buildings, funding, backfilling empty seats, and other issues.

Consider, for instance, the problem of school facilities. In 2015–16, five DCPS buildings sat empty, six were less than half full, three were used for administrative purposes, and two were used by nonprofit organizations or other city departments. DCPS wanted to keep all the empty buildings for future use, because enrollment is expanding. But they belong to the city, not the district. And DCPS educates only 54 percent of the city's public school students, while charters struggle mightily to find facilities they can afford, sometimes settling for warehouses or church basements.

Mayor Muriel Bowser announced in February 2017 that she wanted to increase charters' facilities allotment and make more city buildings available to them, which should help, if the city council agrees. But it won't end DCPS's near-monopoly on traditional school buildings, nor the city's vastly unequal spending on facilities.

The mayor, through the deputy mayor for education, could be given the power to suspend or even revoke an authorizer's right to authorize if it refused to collaborate in solving such problems. This would require a delicate balance: legislation would also need to spell out clear limits on the mayor's and council's authorities, just as Louisiana's legislature spelled out clear limits on the powers of the Orleans Parish School Board.

Such ideas may sound like pipe dreams, but Louisiana has proven that they are possible. The real question is whether D.C.'s elected leaders have the imagination and courage to implement them.

PART III

DENVER: AN ELECTED SCHOOL BOARD ADOPTS A 21ST CENTURY STRATEGY

CHAPTER 8

THE MILE-HIGH CITY EMBRACES CHARTER SCHOOLS

MANY WONDER WHETHER A 21ST century strategy is possible with an elected school board, because closing schools and laying off teachers triggers such fierce resistance. New Orleans and Washington, D.C., have been insulated from local electoral politics by Louisiana's Recovery School District and D.C.'s Public Charter School Board, created by Congress. In other cities that are moving in this direction, such as Memphis, Tennessee, and Camden, New Jersey, recovery districts or state takeovers have driven reforms.

All of which explains why reformers are paying close attention to Denver. With an elected board, Denver Public Schools (DPS) has embraced charter schools and created "innovation schools," district schools with some of the autonomy charters enjoy. Between 2005 and 2015 it closed or replaced 48 schools and opened more than 70, the majority of them charters. In 2010 it signed a Collaboration Compact with charter schools, committing to equitable funding and a common enrollment system for charters and traditional schools, plus replication of the most effective schools, whether charter or traditional.

Of DPS's 204 schools in 2016–17, 56 were charters, which educated 21 percent of its students, and 47 were innovation schools, which educated 20.5 percent. In 2015 the Board of Education voted for a major expansion of successful charter schools. And in 2016 it created an innovation zone, called the Luminary Learning Network, with an independent, nonprofit board that has a three-year memorandum of understanding with the district. Beginning with four innovation schools but able to expand, the zone could help DPS give innovation schools the true autonomy they need to excel.

For years, Denver's reforms stirred controversy. When the Board of Education closed or replaced failing schools, protests erupted and board meetings dragged into the wee hours. During four of Tom Boasberg's first five years as superintendent, he had only a four-three majority on the board. But the strategy produced steady results: In 2005, Denver had the lowest rates of academic growth among Colorado's ten largest districts; since 2012 it has ranked at the top.

Denver still has a long way to go, but its progress offers hope to other urban districts with elected school boards—still the norm in the United States. A combination of courageous leadership, political skill, and positive results has yielded broad support for its strategy of closing failing schools and replacing them with charters and innovation schools. Voters have responded by electing a 7–0 majority in support of this strategy.

The Denver Story

With 700,000 people, Denver is booming. It is the number one destination for the millennial generation and one of the nation's top ten cities for business start-ups. Some 50,000 people a year are moving in, finding jobs in growing sectors such as high tech and craft beer. The city is extremely livable, with a vibrant downtown, tree-lined neighborhoods, and a significant and growing middle class. The front range of the Rockies beckons a few miles to the west, and with 205 parks, the city has the largest park system in the nation. Denverites enjoy sunshine 300 days a year, and they use it: According to one federal study, a smaller percentage of residents are overweight than in any other U.S. city. The city is racially diverse—53 percent white, 31 percent Hispanic, 10 percent African American, 4 percent Asian, and 2 percent Native American. It has one of the highest percentages of college graduates of any large city and very little entrenched, third-generation poverty. There is a sense of opportunity, residents will tell you—people are open to new things, unbound by dogma.

The school district is also growing. Enrollment increased 25 percent between 2007 and 2015, driven by population growth, expanded preschool programs, and more families choosing Denver public schools over private schools or neighboring districts. This growth has enabled Denver's reforms: It is politically easier to close failing schools and replace them with charters in a growing district, because there are jobs waiting for most of the teachers who are displaced.

On the other hand, shortages of money imposed by Colorado's constitutional cap on tax revenues have created hurdles. Colorado cut education spending deeply following the Great Recession, and by 2016, it ranked 42nd in the nation in state spending per pupil. DPS revenue was $2,000 to $2,500 less per student than the national average, and still below its own level of 2009–10. DPS's demographics also pose challenges: Almost seven in ten of its students are poor (qualifying for a free or reduced-price lunch), 37 percent are English-language learners, and 94 percent of low-income students are minorities. Of its more than 91,000 students, 56 percent are Hispanic, 22.6 percent are white, and 13.8 percent are African American. (All these figures include charter students.)

Like New Orleans and D.C., DPS was floundering in 2005. Of 98,000 seats, 31,000 were empty, and many school buildings were half full. Almost 16,000 students chose private or suburban schools instead—through statewide public school choice, which passed in 1990. A financial crisis loomed, in the form of pension contributions the district could not afford. When the superintendent retired in 2005, Board of Education (BOE) members decided they wanted a reformer. Mayor John Hickenlooper urged his 40-year-old chief of staff, Michael Bennet, to pursue the job. A Yale Law School graduate, Bennet had no background in public education, but he had spent time turning around failing companies and restructuring debt for a local investment firm. He also knew the important political players in town. The board chose him over two more traditional candidates.

The political environment was ripe for reform. The previous superintendent, Jerry Wartgow, had negotiated a pathbreaking pay-for-performance system, called ProComp, with the Denver Classroom Teachers Association (DCTA). (For a discussion of ProComp, see appendix B.) He was reconstituting 13 elementary and middle schools, and he had built support for reform among business and community leaders. "There was a consensus that we had to do something," says David Greenberg, who founded the city's most successful charter network. "But there was no consensus about what."

Michael Bennet knew he had to lure students back from other districts to stave off financial ruin. He considered the charter sector too small and ineffective to make a difference: only 7 percent of public school students attended 17 charters, half of which performed below the district average. Up to that point, most DPS leaders had been indifferent or hostile to charters, and the district had done a poor job of authorizing. Bennet was initially hostile as well. According to Greenberg, "He opposed expansion of charters within the district, on the grounds that charters 'stole' students from the district and thus were costing the district money."

Bruce Hoyt, then a BOE member, says Bennet and the board continued with a centralized strategy because the district was in such bad shape. "Given the weak capacity of school leadership, lack of good data systems to have accountability, and concerns over the large mobility rates of our students, the board adopted a 'managed instruction' theory of action," he told me. This meant central control over curriculum, budgets, hiring, and almost everything else. In late 2005, Bennet rolled out *The Denver Plan*, 85 pages of traditional reform initiatives, such as more training for principals and teachers, more summer school, longer school days, and healthier school meals.

Bennet's biggest challenges were the city's many failing schools. One of the most spectacular failures was Manual High School, an older school in the center of town. When forced busing ended, after the 1996–97 school year, Manual changed almost overnight from a middle-class school with test scores at the national average to a school with 86 percent of students living in poverty, scores around the 30th percentile, and 20 kids a year suspended for carrying weapons. By 2000 it had the lowest test scores in the state. With money from the Bill and Melinda Gates Foundation's small schools initiative and leadership from the Colorado Children's Campaign, the district split the school into three small high schools. But teachers felt the plan had been foisted on them, administrators fought over resources and shared spaces, and the experiment failed. By 2005, the school's four-year dropout rate was estimated at 75 percent.

Soon after he released his Denver Plan, Bennet announced that he would close Manual for a year and start over, one grade at a time. Current students would have to attend other high schools, most of which also performed abysmally.

There had been no consultation with the community, and the backlash was fierce. At a packed board hearing, a local minister called the decision racist. Others labeled the district a "dictatorship," and the crowd broke out in "We Shall Overcome." Realizing their error, Bennet and his staff launched a campaign of door-to-door visits to the homes of displaced students, to make sure they found another option. They and the board learned two painful lessons: to consult with school communities before taking such drastic action, and to make sure displaced students had better options to attend.

About that time, Alan Gottlieb, then the Piton Foundation's education specialist, asked Bennet what had been the most surprising thing about DPS. Gottlieb has never forgotten the reply: "How deeply, deeply f—ed up this place is."

DPS was so dysfunctional, he had concluded, that he could not fix it from the inside without significant outside pressure. So in 2006 he asked several foundation executives to create an organization of civic leaders to push for change and support the board when it promoted reform. It was co-chaired by two popular former mayors, Federico Pena and Wellington Webb, Qwest CEO Richard Notebaert, and a parent activist, Anne Rowe, and its members eventually included 100 influential Denverites. They called it A+ Denver, and it has played a central role in advocating reform, along with the Piton, Donnell-Kay, and Gates Family Foundations.

Abandoning Centralization

Bennet's centralized strategy, with required core curricula, benchmark assessments, professional development, and the like, quickly bogged down. The curriculum was over the heads of many kids, who were behind grade level. And the teachers union complained that teachers didn't have enough time to absorb all the new mandates handed down from headquarters.

Back in 2005, Bennet had recruited Brad Jupp, a union official who had led the negotiations for performance pay, to be his senior policy advisor. A former teacher, Jupp was convinced that DPS principals needed more autonomy to improve their schools and compete with charters. In the fall of 2006, he convinced Bennet to create something like Boston's pilot schools—in-district "beacon schools." They negotiated a memo of understanding with the teachers union, then asked teachers and principals to make proposals. We offered "greater resources, the opportunity to have a new school design, and a bit of autonomy," Jupp says. Their offer generated 24 proposals.

In March 2007, Bennet offered the principal's job at Manual High School to Rob Stein, a Manual graduate who had gone on to earn a Ph.D. at Harvard, become principal of a DPS "expeditionary school," then principal of a leading private school in town. Stein told Bennet, "I need to completely hire my own staff, I need my own curriculum and program and discretion over the budget." The school was scheduled to open in five months, and Bennet was desperate. Saying yes was his second big departure from centralization.

A month later, the *Rocky Mountain News* published a week-long series funded by the Piton Foundation, which revealed that almost a quarter of Denver students had left DPS for private schools, surrounding districts, and charter schools in those districts, costing DPS $125 million a year. A disproportionate percentage of those left behind were poor and nonwhite.

Bennet and the board responded with a call for dramatic change, suggesting that the superintendent was not alone in questioning centralization. "It is hard to admit," they wrote, "but it is abundantly clear that we will fail the vast majority of children in Denver if we try to run our schools the same old way." The district should "no longer function as a one-size-fits-all, centralized, Industrial Age enterprise making choices that schools, principals, teachers, and most, most important, parents are in a much better position to make for themselves." Instead, it should "function more like a partner, building capacity and leadership at the school level and serving as an incubator for innovation."

That summer Denver's standardized test scores remained flat or dipped. But two charters were hitting the ball out of the park: West Denver Prep, a middle school full of low-income Latino kids, and Denver School of Science and Technology (DSST), a high school that combined low-income and middle-class students. "Michael basically said, those schools are really great," says Jupp. "And I need something in the pipeline to compete against the beacon schools. He wanted the union to get behind beacon schools, to get going, and he used charters as a way to light a fire under them." So he and Jupp urged West Denver Prep and DSST to expand and offered them empty buildings.

Given the district's finances, Bennet wanted to close 30 half-empty schools. For political cover, he asked A+ Denver to study the oversupply of school buildings. The Piton Foundation hired the Center on Reinventing Public Education (CRPE) to help, and Margarite Roza and Paul Hill—coauthor of *Reinventing Public Education* and the nation's foremost proponent of what he called the portfolio strategy—began to spend time at DPS.

They told Bennet that superintendents did not survive big school closures unless the kids got to move to better schools. So Bennet pared the plan down to eight school closures and announced in October 2007 that DPS would develop "innovative and high-performing schools, especially secondary schools, by conducting a Request for Proposal (RFP) process to solicit new schools for the 2009 school year and beyond." That evolved into an annual "Call for New Quality Schools," which indicates where the district needs what level of schools and invites high-performing institutions to apply to open them.

A month later the board adopted a New School Development Plan, which gave new schools the opportunity to gain some autonomy, in return for accountability for performance. And early in 2008 Bennet created an Office of New Schools, modeled in part on what New York City was doing under Joel Klein and Chicago was doing under Arne Duncan.

This was all controversial, but Bennet had learned from the debacle at Manual. He had begun working with two community organizations, soliciting their views and support. Metro Organizations for People, now called Together Colorado, was a multiracial, multifaith coalition of more than 60 congregations and clergy, schools, and youth committees, affiliated with the national PICO network. Padres Unidos was an organization of Latino activists dating to the 1970s. Both were instrumental in supporting Bennet's reforms, including replacement of failing schools and expansion of charters.

"They really inoculated the district from having the kind of blowback that other districts have had from low-income communities of color," says Van Schoales, CEO of A+ Denver (now A+ Colorado). "It made it harder for the traditional factions—they lost some of the potential opposition to a lot of these reforms."

Back in 2005, a Commission on Secondary School Reform had recommended that the district shift to "weighted, student-based budgeting," in which dollars followed children to their school of choice, and more dollars were provided for children with higher needs. Metro Organizations for People had picked up on this, pointing out that poor and non-English-speaking students cost 20 to 25 percent more to educate than others and demanding the reform. Bennet and the board made the shift; by 2015 about 56 percent of operating money followed the student to the school they chose, and low-income students got 20 to 40 percent more money, depending upon their school level. (There are about ten different classes of students that get additional money.) This also increased the competitive pressures on schools, because losing students meant losing money.

The Emergence of Innovation Schools

Meanwhile, the beacon schools were bumping up against the limits imposed by district rules and the teachers' contract. Frustrated leaders at the Bruce Randolph Middle and High School, led by the principal, Kristin Waters, the union leader at the school, Greg Ahrnsbrak, and a teacher, Chrisanne LaHue—Brad Jupp's wife—proposed a novel use of a waiver clause in the 120-page contract: to waive everything but the provisions that permitted union membership and representation.

"We were a beacon schools but felt like it wasn't enough to give us the flexibility and the freedom to do some of the things that we wanted to do," says Ahrnsbrak. "Mainly, being able to make decisions in real time and being able to implement them in real time, instead of jumping through multiple hoops and different layers of bureaucracy in order to get an answer."

The union objected, but the Bruce Randolph team went ahead anyway. "Some of my union colleagues were very unhappy," says Ahrnsbrak. "People felt like it was weakening the union, making us vulnerable." But in early 2008, the board approved the waiver. Rob Stein, who was enormously frustrated by a school bureaucracy that had no idea how to fulfill Bennet's promises, immediately submitted an almost identical waiver request, and it, too, was approved.

Both schools were in the district of State Senate President Peter Groff, an African American who represented Northeast Denver. He jumped on the idea, and with help from Bennet's staff and others, drafted an Innovation Schools Act and pushed it through the legislature. It allowed waivers to district policies and state statutes governing budgets, hiring, scheduling, school calendars, and tenure for new teachers, if a majority of teachers voted for the innovation plan. If 60 percent voted for it, schools could waive all or part of the union contract. The schools could also decide whether to budget using actual teacher salaries or average salaries. If they chose the former, they spent less than average for young teachers and more for veteran teachers. They could also choose to opt out of a few district services.

"I think it was a recognition that so many of the rules that govern our schools, whether in statute or collective bargaining agreement, are really products of an Industrial Age economy," says Tom Boasberg, then Bennet's deputy. They were not designed for "a knowledge-based economy, where you have an extraordinary stress on creativity and problem solving. So the Innovations Schools Act, which we helped draft, was a response to allow district-run schools significantly greater flexibility from a set of work rules that frankly didn't make sense."

Unfortunately, the district began creating innovation schools without much attention to their design. District staff wrote applications, sometimes before they found a principal. "They opened a bunch of them, pretty quickly," says A+ Colorado's Van Schoales. "Many of them were opened without principals, without much of an idea of what the schools would be. It was mainly a way to get out of the union contract. The problem with doing that without a great leader and a plan in place is that you get another crappy school with a bunch of young, inexperienced people that don't know what they're doing."

The teachers union also resisted. "The union was brutal," says Brad Jupp, the former Denver Classroom Teachers Association (DCTA) leader. It brought "four union attorneys to strong-arm the faculty, as well as the executives." At Bruce Randolph School, union lawyers told the staff they were giving up their legal rights as teachers if they agreed to the innovation plan. "That scares the hell out of a 24-year-old teacher, who doesn't really understand the implications."

Nor did the DPS bureaucracy cooperate. Innovation status required many different parts of the central office to do things differently, and that is still a struggle. "It was a huge cultural shift for the district, and even for the superintendent, initially, it was kind of a struggle," says Mary Seawell, a former school board chair who is now the education specialist at Denver's Gates Family Foundation.

Changing a centralized bureaucracy with many moving parts is extremely difficult, because everything is connected: Change one thing and every other part is disturbed. Those other parts often resist. "I think the further one moves down the hierarchy, the more those challenges become dramatic," says Chris Gibbons, CEO of Strive Prep, the network that evolved out of West Denver Prep. "It's the result of a system that has a bureaucratic structure, set up to do business in a certain manner and ill equipped to do business in a different manner. While I would put Denver far ahead of many traditional districts in that regard, we are not operating like New Orleans or some other examples of real autonomous schools."

Consider what happened to Manual High School under Rob Stein. He and the team he hired created a school he describes as "high structure and high love," the basic model borrowed from effective charter schools like DSST, Yes Prep, and KIPP. Many of their students were dealing with "toxic stress, so we needed to create a place with lots of love and support." Like many charters, they created an advisory system, through which every student had an advisory teacher who was also a counselor, friend, and supporter when they were in need. They also required students and their parents or guardians to sign contracts agreeing to a certain level of commitment and behavior to remain enrolled.

Manual's typical incoming eighth-graders were scoring at fifth-grade levels, so Stein beefed up the core subjects of reading, writing, and math and spent less time on electives. When he tried to get the district to purchase textbooks that met his students where they were, the purchasing office had already pre-purchased textbooks at scale, and they refused to make an exception for Manual. Stein was not satisfied with the part-time school psychologist the district assigned him, so he asked that part of her salary be added to his budget, so he could find someone better. No luck. He felt no need for the instructional leader the district assigned him, so he asked for the money instead. But the instructional superintendent didn't want to lose any of his ten staff members, and he had not been consulted on the school's innovation plan. Another battle lost.

Manual's innovation plan, which had been approved by DPS, said, "Manual will be able to purchase administrative services, such as transportation, food services, facility management, maintenance, student services and substitute teachers from DPS, based on a pricelist that will be provided by DPS to the principal or designee, or from other providers." Yet the district never provided a pricelist and continued to force its services on the school. When the school contracted with Mental Health America of Colorado to provide services, DPS ordered the company to stop.

Being a lawyer, Boasberg had introduced the phrase "unless there's a moral hazard." So over and over, the bureaucrats would tell Stein, "It's a moral hazard." For instance, he wanted the money for security services so he could hire the Denver Police Department, because the district's security guard was eating donuts in the parking lot. But no, that might be a moral hazard.

"Boasberg would say, 'Well, we never said you could control the curriculum,'" Stein remembers. "And I would say, 'Yes, you did, it's here on page two,' and show it to him."

Despite the struggles, Stein turned Manual around. In its first two years, the school rose to third among comprehensive high schools in academic growth. Proficiency scores on state exams doubled in the first three years. Since Stein's goal was to get students ready for college, he is most proud of the fact that the school's average ACT score increased by four points, moving from the lowest to one of the highest in DPS. And in three years, only one student dropped out.

But on March 31, 2010, he turned 50. On his way to dinner with his wife, he was reflecting on his life when he received a call from a security guard, who refused to let a group hold a scheduled student event at the school that evening. The innovation plan gave the school control of such decisions, but the guard refused to let anyone in unless Stein came and personally supervised. "So at dinner my wife and I talked about it, and I thought, what am I doing? I'm playing against my own team. I can't even go out and celebrate my birthday without having the district interfere."

He wrote a letter of resignation. When he left, a dozen of the issues he had been pushing the district to resolve were still stalled.

The district hired an interim principal for the next year, then finally a permanent replacement, who did away with much of what Stein had done. Stein's teaching staff began to depart, and the school floundered. Test scores plummeted.

The Turning Point on Charters

In the spring of 2008, the *Rocky Mountain News* splashed a full-page photo across its front page of the first graduating class from the Denver School of Science and Technology, the charter high school founded by David Greenberg. Every one of its graduates had gained admission to college—the first time that had happened in a school with many low-income students. Bill Kurtz, whom Greenberg hired to run the school, believes that was a turning point. "When I came to Denver," he says, "there was a mindset that not all kids can go to college, that your income and race would determine that." But DSST's accomplishments gave "the leadership of the district an understanding that what was thought impossible was possible."

The charter's success had a big impact on Bennet and the school board. "A lot of people in Denver came to support for charters not because of ideology but because of what they saw," says State Senator Michael Johnston, a former teacher and principal who has been close to Bennet for years. "Michael would talk about visiting schools across the street from each other and seeing a huge difference. The evidence was compelling to people."

Bennet and the board wanted a good way to measure school performance. As early as late 2005 they had developed a draft "balanced scorecard." In 2008, they finally unveiled a School Performance Framework (SPF) that measured test scores, academic growth, student engagement, enrollment rates, and parental satisfaction. Every school wound up with a score that summarized its performance, and charter schools quickly dominated the top ten lists. It has been an important part of district strategy, because it has helped leaders communicate about the quality of schools, make and justify decisions to close, replace, and replicate schools, and demonstrate overall district improvement. (For more on the SPF, see appendix A.)

"As a board member, data allowed me to make bolder decisions," says Bruce Hoyt.

> *To make a tough decision in front of a hostile public crowd is really hard to do unless you are looking at clear data that compels you to move forward. Very importantly, the use of data enabled us to go from forcing decisions on communities to having them come and demand change from us. I will never forget the pain at closing Manual High, with threats of boycotts and boardrooms filled with people protesting us. Fast forward three years to when the West High parents, armed with data showing that West students were underperforming schools with similar demographics, demanded that we take action to change or close West High.*

With the SPF in place, Bruce Randolph and Manual improving, the charter office weeding out low performers, and other charters proving that autonomy worked, the board formally switched its theory of action to "performance empowerment." This meant DPS would move more and more decision-making to the school level, as principals proved their schools could perform. "Eventually the goal was to have the principals control their budget, how they spent their time, and what personnel they had, to the greatest extent possible," says Hoyt.

On top of that, "Bennet in his last year as superintendent moved in the direction of trying to encourage the replication of high-performing charters within his own district," says Greenberg. "He certainly supported West Denver Prep, DSST, and KIPP in their expansion plans."

"We worked really hard to build a very strong coalition of political leaders in the state," adds DSST's CEO, Bill Kurtz.

> *Every single governor has supported us. We have mayoral support, we have city council support. The combination of both rock-solid results with this reality of the political landscape supporting us gave Michael and other leaders cover to say, "Why wouldn't we do more of this?" They had empty buildings and they had political cover. There wasn't a huge political cost. Michael basically said, "How many can you do? If you commit to do this, I'll commit buildings."*

By the time Bennet left, in early 2009, the board had approved eight more DSST schools, on four campuses. But with the union angry about both charters and innovation schools, Bennet did not trumpet his new strategies. His message was simple: DPS would replace failing schools with better schools, regardless of their type.

It was "a conscious decision on his part never to articulate his strategy," says Tony Lewis, executive director of the Donnell-Kay Foundation. "We had this discussion years ago. They feel that setting the vision and goals and strategies out there gives people something to organize against and fight against. So they keep that all internal. You work your strategy, and you never provide enough there there to fight against."

In November 2008, Barack Obama was elected president. In December he picked Colorado Senator Ken Salazar as his secretary of the interior, and on January 3, the governor appointed Michael Bennet to fill Salazar's Senate seat. Bennet urged board members to appoint his deputy and childhood friend, Tom Boasberg, to ensure continuity, and they quickly agreed. Though Boasberg embraced the portfolio strategy, he also eschewed the words, preferring "an intentional strategy to say we are going to focus on great schools as opposed to political arguments about governance structures."

Like Bennet, Boasberg had a background in both business and government, although he was not the politician that Bennet was. After graduating from Stanford Law School, he had taught English at a public junior high school in Hong Kong, then served for three years as chief of staff to Lee Chu-Ming, chairman of Hong Kong's largest political party. He then served as a legal advisor to Reed Hundt, chairman of the Federal Communications Commission, as the Telecommunications Act of 1996 broke up the 100-year-old Bell system's monopoly on land-line telecommunications.

This experience imbued him with a preference for choice and competition. "For me it really comes from a very profound belief that monopoly, whether in the public sector or the private sector, is generally not a good thing," he says.

> *Monopoly stifles innovation, and it generally leads to poor service for customers. It leads to a focus on your own internal stakeholders rather than a focus on whom you're serving, because by definition you're a monopoly; you don't have to serve them well. Maybe there's some areas—I'm not sure I want competing police forces out there, or competing armies—where government being the sole provider does make sense. But in something as decentralized as hospitals or schools or health care, to be able to give choice to the people you're serving, to be able to promote innovation, to recognize there is not just one way of doing things, I think is really important. What we want to do is bring*

*the greatest amount of talent, energy, commitment, and innovation to
education, and to exclude nonprofits like charters makes absolutely no
sense. We've really got to unleash the power and energy of educators.*

In Boasberg's first year as superintendent, the district created an Office of
School Reform and Innovation to oversee its portfolio of charters and innovation schools, recommend which new schools should be approved, and recommend which failing schools should be closed or replaced. That year DPS
opened eight new schools, while planning seven more for 2010.

A Political Donnybrook

As charters proliferated and innovation schools opted out of the union contract, the Denver Classroom Teachers Association (DCTA) mobilized. In the
fall of 2009 it backed a slate of candidates for the school board elections. In a
low-turnout election, three of the union's candidates won, taking a majority
of the open seats. Jeannie Kaplan, an incumbent union ally who held one of
the board's two seats elected citywide, announced in the *Denver Post* that she
would run for board president. Board rules allowed the president to control
the agenda, so it was a powerful position.

But the union had been a bit careless in vetting Nate Easley, an African
American who had grown up in Denver but had recently returned from
Washington, D.C., to help lead the Denver Scholarship Foundation. When
the union president and executive director invited him to breakfast and told
him how to vote on three key issues, Easley didn't appreciate it. Then Kaplan
gave him a list of influential people and suggested he "call each one, and
they'll tell you why I should be board president." When he made the calls,
every person told him to run for board president himself.

Before the new board members were sworn in, both sides jockeyed for
votes. "People were just dealing left and right," says Mary Seawell, who was
also elected that year. Nate Easley is an outgoing man, short and broad like a
sparkplug, with a straightforward approach to people and the kind of smile
that lights up a room. Being the swing vote, he ended up as president, and
suddenly the union's four-to-three majority had reversed, triggering a bitter
divide that lasted for four years. "Jeannie never forgave him," says Seawell. "She was so angry. Arturo Jiminez [another board member] also. You
couldn't even be in a room with him. They felt so betrayed. And the union
was furious."

The next March, Jiminez introduced a resolution to put a moratorium
on the annual "Call for New Quality Schools" for at least a year, "until a

comprehensive analysis of neighborhood school feeder patterns is completed." The reformers took that as an attempt to stop them from approving new charters, and dozens of parents showed up at a board meeting to oppose the resolution. After it failed, the three anti-reform board members tried to delay everything, Easley says, to stall reform until they won the next election. "That's when it really became a four-three board, which the media loved."

Tensions came to a head in the fall of 2010, when the board majority decided to replace a group of struggling schools in the Far Northeast area of the city, including Montbello High School, with ten innovation schools and a handful of charters. Easley had suggested the strategy to Boasberg. "Why don't we start with my neighborhood?" he remembers saying. "And don't just reform the high school. Have a community process, and go all the way down. Just to reform the high school is superficial; it's not their fault that kids come to high school three or four years behind. You need to do surgery, not just put a band-aid on it."

DPS and A+ Denver organized a group of community members, teachers, and principals, who drew up the actual plan. "That was when the controversy really got enormous," says Seawell. "The scale and scope was like nothing the district had ever done before, and there were so many schools impacted. It was a highly charged, emotional political process," with people shouting and chanting at community and board meetings. "That's when it got front-page attention. We had marathon board sessions until one or two in the morning, for months and months."

The anti-reform leaders invited Easley to lunch and warned him that if he voted for the replacement strategy, they would recall him. But he had strong feelings on the subject. He had been a straight-A student at Montbello High, then tested into remedial math at Colorado State College. "What that did to my ego was so insidious that I almost didn't make it," he says. "Because I thought I was good, and here I am, the only black history major on campus, and I find out I'm remedial." He almost dropped out—"came very close, as a teen parent."

Easley thinks the teachers union was behind the recall. "I wasn't the person they thought they were supporting, and it was the best time to get to Tom and kill school reform in Denver. It was miserable: I ran for the same elected seat, that was not a paid position, twice in the first year and a half." His opponents put together a fake website, that was supposed to be his, lampooning him.

I got attacked for being a bad father; the Denver Scholarship Foundation was attacked. They just came one hundred percent after me. It was nasty. The thing that was heartbreaking: There aren't many

African Americans in Colorado; there's a higher percentage in Denver, but there aren't many. And the two people who were the face of my recall were both African American. The media loved that, putting their pictures up there: these black people want to get rid of this black man. That was just ugly.

He unleashes that smile: "But if it doesn't kill you, it makes you stronger."

After all that, his opponents failed to collect the required number of signatures to get a recall on the ballot.

The State Legislature Weighs In

The next year brought two important steps. The first was led by Denver State Senator Michael Johnston, who succeeded Peter Groff in 2009. In 2010 he wrote and convinced the state legislature to pass a reform bill as part of Colorado's effort to compete for federal Race to the Top money. Called Senate Bill 191, it required that districts dismiss teachers rated "ineffective" for two years in a row, even if they had tenure, and quit forcing principals to take on teachers laid off from other district schools. There would be no more layoffs by seniority, and if teachers were laid off because of school closings or reconstitutions and they could not find new jobs within 12 months or two hiring cycles, they would be put on unpaid leave. Districts would be required to conduct teacher evaluations beginning in 2015–16, with half the weight given to measures of student growth. Finally, the state would boost funding for professional development for teachers.

DPS eagerly supported the bill. "They were an example of some of the practices that people really worried about, like forced placement, the dance of the lemons," says Johnston. At one point 80 percent of the staff in Denver's low-income schools had been forced on principals, he says. They were in the poorest schools, the schools full of minority kids, many of them in his Senate district.

Johnston consulted extensively with the teachers unions: "I probably spent more time with the union lobbyists than with any others." The Colorado Education Association opposed the bill, but the much smaller American Federation of Teachers in Colorado, which includes nonteaching school staff in Denver, supported it. "It was from a belief that there were some things that just made sense, to change outdated rules and practices."

About 18 months after Denver implemented the bill, teachers who could not find another principal willing to hire them after their schools were replaced began losing their paychecks. In 2014, a handful of teachers and the Denver Classroom Teachers Association sued, charging that DPS "improperly applied the law to unfairly and systematically remove veteran teachers and hire less-experienced, less-expensive teachers to replace them." They wanted to go back to the old system, under which principals would be forced to take on those teachers. Boasberg and the board opposed the suit, arguing that "forced placements" usually ended up in schools full of low-income students. Boasberg called that "a civil rights travesty." As this goes to press, each side has won once and an appeal is before the Colorado Supreme Court.

Cooperation Between DPS and Charter Schools

In December 2010, DPS and charter leaders signed a District-Charter Collaboration Compact, which brought a $4 million grant from the Bill and Melinda Gates Foundation. The compact committed DPS to develop a citywide enrollment system that included all schools, to share buildings equitably, to provide equitable funding for charters and DPS schools, and to grow successful schools and close or restructure failing schools of both types. Charters committed to share the responsibility for special education, including severely disabled students, and to admit students who arrived in the middle of school years.

Boasberg stresses that the collaboration with charters is built around a commitment to equity for all students: "From the very beginning we worked very closely with our charter sector and said equity is going to be the stake in the ground around which everything else orbits. So all of our decisions are going to be designed to promote greater equity and greater opportunity, particularly for our kids that need it the most."

This includes equity of opportunity, responsibility, and accountability, he explains.

> All our public schools, whether district-run or charters, should have the same access to public resources, be that public funding, levies, federal funds, or other grants. Secondly, all of our schools need to serve all of our kids. That's why the overwhelming majority of our new charters the last four or five years now have boundary responsibilities—they need to serve all the kids in their boundaries. And equity of accountability: that the standards we use for opening and closing schools are exactly the same whether you're district-run or charter schools.
>
> I recognize the very valid concerns that the left of this country has had around charters and around allowing for choice and moving away from monopoly. Their main concern has been that if you move away

from monopoly to greater flexibility and choice, that our highest-need kids will not be served well enough by schools. Because schools might have an incentive to say, "I'm not concerned about these highest-need kids." I think it's a very valid and genuine concern. Our position is not just to say, "We're going to have completely free market competition."

I think we worked very hard, with equity as a cornerstone, to say how do we come up with a set of approaches where greater choice and greater flexibility leads to more equity rather than less.

The compact led DPS to give most charters space in its school buildings. By 2013, 78 percent of them were in DPS facilities. Many buildings are shared between a charter and a district-run school, which has been controversial at times. The compact also led charters to create more centers for students with severe disabilities, and to follow districtwide practices on student transfers and expulsions. Finally, it led to creation of a Collaborative Council, with five charter leaders, four members of the superintendent's cabinet, and one board member, to hash out issues—such as how DPS buildings are awarded—and propose policy changes. It created *one system* out of the two sectors.

Meanwhile Boasberg and the school board continued to approve replications of successful charter schools, while closing low performers. In 2010–11 they closed 25 percent of charters up for renewal; over the next three years, they closed almost 10 percent. And since 2010 they have opened five to six new charters per year.

In 2011 DPS rolled out the new enrollment system, called SchoolChoice, which includes both charter and DPS-operated schools (except for alternative schools). Before then, parents who wanted their children to attend a public school other than their neighborhood school had to research and apply to multiple schools. With a plethora of magnet schools, DPS had more than 60 enrollment systems for its own schools, not to mention the charters. Parents who knew how to navigate the system, or who knew the right people, fared better than those who didn't.

Community organizations such as Metro Organizations for People pushed for a common enrollment system, framing it as an equity issue. They argued that low-income parents found the process confusing and intimidating, and therefore were less likely to apply for charter or magnet schools. In contrast, more educated and connected parents were often able to game the system. Anti-charter forces argued that charters "creamed" the best students, but in reality charters had to use lotteries if they were oversubscribed, and a 2010 study revealed that DPS schools were doing the creaming. The research showed that many parents got their children into their preferred DPS-operated schools by going directly to the principal, circumventing the formal choice process. Middle-class parents used such methods more frequently than poor parents. Worse, principals could handpick early childhood education students, who were then guaranteed a spot in their elementary schools. Some 60 percent of students accepted into elementary schools from outside their neighborhood boundaries were handpicked in one of these two ways. They were far more likely to be white and less likely to be poor than a random selection would suggest.

The new computerized system makes such favoritism far more difficult, leveling the playing field and simplifying the process. Parents only fill out one form, ranking their top five choices. Parents whose children are transitioning to elementary school, middle school, or high school are encouraged to fill out the form. They receive a booklet from DPS reviewing the performance of each school, to help them choose.

A computer algorithm then ranks applications according to seven factors: those in the neighborhood zone and those with siblings in the school get priority, for instance. Some schools (including all DSST charters) also reserve at least 40 percent of their seats for low-income students.

Surveys conducted by the Center on Reinventing Public Education show that DPS parents find the SchoolChoice system easier to use and less confusing than the old one. It has clearly increased equity, leading to a jump in the percentage of low-income students and English-language learners attending charter schools. And it has minimized parents' ability to game the system. As one local parent wrote on a blog after it went into effect, "This is the dumbest system ever! I used to be able to bake brownies for the principal and get into the school, and now I can't do that!"

During the system's first three years, 95 percent of those participating were placed at one of their five preferred schools, and roughly three quarters received their top choice. Generally, higher-quality schools were in greater demand.

To their credit, Boasberg and his staff have also hired dozens of people from charters, while working hard to spread successful charter practices to schools they operate. They have brought in charter leaders from successful networks such as Uncommon Schools and KIPP to lead professional development for DPS principals and teachers. Through something called Compact Blue, they have created a small, professional learning community that includes teachers and principals from 11 charter and 11 DPS-operated schools. Their Residency for the Educational Development of DPS Intrapreneurs (REDDI) has embedded about a dozen aspiring DPS principals in high-performing charter schools for a year—while providing leadership training and encouraging them to visit other high-performing schools around the country—to learn how it's done.

DPS has pursued multiple strategies to develop strong school leaders and have them share responsibilities with co-leaders, as charters often do. By 2015, 84 percent of teachers rated their principals "effective" or "very effective." Though turnover of principals in low-income schools was a big problem for years, by 2016–17 it had slowed dramatically. According to board member Barbara O'Brien, the district has finally succeeded in creating an adequate supply of effective school leaders.

Other practices DPS has adopted from some of Denver's charters include:

- Home visits by teachers
- "Advisories," in which one teacher stays with 10–15 students for a few years and is expected to get to know them well
- Systematic use of math tutors at many schools
- Ninth-grade "academies," in which students begin high school with a week devoted to shaping their expectations and culture
- School uniforms
- Character education, in which schools seek to instill not only knowledge and skill but "personal success factors" such as self-control and perseverance
- Teacher leaders, who spend half their time teaching and half their time leading and coaching other teachers in their subject area
- A planning year for principals who start new schools

Political Victory

The anti-reform block in Denver opposed most of what Boasberg and the board were doing. But with test scores and graduation rates improving, reformers went on a winning streak, beginning with the mayoral election in the spring of 2011. City Councilman Michael Hancock campaigned in support of education reform, as did the other candidate who made the runoff, Chris Romer, whose father had been governor in the 1990s. But when Romer tacked against reform to pick up teachers' votes during the runoff, the move backfired, and Hancock won going away.

Turnout surged in three board of education races that fall, indicating that voters understood something important was at stake. Reformers mobilized, raised money to support their candidates, and recruited a former city council president to run. They won two races and fell 142 votes short in the third, preserving their four-three majority. But the acrimony on the board continued.

Two years later, Democrats for Education Reform and its allies raised significant money and recruited as candidates a former lieutenant governor, another former city council president, and a former chairman of Denver's Democratic Party. All three won, and the logjam was finally broken. With six reformers, the new board initiated a turnaround strategy involving replacement of multiple schools in Southwest Denver and approved another major expansion of DSST schools.

When the board was considering the turnaround strategy for heavily Latino Southwest Denver, board member Rosemary Rodriguez says, the community "was starting to say, should we replace all our problem schools with charters? Can we charter ourselves out of trouble?" They encountered resistance from the teachers union and some political leaders, but "not from mothers and fathers."

In 2015, when an astounding 44 percent turned out for the school board election, a reformer won the final seat. The teachers union, which has lost many members as charters and innovation schools have spread, was hardly a factor. Two of the opponents of reform campaigned to preserve student assignment to neighborhood schools against the encroachments of choice. But it turned out that for their own children, both had chosen options other than their assigned neighborhood schools. "There is philosophy," one admitted, "and then there is your kid." Not surprisingly, both lost.

CHAPTER 9

DELIVERING RESULTS

DENVER'S REFORMERS WON IN part because they had more money and in part because their approach yielded results. With a combination of charter schools, innovation schools, alternative schools, and traditional schools, the district produced dramatic improvement. In 2005–6, 11.1 percent of DPS students dropped out each year, and in 2006–7 less than 39 percent graduated in four years. By 2015–16, only 4 percent dropped out each year, 67 percent graduated on time, and 74 percent of those who entered DPS high schools and stayed for four years graduated on time. The four-year graduation rate for Latinos, the district's largest group, has more than doubled since 2007. In addition:

- Through 2014, the percentage of students scoring at or above grade level in reading, writing, and math increased 15 percentage points (from 33 to 48 percent) over ten years, far faster than the state average (see figure 9-1). In 2015 Colorado switched to the PARCC tests, so comparisons to previous years are no longer possible.
- Since 2014, Denver schools have adjusted far better to the more demanding, Common Core–aligned PARCC tests than schools in the rest of the state, as figure 9-2 shows. Ranked by the percentage of students at proficiency or above, Denver schools in 2014 outperformed only 16.7 percent of Colorado schools on the elementary English language arts test, but in 2015 they outperformed 42.4 percent and in 2016, 43 percent. In elementary math, Denver jumped from the 19th percentile to the 49th in 2015 and 41st in 2016. Middle schools, where a higher percentage of students are in charters, were even stronger: In English they jumped from outperforming 17.5 percent to 51.4 and 56 percent, above the state median. (Middle-school math comparisons are not reliable, because students can take so many different versions of math, including Math 7 and 8, geometry, algebra, and integrated math. But Denver appears to have risen to well above the 50th percentile.)

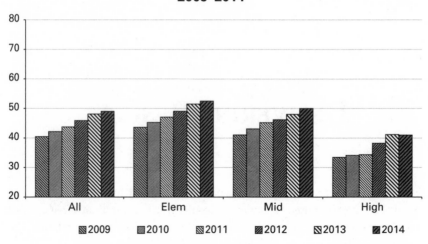

Percentage of DPS Students Scoring Proficient or Advanced, 2009–2014

Figure 9-1 Source: Colorado Department of Education. Does not include alternative schools.

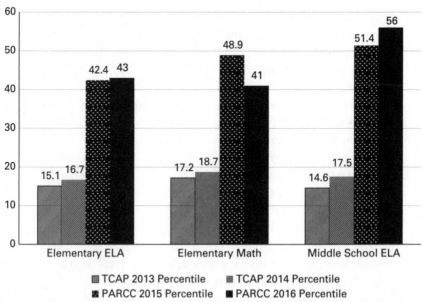

Percentile Ranking of Denver Schools Performance on Standardized Tests Compared to Colorado Schools, 2013–2016

Figure 9-2 Source: A+ Denver, using Colorado Department of Education data. 2014 TCAP tests separated reading and writing; scores on those tests have been combined here.

- In 2005, DPS trailed statewide averages by about 25 percentage points in both English and math. By 2016, that gap was only four percentage points in both areas.
- DPS has tripled the number of students passing Advanced Placement courses, and the passage rate is up to 45 percent. Among low-income students, the passage rate jumped from 21 to 31 percent between 2014 and 2015. DPS was named by the College Board the national leader among districts with 50,000 or more students in expanding access to AP courses while also improving exam performance.
- Average ACT scores have risen from 16 to 18.6, as figure 9-3 shows: twice as fast as statewide scores. (In Colorado, unlike many states, all high school juniors take the ACT. In 2016 the state average on those tests was 20.4.)

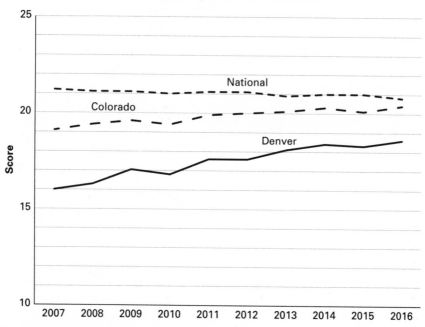

Average Composite ACT Score

Figure 9-3 Source: Denver and Colorado: Colorado Department of Education. National data: ACT.org. Note: the ACT is not mandatory in most states, so non-college-bound students don't usually take it. National data also includes all ACT scores, including senior year; Denver and Colorado data includes only the mandatory ACT exam taken by all students in the spring of 11th grade. Hence Colorado's scores would be expected to fall well below the national average.

- Although only about 48 percent of DPS graduates have enrolled in college in recent years, one in seven low-income students in Denver did so, compared to one in 20 in the rest of the state. And the percentage of enrollees from DPS who are required to take remedial classes in college is dropping, from 64 percent in 2010 to 53 percent in 2014.

Low-income students have shared in this growth. An analysis done by the Donnell-Kay Foundation used data from 2009 through 2013 to show that low-income enrollment in "quality schools" (those scoring 70 or higher on DPS's School Performance Framework) increased from 34 to 49 percent. "For every three students who were newly enrolled at a quality school in the past five years," the study found, "two were low-income."

Despite this progress, however, Denver has not been able to narrow the achievement gap between races and income groups. The gaps have actually widened, because white and middle-class students have raised their scores faster than minority and low-income students, as shown in figure 9-4. In 2014, the gap between the percentage of low-income and non-low-income students who tested at grade level was almost 40 points across all subjects, and the gap between African Americans and Latinos, on the one hand, and whites, on the

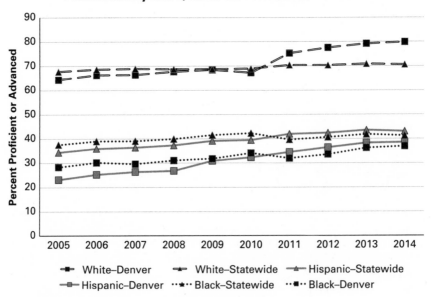

Average Percent of Test-Takers Scoring Proficient or Advanced by Race, 2005–2014: Denver vs. Colorado

Figure 9-4 Source: Colorado Department of Education

other, was 42 points. Even growth scores have increased faster for middle-class than for low-income students. This is similar to the trend in Washington, D.C., suggesting that as reforms spur schools to improve, white, middle-class students are better prepared to take advantage of the opportunity.

Charter Schools Lead the Way

Denver's two largest charter networks are Denver School of Science and Technology (DSST) and Strive Prep. Because these networks started with high schools and middle schools, respectively, the city's charters are unusually concentrated at the secondary level. Though DPS has clearly improved its elementary schools, at the secondary level charters account for most of the academic growth. They also accounted for three quarters of DPS enrollment growth between 2010 and 2016.

In a 2014 study published by the Donnell-Kay Foundation, which used School Performance Framework (SPF) data through 2013, author Alexander Ooms concluded:

> *The decision to close poorly-performing schools of all types appears to be paying dividends and is especially encouraging for low-income students. Likewise the decision to encourage replication of the best charter schools has clearly led to positive results. But the district's attempts to open its own new schools, and particularly to improve its continuing schools serving secondary grades, have yielded remarkably little.*

A year later, my analysis of 2014 SPF scores revealed little change. Six of the top eight schools were charters, and in academic growth all of the top 12 secondary schools were charters. Charters had 13 percent more African American students at grade level than district-run schools, 9 percent more Latinos, and almost 10 percent more low-income students. And though charters made up only 37 percent of Denver's public secondary schools (excluding alternative schools), they accounted for 60 percent of the 20 most sought-after secondary schools.

There were no SPF or growth scores for 2015, because of the switch to PARCC exams, and DPS changed the SPF significantly before releasing 2016 scores, so scores are no longer comparable. But in 2016, five of the six top-scoring high schools were DSST charters. And 15 of the 19 secondary schools with above-average percentages of low-income students and SPF scores at the two highest levels were charters.

A study of test scores from 2010 through 2014, by economists at the

Massachusetts Institute of Technology and Duke University, found that Denver's charters produced "remarkably large gains in math," large gains in writing, and smaller but statistically significant gains in reading, compared to DPS-operated schools. The gains in math were the equivalent of closing almost half the large gap between white and black students in the United States.

DO CHARTERS PERFORM better because they attract better students? They do have advantages over other district schools: More of their families make an active choice to enroll, and they backfill empty seats at a slightly lower rate (80 percent compared to 93 percent).

On the other hand, charters get 19 percent less money per student than district-operated schools, according to one analysis. Although the district strives for equity, charter teachers are not eligible for ProComp bonuses, which average $7,396 for a second-year teacher. Charters also get less district-funded transportation for students.

And by 2014–15, charters served three percentage points more low-income students (those who qualified for subsidized meals) and ten percentage points more English-language learners than district-run schools. A Center on Reinventing Public Education study found that "charter schools are less likely to classify students as in need of special education services, and more likely to declassify them, than are traditional public schools." Yet by 2014–15, charters had almost as high a percentage of special education students as DPS-operated schools did—10 versus 11 percent. Both sectors used the same expulsion guidelines, yet charters expelled students at a lower rate and retained students at twice the rate of district-run schools.

The 2015 CREDO study of urban areas compared charter students to demographically similar students with the same past test scores in traditional public schools. It found that Denver's charter students had gained almost three months more learning in math and 22 days more in reading, each year. The impact was particularly large in middle schools, roughly triple this amount. By a student's fourth year, charter gains across all school levels were huge: five times as great in reading and more than three times as great in math.

Another fair way to compare charters and DPS-operated schools is to analyze school test scores and percentages of low-income students together, on the same scatter plot. This produces the same results we have seen in other studies. There are only 16 elementary charters, and their performance is widely scattered. As a group they perform about the same as district-run schools. But at the middle and high school levels, charters perform much better than either traditional or innovation schools.

Learning from Charters' Success

Charters are successful in Denver for the same reasons they are successful in New Orleans and Washington, D.C.:

- They have true autonomy to design their schools to meet the needs of their students, hire the best and fire the worst, design their own pay and reward systems, and craft their own cultures.
- They experience consequences for their performance. Their funding depends on how many families choose to enroll, and if their students excel they are encouraged to grow and replicate, but if their students lag they are closed.
- Many are schools of choice, encouraged to handcraft their services for particular types of students rather than required to meet the needs of all comers.
- The charter sector puts responsibilities for steering (setting direction and policy) and rowing (operating schools) in separate organizations. DPS does the steering; charter management organizations and schools do the rowing. Unfortunately, DPS also has many rowing responsibilities, which makes it harder to steer well. Jen Walmer was chief of staff to Tom Boasberg for three years, before leaving to run Democrats for Education Reform in Denver. She said she left DPS because it was so "hard to steer when you're managing." In addition to all the political maneuvering with the board and external stakeholders, "what was overwhelming to me was the one A.M. phone call about a threat assessment at a high school, the four A.M. decision to close a school because of snow. That kind of stuff just became overwhelming."
- Separation between steering and rowing gives the DPS board more political freedom to replace failing charter schools, because they are not putting employees out of jobs or closing "their own schools." Although they also replace traditional schools, they have been more aggressive in closing charters. Hence the right to operate a charter school has been more *contestable,* based on performance.

The Story of One Charter Network

To gain more fine-grained insight into why charters perform so well, let's take a closer look. Denver has three strong charter networks: KIPP, Strive Prep, and DSST. The first two are fairly typical no-excuses schools, full of low-income kids, that use no-nonsense academics and behavioral incentives to push students toward college. DSST is less typical: Although more than two thirds of its students are low income, its schools are intentionally integrated by income. Its flagship high school feels more like a private prep school than a no-excuses school.

For the near-decade that DSST has had high school graduates, 100 percent have been accepted to a four-year college or university. At least 85 percent have enrolled in college, the highest percentage of any public school in the city. Although its schools are not selective—unlike many district magnet schools—DSST has the 11th lowest rate of students forced to take remedial classes in college among all public and private high schools in Colorado. As of this writing, 61 and 53 percent of the first two classes had graduated from college within six years, and another 13 and 14 percent were still enrolled. By comparison, 42 percent of all students and only 9 percent of low-income students in the United States finish college within six years.

How does DSST do it? By setting high expectations, finding and developing extraordinary teachers, creating close relationships between those teachers and their students, and molding school cultures around six values: responsibility, respect, doing your best, courage, curiosity, and integrity.

Originally, DSST was not intended to be a charter school. Its founder, David Greenberg, is a Harvard Law School graduate who had served as legal advisor and speechwriter for Governor Richard Lamm, a Democrat, then founded a public policy consulting firm. Two successive governors appointed him to the Colorado Commission on Higher Education, which oversaw the state's colleges and universities. There he was appalled at how few low-income minority students were in the state's public universities. The University of Colorado at Boulder had fewer than 500 African American students out of 25,000 undergraduates. When he asked why the number was so small, a university administrator explained that there was simply no pipeline: Urban districts were graduating very few low-income minorities who could qualify for the university.

That got Greenberg thinking about creating a high school. He went to see Republican Governor Bill Owens, who had reappointed him to the commission, and Owens told him Bill Gates wanted to provide start-up money for a small schools initiative. So Greenberg, the governor's secretary of technology, and several business leaders visited High Tech High, an innovative charter network in San Diego that used project-based learning as its core. "I was totally blown away by High Tech High," Greenberg says. "I came back and said, 'We should do this.'"

The year before, Denver had been among three finalists for Boeing's headquarters, after the company decided to leave Seattle. "We lost in part because we didn't have enough schools they thought they could send their employees' kids to," Greenberg says. "So to me it was both a justice issue and a great economic development engine. The only reasonable place where people were really comfortable making investments to create a more equitable society was public education. I was looking for the next step in my life, and it seemed to be the right thing to do."

DPS had a School for the Arts, and people had long talked about creating a STEM high school. But it had never happened, largely because all five school board members elected from districts wanted it in their district, so they could never agree on a site. Greenberg decided to try. He was close to board President Elaine Berman, so he proposed a "pilot school," on the Boston model—a district school with waivers so it could hire and fire its own faculty and run its own show. (See appendix C.) But DPS would not give him a building.

Undaunted, he decided to create a charter school. He recruited a board and set out to raise $12 million dollars to construct the school. For the first two years, almost everything that could go wrong did. The dot-com bust eliminated an entire category of potential donors he had counted on. The fundraising kickoff, at the governor's mansion, was scheduled for September 14, 2001. "It was like walking into a funeral service; everybody was wondering if the world was going to end," he remembers. "The last thing anyone wanted to focus on was a new school."

The money came in slowly. Compaq donated a $1 million line of credit for computers, so he could have a laptop for every student. A real estate development company called Forest City, which was redeveloping Denver's old Stapleton Airport as a residential neighborhood, offered to donate land and $1 million. "They wanted to have a fantastic lab school," Greenberg explains. "Part of their marketing strategy was to have higher-quality public schools than their competitors." But the area would be 95 percent white and middle class, and Greenberg wanted an integrated school, so he insisted on a floor of 40 percent low-income students. Both DPS and Forest City agreed.

By April of 2003, they were still $5 million short. Greenberg told his board that if they couldn't raise it in the next few months, they would have to fold up shop. They had one "Hail Mary" option left: to convince DPS to include the school as part of its upcoming bond package.

DPS had identified $1.3 billion in capital needs, but it could borrow only $310 million without a tax increase. So it had formed a citizens committee to whittle the needs list down to $310 million. "I spent every waking hour asking the committee to give us $5 million," Greenberg says. To his surprise, they agreed, and the bond measure passed.

To start the school design process, his team did focus groups of potential students—one of boys, one of girls, one mixed—to see what they wanted in a building. "They basically said, we want it to look like a mall, and we want it to have a color scheme like Abercrombie," Greenberg says. "If you look at

Stapleton High School, it *is* designed as a mall. We have a long galleria, and the classrooms are sort of hidden away." The mall is carpeted, with the utilities exposed far overhead, and it has an irregular shape, bulging here to create a wide space for morning meetings of every student, narrowing there to make room for offices and classrooms.

It was probably the nation's first public school specifically designed for a wireless environment in which every student had a laptop. Every part of the building, including the carpeted hallway floors, could be used by kids working on projects or doing homework. Three foundations produced a documentary on it called *Schools Designed for Learning.*

Greenberg had the architects present the plan at neighborhood meetings, where they asked people to vote on designs and layouts. "We broke all the district rules regarding building design," he says. But the district absorbed the lesson: A few years later, it began convening citizen juries when it designed schools.

When it came time to hire a director, Greenberg got a $50,000 grant to do a national search. They received 120 applications, from three continents. "Two days before we closed the search Bill Kurtz applied," Greenberg remembers. "The search guy said, 'Drop everything you're doing, you need to fly to Newark and see this guy's school.'"

Kurtz was a 35-year-old Princeton graduate who ran the Link Community School, a private Catholic middle school in Newark, New Jersey, that took mostly poor, black kids, educated them for two years, then sent them off to elite high schools, most of them private, on scholarships. Link was the model for North Star Academy in Newark, the first school opened by Uncommon Schools, now one of the nation's most successful charter networks. (Later, in 2014, Link itself became a charter school and expanded to cover grades five through eight.) Greenberg was impressed, and Kurtz agreed to come to Denver.

The entire ordeal ended well, but Greenberg paid a high price. "Every single thing was difficult," he says. "For two years we operated out of a double-wide with no running water and His and Hers outhouses. Two years after we opened the school I had a 99 percent blockage of my lower descending artery, the widow maker, and the doctor absolutely said it was stress. It was not cholesterol, it was not genetic. 'Congratulations,' he told me, 'you almost killed yourself.'"

DSST SCHOOLS ARE small, with 450 to 500 students in each one, although each campus has two schools, a middle and a high school. Like most private prep schools, they focus on core academics—reading, writing, math, science, social science, and foreign language—allowing students only one elective per term. They use a lot of the techniques one finds at a no-excuses school, like frequent assessments, constant analysis of data, student dress codes (except for dress-down Fridays), a system of rewards and penalties for behavior, and teaching methods from *Teach Like a Champion,* by Doug Lemov of Uncommon Schools. But they also have competitive sports, a robotics team, a mandatory internship for juniors, and a required final project for seniors.

Every student is expected to meet the school's demanding standards. Students who struggle receive intensive help, and every year a handful are held back. Mark Heffron, who was school director at DSST's Stapleton High for four years before returning to the math department, describes a typical conversation with a struggling student:

> "We're going to be here on Saturday, and we're bringing in an outside tutor to work with you, and in addition to that we've lined up a peer tutor for you, and instead of doing the music elective, you're going to be in a math or an English support class. You need to ultimately hit the high bar, which is seventy percent to pass all your classes. We do summer school, but if you don't meet those things, you will be retained. There is no social promotion."
>
> Those are new conversations for lots of kids, because they've come through systems where every year they may be getting a half year behind. They show up in high school and they're three or four years behind. But we're pretty upfront with kids and parents: Halfway through the year, we'll tell them, "It's not looking great for next year, but we've had kids in your shoes who have made it through the years." And there's lots of kids who spent two years in ninth grade, graduated in five years, or six, and they come back to us and say, "That was the best thing you could have done for me, because I walked into college, and I was the kid that was passing, and I wasn't in remedial classes, and the kids came to me for help. If I wasn't in your program, I would have been one of those kids in remedial classes, and paying for it."

Roughly 40 percent of students who start high school leave DSST for other schools before graduating—a high rate but lower than DPS-operated high schools. Rents have been rising rapidly in Denver, and poor families move a lot. But at DSST, some students also leave because they don't want to work so hard; they know they can get better grades with less effort elsewhere.

Students I interviewed at DSST Stapleton talked about the strong community, their bonds with teachers, how well prepared they were for college, and the values DSST inculcated in them. Zenetta Zepeda is Native American, half Lakota and half Navajo. A thoughtful, attractive 17-year-old when I spoke with her in December 2015, she had a wide face, big, dark glasses, and dark hair she colored partially blond. She had been at DSST since sixth grade. She was taking three science classes—she loved chemistry—and she hoped to go into biochemical engineering or marine biology. When I asked her what she liked best about the school, she talked about the community: "I think it's the richest aspect of our school. DSST is almost like a family. If you're having a bad day, not only your close friends will ask you what is wrong, your teachers will ask you what is wrong, the deans will ask you what's wrong: 'What can I do for you?'"

There is no bullying at the school, she said, and gay and bisexual students are fully accepted. The entire school gathers for a morning meeting on Mondays and Fridays, and juniors and seniors gather separately on Tuesdays and Thursdays. They talk about problems that have occurred at school, or societal issues like race. "Morning meetings are important," she said. "They're something special."

They started discussing the core values in sixth grade, receiving constant encouragement for following them. Their report cards had grades on each value, and awards were given to students who exemplified the values. Gradually it became second nature. "Integrity, doing your best, responsibility, and respect—those words are so haunting," she said. She worked at a fast-food restaurant, and when she saw fellow workers violating the values, she was perplexed: "Why would you do that? DSST has instilled the values inside of us—I don't know how they do it."

In elementary school, Zenetta said, she didn't care much about school. "I had a lot of free time to get in trouble. Without DSST, I don't think I'd be in the position I am today, going to college, being a pretty decent student, being in the position socially I am now, and being a big okay in life. If I didn't go to DSST, I probably wouldn't be college bound."

Other students had similar things to say. Giovanni Venzor Melendez was headed for the University of Colorado at Boulder, where he wanted to major in biochemistry and molecular biology. When he began kindergarten, he spoke no English, and when I met him his family still spoke Spanish at home. DSST is a "very diverse school, where you know the people in your class," he told me. "You just form these amazing bonds with people, and you start to love them." The only segregation at the school, he said, was between grade levels.

When I asked Giovanni what he liked most about the school, he said, "The teachers are not just teachers, they're like friends. They are there for you even in hard times. They will listen to you, to problems at home, to everything you tell them." The others I talked with agreed.

Bill Kurtz says it all begins with the core values. DSST builds them into everything it does. Staff evaluations focus on how people are living the values. Student report cards give grades on values, triggering conversations with students and parents. Jeff Desserich, then director of Stapleton High School, told me, "I had a kid who had all A's and B's, and I'm having a conference with his dad, and the all A's and B's is good, but we can see that courage is pretty low, like two out of five. So that can really frame our conversation around what should the student's development plan be—to speak up in class more, or take on a leadership role or something."

New students get a home visit, where deans and teachers talk about the values, and attend summer school, which is part culture and part academics. Every year all students go through a ceremony at which they sign their allegiance to the core values. Every month each school focuses on two core values, building them into morning meetings, advisory sessions, and other conversations. When there are behavior problems, kids attend "Refocus"— a two-hour session on Saturday, where they write a reflective essay on their behavior, how it affected their classmates and teachers, and what they can do differently next time. "If a kid is suspended for something," Desserich said, "they do a reflection on what core values they violated and how they can do a better job of living those core values, and who could support them in that."

"This is a different approach from the no-excuses, high-accountability model," Kurtz told me.

> We're not just about compliance. We're actually about building a values-driven culture with all of our students, so that they all understand what it means to live a set of values. They may not choose our values over time, but hopefully they will learn to choose a set of values that will guide them in the way that David Brooks would say are the eulogy values, the values that really matter in how you live your life—what you care about when you look back on your life.

DSST is trying to do three things, says Kurtz: give young people a world-class education, help them become the best versions of themselves, and help them become contributors to society. He calls the school "a high-care, high-accountability community."

> It's about understanding and knowing and affirming each individual that comes into our community. Challenging them to be their best, to grow, to develop so that they can choose that significant contribution they want to make to their human stories. Most kids in this country, particularly from low-income communities, never had that choice.
>
> But there is a deeper part that is helping young people discover what it means to live in a community. Our communities in this country desperately need a civic responsibility that says no, your individual

*interest sometimes gets trumped by the collective needs of the commu-
nity in which you live. [You] have obligations to that community. And
certainly we want each kid to discover their own gifts and talents, and
become the best version of themselves, but that is not in absence of all
other expectations.*

World-class teachers are another linchpin. Enormous effort goes into finding the right teachers and developing their talents. "And because of that the
camaraderie between the teachers in the school has been outstanding," says
Jeff Hollenbach, who has taught physics and music for a decade.

In recent years DSST has developed a new career ladder teachers can move
through, based on their evaluations and their students' performance. They
start as "novices," move on to "developing" teachers, then "accomplished,"
then "lead" teachers, and finally "master teachers." Each level comes with a
pay increase, until master teachers are paid on a par with school directors—
$60,000 a year or more. (Teacher salaries are surprisingly low in Denver, no
doubt because school funding levels are so low.)

Low pay and work-life balance for teachers are the biggest challenges the
organization faces. Attracting and retaining great teachers is difficult, when
the district gives DSST only about $8,000 per student per year (or $6,500 if
they lease a DPS building). DSST reports that it usually retains 85 percent of
its teachers from one year to the next, but in 2014 that dipped to about 70,
then rose to 78 in 2015. Exit interviews showed the big reason was people feeling their jobs were not sustainable. While they demonstrated a very high
commitment to the schools' mission, and 93 percent agreed that "someone at
work cares about me as a person," they didn't feel like they had time for other
things, such as fitness, engagement with family, or engagement with community outside of work. The lowest agreement was with the statement, "Last
year, my manager modeled a sustainable way of working."

Still, DSST produces astonishing academic growth, year after year. The
way DPS measures growth has a built-in tendency to revert toward the mean,
as appendix A explains. The higher a student or school scores, the tougher the
competition next year, because students are only compared to those who had
similar scores in past years. But on 2016 growth scores, DSST had three of the
top six Denver public secondary schools. Two DSST high schools were in the
top five in the state on combined math and English growth.

On DPS's School Performance Framework, DSST had six of the top seven
secondary schools in 2016, including the top two middle schools and the top
high school. Four out of the city's five high schools that were rated "distinguished," the highest category, were DSST schools. (The fifth was a KIPP school.)

DSST excels even when one only measures proficiency, despite the fact that 69 percent of its students come from poor families. Among students eligible for subsidized meals, DSST had two of the three highest-scoring schools in the state on the ACT test in 2016. In 2014 its low-income tenth-graders had higher proficiency rates in math, reading, and writing than *middle-income* students in DPS-operated schools. In 2015, with a third high school open, DSST schools outperformed 87, 90, and 96 percent of Colorado's public high schools, measured by the percentage of students at or above proficiency on the new PARCC tests. These are numbers an expensive private school would be proud to have, yet in the three DSST schools, respectively, 72, 69, and 53 percent of the students were low income.

It's no wonder that with 14 DSST schools open or approved by 2015, the school board approved eight more—half of which will focus not on STEM but on the humanities. And it's no wonder that in reporting that decision, *Chalkbeat* referred to DSST as Denver's "homegrown charter school juggernaut."

Can "Charter-Lite" Schools Compete?

Despite the success of individual innovation schools, as a group they have not performed nearly as well as charter schools on standardized tests, according to three separate studies. Scatterplots that compare test scores at schools with similar demographics reveal very little difference between the performance of innovation and traditional schools.

The bad start appears to explain part of the failure, though there is not enough data to prove that. But in 2011 Boasberg hired Alyssa Whitehead-Bust, the founding principal of Denver's Highline Academy Charter School, to run his Office of School Reform and Innovation. She and her staff began to treat the approval of innovation schools much like the approval of new charter schools, though the bar was a bit lower for innovation schools and the acceptance rate a bit higher. Since then new innovation schools have looked more like charters—with a year to plan, clear visions and strategies, and careful hiring of teachers. And DPS actually replicated two innovation schools in 2016.

Some innovation schools have made remarkable progress. One of the more interesting is Denver Green School (DGS), a pre-K–8 school that is organized as a teacher partnership. Three "lead partners" share most of the administrative duties, while still teaching one class a day. But decisions are made by ten partners, as in a law or consulting firm. Each partner is in charge of one area, such as hiring or professional development. The other 32 teachers are employees, who can join the partnership if invited.

As its name suggests, the school's theme is environmental sustainability. Its students tend an organic garden on campus, which provides 80 pounds of food a week to the school cafeteria until the harvest is complete. "They're deeply involved in the farm," lead partner Frank Coyne told me. "They're deeply involved in organic food. They run a farm stand every week. And all that project-based learning is connected back to their reading and writing and math."

The school uses projects as often as possible to engage its students. Just before I visited, the sixth-grade science class had studied the water cycle, from rain and snow falling in the Rockies to rivers running out to the sea and evaporating. They then evaluated the use of drip irrigation in the garden and determined that it saved a million gallons of water a year, compared with when the building was vacant and the district was watering weeds.

One year, teacher Kartal Jaquette's second grade counted every light in the building, as part of a math project to find out where energy was being wasted. They measured the lumens coming from each light, as well as a series of mini-skylights, called solar tubes. Using graphs and charts, they figured out which light bulbs they could unscrew. Then they designed a monitoring system, with a student "light sheriff" in every classroom, to make sure the room had enough light but not so much that it wasted energy. Their recommendations saved $1,200 in electricity and 20,000 tons of carbon dioxide a year, according to Coyne.

Teachers like Jaquette, who constantly weave projects into their teaching, produce some of the school's highest test scores. The year before my visit, 26 percent of his third-graders tested "proficient" and 60 percent "advanced" in math, he told me. Sixty percent of DGS students are low-income, half are minorities, and 27 percent are English-language learners. "There's not another school with that demographic who had that level" of proficiency, Jaquette said.

Projects work best because "we're competing against Xbox 360, and over-scheduled days with soccer practices and very dynamic lives," he said. "Are you almost as interesting as a video game? Are you getting almost as much attention as a soccer coach might? Is it as much fun? Because if not they're going to tune you out."

DGS enjoys high teacher retention rates, and though it prioritizes project-based learning over test prep, its academic results are strong. In 2016, both the elementary and middle schools scored in the second-highest category, "meets expectations." In the SchoolChoice process, DGS was highly sought after.

Grant Beacon Middle School, which has 88.5 percent low-income students and 47.5 percent English-language learners, is another success story. It was struggling in 2009, when the district approved DSST to open a charter middle school down the street. Enrollment at Grant Beacon was already declining. Principal Alex Magana called a meeting of his teachers and staff and told them the news. "I said, 'If we lose ten percent of our kids, this is going to be a bone crusher for us. We've already seen schools close. We can make the changes, or other people are going to make them for us.'"

He took a straw vote on whether to write an innovation plan. Everyone agreed, and he invited every part of the school to send members to a team that worked all summer and the next school year. He also invited a small group of parents who lived in the community to participate. When the faculty was ready to vote on the plan, the union came in with scare tactics, warning the teachers about what they were giving up, including tenure for any new teachers. But 97 percent of them voted for the plan.

It included three major strategies: blended learning, character development, and an extended day. Magana explained:

> At that time, I had computer labs upstairs, and as I was doing the research on blended learning, I was going, "Wait a second, our kids are touching that computer once a month if that, and half the time it's broken." I suggested that we rip those computer labs out and put them in the classroom, so we tore everything down and put computers in the classrooms. I said, "We're going to bring in a software program and then we're going to focus on small group instruction." That's what we did for reading and math.

Today every student has a Chromebook, and the teachers have built a complete learning management system that allows them to personalize learning, to meet every child where they are. At first many of the teachers were afraid of the new technologies, Magana said. But after a big investment in training—and development of an online system that was easy to use—"teachers just took off."

When the district announced a pilot extended-day initiative, which would pay teachers for their extra time, Magana immediately volunteered. Grant Beacon runs from 7:30 A.M. to 4 P.M. four days a week, 10 A.M. to 4 P.M. on Fridays (so teachers can do professional development on Friday mornings, looking at student test data and figuring out how to respond). Between 3 and 4 P.M., the school offers 60 different enrichment classes, many run by people or organizations from the community—everything from sports to arts and crafts to music to STEM to "Girls Are Great!" Kids who are struggling get intervention classes during that time, to pull them up to grade level.

"I have parents that say, 'You know what? This parent here, she's a pilot,'"

Magana said. "'She'd like to teach an aerospace engineering class.'" So Magana asked her what she needed, then bought the materials. "She's shooting off rockets in the back. She's doing propulsion, doing all kinds of fun activities with the kids."

The toughest piece was character development. "I'm a big fan of Google," Magana said. "I've read how Google works—I gave it to my School Leadership Team. I said, 'We need to look at things differently. I don't want you to measure negative [traits], I want you to measure positive." So they defined the character traits they wanted kids to develop: leadership, perseverance, integrity, curiosity, and kindness. And they began to grade students on each trait and give them feedback on how they could improve, just as DSST does.

"You have to have a 2.6 to attend the social," Magana explained. "Now kids are having different conversations. They're not saying, 'I can't go because the teacher sent me to the office.' It's more of, 'I'm at a 2.5. If I do this, I can get up to a 2.6.'"

Before it became an innovation school, Magana said, Grant Beacon was the city's lowest-performing middle school. After one year, it had among the highest academic growth. By 2014 it was in the second-highest performance category, "meets expectations." On the 2016 PARCC tests it outperformed four of six Strive Prep middle schools, which had similar percentages of low-income children, but lagged behind most DSST middle schools, which had lower percentages.

In 2014 Alyssa Whitehead-Bust asked Magana if he would like to open a new school, in addition to Grant Beacon. "I was always worried about leaving here," he told me. "I'd have teachers saying, 'If you leave, everything falls apart.'" But with replication, he can have a principal at each school and oversee both.

The replication process "does make us better," he said. "I've had to reflect on my current practices." He is going head to head with a Strive Prep charter that shares his new building, for instance. "It's forcing me to look at what charter schools are doing. The way I see it is, we need to change the role of the principal. We're pushing too many things at the principals. I'm a veteran, but I see how many principals are dropping off. We're not successful because we're trying to juggle so much." He already had a "teacher leader" for each academic subject, which will continue in both schools. Now he recruited his best people, those who were hungry for new opportunities, to be principals, but told them they only had to focus on academic instruction. A blended learning director would take care of that piece, plus professional development and data teams, at both schools. A director of operations would take care of budget and operational issues at both schools. And Magana would work closely with all of them. The new school opened in August 2016.

Why Innovation Schools Have Not Excelled

Four important differences between innovation schools and charters have probably contributed to the gap in performance—differences that also explain why charters outperform DPS-operated schools in general.

First, charters have faced more consequences for poor performance. The district often filled innovation schools that didn't meet their enrollment targets, whereas if a charter's enrollment lagged, it might have to lay people off. Charters also have explicit performance contracts and are usually closed if they fail to meet their targets. Politically, it is harder for a board to close a school full of DPS employees—and so far, no failing innovation school has been closed. In 2016, however, the board approved a School Performance Compact, which applies the same standards and process to the closure of all public schools, regardless of type. If DPS follows through, that policy will for the first time give all sectors similar accountability.

Second, charters are often run by entrepreneurial leaders. Most innovation schools have been run by principals from within DPS, who may have less inclination to think outside the box. The most entrepreneurial leaders probably gravitate to the charter sector. As Van Schoales says, "You never see a charter person say, 'Oh, I'd like to have half my arm tied behind my back.'"

Third, successful charter schools often replicate, spreading their success and improving the charter sector. DPS only began to do the same with innovation schools in 2016. Unless the replications fall flat, however, Boasberg says he intends to continue the practice.

Fourth, innovation schools have more autonomy from district mandates than traditional DPS schools but far less than charters. Some of the innovation school principals I interviewed were happy with the degree of autonomy they enjoyed, but others were frustrated. In part, it depended on whom they dealt with at the district: their instructional superintendent, their HR partner, their budget partner, and so on. DPS leaders freely admit that employees' views on autonomy vary. Some share Boasberg's vision, which calls for significant autonomy for innovation schools and increasing autonomy for all schools, but others don't.

"It's infuriating to innovation school principals, because they feel like they have the blessing of the top leadership, but it's like cutting through frozen molasses," says Alan Gottlieb, who has been following education in Denver for more than 25 years as a journalist, a foundation executive, and the founder of an online education magazine. "Any little thing—hiring somebody, getting a school bus, ordering new furniture—it's all impossible. And it is because everybody below the top level is operating as though they're still just working for a traditional school district."

Grant Beacon Middle School again offers an example. "You wouldn't believe some of the simple things that we can't get done," Alex Magana told me. "One was as simple as ordering a bus. We said we want to order our own bus, because I have an extended day, we do all kinds of activities, our school year's longer. That conversation's been going on for over a year." The director told him, "'No, you guys can't order a bus. If you do, you have to do this, this, and this. It's going to cost you this.'" Magana agreed to the conditions, but still nothing happened. "Finally, I had a parent that got frustrated and sent an email to the board members. All of a sudden, I had the chief of staff giving me a call: 'What do you need?'"

Even hiring teachers was a problem in their replicated school, because the district wanted Magana to use its hiring process. He wanted to hire early, as charters and some innovation schools do, to get the best teachers. But his new school couldn't become an innovation school until the faculty voted for the plan, and they couldn't vote until they were hired—a classic catch-22. So the district said he couldn't post a teaching position until its regular hiring cycle started.

The same happened when it came to the budget. Magana wanted to budget for the two schools, so he could move money. The bureaucrats said that was impossible. One of them even said his schools couldn't call themselves a "network"—because there were only two of them. She suggested they call it a "circle."

"Thank goodness I wasn't at that meeting," he laughed, "because I would have flipped out."

Magana said Boasberg and the board believe in autonomy, but DPS mid-level staff people don't always get it. The issue is not so much outright restrictions as the constant battles principals must endure. Often they involve districtwide initiatives, such as home visits or a new reading program, in which the innovation schools are expected to participate. Zach Rahn, who runs another innovation school, Ashley Elementary, offered the example of a district initiative to create teacher leaders, who teach half-time and coach other teachers half-time. Ashley was an early adopter, and the initiative has been an "unbelievably huge benefit to our school communities," Rahn told me. "But now, as they seek to bring it to the whole district, they've put all these strings attached to it that actually take away from it. They sent us a 42-slide PowerPoint on how we need to organize the ecosystem in our school." It included a rubric to rate the school's readiness, a survey to fill out, and essays to write on why the teachers they chose were the most qualified—though Ashley was already using teacher leaders.

Rahn, Magana, and some of their peers routinely ignored such mandates, then had to waste precious hours fighting up the chain of command until they got permission. The time they lost troubled him, Rahn said, but "I also think about my colleagues around the district, who are just as capable as I am, and they aren't getting that option" to refuse.

This is the biggest reason innovation schools have not performed as well as charters, he believes. "Hold me accountable to whatever levels you want, but I need to be able to lead, and do my job, and not be stuck in the weeds down here."

Alyssa Whitehead-Bust pointed to another problem, before she left DPS in 2016: districtwide services that were not flexible enough for schools that wanted something different. If an innovation school started three weeks earlier than traditional DPS schools, food services, data services, and transportation might not be ready to start. The school might have to call food services every day, starting in June, to make sure food was there when it opened. Or they might have to pay to get the transportation team to run alternative bus routes, because there was a negotiated agreement with the bus drivers.

Finally, innovation schools don't have independent boards to protect them from meddling, as charters do. One of the advantages of a board is that the members are all advocates for your schools, David Greenberg points out. "But if you're an innovation school, your principal is still hired and fired by the district. There's a limit to how much you can scream if you're upset with the district."

An Innovation Zone to the Rescue?

By 2015, 17 innovation school leaders were frustrated enough with their waivers being ignored by the district—and with DPS changing their instructional supervisors—that they signed a letter to Boasberg asking for a meeting. They met repeatedly and got a few concessions, but by the next fall, things weren't much better. Four of them decided to propose an "innovation zone"—a group of schools with an independent, nonprofit board, which would negotiate flexibilities and a performance agreement with the district. "There's an incredible value for schools to go through the innovation school process," Rahn said, explaining why they took the initiative. But "there also comes a point where you almost hit a ceiling, where the constraints of the public education system don't allow you to actualize your plan."

The idea met a lot of resistance from district staff. Whenever someone pushed for more school autonomy, board of education member Barbara O'Brien explained, the hurt feelings of school supervisors dominated conversations at district headquarters. But in December 2015 the board stepped in and endorsed the idea, even without a specific plan from the staff. Months of negotiations followed, finally resulting in a three-year memorandum of understanding between DPS and the board of the newly named Luminary Learning Network (LLN).

The four schools—three elementaries and Denver Green School, which runs from early childhood through eighth grade—won the right to opt out of some district mandates. "We're not pulled out for the once-a-month, all-day meetings anymore, and we have less people hounding us for things that are required, because they're simply not required anymore," says Frank Coyne of Denver Green School. That "has freed us up to focus on our buildings and our kids—coaching our teachers, giving them feedback," and the like.

They were also able to opt out of additional DPS internal services, receiving the funds instead. Each school got about $425 per student more than they otherwise would have. At Denver Green School, the extra $150,000 allowed them to hire a school psychologist full-time, rather than two days a week, which meant more one-on-one and group work with kids who needed it. Each of the four schools now has a coach for the school leader or leaders, who spends a day a week in the building. They have invested more in training for teachers and hired aides to help with areas such as literacy and special education. One school brought in a full-time substitute teacher, so when there was a substitute she wouldn't be a stranger and the kids would stay focused on learning.

In return, the schools pledged to improve their performance. The SPF has five performance levels, or bands. If they were in one of the top two, they pledged to move up within their band. If they were below those levels, they pledged to move up a full band. If they fail to improve, the Luminary Learning Network board can recommend actions to DPS, such as replacing a school leader or even replacing a school. DPS remains the authorizer; the LLN board is a kind of intermediary, to oversee, support, and protect the schools.

The board of education appears interested in expanding the zone to eight or ten schools—the optimal size for sharing the costs of the board and executive director, as well as for sharing what has worked at different schools, according to the four school leaders. BOE members see the LLN as a good thing in itself, but also as an instrument to force the district bureaucracy to change. "Dramatic change needs to happen at central headquarters" to facilitate school autonomy, Chairwoman Anne Rowe said at a conference in May 2016. She and her colleagues want to see a cultural shift from managing subservient schools to serving autonomous schools. They have begun talking about "the school as the unit of change," and Boasberg has picked up on that rhetoric. But the devil is in the implementation, as always.

Boasberg has supported expanding the LLN and recommended to the board that DPS issue a call for the development of new innovation zones, though without independent boards. The DPS board appears likely to pursue both of these paths.

Giving innovation schools more of the autonomy they have been promised is a good idea, no matter how it occurs, and the creation of the zone is a big step forward. But many of those who pushed for it wanted "independent governance," an LLN board that was actually the schools' authorizer. As I have stressed before, authorizers that don't also operate schools are freer to hold them accountable, without conflicts of interest.

The other risk of Denver's approach is that it could so easily be undone. The agreement with the LLN is for only three years; it would be simple to let it lapse if the political situation changed. A scandal or a populist revolt against the board could always unseat the current majority. The history of autonomous zones within public systems tells us that those in the bureaucracy always resent the "special privileges" granted those in the zone and take them away at the first opportunity. A new board could give DPS staff that opportunity.

CHAPTER 10

DENVER'S REMAINING
CHALLENGES

TOM BOASBERG AND THE SCHOOL board deserve credit for putting in place many of the elements of a 21st century strategy. They have embraced charters, committing to expand their numbers even though they have no more empty buildings. They have finally agreed to be as tough in closing failing district schools as they are with failing charters, and to treat both sectors equally in awarding buildings. (The board voted to replace two traditional schools and close a third in November 2016, and there was no public fuss.) They have created an innovation zone that may finally give district schools the autonomy they need. They are moving more special education centers for extremely disabled students into charters, correcting an imbalance. It runs design challenges in which people compete to develop the most innovative designs for schools and for new educational programs within schools. With facilitated sessions to help and a prize of $100,000 for the best design, it has worked with up to 20 schools at a time.

Meanwhile Denver has accomplished a dramatic expansion of full-day preschool, which is now available for most four-year-olds and a few high-risk and special-needs three-year-olds. Voters have funded the Denver Preschool Program with a sales tax increase for the last decade, and the state and district also provide money. Test scores and evaluations suggest the investment is paying off.

Yet DPS still has a long way to go before most students graduate and most graduates are ready for college or a career. By 2016, only about a third of students met or exceeded Common Core standards. Achievement gaps by race and income were wide and growing wider.

"I don't think we have figured out how to educate low-income kids," says board member Barbara O'Brien, a former state legislator and lieutenant governor who has been at the forefront of education reform for decades. "There are fabulous, charismatic leaders, a Bill Kurtz, a Chris Gibbons [founder and CEO of Strive Prep]—they're out there. But in terms of a whole district of

90,000 students, the change is incremental. We're not moving the needle for the whole district."

In contrast, Denver's charter schools *have* figured out how to educate low-income children. Hence the first two challenges Denver faces, if it wants to accelerate its progress, are to close more failing schools and open more charters.

1. Accelerate the replacement of failing schools.

A recent study by the Center on Reinventing Public Education found that roughly 10 percent of Denver's schools were stuck in the bottom 5 percent of the state in math scores in 2012. Two years later, half remained stuck there. In reading, almost 17 percent were stuck in the bottom 5 percent in 2012; two years later, a third of them still were.

Denver needs to replace these schools faster. Of the five charter public schools on probation in 2010, only one was still open in 2015. But of the 12 traditional public schools on probation in 2010, half were still open and struggling in 2015. Replacement has been far more effective than trying to turn failing schools around, both locally and nationally. In Denver, replacement with charters has worked best—which leads us to the next challenge.

2. Expand the charter sector and ensure that there are adequate facilities for new charters.

To create more quality schools for low-income students, Denver needs more charters. "Quality new charter schools serve 78 percent low-income students," Alexander Ooms found in 2014. "Quality new district-operated schools serve just 18 percent . . . While the strategy of starting new schools is paying dividends for DPS, the success in creating quality schools—as well as serving low-income students within those schools—resides overwhelmingly with charters."

Since DPS no longer has empty buildings, it must replace failing schools with charters and/or finance new facilities for charters. Either way, it should do two things: replicate successful charters in addition to those of DSST, Strive Prep, and KIPP; and recruit outstanding charter networks from elsewhere. Several foundations made an effort to do the latter a decade ago, and unfortunately it did not go well. Yet excellent organizations such as Summit Public Schools, Green Dot Public Schools, and Uncommon Schools are expanding beyond their home cities. Surely Denver, which has a more hospitable environment for charters than most, could attract some of them.

3. Make the Innovation Zone work and expand it.

DPS leaders *and* staff will need to be committed to true autonomy for innovation zone schools if this experiment is to work. That will require a big change management effort within DPS, to shift the mindset and culture. The next strategy should be a big part of the effort.

4. Give schools control of the money for most internal services and let them purchase those services wherever they please.
Internal services are those provided to schools, such as maintenance and bus transportation. In June 2015, DPS announced that all principals could manage their own professional development, curriculum, and assessments and receive a bit of district money allotted for those functions. On short notice, about one in five DPS principals immediately chose to take advantage of this offer.

But if DPS is serious about school autonomy, it should hand principals control of and funding for *all central service functions* other than transportation and telecommunications—but not all *policy* or *compliance* functions. (Transportation and telecommunications are much more efficient if centrally managed, and decisions about policy and compliance with rules cannot be left up to individual schools.) DPS should turn the central offices that provide services into public enterprises that must earn their money by selling their services to schools, and principals should be free to buy those services elsewhere if they prefer. This approach, pioneered 30 years ago by Edmonton, Alberta, has been used by other districts to ensure that principals are empowered and central service offices provide quality services at a market price.

Consider school maintenance. The Denver Green School pays $280,000 a year for facilities, which includes maintenance. They've thought about opting out—hiring one maintenance person and using the savings in the classroom. But it's not easy, says Frank Coyne, because the district requires that they write a detailed plan for how they would handle maintenance. "It's union backed, and it gets real political real fast," he adds. "They can't tell you what you get for two hundred grand, right—there's insurance, there's maintenance—but we still wait three weeks for a plumber."

Rob Stein's success with food services at Manual High School illustrates the power of giving schools control over the money:

> We were really dissatisfied with food services because none of our kids would eat the food they provided. For the first year or two, we continually gave them feedback, but nothing changed. There was a competing food service company trying to move into town, Revolution Foods. We contacted them and held a taste test, asking students which food they preferred. We presented our results to the food service and told them we were going to contract with Revolution Foods. To their credit, the DPS food service director eventually asked if he could work on it and put together a competitive bid. He came back with improved menus and

we decided to go with the DPS food services. That was a win because choice and competition drove the DPS food service to provide a better meal for our students. They had a huge competitive advantage, because they controlled the kitchens and had infrastructure—transportation, bulk purchasing—all on their side. But before we had a choice, they were not responsive to their customers. After we broke their monopoly, they improved the product and provided better meals to the students.

5. Tame "the district monster:" create real autonomy for all schools.
As the discussion of innovation schools in the previous chapter makes clear, DPS schools need more autonomy, and not all central staff are willing to give it to them. High-level officials in DPS freely admit that, as one told me, "We don't have the same level of buy-in across the organization about autonomy."

In the past, even DPS's leaders have been somewhat schizophrenic, with little clarity about which schools should be given more autonomy. As a result, many staff are still acting as if school autonomy should be partial and should depend on the quality of the school—struggling schools should be held on shorter leashes. This is counterproductive. As the charter sector has shown, it is far more effective to let principals and their colleagues make the decisions at their schools, but hold them accountable for performance and replace their team if children are not learning enough. The central office can never know enough to make the right decisions at each and every school.

"There's such a huge gap between the policy makers and the reality on the ground," says Greg Ahrnsbrak, who helped lead the drive for autonomy at Bruce Randolph School. Mary Seawell says she never appreciated the negative role she played when, as a board member, she helped DPS place so many initiatives and requirements on the schools. Decisions that looked perfectly rational to those on the board and at the central office—and were made with the best of intentions—sometimes backfired at individual schools. In their haste to drive improvement, DPS leaders launched so many new initiatives that they overwhelmed some principals and teachers.

"Just yesterday, somebody forwarded me an email they got," Pam Shamburg, executive director of the Denver Classroom Teachers Association, told me in late 2014. "The superintendent has decided he wants 10,000 home visits done, so in their school it means 280 home visits. Not that they're a bad idea, but when? When do we do this? With all the parent meetings we're supposed to have, all the curriculum meetings, all the Common Core training, when do we stop, when is there enough time?"

On DCTA surveys, Shamburg said, teachers continually expressed the same frustration: "'I'm overwhelmed, I'm exhausted, I don't know how to do this.' Our teachers are just: 'Can we stop, can I learn to do one new thing before we add?'"

"It's no wonder that Denver suffers from fairly high turnover among new teachers," added Kerrie Dallman, president of the Colorado Education Association.

I ran into this problem at one of the Far Northeast turnaround schools, which were part of something called the Denver Summit Schools Network (DSSN), managed by a national organization founded by Harvard Professor Ronald Fryer, called the Blueprint Schools Network. These schools had two masters, DSSN and DPS, and they were under intense pressure to improve, quickly. At some schools teachers were told to do new things with no explanation about why and no support to learn how to do them. "There's a huge sense of immediacy—data immediately needs to go up, best practices need to happen in every classroom," one told me. But most teachers were new, and there wasn't much training or professional development. The attitude was, "Fix it now, without knowing how to fix it. And your job is on the line if you don't. People feel a lot of stress, because you know your job is not protected."

"People who are super committed to kids have left this network," another teacher told me. At her school they lost 80 percent of their staff after their first year and 70 percent after their second. "All the systems fall apart because you lose the people who supported them."

Centralized discipline policies also created problems. Over the past decade, DPS has reduced the numbers of suspensions and expulsions by more than two thirds, through new policies. The rates came down, but teachers began to complain about disruptive students who were allowed to remain in their classrooms. In 2013, 60 teachers and staff from Bruce Randolph School sent an open letter to Boasberg. "The disproportionate amount of time and resources that in the past would have been spent on improving instruction," they wrote, "is instead spent by our entire staff, including administrators, instructional team, support staff, and teachers, on habitually disruptive students that continually return to our classrooms. This has now reached a critical point."

Under Kristin Waters, Ahrnsbrak says, Bruce Randolph expelled ten students, the highest number in the district. Because they were serious about turning the school around, they refused to tolerate constant disruption. But that all changed after Waters left and the district changed its discipline policies. By 2013, he says, students had threatened to bring guns to school and kill teachers, even threatened to blow up the school, and received only a few days of suspension.

In March 2015, the union conducted a survey of teachers. A third said they felt unsafe in their schools, and almost 60 percent said they would hesitate to send their own child to their school because of discipline issues.

At a board meeting on the issue, a union representative read a letter from a resigning teacher. At the end of the previous semester, the teacher wrote, administrators told teachers that habitually disruptive students could not be sent to the counselor's office without a call to parents first.

> With 30 students in class, how is it possible for us to make that kind of a call home in the middle of instruction? All of our teachers here are exhausted as we continue to deal with the same issues and same students over and over due to the lack of support and ineffective consequences. We are overwhelmed, security is overwhelmed, and the overall feeling of our entire staff is that we have to take it.

The district was creating a "dangerous and destructive" environment, the teacher said.

After Ahrnsbrak went on public radio and talked about what was going on, DPS created a discipline committee to review its policies, involving the teachers union, the community group Padres Unidos, a consultant from Denver University, and district officials. They are working with a few schools to help them adopt restorative justice. But as of 2017, Ahrnsbrak said, discipline issues remained a persistent problem.

The bottom line: most central initiatives should be voluntary, because schools work best when their leaders decide what changes to implement and when.

6. Align DPS staff around a 21st century strategy.

The struggle over autonomy is part of a larger problem: a lack of alignment within the DPS bureaucracy. The district has had a "strategic plan" since 2005, now called the Denver Plan 2020. But it is primarily a set of goals, with less emphasis on strategies. Because they did not want to give the opposition a big target, Bennet, Boasberg, and their allies on the board chose for years not to use the phrase "portfolio strategy," nor to talk about their intention to increase the number of charter schools.

This silence has been successful, politically. In contrast, when Newark Superintendent Cami Anderson presented her strategies in her "One Newark" plan, it gave her opponents a big, fat target, and she was gone within two years. But the price of Denver's success has been frustration on the part of principals, who have to deal with central office staff who don't share Boasberg's vision.

It is time to lay out that vision, including an explicit 21st century strategy, and invest in a deep effort to bring all employees on board. "From my observations of the district, it would seem that if they were clearer, they could actually move the needle much faster," says Van Schoales, CEO of A+ Colorado.

"I feel that often people are spinning their wheels—working hard, but not necessarily working together to move in the right direction."

"Even if you have aligned vision, the ability to make change in a complex system like this is incredibly challenging," adds Bill Kurtz. "It's close to impossible when you don't have aligned vision. You have a fighting chance if you get that, but it's still hard. That's what I worry about."

7. Expand equal opportunity by expanding public school choice.

Like Washington, D.C., DPS offers both neighborhood schools and schools of choice. By 2016, Denver had the most school choice of any city in the nation, according to the Brookings Institution. Polls showed strong support for public school choice, and participation in the enrollment system had steadily increased. In the first three years, between 55 and 80 percent of those going into key transition years—kindergarten, sixth grade, and ninth grade—participated. (Those who don't participate are assigned to their neighborhood schools.) White students had the highest rates in 2014 (84.7 percent), followed by Hispanics (71.1 percent) and blacks (63.3 percent). Low-income students had slightly lower rates (63 to 67 percent, depending on the year) than others (69 to 70 percent).

As these numbers show, the new system has not fully equalized access. Like other cities, Denver has residential neighborhoods segregated by race and income. To foster integration and encourage more parents to choose schools, DPS has established 11 multischool "shared enrollment zones," which encompass a wider diversity of races and incomes than single-school neighborhood boundaries. Families in these zones are guaranteed placement at a school in the zone but aren't assigned; they can list up to five choices. Unfortunately, by 2016 these zones covered less than a third of the city, and more affluent areas had resisted them, because parents who bought homes where their children could attend a high-performing neighborhood school didn't want to lose that privilege. DPS leaders have to be careful not to go too fast, for fear of pushing middle-class families to leave for private or suburban schools.

Limits on student transportation also cut down the choices available to poor families. DPS creates bus systems families can use within the zones, though only five of them provide fairly full access through a bus system. Outside these zones, at magnet and neighborhood schools, students are only bused if they live more than 2.5 miles from the school. Charters outside the zones are responsible for their own transportation, so many charter parents drive their children across town for school.

Given residential segregation, transportation challenges, and many parents' preference for neighborhood schools, access is far from equal. By 2015–16, close to one in five children was still enrolled in schools where more than 80 percent were low-income minorities and performance was well below the median. Those who were not poor were 6.5 to 8 times as likely as the poor to be enrolled in the top performing 20 percent of elementary and middle schools—the third-highest ratio among 50 cities studied by the Center on Reinventing Public Education.

Solutions include replacing low-performing schools; gradually expanding the shared enrollment zones and their bus systems, to cover most or all of the city; and reserving a certain percentage of seats for low-income students (as DSST does) in more schools. Breaking up the concentrations of poverty in schools will go a long way toward improving the education of low-income children and reducing the number of failing schools.

8. Expand equal opportunity by budgeting for actual teacher salaries rather than average teacher salaries.

Most school districts assign a certain number of teachers per student to each school, then assume in their budgets that each teacher costs the same amount. They also use seniority rules that give veteran teachers an ability to fill open spots in sought-after schools. These are usually the schools with the most "teachable" students. Hence veteran teachers in urban districts gravitate to schools with middle-class students, and schools full of poor students get the new teachers. Denver is no exception: its low-performing schools have many more novice teachers and much higher attrition than high-performing schools. Since most teacher salaries rise based on seniority, not performance, districts can spend almost twice as much on veteran teachers for middle-class students as they do on rookies for poor students.

Denver has given innovation schools the option of choosing to budget on the basis of actual or average salaries. The majority have chosen actual salaries, so they can save money and invest it in more teachers, psychologists, technology, or whatever they feel will most help their students. But the majority of DPS-operated schools still use average salaries, which means the district spends more per student in middle-class schools, because that is where the higher-paid teachers are. If the district truly wants to equalize opportunity for all students, it must eliminate this financial advantage. That is politically difficult, because it means taking money away from middle-class schools, where parents are often more vocal and politically active. Hence DPS would be wise to phase the change in gradually, to minimize the opposition.

9. Fix the School Performance Framework (SPF).

As appendix A argues, Denver's SPF gives too much weight to growth and not enough to proficiency—the opposite of the problem in most districts. In addition, its standards are too low, its five performance bands are not equal in their range, making too many schools look like they are successful, and it is too complex for most people to understand. (See pp. 307–13 for more.)

10. Take a second look at the performance pay system.
In 2005, DPS stepped into the national spotlight by negotiating a districtwide system with the teachers union, financed by a $25 million annual boost in property taxes. The subsequent decade of experience reveals a surprising lesson. No one in Denver thinks performance pay has made much difference in student outcomes, but most agree that charter schools—which aren't eligible for the taxpayer-funded performance pay—have made a big difference.

The lesson: Performance pay can work, but compensation systems are more effective when they are fashioned by individual schools or groups of schools, such as charter networks. Different schools and teachers have widely different needs and attitudes toward performance pay, and fashioning one system for 150 different schools is probably a fool's errand. (For a detailed discussion, see appendix B).

The Secrets of Denver's Political Success

How has Denver managed to pursue a 21st century strategy for almost a decade, with an elected school board, when similarly bold strategies have been turned back in other cities? What could other elected school boards learn from Denver? I believe there are ten principal lessons. Denver has not done every piece well; for instance, it has often been perceived as moving ahead without genuine community input. But the backlash after such failures has only illustrated the importance of that lesson. (The ten elements do not need to be put in place in any particular order.)

Create a respected catalyst for reform. A+ Denver, now called A+ Colorado, included some 100 movers and shakers among its membership. Its mission was "to harness the power of Denver's civic leadership to build public will and advocate for the changes necessary to dramatically increase student achievement in public education in Denver."

Build a broad coalition for reform, including organizations that represent minorities and low-income people. Michael Bennet was wise enough to ally with organizations such as Padres Unidos and Metro Organizations for People, both of which supported key aspects of reform. Their support helped neutralize opposition to school replacements, expansion of charter schools, weighted student budgeting, and expanded choice of public schools.

Create positive examples of success. The success of Strive Prep, DSST, and KIPP charter schools convinced Michael Bennet and board members to embrace and expand charter schools. "If you were a critic," says State Senator Michael Johnston, "we could take you to 20 different charters that would show dramatic results."

Use data to communicate the need for change. The School Performance Framework was indispensable, producing data that justified closing, replacing, and replicating schools. Once ratings became available, community groups began to use them to demand improvements in their schools.

Seek community input before making changes. When Michael Bennet decided to close Manual High School with little public consultation, a huge uproar ensued. He learned his lesson and invested significant time seeking community input thereafter. But even when his successor did so, asking A+ Denver to lead a community consultation on what to do in Far Northeast Denver, it was not enough. The proposal to replace Montbello High School and other schools in that region created huge opposition. The lesson: it is almost impossible to consult too much with the community. At the same time, leaders must be willing to proceed even when significant minorities in the community oppose action. Consultation does not mean capitulation to the loudest voices.

Treat all school types—charter, traditional, and others—with an even hand. Being agnostic about school type played a big role in Denver's success. By signing a compact with the charters but refusing to indicate any preference for them, Boasberg avoided giving the opposition something to rally around. That may have slowed the expansion of charters, but when combined with their strong performance, it neutralized any backlash.

Get serious about winning school board elections. In 2009, reformers took the elections for granted, but the opponents of reform, led by the teachers union, organized and won three open seats. Reformers never made that mistake again. Beginning in 2013, they raised significant money and recruited candidates with enormous credibility. The result was a 7–0 reform majority.

Be strategic about the pace of reform. Former board member Bruce Hoyt points to superintendents who moved too fast: David Hornbeck in Philadelphia, Alan Bersin in San Diego, and Michelle Rhee in Washington, D.C. All three sparked a backlash that undermined reform in the first two cities, and would have done the same in D.C. if Mayor Vince Gray hadn't been a genuine leader.

"We all learned from Alan Bersin," says Senator Johnston. "I think Bennet went and visited with him and took some cues from both his successes and mistakes. He led in a bullish way and let the chips fall where they may. We never did that."

"School systems operate in a complex environment of stakeholders," adds Bruce Hoyt, who now handles education investments at a philanthropic organization called Gary Community Investments. "Tom Boasberg told me once that he would get frustrated one Friday because they hadn't pushed hard enough and would worry the next Friday that they had pushed too hard and burned out the staff or community. Keeping healthy tension on the wire without snapping it is the key balancing act."

Others would disagree, arguing that if most of the academic progress in Denver is coming from charter schools, expanding the percentage of students in charters from seven to 21 over a decade is hardly moving fast enough. But until DSST and Strive Prep proved so effective, Hoyt points out, "There was still a lot of political backlash against the concept of charter schools." If the board had moved faster, "I think we might have lost the board majority and lost the strategy entirely." It is certainly true that since 2009, Denver's reformers have managed to keep moving forward without stirring an electoral backlash.

Don't back down because you have only a 4–3 majority on the board. Often appointed superintendents, city managers, and county executives are extremely cautious when they have only a one-vote majority on the body that hires and fires them. Had Tom Boasberg been that cautious, there would have been no opportunity to demonstrate that expanding the charter sector produced results.

Ensure consistent leadership over time. More than a decade of consistent leadership at the superintendent level cannot be underestimated. Profound change is almost impossible without continuity of leadership. One of the reasons for Denver's and others' success, says Bill Kurtz, is because "we've had a similar vision for ten years under the same leadership, the same vision. When you look at countries in the world who had huge gains in education, that's largely what's happened. In this country, we're often left not clear and aligned on the vision, and it can change every two to four years. If you can't get the vision and the political leadership consistent over ten years, it's incredibly hard, as we see in New York City now, to make any substantial gains long term."

How Sustainable Are Denver's Reforms?

Tom Boasberg is likely to enjoy support from a majority of the board for quite a few years. The opposition is weak and disorganized, and all the momentum is on the side of the reformers. If anything, some on the board are frustrated that Boasberg is not moving *faster*.

Although there is no reason to believe DPS will waver from its current path, only time will tell. A scandal could discredit reform, or Boasberg could leave and the board could make a mistake in choosing his successor. Unlike charters, innovation schools and zones could be easily neutered if the district's leadership changes.

But if the innovation zones work and DPS continues to expand its charter sector, Denver could reach a tipping point where a majority of public school families benefit from 21st century governance, in the form of charters and innovation zone schools. If that happens, the reforms will be difficult to undo. Denver just might prove that an elected board can successfully transform a 20th century school system organized on the principles of bureaucracy into a 21st century system built to deliver continuous improvement.

PART IV

THE REVOLUTION SPREADS

CHAPTER 11

OTHER CITIES EMBRACE THE 21ST CENTURY MODEL

As New Orleans, Washington, D.C., and Denver outpace other cities in academic growth, leaders elsewhere have taken note. The 21st century model is spreading far more rapidly than people realize. Already legislatures in Tennessee, Virginia, Nevada, and North Carolina have acted to create versions of Louisiana's Recovery School District (RSD), though Virginia's Supreme Court ruled the district unconstitutional. A number of other cities—from Memphis to Indianapolis to Camden, New Jersey—are creating 21st century systems. Different cities are inventing their own paths, shaped by their particular histories and political situations. In this chapter we will take a close look at one of them, Indianapolis, and a quick look at others. (Interested readers will find more details in appendix C.)

Indianapolis Blazes Two New Trails

Indianapolis is the only American city where the mayor authorizes charter schools, and Indiana's charter law has been ranked number one in the country by both the National Alliance of Public Charter Schools and the National Association of Charter School Authorizers. Some skeptics doubt that cities other than hotspots that draw millennials, such as Boston, D.C., New Orleans, and Denver, can attract the talent necessary to build large, vibrant charter sectors. But for the last decade, Indianapolis has proven them wrong.

Today the city is innovating again. Indianapolis Public Schools (IPS) is authorizing "innovation network schools": district schools with performance contracts and full charter-style autonomy. Some are charters, some are start-ups, and some are existing IPS schools that have converted. Though they are outside the teachers union contract, all use IPS school buildings. All have independent boards, organized as 501(c)3 not-for-profit organizations. Other cities have their own versions of "innovation schools" or "pilot schools," but only Indianapolis gives them the full autonomy and accountability that charters experience.

The city's charters educated about a third of all public school students in the district in 2016–17, while innovation network schools educated another 10 percent. Soon the two sectors combined will surpass 50 percent.

The roots of all this go back to 1999, when Bart Peterson ran for mayor as a Democrat. Indianapolis was struggling to keep its middle class, and Peterson, who wanted much stronger public schools to attract and keep residents, campaigned for a charter school law. Teresa Lubbers, a Republican state senator, had introduced six previous charter bills, all of which had failed. She came up with the idea of giving the mayor authorizing authority, and Peterson agreed. The combination of a Democratic mayor of the state's largest city and a Republican legislator finally broke the logjam.

Peterson put a young staffer, David Harris, in charge of his new charter office, and Harris put in place a rigorous process to approve charters. When Republican Greg Ballard defeated Peterson after two terms, some worried that the political transition would undermine chartering. But Ballard expanded the number of charters from 16 to 39, while closing seven. His Democratic successor, Joe Hogsett, continues the bipartisan support. By 2016 the mayor authorized 35 schools on 40 campuses, which served about 13,600 students. Six more had been authorized to open in the fall of 2017. The Indiana Charter School Board also authorized seven schools in the city, while Ball State University authorized two, one of which was a virtual (online) school, which drew students from all across the state.

With a few exceptions, most of the charters in Indianapolis are homegrown. A key reason is an organization called The Mind Trust, founded in 2006 by Peterson and Harris as a kind of venture capital outfit for the charter sector, to raise money and recruit talent. The Mind Trust convinced Teach For America, The New Teacher Project (now TNTP), and Stand For Children to come to Indianapolis. It also raised millions of dollars and offered start-up space, grants, and other help to eight nonprofit organizations and 17 schools, with more to follow.

The mayor's office is highly regarded as a charter authorizer. It tracks 27 different performance measures on its schools, does qualitative evaluations, and has closed at least ten schools, often replacing them with a new school by a stronger operator. Over the years, it has rejected many more applications than it has accepted.

By any measure, mayoral charters have outperformed IPS schools. Demographically, they serve a poorer population, but one with slightly fewer English-language learners and students with special needs. As schools of choice, charters may have the advantage of more motivated parents. On the other hand, they have received roughly $4,200 per student less than IPS schools each year, in large part because they do not get free buildings or local property tax money.

Like most states, Indiana debuted a new, more demanding test in 2015, and student proficiency rates dropped precipitously. The state then changed testing companies in 2016, and scores dropped a bit more. So there is no valid way to compare test scores before and after 2014. On the 2014 tests, 71 percent of students at the mayoral charters were proficient in English language arts, compared to 60 percent of IPS students. In math, the difference was 75 to 65 percent. (The same trends continued in 2015, but at lower levels of proficiency.)

According to the mayor's office, the charters outperformed neighborhood schools that students would have otherwise been assigned to by 17 percentage points in English and 16 in math. Their median growth percentile, which measures students' rates of progress, was about five percentage points higher in both subjects, and their four-year graduation rate in 2016 was 89 percent—the state average—compared to 77 percent at IPS schools.

Perhaps because the mayor's office closes failing schools, its charters have also shown more rapid improvement. In 2013, only 35 percent of them received an A or B rating from the state; by 2016, 50 percent did—compared to 18 percent at IPS.

Stanford University's CREDO released a study on charter performance in Indiana in 2012. Compared to their counterparts in traditional public schools, it concluded, every year "charter students in Indianapolis gain an additional two months in reading and nearly three months in math." Those in mayoral charters did even better, gaining two months in reading and 3.6 months in math. In 2015 CREDO published a report on 41 urban regions, including Indianapolis, which also revealed that by students' fourth year in Indianapolis charters, their annual gains were roughly double this amount.

Mayoral authorizing has turned out to be a surprisingly stable and effective strategy, enduring through three mayors from both parties. David Harris believes it is the best authorizing model, because the authorizer is accountable to the families served by the schools:

> *They can be thrown out of office in the next election by dissatisfied parents if they hand out charters to subpar operators. Because of this, mayors have a powerful incentive to rigorously review charter applications and shut down underperforming schools. Under a mayoral authorizer, bad charters won't be allowed to fail with impunity—either the school or its authorizer will pay a price.*

Innovation Network Schools

As in D.C., the rise of charters put enormous competitive pressure on Indianapolis Public Schools, where the state rated 44 percent of schools D or F in 2016–17. In the 1960s IPS had more than 100,000 students; by 2016, it had only about 29,000. Within its geographic boundaries, which encompass only part of Indianapolis, about 14,000 students attended K–12 charters in 2015–16, another 2,339 attended six charter high schools for adults, and more than 3,400 students used state-funded vouchers to attend private schools.

Until the arrival of a new superintendent in 2013, the district was hostile to charters. His predecessor, Superintendent Eugene White (2005–13), knew he had to do something to keep families in IPS schools, so he expanded magnet programs aggressively. He encouraged them to develop unique academic programs, and he let them hire their own teaching staffs. Unfortunately, the magnets have drawn more white, middle-class families than the rest of the IPS schools, raising suspicion in the African American community about a two-tier system.

Two things happened that changed the course of history in IPS. In December 2011 The Mind Trust released a 150-page report, *Creating Opportunity Schools: A Bold Plan to Transform Indianapolis Public Schools*. It called for a switch from an elected school board to an appointed one, with three members appointed by the mayor and two by the city council. More important, it urged that over time *all* Indianapolis public schools be converted to "opportunity schools," which would be treated like charters. They would have a seven-year performance contract with the district that would guarantee the kind of autonomy charters have—over hiring, curriculum, school design, and how they spent their money. If they failed to perform as promised, they would be closed and replaced by a stronger school operator. They would all be schools of choice; every family in Indianapolis would choose its school.

The report generated an enormous amount of attention and controversy. Superintendent White rejected it, and Mayor Ballard chose not to pursue it. But, says Harris, "it really stimulated a conversation about what needed to happen in the district that had never happened before."

An informal group of elected officials, businesspeople, and community activists tried to convince the state legislature to allow mayoral appointment of the school board, but their efforts failed. So they turned their attention to electing reformers. "We had candid conversations with current board members and asked them not to run again, that it was time for a change in leadership," says Sam Odle, a former health-care executive who won a seat in 2012. "Those incumbents all stood down. They knew they were going to be running against candidates that were well funded and had the support of the business community. One of them had been on the board for 30 years, but I think they recognized the winds were shifting."

The reformers won all four seats that were up in 2012, creating a majority on the seven-member board. The new board bought out Superintendent White's contract and hired Dr. Lewis Ferebee, a young African American who had been an elementary school teacher, an administrator, and a deputy superintendent in North Carolina.

Ferebee is tall, bespectacled, and soft-spoken, with an easy smile and a low-key manner. To understand why Indianapolis is creating charter-like district schools, it helps to understand his background. At 25, Ferebee was a middle school assistant principal in Creedmoor, North Carolina, when the superintendent asked him to become principal of the worst elementary school.

> He gave me the keys and said, "Lewis, you have carte blanche authority. If anybody comes to you about a decision you made, have them come to me. This is so important that I don't want anything to get in your way."
>
> And I believe that was why I was successful. At the end of the day, if principals feel handcuffed, if teachers feel handcuffed, you're stifling their creativity. Your best teachers are your most innovative and creative teachers, and they know their learners. So when you don't give them the full opportunity to make informed decisions about what they know, you're limiting the opportunity for them to be successful.

Ferebee also discovered that empowering teachers "was the best recruiting tool I had.

> I had teachers helping me recruit other teachers to my building, because they were excited. From that I learned the power of teacher leadership, so now I'm just anointing and empowering teachers to be leaders among themselves, and then I sit back and watch this amazing work of teachers getting better as they're developing other teachers.
>
> What I learned was you can raise salaries—we can do some of that—but I think there's something to be said for creating leadership opportunities and for agility and autonomy in schools. That is where teachers feel most valued and most respected.

As an elementary principal, Ferebee saw a lot of his graduates fall back academically in middle school, so he asked the superintendent if he could run the middle school. When he turned it around, the superintendent asked him to supervise all the middle schools in the district. Then a new superintendent came in and made him regional superintendent of a feeder pattern of elementary, middle, and high schools that were all struggling. "We outperformed the district in terms of growth," he says.

When Durham, North Carolina, hired the district's chief of staff to be its superintendent, he brought Ferebee along as his chief of staff and asked him to turn around all the district's low-performing schools. Again Ferebee empowered his principals and teachers. He and his partners at Duke University were telling their story at a National Association of School Boards meeting when some school board members from Indianapolis heard them. The next thing Ferebee knew they were inviting him to Indianapolis for an interview.

"I didn't realize until I got here the real thick dividing line between traditional public schools and charters, the contentious relationship," he says. "It was almost as if we were in the same boat with the same mission and the same goals, but there was this huge wall and barrier." There was "a lot of finger pointing" between IPS and the mayor's office and "no collaboration." IPS was "struggling with underutilized facilities, and charter schools were being incubated in old grocery stores and old factories. The whole financial model of that division didn't make sense to me. We're still talking about public schools."

Ferebee also found an unusual degree of centralization at IPS: principals didn't even select their assistant principals and teachers. On his listening tour, principals told him their schools weren't as strong as they could be because they didn't have enough autonomy. So he began to empower them.

He quickly forged a relationship with the mayor's charter office. The deputy mayor for education drafted a bill to create incentives for IPS and charters to work together, by allowing the district to bring outside operators in to run autonomous schools in district buildings. The Mind Trust's vision informed the draft, and the fact that the state was taking over failing IPS schools created urgency. Ferebee signed on and publicly supported the bill. In legislative hearings, the state teachers union suggested allowing traditional IPS schools to convert to innovation status, and Ferebee and the mayor's office agreed. The bill passed in 2014, and in 2015 the legislature added new features and extended the same authority to the state's other districts. When the 2014 elections brought three more reformers onto the IPS board, Ferebee had strong support for the idea.

Innovation network schools are exempt from the same laws and regulations charters are exempt from, and they operate outside IPS's union contracts. They have five- to seven-year contracts with the district, much like charters. If a school fails to fulfill the terms of its contract, the district can terminate it or refuse to renew it, but otherwise it cannot interfere with the school's autonomy.

The principal and teachers are employed by a 501(c)3 corporation, not IPS. The nonprofit's board hires and fires the principal, sets the budget and pay scale, and chooses the school design. All the schools operate in IPS buildings, and IPS handles special education for innovation schools that are not charters.

There are four types of innovation network schools:

1. New start-ups, some of which are also charter schools.
2. Existing charter schools that choose to become innovation schools and are housed in district school buildings.
3. Failing district schools restarted as innovation schools, often in partnership with an outside operator.
4. Existing IPS schools that choose to convert to innovation status.

The new schools tend to build up a grade or two at a time. Some of the restarts (type 3) take on the entire student body, while others phase in a grade or two per year.

All but the second type serve as neighborhood schools, not schools of choice. Ferebee believes in public school choice—indeed, he wrote his doctoral dissertation on the topic—but he also wants to give quality schools to those whose parents don't choose. He's trying to create a system that will provide both. In addition, "There is a symbiotic relationship between a neighborhood and a school," he says. When a school is abandoned, the neighborhood tends to go downhill. He wants innovation schools to have the opposite effect, to revive neighborhoods.

When charter schools become innovation schools, they pay rent to IPS, but at very low rates. Different innovation schools have negotiated different agreements with IPS, but most get free or reduced-price bus transportation for students who need it, free utilities, free student meals, free custodial, maintenance, special education, and information technology services, and a nurse and social worker. These advantages add up to an average of about $2,000 per student per year, according to David Harris—enough to make becoming an innovation school more attractive than just opening a new charter school. "Just having a facility that exists is a $2.5 million fundraising difference," says Earl Martin Phalen, who opened a charter school and later an innovation school in the city.

Though the statewide teachers union opposed the original legislation, the local union has not interfered with implementation. Union leaders were present when IPS leaders talked with the first two schools that wanted to convert to innovation status. In both cases, an overwhelming majority of the teachers supported conversion, including the union representatives, even though it meant leaving union membership and tenure behind. "These are the high-performing schools," says Brandon Brown, who ran Mayor Ballard's charter office and is now at The Mind Trust. "Most of the teachers probably feel pretty confident—and rightfully so—that their situation is going to be fine."

The Mind Trust proposed that it "incubate" innovation schools, by providing grants to leaders to support them through one or two years of planning, and Ferebee agreed. The Mind Trust incubated one of the five innovation schools launched in 2015 and all four that opened in 2016. Of those that began in 2015, the one restart best illustrates what IPS is trying to do.

Francis Scott Key Elementary School 103 had been rated F by the state for five years. In its neighborhood, nearly a third of residents had annual household incomes of less than $10,000. The school had one of the most transient and violent student bodies in the city. In its final year, 2014–15, 73 fights erupted, more than in any other IPS elementary school. Enrollment had fallen from 527 to 341, and only 11 students passed the state exams. "Every single classroom was chaotic," says Earl Phalen, who took it over. "Literally 13 of our sixth-graders, on the pretest, were at kindergarten or first-grade levels. They couldn't spell their names."

Phalen, an African American who graduated from Yale University and Harvard Law School, already ran one charter elementary in town and had charters to open nine more. The Mind Trust had first enticed him to town to create a summer program for thousands of teenagers, then had suggested he launch a charter. Of the innovation school he says:

> We knew it had to be done well, because if it wasn't, the notion of innovation schools would take a severe hit. It was sooner than we wanted to do a turnaround, and everybody said turnaround is tougher than a charter. The risk is that you're taking on the whole school, and you have to believe that you can get third-graders and fourth-graders and fifth-graders who've been in a chaotic environment for five, six, and seven years to actually behave up to your expectations. But we had done summer programs with kids from seven different gangs, and we put them on one campus. So I wasn't scared about being able to set the culture. We can set culture.

Francis Scott Key had 53 teachers. Phalen says he told them kids were going to grow 1.5 years per year, academically, but they didn't believe it. So he didn't hire any of them—"Because they didn't have the fundamental belief in the kids they were serving." He and the principal, Agnes Aleobua, hired 42 new staff members and had the dingy old school renovated, with new desks, carpeting over the old tile, and bright new paint on the walls. They assigned a teacher and an assistant to most classrooms—then let two of them go within the first few months. "We cannot waste a year of a child's life while a teacher tries to figure out if they want to do this," Phalen explained.

They invested heavily in getting parents involved: having teachers do home visits before school started, hiring parent advocates, creating a breakfast program for fathers and their kids (designed by a former Indianapolis Colts coach, Tony Dungy), and inviting parents to regular events at school.

After six months, Phalen told me, "We've got the culture straightened out; now we need to get the academic piece fixed." By the time state testing rolled around, the percentage who passed IREAD—a third-grade test that has not changed in recent years—had doubled, from 30 to 61 percent.

While Phalen reinvents the school, the Glick Philanthropies have launched a comprehensive effort to turn around the broader area. Called the Far East-side Success Initiative, it is a partnership with the United Way of Central Indiana, Central Indiana Community Foundation, and IPS. It will involve housing, free preschool, college scholarships, a food pantry, adult education and training programs, and health care and public safety initiatives.

Gene B. Glick was a builder who constructed many of the homes and apartments in the neighborhood, beginning in the 1950s. His family says it is prepared to make a 20-year investment in the area, which also houses a high school. Already it has purchased an apartment complex he built and invested $5 million in improving it. It has given School 103 more than $1 million over the first two years to help with renovation, staff recruitment and training, parent advocates, and preschool. At the high school it has invested $40,000 in college scholarships and $60,000 to support a restorative justice discipline program.

In 2016–17 Phalen took a second innovation school under his wing, but on a slightly different basis. School 93 is run by a group of teachers who call themselves Project Restore. As Phalen tells it, this is "an incredible group of teachers who eight years ago were at another school, School 99, and said, 'You guys keep handing us down all these initiatives. You don't have any idea what works or doesn't work because your feet have been so far from the ground. Let us run the school.'" The principal agreed, and "with the exact same teachers, they took the school from an F-rated school to an A-rated school in one year. So the superintendent, Dr. White, said, 'Why don't you try that again?'" They turned that school from an F to a B in one year, an A the next year.

Ferebee encouraged them to bring their model to School 93, which they moved from an F to a C in their first year, 2014–15. When they decided to pursue innovation network status through a Mind Trust Educator Empowerment

Grant, they didn't want to spend time building a new 501(c)3 organization and a board. So they joined Phalen Leadership Academies, reporting to its board.

ANOTHER INTERESTING RESTART is Global Preparatory Academy, a K–2 school that will gradually grow to be K–8. The first dual-language immersion school to be chartered in Indiana, it was started in August 2016 by Mariama Carson, an African American former teacher and principal in Pike Township, one of ten other districts within Indianapolis's borders. It offers instruction in both English and Spanish, to native speakers of both languages.

Originally Carson intended to create an independent charter school, but when the innovation path opened, it was financially more attractive. So her school is both a charter, authorized by the mayor's office, and an innovation network school, located in an IPS building. "I thought I would never again work inside a district," she says, "but I think this way of working inside a district will work for us."

The school Global replaced was one of the worst in IPS. Only one teacher applied to stay, and Carson hired her as an assistant in the behavior room. "Kids are easy to change," she says. "It's adults that are hard." She had to recruit teachers worldwide, to get 50 percent native Spanish speakers. One came from Spain, another from Mexico.

Students spend half the day with a teacher in each language, so every student has two teachers. With both English and Spanish speakers in each classroom, Carson says, "Kids help each other a lot. That's why the two-way language immersion is so powerful."

There are six interdisciplinary units of study, on topics such as family, science, money, and "Who am I?" "That's how I've always taught," says Carson, who won a $25,000 Milken Educator Award during her teaching days. "There's tons of research: When you make connections for kids, it has more meaning and it sticks with them."

The teaching is project-based, so kids do explorations within each unit. They develop expertise on a topic, and every 12 weeks they do a presentation to showcase what they've learned. That motivates them to learn, while teaching them how to speak in front of a group.

The school takes only seven weeks off in the summer, two in the fall, two in the winter, and two in the spring; it offers ten more days than a normal IPS school. Any child not at grade level stays for an additional week during the spring and fall breaks, to work in a small group.

* * *

IT IS FAR too early to judge the results of the innovation network schools, and test scores are no help, because the state changed its test in 2015 and its vendor in 2016. But there are glimmers of hope in attendance data. The first restart, Phalen Leadership Academy 103, saw its enrollment increase by 17 percent in its first year and 15 percent in its second. In the two innovation schools that opened as restarts in 2016, enrollment was up by 20 percent at Global Prep Academy and 27 percent at Kindezi Academy.

As of 2016–17, more than 10 percent of IPS students attended nine innovation network schools, six of which were also charter schools. That percentage will increase as these nine build out their grade levels and four more innovation schools launch in August 2017. Another year or two at that pace and a full quarter of IPS's students will be in innovation schools.

Meanwhile, Superintendent Ferebee has announced a three-year plan to close several existing IPS high schools. In his first three years, Ferebee estimates, IPS has weeded out 56 percent of its failing schools. "My philosophy is this," he says:

> *You can have a bad year, but we know those schools, and they exist all across the nation, where every year is a bad year. The outcomes and challenges of those situations are very steep to overcome for the students and their families. It's typically the neighborhood schools, where students are required to attend. That's a social justice issue, an equity issue. I am of the belief that we get students out of those situations by any means necessary.*

There are constant problems to be worked out, acknowledges Aleesia Johnson, a former KIPP principal who oversees the innovation network for Ferebee. Will there be enough money to support the growing number of innovation schools? And what does IPS do with teachers the innovation schools don't want? The teachers' contract doesn't let the district lay people off if their school is replaced by an innovation school. So far, most of them have found positions at other IPS schools. But when IPS gets to 20 innovation schools, what will it do with surplus teachers? Right now, if principals at traditional schools still have vacancies the first day of school, they are forced to take surplus teachers. Unless that policy is changed, the expansion of innovation schools could undermine other IPS schools by forcing inferior teachers on them.

Johnson has confidence that they'll figure it out. Dr. Ferebee has "created the mindset, 'Figure out how we can do it.' It's never, 'No, we can't do that.' It's, 'Oh, we've never done that, so let's talk about it and figure out how to get it done.'"

"This is all so new," she adds. "We believe we can be a proof point for the country, quite honestly, but we're still new."

Other Initiatives to Create a 21st Century System

Ferebee and the board are rolling out a series of other initiatives. They have created a category of "autonomous schools," which get more control over their budgets and hiring than traditional IPS schools but remain within the teachers union contract. In the first year, Ferebee chose six of the eight schools that applied for the new status. He sees autonomous status in part as a transition for principals before they pursue innovation status. He won't force autonomy on principals, he says, but he'll give them all they want. Indeed, in late 2016 he decided to extend budget autonomy to every IPS school. His long-term goal, supported by the board, is to convert all IPS schools to autonomous or innovation status.

IPS also has a contract with a school turnaround organization called Mass Insight to work with two failing high schools and their feeder middle and elementary schools, in what they call a "transformation zone." These schools were all at risk of state takeover, according to Mary Ann Sullivan, president of the school board. Ferebee has given them some degree of autonomy, and they are developing teacher leaders who teach part-time and coach other teachers in their subject matter and grade levels, through a national initiative called the Opportunity Culture, run by Public Impact.

IPS is planning a unified enrollment system for all public schools in the city, including the independent charters, as in Denver, New Orleans, and Washington, D.C. In 2017–18 the district is shifting to weighted student budgeting, in which most of the money allocated for children follows them to the school and the principal and staff decide how to use it. Students living in poverty bring greater resources. IPS is also working with the mayor's office and state charter board to develop a "common performance framework," by which all public schools will be measured. Aleesia Johnson explains that not all schools will be held accountable for the same things, but there will be a common measuring stick, to help parents make their choices.

Finally, The Mind Trust, IPS, and the mayor's office are working on "equity reports," modeled on those in Washington, D.C. They will cover all charter, innovation, autonomous, and traditional schools. If they follow D.C.'s format, they will give people information about schools' attendance rates, suspension and expulsion rates, midyear entries and departures, standardized test scores, and graduation rates, broken down by gender, race, poverty levels, and special education status.

If all these plans are realized, most public schools in Indianapolis will have the autonomy they need to succeed, parents will have choices and good information with which to make those choices, and schools that lag behind will be replaced by stronger models. Like New Orleans and Washington, D.C.'s charter sector, Indianapolis will have a self-renewing system in which every school has incentives and the autonomy to continuously innovate and improve.

The innovation network schools are the most promising of the in-district autonomous schools around the country, in my opinion, because they start with true charter-like autonomy. The model does have one flaw, however: IPS will try to steer and row at the same time. It will steer the entire district while operating some schools and employing their staffs. Doing both well is difficult, because operating schools tends to consume all the leaders' energy. And when schools full of IPS employees compete with independent schools for students, buildings, and funds, will the elected school board be able to treat them equally? If IPS employees get angry, will the board be tempted to go easier on their schools?

If it can treat them equally—if IPS holds all schools accountable for performance, replaces those that fail, and replicates those that succeed—the innovation schools could change the district's performance dramatically. And if they prove to be a viable alternative to independent charters, they might have enormous impact nationwide. In most places, it is far easier, politically, to create in-district innovation schools than independent charter schools.

The risk is that the independent charter sector in Indianapolis will stop expanding, because charter operators can get a better financial deal as IPS innovation schools. Then, after the political winds shift or there is some kind of scandal at an innovation school, the board could nibble away at their autonomy. Each school has a contract, which will protect it for a few years. But a hostile board could refuse to renew contracts or allow continued use of its buildings. It would take a change in state law to undermine independent charters, but to undermine innovation schools, all it would take is a reversal of the school board majority. In other words, charter schools' autonomy is protected by law; innovation schools' autonomy is subject to shifting political winds.

For now, the majority on the school board for reform is solid. Although anti-reform activists from two groups, Concerned Clergy and OurIPS, ran candidates for all four board seats up for reelection in November 2016, they fell far short. Reformers backed by Stand For Children won three of the seats, and a former board president who falls somewhere between the two camps won the fourth.

The next few years will be critical: If IPS can produce results, the sky is the limit. Indianapolis is fortunate to have a superintendent who knows, from his personal experience, the value of giving principals and schools autonomy and holding them accountable for results—a rare commodity in the world of superintendents. His presence, and the board that hired him, make Indianapolis a city to watch.

Rockin' and Rollin' in Memphis

Since Tennessee legislated its Achievement School District (ASD) into existence in 2010, Memphis has followed in New Orleans's footsteps. Modeled after Louisiana's Recovery School District, it has turned some 26 failing Memphis schools over to charter operators. The legislature also allowed districts to create innovation zones for low-performing schools and grant them significant flexibilities, to help turn them around. Memphis seized the opportunity, and by 2016–17, roughly 30 percent of the city's public school students attended charter or innovation schools.

The ASD can take over schools that score in the bottom 5 percent on state tests. By 2016, ASD schools in Memphis educated about 12,000 students. They will stay in the ASD for at least ten years, at which point they will return to Shelby County Schools—if they perform in the top 25 percent statewide.

In 2012, when the state put together its list of these "priority schools," 69 of the 85 were in Memphis. That "was like someone had pulled the fire alarm and we all needed to pitch in," says Chris Barbic, the ASD's first director. "It was this rallying call for everybody to come together."

Four years later, Memphis's Shelby County Schools (SCS) authorized 45 charters and had 21 innovation zone schools it treated somewhat like charters. The ASD authorized 26 charters and five direct-run schools in Memphis, which it operated much like charters. Of 205 public schools in the city, in other words, 97 operated with significant autonomy and accountability.

As in most cities, Memphis's charters outperform traditional public schools. The 2015 CREDO study found that from 2006–7 through 2011–12 charter students in Memphis gained almost two thirds of a year of learning in reading, compared to demographically similar students with similar past test scores in traditional public schools, and more than half a year in math, *every year.* Charters have also had lower attrition rates and higher graduation rates. Four of the six charter high schools had graduation rates of 90 percent or higher in 2013; a fifth was just below 90, and the sixth was at 75 percent. SCS high schools averaged 75 percent.

In early 2016 the district board voted to adopt a district-charter compact and create an advisory committee to improve collaboration. That committee is working on resource issues, such as the use of facilities and the location of new schools, and developing a common performance scorecard to rate the quality of all schools.

Unlike Memphis's other charters, ASD charters are neighborhood schools, not schools of choice. And many ASD charters have taken over entire student bodies, rather than starting one or two grades at a time. Most of these struggled during their first years with high student turnover and discipline issues, but later thrived. Tennessee's Value-Added Assessment System (TVAAS), which measures student growth while factoring in socioeconomic status, rates schools on a scale of one (slowest growth) to five (fastest). In 2016 the state's new online tests ran into technological problems, so the most recent data at this writing is from the spring of 2015. That year second- and third-year ASD schools averaged level 5, but first-year schools averaged level 1.

In addition to SCS charters and the ASD, the third leg of the 21st century stool in Memphis is the district's innovation zone, or iZone, which by 2016–17 included 21 schools. The district lengthened their school day by an hour, using federal School Improvement Grant funds to pay for it. After that money ran out in 2015, it turned to grants, donations, and the regular district budget.

District leaders recruited their best principals to take over iZone schools and gave them the authority to hire staff, and those principals recruited the best teachers they knew. Teachers could earn bonuses for improved student performance, and their schools provided intensive support and coaching. Principals were not constrained by union contracts, because Tennessee teachers no longer have collective bargaining rights. All teachers had to reapply for their jobs once their school entered the iZone, a reality that led to hundreds of layoffs. But once a teacher was hired and had tenure, firing was still difficult.

There were other limits on autonomy: Principals didn't control most of their budgets, and they could choose their own curricula and assessments only if their first-year test scores were above a certain threshold. Antonio Burt, then principal of Ford Road Elementary, told me he had only about half of the important autonomies a charter principal would enjoy. He didn't have the budgetary freedom to put aides in every classroom, for instance. He wanted a full-time psychologist, but the district gave him one only one day a week. He needed an operations manager but couldn't move money to fund that position. He had no power to replace his custodial staff. And when he took over his school it needed repainting, but he could not move funds to have it done—so he and the teachers did it. If he had all the autonomy he needed, he said, "I could do some amazing things."

Despite the limitations, iZone schools have shown impressive results. For their first two years they showed faster academic growth than the ASD schools, but in 2014–15 the ASD outpaced them. By 2016, seven iZone schools had improved enough to jump off the priority list. Four of seven elementary schools and five of seven middle schools were on track to be among the top quarter of schools in the state, on test scores, within five years.

Unfortunately, the results came at the expense of schools that lost principals and teachers to the iZone. As John Buntin reported in *Governing*, "While iZone students showed big gains in test scores, the schools that iZone principals and teachers had left behind showed declines. The benefits of good leadership and good teaching had seemingly just been redistributed from one group of schools to another."

Still, the combination of the iZone and the ASD has given Memphis a more aggressive strategy to deal with its worst public schools than almost any other city. Of the 69 priority schools identified in Memphis in 2012, only a handful had escaped some intervention by 2017: 31 had been taken over by the ASD, 21 had been moved into the iZone, and 13 had been either closed or consolidated with other schools. A Center on Reinventing Public Education study published in late 2015 found that none of the Memphis schools that tested in the bottom 5 percent in reading and math stayed there for three consecutive years. Of 50 cities studied, New Orleans was the only other one with that record.

Camden and Newark, New Jersey

In 2013, the state of New Jersey took over the Camden schools. Just across the river from Philadelphia, with 80,000 residents, Camden had long been one of the poorest cities in America. Only 8 percent of adults over 25 had a four-year college degree, compared to 36 percent in the state. Violent crime rates were the highest in the nation among cities of its size. The murder rate was nearly twice that of any other city its size.

The school system was both dismal and corrupt. Before the state took over, 90 percent of its 26 schools ranked among the lowest 5 percent in the state on test scores, despite district spending of more than $25,000 per student. The four-year graduation rate was 49 percent, compared to 86 percent statewide.

Two local Democratic Party leaders, George and Donald Norcross, had long advocated for charters, which by 2012 educated a quarter of the city's public school students. That year Donald Norcross, a state legislator, sponsored the Urban Hope Act, which provided funding for school renovation and construction to failing districts that created "renaissance schools"—charter schools that replaced failing schools but continued to operate with neighborhood boundaries.

State leaders hired Paymon Rouhanifard, a 32-year-old Iranian-American who had spent three years working for Chancellor Joel Klein in New York City, to run the district. Rouhanifard put together a plan that would award up to 16 renaissance schools to KIPP, Uncommon Schools, and Mastery Schools, an outstanding charter network from Philadelphia that already had schools open in Camden. He also launched a unified enrollment system for any family that did not want its children to attend a neighborhood school. If carried through, Rouhanifard's plan would put more than 13,000 of the city's 16,000 students in charters. It was hard to argue with him: Fewer than a third of test takers attended charters in 2014–15, yet they made up more than two thirds of those who scored "proficient" or above.

By 2016, surveys showed that students felt safer in their schools, and the dropout rate was down from 21 percent in 2011–12 to 12 percent. Proficiency rates in English language arts had risen 17 points at KIPP's renaissance schools, 24 points at Uncommon Schools' Camden Prep, and five points at four Mastery renaissance schools. Camden still had long way to go, but serious opposition had not surfaced, and the city appeared poised to follow New Orleans down the path toward a nearly all-charter district.

An earlier state takeover did not fare so well in Newark, Jew Jersey. As *Washington Post* reporter Dale Russakoff described in her book, *The Prize*, aggressive reforms under state-appointed superintendent Cami Anderson triggered a huge political backlash. When Governor Chris Christie decided to run for president, in the spring of 2015, he cut a deal with newly elected mayor Ras Baraka to hand control back to the local district. In 2016 and 2017, after charter supporters registered more than 3,000 parents of charter students to vote, Baraka backed "unity slates" that included charter advocates for the advisory board, which may take control in 2017–18. Both states won all open seats, so they control six of nine seats. By then, 30 percent of Newark's public school students were in charters, which were among the strongest in the nation, according to CREDO data. Though charters received roughly 83 percent of district funding per student, their students gained 168 days of learning per year in math and a full school year in reading every year, compared to students with similar demographics and past test scores in traditional Newark public schools. It will be interesting to watch what direction the city's new school board takes.

The Cleveland Plan for Transforming Schools

Cleveland Metropolitan School District (CMSD) has long been among the lowest-performing big-city districts in the nation. In 2013, it scored 20th of 21 large cities that took NAEP tests. Only 13 percent of public school students tested "proficient" or higher, compared to a national average of 29.5 percent for cities with more than 250,000 residents. Among Ohio districts, Cleveland ranked 608th out of 611 in academic performance. Even charters, which educated almost a third of the city's public school students, showed mixed results. Authorized by more than ten different "sponsors," they included both strong and weak schools, and their sponsors let both kinds survive year after year.

By 2011, the district was in financial crisis, and it needed only one more F rating from the state to trigger a takeover. Democratic Mayor Frank Johnson, who appoints the school board, asked the newly elected Republican governor, John Kasich, to let him come up with a plan to turn things around. The mayor pulled together the business community, the district, several major foundations, and a coalition of high-performing charters called Breakthrough Schools. They examined what was working in other cities, then crafted a plan to turn Cleveland into a portfolio district. In Superintendent Eric Gordon's words, their plan would "completely reinvent a school system governed by laws and workplace rules designed for another era.

> Prior to the Cleveland Plan, CMSD had evolved into a bureaucratic, standardized, tightly controlled school system that, from its central office, managed everything in its schools, from staffing to scheduling, curriculum, operations and budgets. The result? A system where no one, not a teacher, not a principal, not a central office administrator, not even the CEO, felt empowered to take the actions needed to improve outcomes for kids. No one felt accountable for results in a system that didn't allow anyone to make decisions and be responsible for them.

The Cleveland Plan called for:

- Replacing failing schools with stronger magnet and charter schools
- Shifting control of nearly 70 percent of the resources from the central office to the schools
- Focusing the central office on governance and support rather than school operations
- Creating a Cleveland Transformation Alliance, chaired by the mayor, with the power to rate schools, close charters that were performing poorly, and replace them with better schools
- Reforming district teacher evaluations, seniority, tenure, and pay policies, lengthening the school day and year, increasing preschool, and recruiting stronger teachers and school leaders

To finance the plan, the mayor proposed a 15 mill increase in the property tax, to produce $85 million a year. It quickly passed, and the mayor shared

$5.7 of the $85 million, as well as facilities, with 17 charters that partnered with the city. In return, the district got to count their scores and graduation rates in district totals. The goal was to triple the number of students in high-quality seats by 2018.

Although the legislature passed most of the plan, it refused to give the Transformation Alliance power to close charter schools. Three years later, reformers finally got a state law passed amending the charter statute, to crack down on authorizers sponsoring low-quality charters. After it passed, seven charter schools in Cleveland closed in the next 12 months. In 2016 the state rated 21 sponsors "poor," which began the process of removing their authority to sponsor.

Superintendent Gordon has embraced the district's partnership with charters. Like Tom Boasberg in Denver, he is publicly agnostic about school type: He says he wants high-quality schools and doesn't care if they are district or charter schools. Enrollment is rising for the first time in decades, and the four-year graduation rate is up from 56 percent in 2012 to 69 percent in 2016. (The five-year rate reached 74 percent in 2016.) Test scores are still low, but academic growth is encouraging: By 2015 Cleveland had risen from 578th to 254th out of 611 districts in academic growth, based on the state's value-added measures. On the 2015 NAEP exam, Cleveland was one of only three big-city districts that increased its scores on all fourth- and eighth-grade math and reading tests.

Cleveland still has a long way to go if it is to follow in Denver's and Indianapolis's footsteps. But the reforms passed a political test in November 2016, when another four years of tax levy passed with more than two-thirds of the vote.

Smaller Cities and Counties

Most school districts that have moved toward 21st century models have been in big cities, where academic failure has created undeniable urgency. But a few smaller and less urban jurisdictions have also embarked on the journey. In the early 1990s, Hurricane Andrew triggered a population explosion north of Miami that left Broward County Public Schools, the nation's fifth largest district, severely overcrowded. Leaders in Pembroke Pines, a racially mixed city in the county that had 65,000 residents in 1990 but had grown to 137,000 by 2000, decided to create their own all-charter school system. Today it has four elementary schools, three middle schools, and a high school. (Broward County Public Schools still operates schools in Pembroke Pines as well.) The charters receive less per-pupil funding than Broward County schools but have consistently earned A ratings from the state, outperforming county and state averages on reading, writing, and math tests. The charter high school, though 52 percent black and Hispanic and 58 percent "economically disadvantaged" (in 2012–13), was named by *U.S. News and World Report* as one of the nation's best in 2014. Two other schools have been named National Blue Ribbon Schools of Excellence. Not surprisingly, demand is high, with a waiting list of more than 4,000 in June 2016.

Hall County, Georgia, about an hour's drive northwest of Atlanta, is a growing suburban and exurban county that had 194,000 residents in 2015, 28 percent of them Hispanic. As the population of English-language learners soared, the Hall County School District embarked on an effort to offer families "personalized education pathways that include both charter schools and programs of choice." By 2014 these included nine magnet schools, 14 selective "programs of choice" within district schools, and 12 charter schools. By 2012–13 almost a third of public school students in the county attended charters, all of them schools of choice that used lotteries if there was more demand than they could accommodate. The first, World Language Academy, was a dual-language-immersion middle school. Others focused on performing arts; project-based learning; science, technology, engineering, and math; digital citizenship; and career opportunities in hospitality, culinary arts, marketing, and cosmetology.

The list of districts moving in this direction is long. Thirty districts belong to a network of "portfolio districts" organized by the Center on Reinventing Public Education, and 19 of them have signed district-charter compacts, pledging to work together to improve education in both sectors.

Charter-Lite Models

Many districts are also attempting to reproduce charter conditions in district schools, as in Denver's, Memphis's, and Indianapolis's innovation schools. On average, these schools appear to perform a bit better than traditional schools but not as well as charters, perhaps because they don't have as much autonomy, accountability, or parental choice as charters do. Memphis is an exception, but the innovation schools' growth there has come at the expense of the public schools their leaders and teachers left behind.

Boston has tried multiple models, including in-district charters, pilot schools, innovation schools, and turnaround schools. As of 2015, almost a third of its 57,000 public school students attended these or charter schools. In general, the more autonomy Boston schools have, the more academic growth they have produced, though there are exceptions. Boston's charter schools are the strongest in the country, according to CREDO, producing 12 and 13 months a year more learning, every year, than Boston Public Schools for similar students. They have been studied intensely by a variety of researchers, and on any measure they produce far stronger results than charter-lite schools. (For more on Boston and Los Angeles, see appendix C.)

Los Angeles has even more charter-lite models than Boston. Since the early 1990s, repeated efforts have been made to decentralize the massive district and give schools much more autonomy. But district leaders have not changed the organization's underlying DNA, and the bureaucracy has always managed to reassert its central control. Still, several initiatives have survived. District schools have been converted to in-district charters, pilot schools, network partner schools, local initiative schools, and expanded school-based management models. As in Boston, independent charters perform better than all these alternatives. According to CREDO, every year their students gain 79 days of learning in math and 50 days of learning, compared to demographically similar students in district schools. Latino students living in poverty do even better in charters. In addition, 75 percent of students at charters complete the courses needed for college admission, compared to just 28 percent in district schools. Still, several charter-lite models have performed better in L.A. than traditional public schools.

Other charter-lite models continue to pop up around the country. Massachusetts took over the Lawrence Public Schools in 2012, and a state-appointed superintendent shifted significant control to the schools, raised teacher pay, and recruited high-performing principals and teachers. He created consequences by turning three of 33 schools over to charter operators and replacing half of the principals and about 10 percent of the teachers in the first two years, while also creating rewards for outstanding teachers. Although it has made only minor improvement in English-language arts, no doubt because English was not the first language for the majority of its students, the percentage of students scoring "proficient" or above in math increased from 28 in 2011 to 44 in 2015 (the last year before the state changed tests). The four-year graduation rate has also increased, from 52 percent in 2011 to 75 percent in 2015.

In Springfield, Massachusetts, the state and school district in 2014 created an Empowerment Zone Partnership, in lieu of a state takeover of failing schools. With a seven-member board appointed by both state and local officials, it assumed control over six struggling middle schools, beginning with the 2015–16 school year. The zone board negotiated a new labor agreement with the teachers union, which includes longer hours and a bit more pay, and gave teachers the right to elect leadership teams that work with the principals to run each school. The board also split two campuses into smaller schools. (After the second year, it added a failing high school and launched an Honors Academy, the district's first selective high school.)

Earlier, the zone board turned the lowest-performing school over to an in-district charter operator from Boston, UP Academy, and brought in veterans from the charter sector to restart two others, one grade per year. After the second year, it replaced two more principals. Hence all principals and teachers know that if their students don't make enough progress, they may be replaced. New operators and restart principals can hire entirely new staffs, if they choose to do so. Tenured teachers who are replaced can move to other positions in the district with the same pay, so they won't be unemployed, but they may have to become teacher's aides if no principal wants them as a full teacher.

Tulsa, Oklahoma, has negotiated a compact with the six charter schools it authorizes, and it contracts with a few outside organizations to operate alternative schools. In 2015, the state legislature passed a bill allowing large urban school districts to use outside operators to run "partnership schools," with the same flexibilities as charter schools. Tulsa's leaders have begun to use this model to bring in charter operators to run district schools.

San Antonio Independent School District is opening two dozen in-district charters and launching an as-yet-undefined innovation zone. Its leaders are also working to create partnerships with some of the 25 independent charters in the city.

Some districts that have embraced 21st century strategies—such as Philadelphia and Chicago—have later backed off. As Shakespeare wrote, "The course of true love never did run smooth." But while setbacks happen, the overall direction is clear. For every Chicago or New York, there is an Indianapolis, a Memphis, a Springfield, or a Hall County. From New Orleans to Boston, D.C. to Denver, charter schools have produced the largest broad-based increases in student performance researchers have ever seen. Teachers unions and their allies are fighting hard to stop charter expansion, but it's impossible to bottle up reforms when they produce such dramatic results.

PART V

THE KEYS TO SUCCESS

CHAPTER 12

THE DNA OF 21ST CENTURY SYSTEMS

"EDUCATION REFORM" HAS BEEN the name of the game in urban districts for more than three decades. There has been improvement, but in most places the pace has been glacial. Why? Because most districts have not pursued the reforms with the highest leverage, those that force everything else in the system to change. "Reform du jour" has been the norm, quantity more important than quality. Professor Jeffrey Henig and three colleagues, who wrote about reform in four urban districts in the 1990s in *The Color of School Reform: Race, Politics, and the Challenge of Urban Education,* put it well:

> In spite of frequent charges that the education community is reflexively resistant to innovation and reform, we find that the school systems in Atlanta, Baltimore, Detroit, and DC are virtually overrun with reform initiatives. Some of these efforts may represent political posturing or efforts to substitute the appearance of reform for the genuine article, but we find many signs of sincere efforts in which committed educators and parents are investing time, energy and emotional capital. The problem, we suggest, is less an unwillingness to try something new—in this respect school professionals seem more like gullible consumers than complacent bureaucrats—than a fragmented, episodic effort.
>
> . . . the typical pattern is for initially vibrant reform movements to sputter and run out of steam.

The late Gene Maeroff, a former *New York Times* correspondent, author of 15 books, and one-time school board president, wrote a book about reform in Syracuse and came to similar conclusions. "School reform has proved itself more difficult than getting a man on the moon," he wrote. "Failures and mixed results predominate. It puts one in mind of the exploits of Don Quixote, with reformers at times seemingly tilting at imaginary windmills."

Charles Taylor Kerchner and three academic colleagues wrote a similar account of education reform in Los Angeles. Like so many of their colleagues elsewhere, reformers in Los Angeles failed to permanently change the behavior and attitudes of the thousands of people who made up the school district. Somehow, none of their efforts got at the most fundamental pieces of district DNA.

Over the past three decades, I have researched and written about the most dramatic examples of transformation in post-bureaucratic public organizations and systems I could find, in multiple countries and at every level of the public sector. I have constantly asked: What strategies made the most difference? What pieces of DNA had to be changed to get fundamentally different behavior? In the answers I have received, the patterns have been striking. Whether in public education, the Department of Defense, city government, or state government, the fundamental DNA of bureaucracy is the same—which means the strategies required to transform it are the same.

Traditional public bureaucracies centralize authority, organize in hierarchies, use rules to control behavior, avoid competition, treat those they serve as dependents, not customers, and produce standardized services for mass markets. A century ago, bureaucracy was perhaps the most effective form of organization possible, given the low levels of education in the workplace, the communication technologies available, and the expectations of the public. But in the Information Age, these bureaucracies are dinosaurs. They are too slow, too rigid, too inward-looking, and too indifferent to the quality of their performance. They frustrate a public accustomed to choices and quality service from the private sector—where the most innovative firms have moved beyond bureaucracy, to new forms of organization.

In *Banishing Bureaucracy*, Peter Plastrik and I explained the five fundamental strategies that we found reformers using to reinvent their bureaucracies, around the globe. We called them the five C's: the core, consequences, customer, control, and culture strategies. By now they no doubt sound familiar, because well-run charter systems embody all five. In this book I have been careful to highlight both aspects of the core strategy—contestability and clarity of purpose and role—because both are so important in 21st century education systems. I have also discussed another strategy that becomes central when the task is as difficult as educating poor, inner-city children: creating talent pipelines and building the capacity of school leaders and personnel. This strategy—though always useful—is less critical in many public functions, because average public servants operating in 21st century systems can perform well. But inner-city schools are extremely challenging terrain, so I have lifted capacity building up as a key strategy.

The Seven Key Strategies

I believe there are seven strategies that hold the key to transforming performance in urban school systems, that have the most *power* to drive improvement. Think of them as the seven C's of 21st century education systems:

1. Creating *clarity* of purpose and role by separating steering from rowing, so those doing each can concentrate on their core purposes.
2. Creating *contestability*, so no public school has a right to continue if it consistently fails its students.
3. Creating *consequences* for performance, through competition, rewards, and penalties.
4. Empowering *customers* by giving them choices of different kinds of schools, with public dollars following their choices.
5. Decentralizing *control* over operations (but not steering), to give those running schools the authority they need to succeed.
6. Using this freedom to transform the *culture* of public schools.
7. Boosting the *capacity* of school leaders, teachers, and other staff.

Others have come to similar conclusions. William Ouchi, the UCLA business professor and author of *Theory Z, Making Schools Work*, and *The Secret of TSL*, studied a number of school districts and concluded that the keys to high performance were school autonomy, school choice, accountability for performance, weighted student budgeting (which heightens both school autonomy and competition), and the development of effective principals. Since he was studying traditional districts, not 21st century districts, he missed the critical importance of separating steering and rowing.

Amanda Ripley studied three countries—Finland, Poland, and South Korea—that had some of the highest scores on the PISA exam, which stresses critical thinking and problem solving. Her book, *The Smartest Kids in the World*, pinpointed clarity of purpose, cultures of high expectations, and high-quality teachers as three of the keys to success. She added "more accountability for results, while granting more autonomy for methods. That dynamic could be found in all countries that dramatically improve their results, including Finland and, for that matter, in every high-performing organization, from the US Coast Guard to Apple Inc." Like Ouchi, she found all of the C's except those involving separation of steering and rowing—since none of her three countries had taken that step.

Charles Glenn, an education professor at Boston University, and Jan De Groof, a Belgian professor of comparative educational law and policy, are the editors of *Balancing Freedom, Autonomy, and Accountability in Education*, which has chapters on 65 countries. In summing up their findings, Glenn quoted a chapter by the Harvard education professor Martin West and the German economist Ludger Woessmann. They had come to similar conclusions: "Studies using student-level data from multiple international achievement tests reveal that institutions ensuring competition, autonomy, and accountability within national school systems are associated with substantially higher levels of student performance."

The Dutch are rated near the top, for instance. They have high national standards, significant autonomy for schools, and full school choice, and they employ many different models, from publicly funded but privately run religious schools to Montessori programs, from Waldorf schools to career and technical high schools. There is so much choice that groups of parents can demand that the government create and fund a new school for their children. Schools are held accountable through competition for both students and funding and through qualitative school assessments, while students must pass standardized tests in multiple subjects to graduate from high school. "In some ways," wrote one American observer, "the educational system in the Netherlands, a country that's comparable in size to Massachusetts and Connecticut combined and serves a population of 17 million people, functions like a group of 8,000 charter schools."

In the United Kingdom, Prime Minister David Cameron, in a national televised 2015 address to his party, urged the British to convert their entire public school system to academies, the British version of charter schools.

We are not alone in learning the lessons taught by well-run charter systems, then. And if we fail to embrace those lessons, our education systems will fall even further behind those of our foreign competitors.

Creating Clarity of Purpose and Role
by Separating Steering and Rowing

Cathy Mincberg, a veteran of 14 years on Houston's school board, recently expressed her frustration at being responsible for both steering and rowing—setting direction and policy for a large school district while also operating schools. Her observations are worth quoting at length:

> School boards have a difficult task. They are expected to oversee a vast number of details for their districts: handle business operations, decide which e-tablets to buy, keep constituents happy, and spend hundreds of hours dealing with such mundane issues as choosing between paper towels and hand dryers for school restrooms. It's no wonder school boards find it hard to focus on what really matters . . .

> *More and more, school board members feel as if they're running on hamster wheels. They must jump from subject to subject and are expected to either contribute an educated opinion or just trust the administration's recommendations. School boards . . . spend huge amounts of time talking about what they know or can easily grasp, such as how long a student's suspension should be. But the difficult discussions— how to reduce the dropout rate or implement meaningful professional development—get short shrift.*
>
> *We have charged school boards with an overwhelming responsibility, and consequently, they cannot make real progress for their districts.*

In New Orleans and Washington, D.C.'s charter sector, by contrast, boards and superintendents no longer have to operate schools and employ thousands of staff. They don't have to worry about e-tablets or paper towels. Their role is clear: to focus on their core purpose, improving student outcomes. They have time to address the issues that get in the way of progress: how to create enrollment systems that prevent "creaming" of the best students and give poor families an equal shot at quality schools; how to ensure that students with disabilities find programs that fit their needs; how to offer educational programs that engage all students, whether they are college bound or not. They can even figure out how to use enrollment systems to boost racial and economic integration, or how to fund new birth-to-five initiatives to help poor families better prepare their children for school. Free of rowing obligations, they can devote their full attention to steering.

And they can do so with far fewer employees than traditional districts. The charter board in D.C. does an outstanding job with 38 employees (as of 2017), while the central administration in DCPS has 902.

In an effective 21st century system, those doing the steering play four key roles: authorizing, regulating, managing resources, and speaking up for the needs of families and children.

Authorizing functions include:

- Negotiating, approving, and renewing charters
- Holding school operators accountable by measuring and reviewing their performance
- Revoking charters and replacing failing schools
- Making sure that children get access to better schools when theirs are closed
- Making sure there is capacity to handle students when a school suddenly closes during the school year
- Replicating and expanding successful schools

- Adjusting supply to demand—for example, by filling niches in the market with new schools

Regulating ensures equity of access to schools, resources, and opportunities by:

- Establishing the rules of the game regarding choice, neighborhood schools, the admissions process, student transfers, transportation, discipline, accounting, purchasing, measurement of performance, provision of information to parents and others, adjudication of disputes, and meeting the needs of special populations such as students with disabilities, English-language learners, gifted and talented students, and former dropouts
- Enforcing compliance with these policies and rules—for instance, to prevent schools from discouraging or pushing out students they don't want, and to prevent self-dealing (self- enrichment of those who control the school, contracting with family members for transportation and other services, and the like)

Managing resources means making sure schools have what they need to succeed:

- Creating a funding formula that provides adequate resources to educate each kind of student (including those with severe disabilities) at each level of schools (elementary, middle, and high, plus alternative, adult, and preschools, if they are included in the system)
- Ensuring that adequate facilities are available to all schools
- Ensuring that support services schools need are available to them
- Ensuring that schools have an adequate supply of effective personnel (teachers, school leaders, psychologists, and so on) available to them
- Ensuring that systemwide resources needed are available, such as health insurance and pensions or 401(K) accounts for school staff
- Securing any new revenues needed to make these things happen or to provide new services or schools, such as preschools or adult schools

Speaking up for the needs of families and children involves:

- Lobbying the state legislature to change laws when necessary—to equalize funding between charters and traditional schools, for instance, or to give charters access to existing public school buildings and/or public funding for facilities

- Lobbying for more resources for schools or for steering, when necessary
- Bringing leaders and institutions in the community together to address problems and opportunities that the schools cannot address on their own, such as providing mental health services
- Lobbying public and private sector leaders to create new supports for children and families, such as support for poor families beginning at the birth of their children, free tuition for low-income high school graduates at public institutions of higher education, or apprenticeships for those who want to learn a trade

State legislation must not only empower charter authorizers to play these roles, but also restrict their ability to step over the line into micromanagement of schools, as Paul Hill and Ashsley Jochim point out in their book, *A Democratic Constitution for Public Education*. We need the kind of checks and balances Louisiana worked out in its legislation to return RSD schools to the Orleans Parish School Board (pp. 76–7).

Early in the evolution of charter schools many advocates pushed hard for states and cities to have multiple authorizers, so the supply of charters would not be choked off by one stingy authorizer. Some advocates still argue this case. If a traditional school district is the only authorizer, having another makes perfect sense, since most districts are leery of charter schools, which take students and money away from their own schools. But experience has shown that having more than two authorizers doesn't work so well, for two reasons. First, when there are multiple authorizers no one has the power to steer, so citywide needs often remain unaddressed and problems unsolved. Second, when one authorizer revokes a school's charter, the school may be able to shop for a more lenient authorizer and stay open. Both of these problems have bedeviled cities in Michigan and Ohio, although Ohio may have ameliorated them with 2015 reform legislation. CREDO's first national charter study, in 2009, noted this phenomenon: "States that empower multiple entities to act as charter school authorizers realize significantly lower growth in academic learning in their students, on the order of -.08 standard deviations. While more research is needed into the causal mechanism, it appears that charter school operators are able to identify and choose the more permissive entity to provide them oversight."

We have seen how effective one authorizer can be in Washington, D.C.— although it has required collaboration with DCPS, which has sometimes resisted. Massachusetts, New Jersey, and D.C. have all had one authorizer for some time, and New Orleans has had only two. According to CREDO studies, their charter sectors are among the highest-performing in the country.

The ideal situation appears to be one authorizer in a city, with appeals possible to another body—such as a state board—if a charter school feels its application was denied unfairly or it was closed for the wrong reasons. CREDO's 2009 study also found evidence to support the value of such appeals: "Where state charter legislation provides an avenue for appeals of adverse decisions on applications or renewals, students realize a small but significant gain in learning, about .02 standard deviations."

Cities with multiple authorizers need some way to create unified steering capacity, either through coordination, as the RSD and OPSB finally managed in New Orleans, or by creating a board or commission with the power to oversee authorizers and make steering decisions for the system. In recent years, district leaders in both Detroit and Cleveland have tried but failed to get their state legislatures to create such commissions. In Michigan, the state charter association opposed the effort, because most of its members worried that the commission, to be appointed by the mayor, would favor traditional district schools. Charter advocates in Ohio similarly opposed giving Cleveland's Transformation Alliance the authority to close failing charters. Though there may have been good reasons for the misgivings in both cases, the charter community should welcome effective steering bodies. Otherwise, failing charters will survive and problems that discredit charters will remain unaddressed.

Creating Contestability, So Failing Schools Are Replaced

As I have repeatedly pointed out, those doing the steering in traditional districts are often politically captive of their employees in the schools. Turnout of voters to elect members of school boards is notoriously low, often below 10 percent. If reformers on a board get enough employees riled up, they risk defeat. And there is no better way to get them riled up than to eliminate their jobs by replacing their schools.

As the examples in this book show, this is not the case in 21st century systems. Once there are enough charter operators, replacing a failing school with a better one becomes fairly easy. There are still losers in one school, but there are also winners throughout the system. In New Orleans, D.C., Denver, and Indianapolis, failing charters are regularly replaced with little public protest.

Not so in most traditional districts. Denver and D.C. have become exceptions, but it took Denver almost a decade to reach the point where it could close traditional schools without much fuss, and Kaya Henderson managed to close 15 schools in D.C. only after spending an entire year working with the community to get its input and prepare it for the change. Nor would reformers have ever reached that point without luck—namely, that Nate Easley broke with his union backers after he was elected in Denver, and that Mayor Gray did not undo most of Michelle Rhee's reforms in D.C. Otherwise reform in both cities would have ended in 2010.

When those steering do not employ those rowing, in contrast, they have the political freedom to do what is best for children, including replacing failed schools. That changes everything—which brings us to the next strategy.

Creating Consequences for Performance

In a typical public school, everyone knows there are a few problems. There might be a fourth-grade teacher with tenure who shouldn't be teaching because he doesn't like kids, or a high school chemistry and physics teacher who is senile. Perhaps no one is really teaching children to write well—or perhaps some teachers are, but they stress creativity and skip grammar and punctuation.

These aren't hypothetical problems; I've encountered each one in a school I or my children attended. In a typical public school, no one does anything to solve these problems. Removing a tenured teacher for performance is impossible in some states. In others it takes hundreds of hours of work over several years, involving careful documentation, then a grievance filed by the union, and finally multiple appeals. And fixing a school's approach to something like writing requires the cooperation and commitment of many teachers over a long period of time. The adults in the building know there will be no negative consequences for them if they simply ignore the problem—so nine times out of ten, they do.

The dynamics are entirely different when all the adults know the school could be replaced and everyone could lose their jobs. Most of the time, people find a way to come together and solve problems.

Al Shanker, the long-time American Federation of Teachers president who helped birth the charter idea, understood the importance of consequences. "Something has to be at stake," he said in 1991.

> *There is, in other fields. Your organization could fail. People in these fields dislike change too. But they have to do it. We in education don't, because for us nothing is at stake. If our kids do brilliantly nothing particularly good happens. And if we don't push we can count on remaining popular with our colleagues . . . We have got to deal with this question of consequences for adults. Educators are simply not going to take the risks of change, against the pressures of everyday popular feelings, unless they have to.*

Shanker was right. But it's not just the threat of negative consequences that improves schools; it's also the possibility of positive consequences. In New Orleans, D.C., Denver, Indianapolis, Memphis, and Camden, people running schools know that if they succeed, they may be able to expand and/or replicate their school. For those who care about educating children, this is a handsome reward.

Many believe that failing schools can be turned around if we just give them enough money and support, and occasionally that does happen. But as study after study shows, most such efforts fail. It has been far more effective to *replace* a failing school with a better one. Doing so every year yields continuous improvement.

Many also assume that we should hold individual *teachers* accountable for student learning, but in reality it is far more effective to hold *schools* accountable. Since President Obama's Race to the Top competition made teacher evaluation systems based in part on academic growth a central requirement of winning, most states have mandated them. Making teachers accountable for the success of their students is a laudable goal, but it hasn't worked very well. In state after state, less than 1 percent of teachers continue to be rated "unsatisfactory." Meanwhile, the mandates triggered a fierce backlash against standardized tests, led by teachers.

Top-down mandates simply aren't very effective. Often school personnel jump through hoops to comply with rules without truly embracing their purpose. But even where local leaders have embraced teacher evaluation, as in D.C. Public Schools, charters have performed better with no such mandate.

Neerav Kingsland, the former head of New Schools for New Orleans, points out that roughly 4 percent of charter schools close each year and 7 percent are closed during formal evaluations, whereas only 2 percent of teachers are terminated every year and less than 1 percent are rated in the lowest evaluation category. Why? Human nature:

> *Charter schools are evaluated by outside entities that are separated by governance structures. Teachers are evaluated by their bosses, who work with them every day. As a manager, I get it. It's very difficult to give extremely low ratings to employees, especially those you don't plan on firing. It's still hard, but less difficult, to review the performance of an entire organization that exists at an arm's length from you.*
>
> *This is one reason among many that legislative mandated accountability is best implemented at the organizational level rather than at the employee level. Quite simply: It is more congruent with human nature.*

Data, logic, and experience all suggest that states and districts should hold *schools* accountable for performance and let them figure out how to hold their teachers accountable. This is true for several reasons, in addition to human nature.

First, teacher quality is important, but mandating penalties and rewards for individual teachers risks undermining their morale. Indeed, it appears that evaluation mandates did just that: according to a MetLife survey of teachers, between 2008 and 2012 the percentage of teachers "very satisfied" with their jobs fell from 62 to 39, the lowest level in a quarter century.

Second, the shibboleth that teacher quality is the single most important element of school success, though suggested by academic studies, is probably false. None of the studies consider school design as one of the alternate drivers of success. Instead, they take school design—the traditional ways schools are run and teaching is done—as a given. But school design is crucial, as those who run effective charter schools know.

Like other institutions, public schools are perfectly designed to produce the results they achieve. Unless we redesign them, we will continue to get those results. The success of charter schools has largely been a success of redesign: longer school years and days, advisories, blended learning, project-based learning, student internships, intensive tutoring, new approaches to discipline, and dozens of other design innovations.

But individual teachers cannot redesign schools. That requires a team. We want teachers working together to improve their schools, not working alone to get higher evaluations than their peers. We want the gifted ones to share their magic, not hoard it. Just as in many team sports, the quality of a school's teamwork is usually more important than the individual quality of its stars.

But without a mandated evaluation system, how can we be sure that schools weed out the failing teachers? Not a problem. Where charter authorizers weed out failing schools, most schools routinely weed out their weaker teachers. And surprisingly to some, other teachers are usually happy to see the weak links go.

Finally, cookie-cutter evaluation methods push schools to do cookie-cutter teaching. Would traditional evaluation work for project-based education, in which teachers are more coaches than instructors? How about for student internships, or personalized learning? "For blended-learning teachers, the problem with many teacher evaluation systems is that they assume too narrow a concept of teachers' roles and of effective teaching practices," says Thomas Arnett of the Clayton Christensen Institute, which promotes innovations in education. They simply don't apply to the many ways teaching is done in innovative schools.

Giving "Customers" a Choice of Different Schools

There are many reasons why public school choice improves student outcomes. For starters, those who are able to choose their school often show more commitment to it. Furthermore, all parents should have the freedom to get their children out of bad situations, whether the problem is bullying, violence, cliques, frequently disrupted classes, or schools with poor teaching. Most parents who can afford it choose, by moving into a neighborhood with good schools or sending their children to private schools. Low-income parents deserve the right to choose as well.

But even more fundamental, different children flourish in different environments. Students arrive at school with different backgrounds, different interests, different forms of intelligence, and different learning styles, but traditional schools treat most of them the same. "With its model of courses and classes school is a kind of batch-processing," writes Ted Kolderie, "a bus rolling down the highway with 30+ students on board, moving too fast for some and too slowly for others. An adult points out interesting and important things along the way. But there is no opportunity for a student to get off to explore what she finds intriguing."

The Harvard psychologist Howard Gardner established that different people have different forms of intelligence, which he described as linguistic, logical-mathematical, spatial, bodily-kinesthetic, musical, interpersonal, intrapersonal, and naturalist. The Ball Foundation and psychologists at the University of Minnesota developed the Ball Aptitude Battery, which measures different aptitudes, such as speed, accuracy, motor skills, memory, reasoning, vocabulary, numerical computation, numerical reasoning, spatial aptitude ("visualization"), and creativity.

In addition to different intelligences and aptitudes, students have different learning styles. A minority of people are conceptual, abstract thinkers, who do well learning from books. Others are verbal learners, who learn by talking things through, or visual learners. Children also have different noncognitive skills, such as persistence, self-control, curiosity, and self-confidence. Some can sit still and listen for much of the day; others learn far better if they are active. They also come from different backgrounds: cultural, linguistic, socioeconomic, and psychological. Finally, boys and girls mature at different ages; their brains are ready for complex subjects at different stages.

If our schools treat most children the same, the outcomes are bound to be very different. But there is a way out. There are dozens of different kinds of schools already in existence, as the box on pages 235–7 shows. When families can choose one that fits best, their children are less likely to resist school and more likely to be motivated. When children land in the right school, they can blossom in surprising ways. Look at Troy Simon, who went from being a troublemaker who could barely read in middle school to a lover of literature at Sci Academy in New Orleans and Bard College (see pp. 47–8). And when communities can help choose which model they would prefer to replace a failing school, as in New Orleans and Denver, parents are more likely to feel committed.

Of course, for many families the best choice is a neighborhood school to which their children can walk, particularly in elementary school. Because this is true, most 21st century districts have either reserved half their seats in K–8 schools for those who live nearby, as New Orleans does, or have designated some of their charter schools to be neighborhood schools with geographic attendance zones, as Denver, Indianapolis, Memphis, and Camden do.

Different School Models

By Pedagogical Approach:

- Project-based education encourages active learning through projects, at times in the community outside school
- Community schools include "wrap-around" social services for students and families, such as health care, psychological counseling, and parent education
- "No-excuses" schools usually have longer school days and years, high expectations, an incentive structure with clear rewards and punishments, and an unrelenting focus on college
- Competency-based learning allows children to move on not when the teacher does or the calendar flips over but when they prove they have mastered particular content
- Personalized learning usually involves educational software to help students learn content at their own pace; it is often combined with competency-based learning
- International Baccalaureate schools offer rigorous, exam-based curricula that help develop language abilities, international understanding, and critical thinking
- Montessori schools group three grades together in each classroom and engage students in self-directed learning, at their own pace, for much of the day

---

(continued)

- Waldorf schools focus preschool through age six or seven on creative play and hands-on activities, elementary education to age 14 on developing artistic expression and social abilities, and secondary education beginning at age 14 on developing critical reasoning and empathic understanding
- "Early-college" high schools engage motivated students in college-level work and allow them to earn as much as two years' worth of college credits, through Advanced Placement courses and dual-enrollment programs with colleges
- Virtual, online schools let students take all courses online, often using educational software
- Internship-heavy high schools, such as the Big Picture Learning schools, have all their students spend some time every week in internships at businesses, nonprofits, or government offices
- Tutoring-intensive schools, such as Match Charter Schools in Boston, provide as much as two hours a day of tutoring to students
- Peer learning schools involve students in teaching one another as a central part of the curriculum
- Intensive writing schools use a curriculum in which students write every day, in multiple classes

By the Type of Students They Target:

- Neighborhood schools
- Schools for gifted students
- Single-sex schools
- Schools that offer increased support for English-language learners
- Schools for adults
- Preschools
- Schools with intense therapeutic help for children (and families) who need it
- Schools for students with disabilities, some of which target a particular disability, such as autism, and some of which integrate regular students and those with disabilities
- Schools that seek to preserve a cultural heritage, such as Afrocentric schools, Native American schools, and schools that stress traditional culture in Hawaii

(continued)

- High schools for those who have dropped out or are over-age
- Alternative schools for "at-risk" children: those who are chronically truant, coming back from the criminal justice system, or otherwise struggling
- Residential schools for high-need students, such as SEED schools in Washington, D.C. and elsewhere
- Schools for children who have experienced trauma or been in foster care, such as Monument Academy in Washington, D.C.
- Recovery schools for students with addictions
- Schools for adults and their young children, such as Briya Public Charter School in Washington, D.C.

By Particular Content Areas:

- Bilingual immersion schools
- Science, technology, engineering, and math (STEM) schools, and STEAM schools, which add arts
- Career and technical high schools, which prepare students for college or technical careers right out of high school
- Arts-intensive schools
- Drama-intensive schools
- Military academies
- Military and maritime academies
- Athletics-intensive schools, such as Denver's Girls Athletic Leadership School

Once choices are available, families need enrollment systems that help them find the right match. As we have seen in New Orleans, D.C., and Denver, computer algorithms can create effective systems, but some families need hands-on help. The Center on Reinventing Public Education (CRPE) surveyed 4,000 public school parents and concluded:

> *One-in-three reported difficulty understanding eligibility requirements. One-in-four reported struggling to get information about their public school options and to find transportation. One-in-five reported trouble with the enrollment system. Families with lower levels of educational attainment were much more likely to report difficulty with all of these issues.*

Districts and authorizers should create places where parents can sit down with counselors to sort through their options, as the RSD did in New Orleans, or make sure one or more organizations in the city are playing that role, as in D.C. Some families will need even more help, such as those that use the EdNavigator in New Orleans. Authorizers must also ensure that transportation is equally available to all students.

Giving families a choice of different kinds of schools has several other advantages over assigning all students by geography. First, schools have to compete for their students and money, so they pay more attention to what parents want. Parents have much more leverage in demanding what their children need, because they can leave, and the money follows them. So schools are accountable in two ways, just like private businesses in competitive markets: to their customers (students and parents) and to their owners (citizens, represented by a district or authorizer).

This competition works even if less than half of families make active choices. As economists have long explained, even if only 15 percent of customers pay attention to information about the quality of products or services, those producing them will strive to satisfy the active choosers—thereby helping all customers.

Second, information about the demand for schools can help authorizers make decisions about renewing charters and replicating schools.

Third, choice can help keep middle-class families in cities, which is important for the quality of city life and the effectiveness of public schools.

Fourth, choice can help stabilize school populations. Low-income urban families tend to move often. In some cities, landlords even offer the first month's rent free, which lures people into moving when they run short of money. Up to a third of students at any given school can be new in any school year. But if families can choose their schools and transportation is provided, their children don't have to switch schools every time they move. In New Orleans, mobility between schools actually decreased as choice exploded in the years after Katrina.

Finally, choice makes integrating schools by race and income easier. Research has shown that low-income children benefit from being educated with children from families that don't live in poverty, while the higher-income students lose nothing. Some districts have used "controlled choice" to integrate their schools by race for decades. Others, like Denver, use quotas in some schools to guarantee economic integration.

Empowering School Operators by Decentralizing Control

To create different school models, it helps to give those running schools the authority to control their operations. It's silly to expect unique and innovative models to appear when schools have to use the same staffing patterns, pay scales, hiring methods, school calendar, and curriculum.

Successful schools also require real commitment from their leaders and staff, and that is much more likely if they control their own schools. Someone taking orders from central headquarters is seldom going to give 100 percent, particularly when they question some of those orders.

This is common sense, long understood by educators. But it is shocking how little control traditional districts give their principals and teachers. Paul Hill, Christine Campbell, and Betheny Gross, the authors of *Strife and Progress*, put it well:

> *It may come as a surprise to readers that, in many districts, principals have control over almost nothing. Teachers are hired to work at a school without the principal's consent, and senior teachers from another school can bump incumbent junior teachers if there are lay-offs. If a principal has an open teaching position, a teacher without an assignment gets first choice. In addition, principals have little say in hiring their administrative, cafeteria, or janitorial staffs. While they may be given a budget, most everything on it is already allocated to teacher salaries and central office services, such as teacher professional development or building maintenance. In traditional districts, a school of 500 students can have an operating budget in excess of $5 million, but principals have told us that they actually control only $30,000 to $70,000 for field trips, copying, presenters, and so forth.*

When my eldest child was ready for kindergarten, my wife and I met with the principal of our local public school to investigate it. He was a wonderful man, beloved in the community, and an effective school leader. One of his virtues was honesty, and he told us that he couldn't fire any teachers because of tenure and couldn't hire any because if there were an opening, the district would send him the teacher with the most seniority who had been laid off in the past.

"Forced placement" of teachers by central headquarters is common, often required by union contracts that honor seniority. In addition, lockstep pay systems give great teachers an incentive to leave for better pay in another industry and poor teachers an incentive to stay. They also make it hard for principals to recruit top talent. Finally, they send a message to every teacher that, in TNTP's words, "In this profession, great work isn't valued."

Tenure policies, union contracts, and appeals processes also make it difficult to fire ineffective teachers in most states. The Fordham Institute recently studied 25 large school districts and found that despite recent reforms eliminating tenure in a few states, it still took at least two years to dismiss a veteran teacher for poor performance in a majority of them. In 11 others, it took up to a year. "Most states continue to confer lifetime tenure on teachers, weak teachers still take years to dismiss if they achieve tenured status, and any attempt to dismiss an ineffective veteran teacher remains vulnerable to challenge at every stage in the process—from evaluation, to remediation, to the dismissal decision, and beyond," the authors concluded. "Consequently, in most districts and schools, dismissing an ineffective veteran teacher remains far harder than is healthy for children, schools, taxpayers—and the teaching profession itself."

Union contracts often take away many normal management powers, such as choosing staff and reassigning them. Some even control when teachers can be hired, because they mandate that no new teacher can be hired until all current teachers have been placed. That is usually late in the summer, when all the best new teachers have already found jobs elsewhere. In New York City, the United Federation of Teachers contract even forbade the chancellor from sending an email to teachers or inviting them to a brown-bag lunch in their teachers lounge.

Sometimes principals are unionized, too, which makes firing them extremely difficult. Even in the model district of Union City, New Jersey, the subject of David Kirp's *Improbable Scholars*, the district can't fire poor principals, assistant principals, or tenured teachers. They can only ship them to another district school or wait until they retire.

Procurement—the process of buying supplies and equipment—is also controlled centrally in traditional districts, which creates enormous frustration in their schools. A story from Newark illustrates the problem: When a KIPP school that shared a building with a district school bought air conditioners, those still sweating at the district school downstairs resented it. So KIPP's board bought air conditioners for that school, too. They paid $400 apiece to buy and install their own units, but because they had to use the district's procurement system, they paid $700 apiece and it took a year to get them installed downstairs. The district had to solicit bids, then follow the union's rules and pay union wages for installation.

Centralized professional development has long been a joke for most district teachers. Every so often they are all marched off to spend a day or half a day in an auditorium, to listen to yet another presentation that may or may not be relevant to the challenges they face. On surveys, most teachers with more than 20 years of experience say professional development has had zero impact on their teaching.

Finally, centralized discipline policies often undermine schools as well, as we saw in Denver (pp. 188–9) and D.C. (p. 131).

Because centralized control through rules doesn't work well in today's world, 21st century systems shift the primary mechanism of control from rules to accountability for results. Some advocates for children worry that without all the rules, schools will not treat poor children and minorities equitably—avoiding them, suspending them too often, giving them inferior courses, and the like. What they don't understand is that our centralized districts *systematically* treat poor and minority children like second-class citizens. Those children get the most inexperienced and lowest-quality teachers, because stronger teachers and those with seniority use the centralized rules to migrate to middle-class schools, where it is easier and often more rewarding to teach. But as our 21st century systems have shown, it is entirely possible to create decentralized systems of choice that are far more equitable than traditional districts.

IF WE WANT to hold principals accountable for student learning in their schools, we have to let them control what goes on there. Otherwise, they have a ready excuse for failure: They blame central headquarters with its silly rules.

But we shouldn't stop at empowering principals. Running a school is too big a job to leave all the decisions in the hands of one person. In the 2012 MetLife Survey of the American Teacher, three of every four principals agreed that their jobs had become "too complex."

Many charter schools have an instructional leader and an operational leader, and sometimes a third leader who focuses on school culture. More and more also use distributed leadership, with "teacher leaders" for each subject and grade level or levels. Typically, teacher leaders teach part-time and coach, instruct, facilitate, and/or evaluate their team the rest of the time. As Michael Petrilli and Amber Northern of the Fordham Institute report:

> *The KIPP network, for instance, has developed multiple levels of leadership for its schools, from executive directors of citywide clusters to school principals and vice principals to deans, department- and grade-level chairs, as well as rank-and-file teachers who assume additional leadership or coaching responsibilities. This makes sense for at least two reasons. First, by truly distributing leadership, it makes the job more doable by non-super-humans. Second, it provides a clear career trajectory for KIPP's teachers—the kind of "career ladder" that reformers have been promoting at least since Lamar Alexander was governor of Tennessee.*

In the MetLife survey, nearly a quarter of teachers said they were very or extremely interested in serving as teacher leaders. This is particularly important, because so many teachers feel that they are treated like children. Gallup has found that teachers are the least likely of 12 professions surveyed to agree that "my opinion seems to matter at work."

This may seem odd, given that teachers control their own classrooms. But they are subject to dozens of district rules and policies that undermine them. This complaint from an anonymous teacher was republished in the *Washington Post*. She was leaving her position at a "high-needs school" in frustration, and she wrote about what she wanted to tell Americans about their public schools.

> *I would tell them about the bright bulletin boards, posters, and student work that are either taken down or covered with white butcher paper for most of the spring semester, because the state mandates that there can be no words of any kind on the walls during one of the fourteen standardized tests . . .*
>
> *I would tell them about how I'm not allowed to fail a student without turning in a form to the front office that specifies all instances of parent contact, describing in detail the exact accommodations and extra instruction that the child was given. I would tell them about how impossible this form is to complete, when leaving a voicemail doesn't count as contact and many parents' numbers change or are disconnected during the school year. I would tell them how unrealistic it is to document every time you help a child when you have a hundred of them, and how this results in so many teachers passing students who should be failing.*

Richard Ingersoll, an education professor at the University of Pennsylvania who specializes in research on teachers, says being treated this way explains why so many teachers leave the profession. "Buildings in which teachers have more say," he says, "have distinctly better teacher retention." Creating a more supportive, professional environment for teachers also yields more effective teaching—an obvious reality that, like many, has been proven by academic studies.

Schools actually run by teachers can yield even more, though not every teacher wants that extra responsibility. There are about 110 public schools in the United States run by teacher partnerships of one kind or another, almost half of them charters.

The advocacy group Education Evolving, which has published a guide to creating teacher-run schools, released a poll of teachers and members of the public in 2014. After hearing a description of teacher-run schools, 78 percent of teachers surveyed liked the idea. More than half of non-teacher respondents were "very interested" in seeing one in their community, and one in five teachers wanted to implement the idea immediately. Interestingly, those sentiments didn't change among union members.

Many union leaders love the teacher-run model as much as they hate charters. They constantly argue that teachers should be treated as professionals, and there is no more professional model than a teacher-run school. The National Education Association gives grants to members to create such schools. And in Minnesota, the Federation of Teachers has created the Minnesota Guild, which authorizes about a dozen charters, two of them run by teachers. In that state, and perhaps in others, teacher-run charters might carve out some islands of truce in the war between unions and charters.

Transforming School Cultures

The five strategies just discussed will change school cultures, but experience teaches that these changes never come fast enough or go far enough without a deliberate push. In public bureaucracies, cultures become deeply engrained. Being relatively powerless, people become invested in being victims. To avoid any sense that they are responsible, they blame others for all problems—district headquarters, the principal, parents, even the union. Those bent on reinventing public schools have learned that they need deliberate strategies to reshape these cultures. They need to create cultures that embrace innovation, responsibility for meeting students where they are, and accountability for results. They also have to reshape students' habits, attitudes, and expectations.

The best charter schools have figured this out. Robin Lake at CRPE cites a two-year Harvard study of five high-performing charters in Massachusetts:

> This study found that these schools achieve strong results not because of particularly innovative instructional practices, but because of coherent, schoolwide cultures focused on hard work and student outcomes. Findings from the study documented several essential elements that contributed to the academic success of these schools:
> - A clear sense of mission and a broadly shared institutional culture;
> - Purposefully chosen teachers and administrators who "fit" the organization's culture;
> - Organizational structures designed to support student learning;

- *Behavioral systems and codes of conduct that enforce a "No Excuses" commitment to hard work and a palpable sense of urgency.*

Creating motivated learners is a big part of it. Gordon MacInnes, a former state legislator and assistant education commissioner in New Jersey, wrote an insightful book about his state's court-ordered commitment to raise achievement levels in low-income districts. "For years, researchers have noted the plateau of improved results that appears to set in at about fifth grade, producing national results that are encouraging on fourth-grade tests, begin to fade by the middle grades, and disappear in high school," he noted. I believe this is because young children are naturally curious and motivated, but as they approach adolescence—at just the moment we expect them to start doing abstract learning, like studying algebra and reading Shakespeare—their motivation dwindles. Traditional schools barely recognize the challenge, doing nothing special—other than the efforts of individual teachers—to create motivation. But many charters make building motivation job one. They focus everyone on college, beginning in kindergarten. They spend the first week of school setting the culture, the expectations. They create systems of rewards and penalties to heighten motivation. They take students to visit college campuses, to bring the possibility alive. And some of them create internships for their students, so they can experience what life on the other side of college looks and feels like.

Shaping the culture of adults in a school is equally important, since they in turn shape student culture. People who run charters talk constantly about a "growth mindset"—the belief that every child and teacher can learn and grow. A commitment to use data and adjust instruction to meet children where they are is critical in most high-performing charters. Building a culture based on trust and collaboration is essential. "When the relationships among teachers in a school are characterized by high trust and frequent interaction—that is, when social capital is strong—student achievement scores improve," writes Carrie Leana, a University of Pittsburgh professor who has studied the connection between adult relationships and student outcomes in schools.

In other words, culture matters.

Building the Capacity of School Leaders and Teachers

Leaders with the ability to create outstanding schools in the inner city are precious and rare. Teachers with the skill, commitment, and stamina necessary are also in short supply. Yet the programs we usually rely on to train our teachers and principals stress academic study far more than practical skills.

Then, most school systems just plug their graduates in, based on their degrees, as if they were interchangeable parts.

Our traditional teachers colleges are failing us. Careful studies show three things: experience matters in developing high-quality teachers; their verbal or cognitive ability matters more than any other measured characteristic; and degrees and certification from teacher training schools contribute almost nothing. According to Frederick Hess, in his book *Education Unbound*:

> *More than 60 percent of alumni from schools of education report that the schools do not prepare graduates to cope with the realities of today's classrooms. Just one-third of principals think schools of education prepare teachers even moderately well to instruct students with disabilities, diverse cultural backgrounds, or limited English proficiency. Fewer than half of principals say education school graduates are even modestly prepared to use instructional technology, employ performance assessment, or implement curriculum and performance standards.*

Almost two thirds of education schools fail to give their students feedback on techniques for managing classrooms, according to a 2014 review by the National Council on Teacher Quality. And most don't check to see how their graduates perform. Peter Hutchinson once ran the Bush Foundation, in Minnesota. In preparing to launch an effort to improve teacher preparation and retention in the region, in 2008, he met with virtually every dean of every teacher preparation program in Minnesota and the Dakotas.

> *Early in my first conversation with each of them, almost as an off-handed question, I would ask, "What can you tell me about your recent graduates—where are they, how well are they performing?" In over a dozen such conversations the virtually unanimous response was, "Actually, we don't know." Most of the deans knew how many students passed their licensing exam or even how many got licensed. Many knew how many got hired into teaching positions. That's not what I was after. I wanted to know, how well were they doing in the classroom. How, I wondered, could these programs get better if they had no real time information on the performance of their graduates?*

In the 21st century, this is malpractice. A century ago, when most students went on to menial work or childrearing, teachers didn't have to excel. Principals weren't expected to be instructional leaders; even in recent decades, their days were given over to facilities management, discipline, parent and community interaction, and gathering evidence of compliance with federal, state, and district requirements. But in the 21st century, the majority of jobs will require some technical skill and the ability to analyze and solve problems. Today we *do* need excellent leaders and teachers, particularly in urban schools.

Hence those creating 21st century systems realized early on that they needed deliberate strategies to build new talent pipelines. They brought in Teach For America, The New Teacher Project, and New Leaders. The Mind Trust in Indianapolis and New Schools for New Orleans created fellowships for aspiring school leaders. KIPP and E. L. Haynes Public Charter Schools in Washington developed the Capital Teaching Residency, which Kaya Henderson then adapted for DCPS. Denver Public Schools set up the Denver Teacher Residency, in which aspiring teachers work for a year in a classroom alongside a mentor teacher while earning a master's degree from the University of Denver. DPS also created the Residency for the Educational Development of DPS Intrapreneurs (REDDI), which trains aspiring DPS principals at high-performing charters for a year.

The leaders of three of the best charter networks, KIPP, Uncommon Schools, and Achievement First, created Relay Graduate School of Education and built a two-year master's program that teaches best practices developed in their schools and involves almost two years of actual teaching. It now trains more than 2,400 teachers and principals each year, on 13 campuses around the country. High Tech High in San Diego, Match Public Charter School in Boston, and Aspire Public Schools in California also created graduate schools of education to train teachers. Building Excellent Schools created a development program for aspiring school leaders. The Eli and Edythe Broad Foundation set up an academy for aspiring superintendents.

And yet we need much more. If we want to compete with other high-performing nations, we must reinvent or replace the education schools that prepare and certify most of our teachers and principals.

We also must build the capacity of school governing boards. As discussed in chapter 6, they are often a weak link in the charter chain. We need training programs for members of boards, and authorizers need to pay more attention to the quality and mix of skills on their charter school boards.

Multiplication, Not Addition

Seven strategies, then, hold the key to reinventing our schools: clarity of purpose and role, contestability, consequences, choice, control, culture, and capacity. Are all seven necessary? Yes, if we want dramatic improvement. The formula for success is more like multiplication than addition: if too many are zeroes, the outcome is going to be zero, or close to it. Changing half the DNA of a bureaucratic system is a recipe for internal conflict, not transformation: while 21st century DNA tells people to innovate and behave like social entrepreneurs, the old DNA holds them back. Denver has lived with this tension for years.

When system DNA is coded for bureaucracy, innovators swim constantly against the current. Most of them either wear out or give up. But when the key pieces of DNA are recoded in the ways I have described, innovators get to swim with the current. The entire system supports them.

Are strategies as radical as these seven really necessary? Only if we want world-class public schools. If districts have political stability over a long period of time—which is difficult with elected school boards—they can make incremental improvements using the old model. In *Improbable Scholars* David Kirp describes how Union City, New Jersey—motivated by the potential threat of a state takeover—did just that, finally reaching the state average in performance. But it had the advantage of dealing with a tightly knit Hispanic community that had mostly healthy, two-parent families and high levels of social trust. Even so, the district took 20 years to get to the state average, because it was held back by its bureaucratic systems.

In tougher environments, where we want faster improvement, we need new DNA. As visionary AFT President Al Shanker said back in the 1980s, "It's no wonder our school system doesn't improve. It more resembles the communist economy than our own market economy."

What about suburban and rural communities? Are bureaucratic systems adequate there? Well, ask yourself: Do we want most suburban and rural schools to be cookie-cutter models? Should we allow them to survive year after year if their students are falling behind? Should their principals have little power to select their teachers, fire the incompetents, or control their own budgets?

I would answer "no." The new model is emerging first in urban districts, because they are desperate. Small, rural bureaucracies tend to be far less constraining than large ones, and there are geographic limits on how many choices students can have in rural areas. But rural districts and authorizers can use most of the seven C's. They can empower their principals and teachers. They can give schools five-year contracts and bring in replacements if they don't perform up to expectations. They can use online resources to give their students more choices. And even with less real choice, they can use other tools to listen to their students and parents and make their schools more accountable to their customers.

By 2050, I believe the 21st century model pioneered by New Orleans and the

D.C. Public Charter School Board will be the norm, just as the bureaucratic model became the norm between 1900 and 1950. There were still one-room schoolhouses in a few rural areas in 1950, but they were exceptions. And there will still be 20th century school districts operating in 2050, but they too will be exceptions. There is simply too much at stake to maintain systems that don't prepare students to thrive in today's world.

CHAPTER 13

You Get What You Measure: Defining School Quality in 21st Century Systems

IF WE WANT 21ST CENTURY SCHOOLS, we must hold them accountable to 21st century standards. For too long we have defined and measured school quality in a way that encourages cookie-cutter schools, all focused on preparing students for tests. Instead, we need diverse schools that cultivate the joy of learning, engage their students in deep learning, and help them develop "character skills," such as conscientiousness and self-control, that lead to success in life.

Our dominant school accountability systems were shaped by President George W. Bush's No Child Left Behind (NCLB) Act. Fortunately, the Every Student Succeeds Act, passed in December 2015, altered the rules, requiring states to have measurement systems but leaving them freer to modify them and handle accountability as they please.

Most states have changed their approach, and some will continue to do so. As they do, it would be helpful for them to get clear on the purposes of their accountability systems. Their first purpose should be to ensure that all schools produce at least a minimal level of student learning, by imposing consequences for repeated failure, including replacement of the school. Their second purpose should be to give parents the information and power they need to choose effective schools for their children. Their third should be to motivate districts, schools, and their staff members to improve student learning.

Each of these purposes is best served by a different form of performance accountability. Let's call the first "formal accountability systems": measurement by the state and/or district and consequences of some kind if performance falls below minimum standards for several years in a row. The second is accountability to customers: consequences imposed by parents who react to performance information by moving their children to different schools, taking public dollars with them. The third is the pride or embarrassment administrators and teachers feel when their schools are shown to be of high or low quality. All three can stimulate school leaders and their staffs to work together to improve student outcomes.

Formal accountability systems serve the first purpose well, and they can also help parents make wise choices, though they are not sufficient to ensure that outcome. They are less effective at the third purpose, motivating staff members. Most school personnel feel no real ownership of state standards, particularly when they include "value-added" scores that teachers and administrators cannot calculate or comprehend. Performance agreements negotiated between authorizers and charter schools or districts and traditional schools are more effective at motivating staff. School leaders and staff have some say over those agreements, so they often feel more ownership and more responsibility to fulfill them. Such agreements can also reflect the unique characteristics of a school far better than statewide standards can.

This is the first major point I will make in this chapter: We need more than one way to hold schools accountable for their performance.

My second point is related: To accomplish the second and third purposes, we need more data than we include in formal accountability systems. School personnel need information that helps them figure out how to improve student learning, and parents need information that helps them choose the best schools for their children. Measurement systems, in other words, should be broader than accountability systems.

My third point is that we need a much broader picture of student learning than standardized tests can provide—and when we use tests, we need to put more emphasis on student growth than on current achievement levels. This chapter will discuss several things we should measure in addition to test scores and propose how much weight we should give each one in our statewide accountability systems.

Fourth, there are some extremely important aspects of student learning that we don't yet know how to reliably and objectively measure, including "deeper learning" and character skills. Though we should not yet include them in state accountability systems, we *should* experiment with them, to hasten the day when we can include them. States should treat their measurement and accountability systems as works in progress, to be improved as we learn more.

Finally, as I argued in chapter 12, state systems should not be used to hold teachers accountable for performance. States and districts should hold *schools* accountable and let the schools figure out how to evaluate their teachers and hold them accountable. As I hope this book has demonstrated, we should leave as many operational decisions as possible to those who actually operate schools.

Readers with little interest in how to measure school quality should feel free to move on to chapter 14.

Two Formal Methods to Hold Schools Accountable

The common belief that the same formal accountability system should be applied to every public school is an outdated holdover from the Industrial Era. In a traditional 20th century district, in which all schools operated in similar fashion and sought to educate all types of children, it may have made sense. But in 21st century systems, with parents choosing between many diverse schools hand crafted for different kinds of learners, it no longer does.

It is still important for states to use the first method: minimum standards that will trigger consequences for most schools if they consistently fail to meet them. Rather than measuring these things only in grades three through eight and then once in high school, as required by federal law, states should measure annually, in all grades. After all, we want every child to read, reason, do basic math, write coherently, and gain some familiarity with science, technology, history, geography, and civics. If children are not learning these things, should we really be using taxpayers' dollars to fund their schools?

We must always remember, though, that these are only *minimum standards*. Beyond them, states should also encourage districts and authorizers to use a second method of holding schools accountable: negotiating more specific performance goals that reflect the missions of individual schools. If a school is designed to provide STEM education, for instance, it should be judged in part on how well it does so. If it is designed to provide dual-language immersion, or career and technical education, its performance measures should reflect those goals.

Should alternative schools for dropouts and over-age students be held to the same standards as ordinary high schools? How about schools designed specifically for students with disabilities? Or schools for students returning from the criminal justice system? Obviously, we need different standards for such "alternative" schools. States should measure and rate these alternative schools, just as they do all others, but they should not impose consequences. Instead, districts or authorizers should hold alternative schools accountable for performance goals and measures they have negotiated with each individual school or group of schools, if more than one use the same model.

Holding each school accountable to its own standards has always been the heart of the charter model, although not all states are faithful to that model. A charter should be a performance contract, which spells out what the school intends to accomplish, how it will be measured, and what will happen if the school fails to achieve its goals. When schools are held accountable to their own goals, negotiated with their own authorizer or district, their leaders and staff members are far more likely to embrace responsibility for accomplishing them.

Such performance agreements can also motivate *every* school, whereas minimum state standards have little effect on schools whose students regularly score above the minimums. Our accountability systems should motivate everyone in every school to seek improvement in student outcomes—even those who work in schools for gifted students.

Finally, by crafting different performance goals for different kinds of schools, we encourage people to open innovative schools designed to serve different kinds of students. When we apply standardized accountability to all schools, we do the opposite, and we get far less innovation.

Consider University Preparatory Academies, in inner-city Detroit. When founder Doug Ross opened his first high school, in 2003, he adopted a model heavily influenced by Big Picture Learning—particularly Providence, Rhode Island's MET School. Aware that his biggest challenge was creating motivation for college among inner-city, African American teenagers who had rarely met anyone, other than their teachers, who had been to college, Ross decided that every high school student would spend two days a week in internships, with local businesses, public agencies, or nonprofits. It worked: When students saw African American adults who had graduated from college and had good jobs, nice houses, and nice cars, a light bulb often went off. On top of that, they discovered that they could contribute in meaningful ways, which boosted their confidence, and some of them fell in love with particular fields of work. But when Michigan adopted statewide standards and imposed them on all schools, prompted by NCLB, University Prep had to cut internships back to half a day a week, to ensure that students covered all the material on state tests. Other Big Picture schools had similar experiences.

Make Accountability Real By Replacing Failed Schools with Proven Models

Another mistake NCLB made was allowing states and districts to impose consequences for failure that had few teeth. The new federal law, ESSA, could well make the problem worse. But if states want to improve student learning, real accountability is one of their most powerful tools. As argued in chapter 12, experience has proven that the most effective way to turn around a failing school is to replace it—to bring in an entirely new team with a strong track record and a new vision for the school.

When schools fail to meet state standards or charter goals for two or three years, resources should be provided to help them hire the help they need to turn things around. If failing schools cannot turn around within two more years, authorizers and districts should replace them with more effective school operators, as they do in New Orleans, D.C., Denver, and other cities. Before pulling the trigger, however, authorizers and districts should give the schools a chance to appeal—to provide compelling evidence that they are actually succeeding, given the students they educate. A school may be working under significant challenges, such as a high percentage of children with serious disabilities, or a high percentage of former dropouts or homeless children. Sometimes a middle school or high school may be helping children who arrived three or four years behind grade level achieve decent academic growth, while missing minimum state standards.

If it's a close call, the district or authorizer might want to renew the school for only a year or two, to give it time to solve whatever problems exist. But if the school's argument is not compelling, or if it fails to turn things around during its extension, authorizers should replace the failing school with a better one.

Accountability Is Not the Same as Measurement

People often forget the distinction between measurement and accountability, but it is critical. Accountability systems create consequences for school performance: both rewards and penalties. Measurement systems provide information about those schools, without consequences attached. Both are necessary, but they are hardly identical.

There are many things we measure about schools—and some we should begin measuring—because the information is useful. Some information helps parents make better choices, such as the number of advanced placement courses a high school offers. Other information also helps districts, authorizers, and schools learn what works and what doesn't, such as data on parental involvement, or student surveys about teacher and school quality, or student and teacher assessments of character skills like persistence and conscientiousness. Such data may even play a role in school, district, and authorizer decisions about where to invest and what policies to adopt. But there are good reasons to keep it out of a statewide accountability system.

Formal, statewide accountability systems should focus on what we as a society most want our schools to accomplish: real-world *outcomes* such as graduation rates, college-going and employment rates, and student acquisition of knowledge and skills. But to help those who manage schools, districts, and charter networks—as well as parents facing choices—we also need information about *inputs* and *outputs*, such as attendance rates, teacher absenteeism and turnover, student-teacher ratios, numbers of AP courses, and so on. Indeed, every school should track its own "balanced scorecard," including data about student results, employees' views and experiences (morale, turnover), operational issues (spending, learning time, productivity), and customers' views (parental satisfaction, student engagement). Principals and teachers should examine such data in regular group sessions and use it to make changes that will improve performance.

States should require districts and authorizers to measure this kind of data but should *not* include it in statewide accountability or rating systems. Here are a few examples of such metrics:

Attendance rates. These are an important measure of student engagement, but they are easily manipulated by schools and difficult to audit effectively. It would be quite expensive to make them cheat-proof, so while we should collect the data, we should not tie consequences to it.

Student demand. For most schools, demand reflects parental judgments about the school's quality. But some schools are designed for specialized populations, such as pregnant students or dropouts. It would be silly to punish such schools because demand was low or dropping, since lower pregnancy or dropout rates might be a sign of success, not failure, for the school system. However, districts and authorizers should feel free to include negotiated goals about demand in their performance contracts with individual schools, where it makes sense.

Retention rates. Some districts and authorizers measure the rate at which schools retain students, but this is another number that should not be attached to ratings or consequences for every school. As discussed in chapter 9, DSST charters in Denver lose some students because the schools are so demanding, compared to the traditional public schools nearby. It would be insane to punish DSST for that.

Discipline rates. The same is true of rates of discipline. How could one statewide standard ever apply to every public school? How could a state or district judge whether a school was using the ideal type and amount of discipline? As D.C.'s charter board has shown, publishing data on discipline rates is useful—to keep schools honest, to encourage them to recognize the trauma that often underlies student misbehavior, and to nudge them to use methods such as restorative justice rather than suspensions and expulsions. But as Denver has learned (see pp. 188–9), we need to leave judgments about discipline up to the people who run schools. Students in one school may disrupt class frequently, so high rates of discipline may be required to ensure that students can learn uninterrupted. Students in another school may rarely disrupt class and thus need little disciplinary action. Any effort to punish schools for high rates would undermine their ability to deal with the realities in their classrooms.

College-level courses. Some states, districts, and authorizers also give credit in their performance frameworks for the number of advanced placement classes, International Baccalaureate programs, and high school students taking college classes through dual enrollment. Again, this is good information to measure and publicize, because it helps parents and students make informed choices. But how can anyone say that all schools should offer such opportunities? Big Picture Learning schools have concluded that internships in local businesses, nonprofits, and government offices are more valuable for their students. Given their impressive outcomes, they are surely correct. It would be silly to create incentives for them to limit internships and offer more AP courses. Different schools, with different kinds of students, need different methods. Statewide accountability systems should focus on outcomes and leave the choice of methods to schools.

If schools or networks of schools choose to use data about such things for internal accountability, that is their prerogative. Districts and authorizers may want to include any of these measures in performance agreements with particular schools, where it makes sense. But states should limit what they hold *all* schools accountable for to a handful of key outcomes that truly matter in all students' lives. And they should give schools the freedom to figure out the best methods to achieve those outcomes, given the particular students they educate. This is the formula that has worked so well in our fastest improving school systems.

How Heavily Should We Rely on Test Scores?

Since the mid-1990s, our state accountability systems have been dominated by test scores. No Child Left Behind (NCLB), which required states to hold their schools accountable for delivering "proficiency" on standardized tests, intensified the problem. President Obama's Department of Education gave all but a handful of states waivers to NCLB, to measure student growth as well as proficiency levels. But by 2016, according to a study by the Center for American Progress, the average state gave test scores (achievement and growth combined) 91 percent of the weight in elementary and middle school ratings and about 70-75 percent in high schools. Those numbers are far too high.

Don't get me wrong: Test scores are important measures of success. Without them, how will we know if students are learning to read and write and do math? Beginning with sixth grade, we should also test writing (tested by at least five states by 2015), science (at least 13 states), and the social sciences (a majority of states). If we don't measure these things, how will we know whether students are learning the basics? How will we know which schools are failing and need to be replaced?

But that doesn't mean we should rely on test scores for three quarters or more of what matters. Testing experts agree that test scores bounce around from year to year, so we need to be careful how we use them.

Relying so heavily on test scores creates myriad problems. One of the most important, articulated by social scientist Donald Campbell in 1976, has become known as Campbell's Law: "The more any quantitative social indicator is used for social decision-making, the more subject it will be to corruption pressures and the more apt it will be to distort and corrupt the social processes it is intended to monitor." We have seen both corruption and distortion resulting from NCLB's accountability system: adults cheating on standardized tests and schools concentrating on rote learning to drive up test scores, in the process undermining children's natural love of learning. That does not mean we should *stop* standardized testing. Campbell was not discouraging *measurement*; he was warning us not to rely on a single measure of quality. "Many commentators, including myself, assume that the use of multiple indicators, all recognized as imperfect, will alleviate the problem," he added in the very same essay.

In addition, we all know people who perform well in life and work but who did not test well, because of stress, learning disabilities, trauma, or myriad other issues. As one teacher told David Kirp, author of *Improbable Scholars*, about Union City's schools in New Jersey, "The expectation is that 10-year-olds can write five paragraphs in half an hour, solve complicated math problems and have a wealth of knowledge about science, and do it all entirely on their own. But these youngsters freeze up under stress—one word on a question can throw them off . . ."

My daughter's K–8 school in New Orleans, where students had to achieve certain test scores to move from fourth to fifth grade and eighth to ninth, gave teachers rubber gloves along with the testing materials, because students often threw up from the stress. Fights were always more common during testing week, because students wanted to be suspended and sent home so they could avoid the test.

Many of us have also seen questions that unconsciously assume the test takers are from a white, middle-class culture. When my daughter taught fifth- and sixth-grade English, one test prompt asked students to write about the difference between how they and their friends talked and how their parents talked. Her African American students looked at her in puzzlement. "We talk the same way our parents do," they told her. Another question mentioned snow, and some of her students had no idea what it was.

Yet another problem is that standardized tests often give misleading signals about students who are still learning English. Kristina Rizga, author of *Mission High*, describes a student at San Francisco's Mission High School named Maria, from El Salvador. For years, Maria failed standardized tests because she struggled with English. But by the time she applied for college she had mastered the language, and she won two scholarships and was accepted at five schools, including the University of California at Davis.

Some studies find a correlation between good test scores and success in adult life, but others find no connection, and the question is still hotly debated. In 2012 Education Sector compared college enrollment rates at 21 randomly selected California high schools with their state Academic Performance Index (API) scores, which were based almost entirely on test scores. "In the sample of 'typical' schools," they found, "there is a positive relationship between API and postsecondary enrollment. In other words, most high-scoring API schools also tend to have higher postsecondary enrollment and most low-scoring API schools have lower postsecondary enrollment. But in the sample of high-poverty schools, the relationship between high API scores and high college enrollment rates all but disappears."

They described San Francisco's June Jordan School for Equity, "a 250-pupil school founded in 2003 to serve some of the city's poorest neighborhoods," which had a "dismal" API in 2010 of only 568 out of 1000. (The state considered 800 an acceptable score.)

> But also that year, June Jordan ranked second among San Francisco high schools in the percentage of students eligible for the UC/CSU system, behind only the prestigious, admissions-based Lowell High School. Among its 2009 graduates, 70 percent enrolled in college overall, and 49 percent enrolled in four-year colleges—higher enrollment rates than the district average. The graduates are also persisting in college.

Even if they did not put schools full of poor kids at such a disadvantage, standardized tests can push schools to concentrate more on memorization than on deeper learning. As one superintendent put it during the NCLB era, "My concern is that while scores are going up, learning is going down."

Tests developed to measure the Common Core standards now embraced by a majority of states have improved the situation. Tests can measure rote memorization, but they can also measure aspects of deeper learning. When

Massachusetts adopted its MCAS (Massachusetts Comprehensive Assessment System) tests in the 1990s—the closest thing to Common Core exams at the time—they pushed my children's K–8 public school to focus more, not less, on writing, reasoning, and other aspects of deeper learning. Most experts believe the Common Core tests move in the same direction, though some argue that they still need more questions that show how deeply students can apply, analyze, and evaluate what they know.

The more tests focus on aspects of deeper learning like writing, however, the more their scoring becomes subjective. Tests that require students to write essays are typically scored by people who are under time pressure and are being paid by the hour—or, worse, by computers. The results may not be entirely objective.

Schools that focus deliberately on deeper learning often sacrifice their standardized test scores, because they don't prepare their students for such tests. For instance, a dozen teacher-run charter schools in Minnesota, operated or assisted by a teacher cooperative called EdVisions, use project-based learning to maximize student engagement. According to a 2010 study, they had lower scores on standardized tests than the state average but higher ACT and SAT scores. More than 82 percent of their graduates entered two- or four-year colleges, compared to a national average of 68 percent.

When I visited one of these schools, St. Paul's Avalon School, it was obvious that students were immersed in their education. One girl I met had adapted a book into a play and directed it when she was in ninth grade. Another wrote an interactive murder mystery and produced it with a classmate, raising $200 for their prom through ticket sales. When projects don't cover all related state standards, teachers—who work more as coaches than instructors—intervene. One student, concerned by the mass die-offs of bees, did a project on bees rather than take biology. He researched threats to bees; visited beekeepers, apiaries and a state bee lab; and listened to TED talks on the subject. Once he was done, his teacher identified the state standards on water and carbon cycles he had missed, asked him to research them, then required him to demonstrate mastery.

Standardized tests also fail to measure "noncognitive" or "character" skills that are important for future success, such as self-control, conscientiousness, and the ability to work well with others. Former Minnesota governor Rudy Perpich, who in the 1980s brought public school choice to Minnesota—and hence to America—used to say, "I've seen too many people who passed tests and failed life. And too many people who failed tests and passed life."

Finally, too-heavy reliance on standardized testing in accountability systems can discourage people from creating schools for particularly challenging students, such as dropouts, children with disabilities, those convicted of crimes, or those who don't speak English. They also discourage schools from trying new methods, such as project-based learning, student internships, or career and technical education, that might deepen learning but hurt test scores. We need *more* innovation in education, not less; we need to encourage people to start schools that are unique, aimed at students who do not fit well in cookie-cutter schools.

The American people understand this. Every year Gallup and Phi Delta Kappa collaborate on a survey to measure public opinion about education. In 2015, 64 percent of those surveyed agreed that there was too much emphasis on standardized testing in their public schools. When asked about different measures of school effectiveness, almost four in five said "how engaged students are with their classwork" and "the percentage of students who feel hopeful about their future" were "very important," and 69 percent mentioned "high school graduation rates." More than twice as many said the percentage of graduates going on to college or jobs was "very important" than said the same about standardized test scores. But 48 percent agreed that test scores were "somewhat important" in improving schools, and another 19 percent said they were "very important." Less than a third said they were not important or "not very important."

In other words, Americans see the value in standardized testing, but they see more value in measuring graduation rates, employment rates, and student engagement and attitudes.

There is wisdom here. I believe that standardized test scores (including college readiness tests such as the ACT and SAT exams) should be given roughly half the weight in statewide measurement and accountability systems, depending on the school level. But they should be balanced by other important measures.

Under the Every Student Succeeds Act of 2015, states are still required to give greater weight to test scores than other indicators in their measurement systems, but they have significantly more leeway. The new law requires that they measure (1) student performance in math and English language arts, or ELA, (2) a second academic indicator, such as growth in math and ELA, (3) English-language learners' progress toward proficiency in English, (4) high school graduation rates, and (5) at least one other measure of school quality or student success. (States can include other measures as well.)

States have to publish the results (excluding number 3 above) for each school and for these subgroups at each school: students with disabilities, students from low-income families, students from major racial and ethnic groups, and English-language learners. In rating schools, states must give "substantial weight" to categories one through four and "much greater weight" to those four combined than to category five. In other words, assigning 50 percent for the first two categories should pass muster.

States may set "alternate academic achievement standards" for students with the most significant cognitive disabilities and give them alternate tests, provided no more than 1 percent of all students in the state are assessed this way. This accommodation will thus apply to less than 10 percent of students who receive special education. States may also allow multiple student assessments through the year rather than one year-end test, and they may include student portfolios in the assessments. Up to seven states will be allowed to pilot competency-based assessments and other innovations.

The new law requires that this framework be applied to all schools and 99 percent of students, but it leaves it up to states to define how they will use the measures to create consequences, within broad guidelines. In other words, it dictates at least part of a state's measurement and rating systems, but not the rest of its accountability system.

In rethinking their approaches, states have an opportunity to undo several of NCLB's biggest mistakes.

Give More Weight to Students' Academic Growth than their Achievement Levels

Standardized tests usually measure the level at which a student performs, not the gains he or she has made over the past year. Yet we cannot judge the performance of a school or teacher without the latter data. If a school's students arrived four years behind grade level, on average, and two years later they are only one year behind grade level, is the school failing? Of course not. This was perhaps NCLB's biggest flaw: it required states to measure students' test scores but not their rate of growth. This put schools with high percentages of low-income students at a huge disadvantage, because those students' average test scores were much lower.

Under waivers granted by the Bush and Obama administrations, all but five states added growth measures in English and math. But the majority of states still give greater weight to proficiency than growth in their measurement systems—and in making decisions about intervening in low-performing schools.

There are many different ways to measure student growth. Appendix A discusses the flaws in one popular method, the Colorado Growth Model. Jurisdictions using this model and relying on student growth percentiles need to balance it with roughly equal weight for proficiency, as D.C.'s Public Charter School Board does.

Another popular option is a "value-added model," which attempts to isolate the contribution the school makes to student gains by controlling for student characteristics such as socioeconomic status—thus putting all schools on an equal playing field. Whatever method a state chooses, models that take at least two prior years into account, rather than one, are considered more accurate and reliable.

Quit Focusing Only on the Percentage of Students who are "Proficient" or Above

Under NCLB, states were required to measure the percentage of students who reached some cut score, usually labeled "basic" or "proficient." To make their schools look better, too many states lowered the proficiency bar. States must avoid this temptation under the new law.

Putting all the weight on proficiency has myriad other flaws, as more than forty experts in testing argued in a letter to Education Secretary John B. King Jr. in 2016. It fails to distinguish between students who are right at the cut score and those who are far above it. It gives no credit to gains made by students who remain below the cut score, no matter how large. And it creates incentives for schools to concentrate on raising the scores of those just below the cut score, the "bubble kids," as they have become known. My daughter's school created a special two-month-long elective before the state tests just for bubble kids.

In addition, some states use growth models that only include "growth to proficiency," excluding all students who are already above proficient levels. Schools that know they are being judged this way tend to ignore the needs of advanced students. "If you don't measure it, it doesn't count," says Leslie Jacobs, who has watched school and district behavior closely for three decades. "And if kids don't count, they will be ignored."

Focusing only on proficiency leads to neglect of both the lowest- and highest-achieving students. If schools are held accountable for the growth of all their students, in constrast, they will feel pressure to help those who are far behind while also providing challenging material for their advanced students. There are a surprising number of the latter—two million students in California alone perform at least one grade level above their grade in math or reading. NCLB gave schools incentives to ignore such students, and some of them did. According to the Fordham Institute:

> Research has demonstrated that students just below the bar were most likely to make large gains in the NCLB era, while high achievers made lesser gains. Those most victimized by this regime were high-achieving poor and minority students—kids who were dependent on

the school system to cultivate their potential and accelerate their achievement. (Equally able youngsters from middle-class circumstances have other people and educational resources to keep them moving forward.)

In their letter, the experts urged the Department of Education to write regulations allowing states to use either of two approaches under ESSA: (1) average scores for each grade and subject, or (2) achievement indexes, which would reflect the percentage of students who reached each level in the scoring system, not just proficiency. (Eight states already used this kind of index, under NCLB waivers.) Fortunately, the department agreed.

The Fordham Institute also recommended that states add "high-achieving students" as a subgroup on which they report results, just like the other subgroups required by ESSA. It found "that just four states—Arkansas, Ohio, Oregon, and South Carolina—have truly praiseworthy systems when it comes to focusing attention on these students."

What Else Should We Include in Statewide Accountability Systems?

Formal, statewide accountability and rating systems should include the following:

Graduation Rates. NCLB required states to measure graduation rates, so most use a four-year adjusted cohort graduation rate, which includes all those who start ninth grade at a particular high school but subtracts those who transfer to another. Some states have included five-year, six-year, and even seven-year rates. This is wise, because we want high schools to work hard to help students graduate, even if it takes longer than normal. An estimated 42 percent of those who enroll in college are not ready: They have to take remedial courses, and many of them later drop out. Some of the nation's best charter schools require students who are not ready for college to do an extra year of high school. We should reward such behavior, not punish it. Extended-year graduations should receive equal weight with four-year graduations; there should be no assumption that one is better than another.

Some states award special diplomas to recognize high achievement: "distinguished achievement" programs in Texas, for example, and "regents diplomas with advanced designation with honors" in New York. Some of them award points in their performance indexes for the number of high-achievement diplomas. Florida, Indiana, Louisiana, Maryland, New Mexico, Oklahoma, and

New York City also give credit for students who have earned industry-based certifications, to spur schools to make such options available. Both are excellent ideas.

College Entrance and Persistence Rates. Ultimately, the most important factor in judging schools should be how they prepare students for success in life. We need to learn how to measure these real-life outcomes and include them in our accountability systems. Graduating from college is one important outcome. Indeed, the value of a college degree has increased in the Information Age, while the value of a high school degree has fallen, as figure 13-1 demonstrates. (It shows male earnings, but the data for female workers looks much the same.) For most, college has become the gateway to a middle-class career.

Hence many charter authorizers and a few states include the percentage of graduates who enter college in their high school metrics. In addition, Denver measures the percentage of college entrants who must take remedial classes, an important indicator everyone should use.

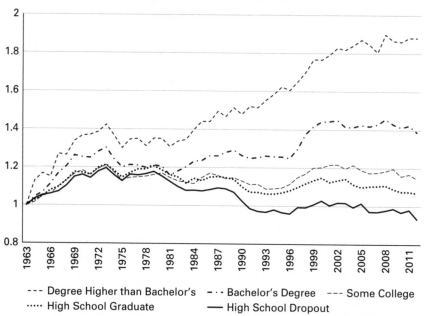

Change in Real Wage Levels of Full-Time Male Workers by Education, 1963–2012

--- Degree Higher than Bachelor's   -··Bachelor's Degree   --- Some College
·····High School Graduate   —— High School Dropout

Figure 13-1 Source: David H. Autor, "Skills, Education, and the Rise of Earnings Inequality Among the 'Other 99 Percent,'" *Science*, 23 May 2014: 344 (6186), 843-851, Figure 6a. Used with author's permission.

College persistence is also important. We should give all high schools an incentive to actively help their graduates make it through college, as many of the best charters do, by measuring the percentage who move on to a second year, the percentage entering a two-year college who earn a two-year degree or credential, and the percentage moving on to a third year. Unfortunately, using college graduation rates is probably unfair, because college graduation occurs so long after high school graduation. A high school might have made huge strides over the past three or four years in helping its graduates prepare for and get through college, but that would take four to six years to show up in college graduation rates.

Training and Employment Rates. Many skilled positions in our economy do not require college degrees; instead, they require some technical training, whether through an apprenticeship, a training program, or a community college. And many students have no desire to go to college. For some, finding a full-time job (or joining the military) after high school is an indicator of success. States should measure employment and training rates (including military service) for graduates who do not go on to college and include them in their accountability systems. They should be careful not to put so much weight on college enrollment that they give high schools an incentive to ignore career and technical education that leads to further training, apprenticeships, and jobs. They should also include the income levels of graduates from the past two years who are employed full-time. A majority of states now track the wages of recent college graduates in their state; they can do the same for high school graduates.

Qualitative Assessments by Experts. In England and Scotland, small teams of experts, many of them former school leaders and teachers, visit each school roughly every three years, with two days' notice, and spend two to three days gauging its quality. They sit in on classes, examine student work, talk with groups of students, staff, and members of the governing board, look over documents, records, and test scores, review parent surveys, solicit written input from parents, and often meet with parents. Then they publish reports full of qualitative judgments and distribute them to all parents. They rate areas such as "quality of teaching, learning and assessment," "outcomes for pupils," "early years provision," "effectiveness of leadership and management," and "personal development, behavior and welfare." There are four possible ratings in each category: outstanding, good, requires improvement, and inadequate. The work in England is overseen by the Office for Standards in Education, Children's Services and Skills, an independent government agency created in 1992.

New York City, Denver, and Charlotte-Mecklenburg School District (North Carolina's second largest) have adopted a similar model to evaluate their schools. Massachusetts, Indianapolis, D.C.'s Charter Board, and other authorizers use visits based on the English model in reviewing their charter schools, and large charter networks such as KIPP have done the same. This approach can yield valuable information about school quality that test scores don't reveal, particularly about the school culture and aspects of deeper learning, such as critical thinking, problem solving, researching, and speaking skills.

Evaluations suggest that the English inspection system is effective in identifying low-performing schools. It also differentiates effectively between outstanding schools, good schools, those that require improvement, and those that are "inadequate." In England, schools rated in the two bottom categories have responded by raising student achievement.

Obviously, assessments such as this are more expensive than standardized tests, though they don't have to be done every year. But they are indispensable if we want a balanced set of quality measures that reflect the whole child's experience. We already spend money accrediting public schools every six to ten years (depending on the region), paid for by the schools. Accreditation is a voluntary process that relies heavily on a "self-study" by the school, and in some regions it focuses less on academic outcomes than on facilities and process (guidance services, curriculum, instructional model, and so on). Whether school leaders implement the accrediting agency's recommendations depends entirely on them, and accrediting agencies rarely refuse a public school accreditation. Without real consequences, accreditation has far less impact on most schools than a charter renewal review process does.

Ted Sizer, the late headmaster of the elite Phillips Academy Andover, author of *Horace's Compromise*, founder of the Coalition of Essential Schools, and chair of the education departments at Harvard and Brown universities, told me that the assessment done when he ran a charter school, at the end of his career, was far more valuable than any accreditation process he had ever been through. In some regions, what we spend on accreditation would be far more productively spent on an English-style assessment of each school every three years. If it costs more than accreditation every six years (which is unlikely), the investment would still be worthwhile. Accountability is an arena in which we should never be penny-wise and pound-foolish.

In large states, the scale of these qualitative assessments might require that they be phased in over multiple years. But organizations already exist that know how to do them, and there are plenty of retired teachers and administrators who would be happy for the part-time work. With 53 million people, England is far larger than any American state, and the English government has managed its system for decades. New York City is larger than most states, and it has also managed.

Student Engagement, Measured by Parent Surveys. In most industries, customer satisfaction is a key indicator of quality. Education is no exception: both parents and students have informed perspectives about the quality of their schools. There is some risk in using student surveys, as I will discuss below. But there is less risk with parent surveys, because parents are more likely to express their true feelings about their children's schools and less likely to comply with principals' and teachers' wishes.

Important Measures Not Yet Ready for Prime Time

Many critics of standardized testing rightly point out that tests cannot capture many valuable aspects of student learning. As our economy requires more and more knowledge workers, deeper learning becomes more important, but even a good test cannot capture all of its aspects. Some schools and districts use methods other than standardized tests, such as the qualitative assessments discussed below. Unfortunately, they are difficult to standardize when applied to thousands of schools. For these and the two other forms of assessment I discuss, we should experiment, moving as fast as possible to develop reliable, objective measurement methods.

Qualitative Assessments of Student Performance. New Hampshire is gradually moving to a system in which students advance by proving their competence in a subject matter, rather than putting in seat time and passing courses. In 2015, the state received a federal waiver to work with eight school districts to develop performance tasks to assess student learning, in place of standardized tests. Some grades take the state's standardized (Smarter Balanced) tests, but others are assessed with multistep tasks that seek to measure deeper learning. For instance, geometry students at Spaulding High School were asked to design two water towers that would each hold about 45,000 cubic feet of water—one a simple solid and one a compound solid—with the fewest construction materials possible, then to write a proposal recommending the best approach.

Deeper learning assessments are common in other developed countries, but they're just beginning to spread in the United States. The Council of Chief State School Officers' Innovation Lab Network is working with schools and districts in a dozen states to assess Common Core skills through "performance-based measures of deeper learning." And the New York Performance Standards consortium, a group of 38 small high schools that focus on deeper learning, has a state waiver allowing them to use continuous, project-based assessments. Students write essays and research papers, solve math problems, do science experiments, and orally present their work to external assessors. All but two of the schools are in New York City. With demographics similar to the rest of the city's high schools, their dropout rates are half the city average and their college acceptance rates are almost 30 percent higher.

All such approaches involve subjective assessment of student work, and it is difficult to ensure that such assessments are standardized across thousands of schools. Other nations, including the Netherlands, Singapore, and parts of Australia, train teachers and education professors who serve on assessment panels, using common rubrics. The results are audited to ensure that roughly the same standards are being applied in all schools. We should research their methods and experiment with them here, as fast as we can. If we find methods that prove objective and reliable when used statewide, they would enrich our accountability systems.

Student Surveys. Most American colleges use student surveys as part of professors' evaluations, but K–12 schools rarely do. Yet when students respond to surveys honestly, their assessments have proven to be very accurate barometers of teacher and school quality. Starting in 2010, the Bill and Melinda Gates Foundation funded research involving 3,000 teachers in six urban school districts to identify the most accurate measures of teaching quality. They analyzed test scores, videotaped 20,000 teacher lessons, studied thousands of classroom observations of teaching, and implemented dozens of student surveys. They asked tens of thousands of students to respond to 36 statements on a survey developed through a decade of research by Professor Ronald Ferguson at Harvard University, in collaboration with teachers, students, and colleagues. The survey asked students to agree or disagree with statements like, "My teacher knows when the class understands, and when we do not," "When I turn in my work, my teacher gives me useful feedback that helps me improve," and "In this class, the teacher accepts nothing less than our full effort." Students' answers correlated well with how much they learned as measured by growth on standardized tests. Indeed, they were more reliable than ratings by trained observers who watched videos of classrooms. And they bounced around less than test scores, over time.

At least 100 districts and 1,000 schools are now using the Tripod survey, as Ferguson and his company call it, as part of their teacher evaluation systems. Some are attaching consequences. In Pittsburgh, Pennsylvania, for instance, survey results collected multiple times over two years account for 15 percent of a teacher's overall evaluation score. Tripod Education Partners has also developed and used student surveys to deliver feedback on school climate, student engagement, peer support, and character skills.

"We believe our measures are the most effective measures of teacher effectiveness," says Ferguson's Tripod partner, Rob Ramsdell. "If surveys are administered systematically a couple of times a year, and we're using the data to support improvement, while tracking those results over time, it's an incredibly powerful tool that can drive improvement efforts and be relevant to accountability decisions."

If surveys are used widely to create consequences, however, a few schools and teachers may push students to emphasize the positive. (If you've ever bought a new car and had the salesmen tell you to expect a phone call from the company asking you to rate his performance—and that his *entire* bonus rests on your answer—you're familiar with the potential problem.) Some students may also use their answers to punish teachers who are more demanding or tougher graders, a phenomenon well known to college professors. Tripod finds very consistent patterns across classrooms, even in districts that give 15 percent of the weight in teacher evaluations to surveys. If students were not answering honestly, Ramsdell says, this would not be the case. But he agrees that we can't rule out the possibility of such problems.

To detect cheating on standardized tests, states analyze data and investigate instances where the unexpected happens. They could do the same with student surveys. Normally, survey results are fairly consistent over time, and they correlate closely with students' academic gains on tests. When surveys suddenly showed a big change, or more positive results than tests, states could investigate.

For now, every school should use feedback from its customers—its students and their families—to improve its performance. If the data is trustworthy, there are few better measures of school quality. States should require that the data be collected and distributed to schools and parents, to help them choose appropriate schools for their children. But given the slight risk of schools influencing student responses or students punishing demanding teachers, states should not yet include student surveys in their formal accountability systems. Instead they should experiment, to learn what works, where the pitfalls lie, and how to overcome them. If some authorizers or districts want to include survey results in their charters and performance agreements, and the schools agree, states could also learn from their experience.

Finally, if states use qualitative assessments by experts, as the English do, assessment teams could include parental and student survey data in their analyses. If the data looked fishy, they could discount it and ask the state, district, or authorizer to investigate.

As with qualitative assessment of student performance, states and the federal government should fund experiments with and research on student surveys as soon as possible.

Assessments of Noncognitive Skills. In recent years scholars have focused increasing attention on character skills not measured by standardized tests, such as self-control, persistence, and conscientiousness. These are also known as noncognitive skills, social-emotional skills, and habits of success. Both common sense and academic research suggest that they are extremely important in determining whether a student will succeed in later life. In a recent paper, Transforming Education's Chris Gabrieli, Dana Ansel, and Sara Bartolino Krachman recounted the research findings:

> In the Dunedin Multidisciplinary Health & Development Study [in a city in New Zealand], 95 percent of the young people in the top quintile of self-control were likely to graduate from high school, compared with 58 percent for those in the lowest quintile and about 80 percent for those in the next two quintiles. In James Heckman's 2006 analysis of the [U.S.] National Longitudinal Survey of Youth from 1979, non-cognitive factors were equally as predictive as cognitive factors in accounting for which young men earned a college degree by age 30. In the Fast Track longitudinal study, kindergartners with high social competency were 1.5 times more likely to graduate from high school and twice as likely to graduate from college . . . Among the Dunedin Study cohort, those from the lowest quintile of self-control in their elementary school years were more than three times as likely as those in the highest quintile of self-control to ever have been convicted of a crime (43 percent versus 13 percent).

According to the authors, noncognitive skill levels predict academic achievement, school completion, employment rates, earnings, financial stability, and the likelihood of committing crimes and being a single or unplanned teenage parent. "The positive health effects associated with stronger non-cognitive skills include reduced mortality and lower rates of obesity, smoking, substance abuse, and mental health disorders." Fostering these skills, as early as preschool, actually works, with "both immediate and long-term impact."

Educators have long understood the importance of character skills. A 2013 national teacher survey found that 93 percent agreed it was important for schools to promote these skills, while 88 percent said their schools were already trying to do so. Indeed, schools have long graded students' conduct, and increasingly they create incentives for good behavior and penalties for poor behavior. Many charter schools focus students on a series of values, as we saw with DSST in Denver (see pp. 172–4). Summit Public Schools, a charter network in California and Washington State, asks students and their teachers to fill out surveys on students' habits of success twice a year; mentors then initiate discussions about them with their students.

According to Ted Dintersmith and Tony Wagner, authors of *Most Likely to Succeed*, employers also recognize how important social-emotional skills are:

> *Google . . . changed its hiring strategies after Laszlo Bock, senior vice president of people operations, analyzed their data and found no correlation between job performance and an employee's GPA, SATs, or college pedigree. Google now considers an applicant's ability to collaborate and to perform authentic job-related challenges. Now, they hire many new employees who never went to college.*
>
> *Our education goals have lost touch with what matters most—helping students develop essential skills, competencies, and character traits. It's time to reimagine the goals for U.S. education, and hold all schools—from kindergarten through college—accountable for teaching the skills and nurturing the dispositions most needed for learning, work, and citizenship.*

Who could disagree? The problem is that almost all measurement of noncognitive skills is done through surveys. (The other option is observations by trained personnel, which is quite expensive.) Surveys raise several issues, one of which is known as reference bias. Imagine a demanding school like DSST, with a lot of homework, and another school that is more laissez-faire, with little homework. If we ask students and teachers at both schools to rate kids on conscientiousness, those at DSST will likely have much higher expectations, so they will not rate themselves as highly as those in the laissez-faire school.

And what would happen if teachers started talking with students a great deal about things like self-control, conscientiousness, and persistence? Would some kids decide they are simply lacking in persistence and always will be? Experts who promote the development of noncognitive skills worry about that. According to Gabrieli, lowering students' perception of their capacity with these skills leads to lower grades, lower test scores, and worse behavior.

Finally, if a state made school scores on these skills part of the measurement of school quality, would teachers start coaching students to influence the way they answered surveys? Would other perverse behavior emerge?

We don't know the answers to these questions. But we may soon begin to find out, because six large districts in California, including San Francisco, Los Angeles, Oakland, and Fresno, volunteered to measure noncognitive skills as part of their measurement and rating system, and the Obama administration gave them waivers to do so. In 2016–17, the experiment was in its third year. These CORE Districts use a School Quality Improvement Index that includes test scores, graduation rates, suspension and expulsion rates, chronic absenteeism, and school culture and climate surveys by students, teachers, and parents. But it also includes student surveys on four habits of success: growth mindset (the belief that one's abilities can grow with effort); self-efficacy (a belief in one's ability to meet goals); self-management (the ability to control one's emotions); and social awareness (interpersonal skills such as empathy, collaboration, and the ability to listen). The results account for 8 percent of the School Quality Improvement Index, though by 2016 the districts had not attached any consequences. According to Harvard Professor Martin West, who led research efforts examining the results, the first year of noncognitive skills data showed the expected correlation between social-emotional skills, grade-point averages, standardized test scores, absenteeism, and suspensions, suggesting that the measures were fairly accurate.

Clearly, we don't know enough yet to use such data as part of accountability systems, with consequences for schools. But these skills are critical to success, and the best way to learn about measuring something is to start doing so. We need to measure student progress on social-emotional skills, learn more about these skills' role in future success and the relative impact of home life versus school life on them, develop better ways to measure them, and figure out how schools can improve them.

Already NAEP and PISA are adding measurements of noncognitive skills to their assessments. In August 2016 the Collaborative for Academic, Social, and Emotional Learning (CASEL) announced that it will help eight states "create and implement plans to encourage social-emotional learning in their schools." But CASEL also warned that it was too early to begin attaching consequences or including the data in rating systems. For now, states should only include noncognitive skills in their measurement systems. This information would be valuable both to schools and to parents when choosing schools. Imagine a high school that discovers a big drop in self-efficacy among ninth grade boys. Wouldn't the staff want to know that and try to figure out what to do about it?

Districts that want to experiment with including the data in their rating and accountability systems, as the CORE districts are, will speed up our learning curve. Charter authorizers should also be encouraged to negotiate performance goals that include such measures with schools that are interested in being accountable for improving students' noncognitive skills. But it is too early to force accountability for such improvement on schools that don't want it.

Ideal State Rating and Accountability Systems

I suggest that tomorrow's statewide rating systems—applied to all schools—should have five or six basic elements, weighted roughly as follows. (The balance between achievement and growth should depend on which method states use to measure growth; with some value-added methods, achievement and growth can be combined in one value-added score.) ESSA requires that states also test English learner progress toward proficiency, but I have not specified a recommended weight because it should vary by school. In some, with many English-language learners, it would be quite important; in others, with none, it would be unimportant.

For high schools:

- Student academic achievement: 20 percent*
- Student academic growth: 25 percent
- English learners' progress toward proficiency: variable
- Student engagement: 10 percent
- Qualitative school assessments by experts: 15 percent
- Student outcomes: 25 percent

Elementary and middle schools would use only five elements:

- Student academic achievement: 20 percent*
- Student academic growth: 30 percent
- English learners' progress toward proficiency: variable
- Student engagement: 10 to 20 percent
- Qualitative school assessments by experts: 20 to 30 percent

Suggested indicators for each element can be found in the box on p. 273–4.

In all cases, states should average two years of data whenever possible, to smooth out annual variation and more accurately reflect school performance. Students who arrive at a school more than six weeks into an academic year should not be included. Schools should not be held accountable—or even measured—on the basis of students they have not had an opportunity to educate for at least six months before a test.

Nor should students with severe learning disabilities be included in these measurement and accountability systems, for obvious reasons. States should create separate systems for them that use different indicators and give less weight to academic achievement and growth. But most students receiving special education services should be included. Students without severe disabilities may learn differently from others, but they can still learn. Some may

---

*Can be eliminated using certain value-added models for measuring growth, in which case all 45 or 50 percent of the weight would go to the value-added score.

Indicators Recommended for State Accountability Systems, Measurement, and Research

Include in Formal Statewide Accountability and Rating Systems:

- Student academic growth and achievement, measured by:
  - Test scores in math, ELA, writing, science, and the social sciences
  - For English-language learners, scores on tests designed to measure their progress in learning English
  - PSAT, SAT, ACT and/or state-approved international test scores
  - Industry certifications
  - Progress toward proficiency of English-language learners
- Qualitative assessment, measured by:
  - Expert site visit assessments
- Student engagement, measured by:
  - Parent survey
- For high schools only: student outcomes, measured by:
  - HS graduation rate: four-year, five- to seven-year, and with GED
  - Quality of diploma, if states offer different diplomas
  - Percentage of graduates enrolling in college
  - Percentage of enrollees required to take remedial classes in college
  - Percentage of college enrollees persisting to second and third years
  - Percentage of two-year college enrollees completing a two-year degree or credential
  - Percentage of non-college-bound graduates employed, in training, or in the military
  - Income levels for non-college bound graduates employed full-time

(continued)

Require Districts and Authorizers to Measure but Don't Include in Statewide Accountability and Rating Systems:

- Student attendance rates
- Rates of chronic student absenteeism
- Rates of teacher absenteeism
- Student surveys
- Parent surveys
- Student demand
- Student-teacher ratios
- Student retention
- Teacher retention
- Safety
- Discipline rates
- Numbers of advanced courses (AP, IB, dual credit, etc.)
- Numbers of student internships

Fund Research to Find Objective, Reliable Ways to Use:

- Qualitative assessments of student performance (performance tasks, portfolios, etc.)
- Student surveys
- Assessments of non-cognitive "character" skills

need accommodations during tests, such as more time. But we don't want to exempt all students receiving special education services, because that would give schools incentives to label students as needing special education. It would also be illegal, under ESSA.

States must ensure that the data is audited, analyzed, and spot-checked, to detect cheating. Districts and schools have been caught cheating on standardized tests and manipulating attendance, graduation, and dropout rates. The lesson: we must be on alert for efforts to manipulate all indicators.

To Grade or Not to Grade?

Ideally, states should give various weights to each indicator and sum them to give a grade for each area, plus an overall grade. Some states use colors (as in Denver) or phrases, such as "meets expectations." But parents understand grades on an A–F scale better. If we use grades for our children, we should have the courage to use them for the adults who run our schools. (I would urge states to use pluses and minuses for more precision, just as schools do.)

Some experts argue against one summative grade for each school. California's superintendent of public instruction, Tom Torlakson, and the president of its state board of education, Michael Kirst, expressed this view in a 2016 letter to the U.S. Department of Education: "A summative rating . . . necessarily glosses over differences in performance across indicators and inappropriately draws school leaders, stakeholders, and the public to focus on the single rating rather than a more robust reflection of performance demonstrated by the individual indicators. We reach this conclusion having over 15 years' experience with a single rating where the public paid little attention to the individual components that comprised that single rating."

Without a single, summative grade for each school, however, accountability becomes squishy: schools face much less pressure to improve. "After New York City dropped its A–F rating system and stopped applying pressure on low-performing schools, achievement in F-rated schools immediately fell," reports Chad Aldeman of Bellwether Partners. And to say that parents don't have the ability to look at the five or six grades that sum to the final grade sells them short. Most parents can understand where a school is strong and where it is weak and make their decisions accordingly.

"Summative ratings are all around us," Aldeman points out.

> *If you want to go to a movie, you might consult a site like IMDb or Rotten Tomatoes. Cars, colleges, neighborhoods, restaurants . . . if there's some sort of choice that people can make, there's probably at least one, if not more than one, rating system to help them decide. Even the National Education Association, which opposes the idea of rating schools, has its own A to F grading systems for individual legislators . . .*
>
> *Summative ratings exist; they're also extremely popular. Consumer Reports is an entire magazine devoted to rating everyday household products, and it's been around since 1936 for a reason.*
>
> *Summative ratings are simple and easy to understand, but they're not one-dimensional. All of the rating systems mentioned above have various factors that go into them (in education-speak, we might say they're based on 'multiple measures'). And, while the overall rating provides a useful method for people to make decisions, none of these systems stop at a numeric rating. They all include much more information for people who want to dig in further.*

To put school grades in perspective, states and districts could also give schools a percentile rating based on their overall score. An elementary school that outperformed 62 percent of all elementary schools would have a rating of 62, for instance. (Utah, New York City, and Philadelphia have all done this in the past.) States could also divide schools into groups with similar demographics, then provide bar graphs to show how all those schools compare. Bar graphs give readers visual evidence of how a school stacks up against schools with similar students. One might be rated at the 62nd percentile but be very close in performance to schools at the 90th percentile. Another might be at the 62nd percentile but be quite close to those at the 40th percentile, because schools are bunched around the middle. Bar graphs reveal this, whereas percentiles do not.

Presenting the Data to the Public

States, districts, and authorizers should publish brief performance reports on each school, showing their scores and grades, as Louisiana, D.C., Denver, and other states and districts do. These reports should include other information that is of value to parents and the public but is not included in the ratings, such as the number of students, the student-teacher ratio, demand for the school, the school's mission and focus, the percentage of students receiving special education, and so forth.

As argued earlier, individual schools should also have their own performance agreements, which would include other goals aligned with the school's particular mission and focus. Performance reports should give equal space to performance against these goals, so parents and others can see what the school feels is most important and how well it achieves those goals. Some schools might be just average when it comes to state standards but be outstanding in their own focus areas, whether music, drama, debate, STEM, languages, or real-world internships. Performance reports should reflect these realities.

On the other hand, parents have indicated their strong preference for brief reports—no more than four pages. More in-depth information can be provided on websites identified on and linked to the reports.

Finally, districts and authorizers need to give families help in understanding the data. They should publish explanatory material, as the D.C. Public Charter School Board does with its "Parent Guide to Public Charter School Performance." They should also create or contract for information centers where parents can get help choosing a school for their children, as the RSD has in New Orleans. When we buy houses, most of us use real estate brokers to help us sort through the plethora of options and make the best choice. Our decisions about our children's education deserve equal care, if not more.

In Conclusion

The kinds of systems I have described may seem like fantasy to those steeped in the world of NCLB, but they already exist. In Massachusetts, charter schools must meet minimum state standards, but their charters also include specific goals. When their charter is up for renewal, a team of experts visits for a day and a half and writes a qualitative assessment report on the school, which the state board uses in making its decision. In Washington, D.C., the Public Charter School Board uses a performance framework much like I have advocated (see appendix A), but individual charters include goals specific to the schools and reviews include multiple site visits to assess the quality of schools. Denver Public Schools does much the same thing with its charters. In New Orleans, charters must meet minimum state standards, and both the RSD and OPSB do on-site reviews every year, plus a high-stakes review when schools are up for renewal.

As we have seen, the results in all three cities are outstanding. They are equaled or more by Massachusetts' charter sector, which according to CREDO data is one of the strongest in the nation. Are these not the kinds of results we want in all our public schools?

CHAPTER 14

STRATEGY: GETTING FROM HERE TO THERE

THERE IS NO ONE BEST PATH FROM a 20th to a 21st century education system. Some will evolve slowly; others, like New Orleans, will make a rapid leap. Those who are furthest along—New Orleans, D.C., Denver, Indianapolis, Memphis, and Camden—have all taken different routes. The seven C's apply everywhere, but tactical paths will reflect local circumstances.

Given the unions' resistance to charter schools, much will depend on the political environment. As Ashley Jochim of the Center on Reinventing Public Education has written, big reforms do not succeed without four things: political will, sufficient authority to implement effective strategies, adequate capacity to execute, and political support to sustain changes over time. The last two can be built up over time. In New Orleans, D.C., and Denver, local political support was weak initially but grew as the charter sector delivered results. Similarly, all three cities built capacity along the way. But political will and authority must be present from the start.

When they wrote the Constitution, the Founders left education to the states, so public education systems are formed—and reformed—by state legislation. Districts operate according to the rules laid down by state law. Hence, those who have the most leverage to introduce 21st century systems are state legislators and governors. The media is obsessed with the federal government, but it provides only 10 percent of public K–12 education funding and fewer of the rules. Federal leverage will be limited unless Congress is willing to return to the activism of No Child Left Behind or the Race to the Top, which it rejected when it passed the ESSA.

What Can State Leaders Do?

The most obvious strategy available to state leaders is Louisiana's: create a turnaround district to take over failing schools and hand them to charter operators. Tennessee and Nevada have already done this; Michigan tried but failed (see p. 331); and North Carolina is in the process. The beauty of turnaround districts is that they create 21st century systems to compete with urban districts, in the process demonstrating the superiority of the new model. Tennessee added a nice wrinkle when its bill empowered districts to also put failing schools in innovation zones, with increased funding and autonomy.

Another strategy that has been employed successfully is to take over a failing district and use the seven C's to turn it into a 21st century system, as New Jersey is doing in Camden (pp. 214–15). Already, 25 states have the authority to take control of districts, though some may need additional legislation to turn the schools over to charters. Massachusetts has used the threat of takeover to create an independent authorizing board to oversee ten struggling schools in Springfield, which the board treats much like charters (p. 219). Ted Kolderie, a principal founder of the charter movement, has suggested that state legislation could give failing districts a year to design and adopt their own 21st century arrangements. If they failed to do so in good faith, the state could impose a model.

Congress gave us a third proven route by legislating the Public Charter School Board into existence in the nation's capital. A state could create a new board dedicated to authorizing charters in a city (hopefully with start-up funding for schools). In a state with a lot of cities, it could even let cities compete for the privilege of hosting a charter board.

Ohio and Michigan have too many authorizers, some of which do a terrible job. In such situations, state legislators could create an education commission in a city with the authority to steer the entire public system, charter and traditional. The district would continue as a school operator, but the commission would have the power to open, close, replace, expand, or replicate both district and charter schools, as well as to set policy and enforce compliance with it. Existing authorizers could also continue, but the commission could supersede their decisions. The members of such a commission could be elected, but appointment by a mayor to staggered terms would work better to keep local patronage and political shenanigans to a minimum.

Short of these alternatives, states could at a minimum pass legislation removing barriers to and creating financial incentives for 21st century models, as the Center on Reinventing Public Education has recommended. One such incentive might be a nonprofit investment fund, modeled after the New Schools Venture Fund, the Charter School Growth Fund, and the Chicago Public Education Fund, which could invest not only in schools and districts but in building an ecosystem of nonprofit organizations to support charter schools.

Some states allow districts to convert to "charter district" status, which gives the district more freedom from state rules. Such a move could help districts trying to cross into the 21st century.

Finally, states could support innovations such as the Harlem Children's Zone and the Promise Neighborhoods, funded by the Obama administration to provide comprehensive "cradle-to-career" services in poor areas. Such initiatives include charter schools in a web of broader support for families, increasing the odds that their students will succeed in climbing out of poverty

State Initiatives To Improve Chartering

If political support is lacking for such bold initiatives, states could simply focus on improving their existing charter sectors. Most state legislatures could strengthen their charter laws in a variety of ways:

- Automatically waive most state and district laws and regulations, something most states still don't do for charters
- Remove caps on the number of charter schools
- Equalize funding between traditional and charter schools, including funding for facilities
- Require districts to let charters buy or lease vacant district school buildings
- Give charter schools equal access to public financing and bonding for facilities
- Allow charter preschools and adult schools

Most states could also improve things by making authorizers accountable for the performance of their schools. In systems that are supposed to be built on accountability for performance, authorizers are the exceptions: Often they are accountable to no one. A few states have changed that in recent years, but most have not. Ideally, the state should rate authorizers, primarily based on the performance of their schools. If they fall below a certain level for two years, it could eliminate their right to authorize new schools, and if they fall below for four years, it could ban them from authorizing and force their schools to find new authorizers. Since many in the charter world would not trust state departments of education to play this role, legislators could create a special authority—its board appointed by the governor and legislature to staggered terms to insulate it from political pressures—to ride herd on authorizers. This body could also be tasked with investigating authorizers and charters that are cheating in one way or another and enforcing compliance.

Some states and D.C. already have politically independent, single-purpose organizations dedicated to authorizing charters, such as the Charter School

Institute in Colorado. Research suggests that such organizations tend to out-perform school districts, state education agencies, and nonprofit organizations, which usually have other core purposes and authorize charters on the side. States that don't have such a body should create one, with the license to charter schools statewide. In a large state, legislators could create multiple single-purpose authorizers, each focused on a region.

States could also use grants to build a more effective charter sector. In Florida, where districts authorize almost all charters, the state has awarded grants to help districts recruit outstanding charter networks. Nevada has funded charter incubators to help people plan and launch charters. States could even give teachers unions grants to create boards that would authorize teacher-run charters, as the Federation of Teachers has in Minnesota.

Finally, states could extend their teachers' pensions, health insurance, and other benefits to teachers in charter schools, to neutralize this advantage for traditional district schools.

General State Reforms That Would Help

Reforms don't have to target the charter sector explicitly to spur the evolution of 21st century systems. If states adopted the measurement and accountability systems described in chapter 13, for example, it would help everyone create more effective schools.

Like the federal government, states also need to reform their categorical funding streams, which sometimes make it difficult to do what's best for children. One study, published in 2002, found that the use of up to 70 percent of the money in districts was restricted by formula. Denver Public Schools has tried mightily to create a weighted student funding system in which dollars follow children to their schools, but largely because of state and federal categorical funding, only 56 percent of the money does so. States should meld their categorical funding streams into broader grants, while also allowing districts to combine funds from different streams if they are under a set amount.

States could also follow in England's footsteps and require local districts to distribute at least 80 or 85 percent of total education funds to schools, using a weighted student funding formula that allocates more for those who cost more to educate. Giving schools control of their money would go a long way toward empowering them to improve. (In New Orleans, 98 percent of the money goes to the schools, and in D.C.'s charter sector, 99 percent does.)

States should also reform or, even better, eliminate their teacher tenure laws. Those laws were passed a century ago, when partisan majorities on school boards routinely fired or harassed teachers of the wrong party and hired teachers of the right one, regardless of their qualifications. Today court rulings make such behavior illegal. Still, teachers and their unions argue that without tenure, vindictive principals would get rid of teachers they didn't like. But wouldn't it be better if teachers who found themselves working under such principals had the freedom to land jobs at other public schools, where they might be happier? That's what happens in other professional fields, where tenure is unknown. In such a system—as in New Orleans, D.C., and Denver—principals who kept losing good teachers would lose their own jobs in fairly short order. If we transform a system that tolerates small-minded, vindictive school leaders into one that holds them accountable for performance, in other words, we won't need tenure. I've never heard teachers at charters in New Orleans, D.C., or Denver complain about not having tenure. But I have heard of them leaving for better pay or conditions at other schools.

To encourage more committed teachers, states could also eliminate barriers to teacher-run schools—and perhaps even create incentives for teachers to create such schools.

Many states need to make it easier for talented people to move from other careers into teaching or administration without returning to college for a credential. A decade ago all 50 states had alternative certification for teachers, but according to the National Council on Teacher Quality, only six provided truly alternate routes. Only two states allowed people who had not been formally licensed as principals to run nonchartered district schools.

What Can Mayors and City Councils Do?

City leaders could follow in former Indianapolis mayor Bart Peterson's footsteps and ask the state legislature to give them the power to authorize charters. Peterson succeeded in creating an alternative system that competed with the traditional district and pushed it to change. Mayors have every incentive to authorize well, because their constituents can punish them at the voting booth if they do a poor job. And when political winds shift, charter systems are far harder to undo than district reforms.

With state legislative permission, cities could also create commissions to steer their entire public education systems—both charter and traditional—as outlined earlier.

Cities could help resolve the battles between districts and charters over school facilities by creating new public authorities, perhaps structured as real estate trusts, to own and manage school buildings and grounds. By creating a neutral organization with its own board, with staggered terms, the mayor and city council could take the politics out of decisions about school facilities. The trust would lease facilities to school operators, both traditional and charter. It would have a financial incentive to renovate buildings and keep them in good shape, because it would have trouble leasing run-down facilities. If it were allowed to operate in a businesslike manner, as a quasi-public organization, it could do a far better job than most districts do of managing and preserving this valuable real estate. And if structured to be politically neutral, it could ensure that the system's assets are shared evenhandedly.

Cities could also provide more job security to both charter and district teachers by funding a pool to continue paying for a year those whose schools were closed or replaced, while they looked for a new job. Denver Public Schools does this for the schools it operates, but not for charters. Eliminating tenure and replacing failing schools make teaching a less secure profession, but this kind of safety net would make it more attractive. It would not eliminate risk: Those who could not find new jobs within a year would lose their salaries. This is a good thing, since we want teachers to feel urgency about improving student learning. But a year's grace period would give some security to good teachers whose schools were closed for reasons other than the teachers' performance.

Finally, cities could catalyze the formation of support organizations like New Schools for New Orleans, D.C.'s FOCUS, A+ Denver, and The Mind Trust in Indianapolis. Mayor Peterson and his charter director launched The Mind Trust, so there is precedent for such action. Cities could even provide continuing funding if they felt it was necessary.

What Can School Districts Do?

Districts could also support organizations like those just mentioned. In Indianapolis, for instance, the district works closely with The Mind Trust, which is incubating most of the district's innovation network schools. Districts could also set up public real estate trusts to manage their buildings without bias toward either sector.

School boards that want to take their districts into the 21st century have a number of other options. In many states school boards can begin authorizing charters, but it would be far wiser to set up a separate, appointed authorizing board that has no responsibility to operate schools. That way the new board could concentrate solely on authorizing and not be distracted by the operating crisis of the day. And when a situation arose in which a charter was competing directly with a district school, the authorizing board would not face a conflict of interest.

Districts can do the same for "innovation schools," as Springfield, Massachusetts, has done. They can also shift to weighted student funding, to increase school autonomy and competition between schools. They can create universal enrollment systems, and if they want to spur integration by income, they can require that some or all schools have a certain minimum of low-income students, as Denver has in some schools.

David Riemer, a former budget director and chief of staff to the mayor of Milwaukee, suggests an approach that might augment such policies, given that middle-class families often resist efforts such as Denver's, because they have bought homes in neighborhoods with good schools and want to keep their children's rights to attend them. Low-income children cost more to educate effectively, Riemer points out. So, in a public school choice system, why not increase per-pupil funding for schools that have a significant portion of low-income students? If the "optimal" share in a district were 50 percent, given its demographics, the board might set a target range of 35 to 65 percent. It could provide more money per student for schools with at least 35 percent low-income children and increase the dollar amount until the share reached 50 percent. Above that percentage the incentive would decline, and at 65 percent it would disappear entirely, to discourage schools from becoming dominated by low-income children. If the base amount per child were, say, $10,000, schools with an "optimal" share of 50 percent low-income kids might get $13,000 per child. (The amounts and ranges could vary, of course, depending on the finances and demographics of the district.)

"It's the overall incentive structure that counts," Riemer says.

> The clear message that it sends to school administrators and communities is: Keep out low-income children, or fail to attract middle-income kids, and you will have a lot less money. Attract a very large percentage of low-income children, but avoid having a school that is predominantly low-income, and you will have a lot more money. All children will be backed by a goodly amount, but schools that promote economic diversity (which in most places means racial diversity) will have an especially goodly amount for each student.
>
> Follow the money is the first principle of American public policy. If, rather than attempting futilely to force economic diversity, we reward it—big—might we get a better outcome? Are not incentives worth trying?

Finally, districts can increase school autonomy by taking the monopoly away from most of their internal services, such as professional development, food services, and school maintenance. This approach, called "enterprise" or "entrepreneurial" management of internal services, empowers schools to purchase most services wherever they find the best deal. (Some, like transportation, may be more efficient if they remain a monopoly, as I noted in chapter

10, and policy and compliance functions should never be handled this way.) Districts would shift the funding for selected services to the schools and, after capitalizing their internal service shops as public enterprises, force them to earn their revenue by selling to their customers, the schools. Edmonton, Alberta, pioneered this approach; Minneapolis Public Schools did it in the 1990s; and other public jurisdictions, including the states of Minnesota and Iowa and the city of Milwaukee, have also used it. It is the single fastest way to make internal services more effective while also reducing their costs, because internal service shops have to sink or swim in a competitive market. They almost always swim, because they are so much closer to their customers than private competitors are. But in the process, they increase their quality and reduce their costs. If they don't, the schools are free to buy services elsewhere.

What Can the Federal Government Do?

The federal government could do something to encourage the creation of 21st century systems, just as it has encouraged the creation of charter schools under Presidents Clinton, Bush, and Obama. Congress could meld its many categorical grant programs into a few big block grants, so districts would have the flexibility to use the money in more productive ways. While doing so—or instead of doing so, if Congress balked—it could allow districts to combine certain kinds of categorical funding without permission, below a set amount.

Just as President Obama's Department of Education created financial incentives for states to lift charter caps, require teacher evaluations based in part on student test scores, and embrace higher academic standards, Congress and the department could create financial incentives to encourage 21st century systems. For example, it could reward states that improve their charter laws in the ways discussed earlier. It could reward districts that create separate authorizing boards, as Springfield has. It could reward districts that use contracts, charters, or performance agreements to hold their own schools accountable, as Indianapolis Public Schools has with its innovation schools. It could reward districts that replace failing schools. And it could reward districts that give their school leaders the power to control their budgets and to hire, fire, and reward employees.

What Can Foundations and Philanthropists Do?

Every year, philanthropists invest hundreds of millions of dollars in public education. A few of them have figured out that there are three big cities with high poverty rates that appear to be improving faster than any others—New Orleans, Washington, D.C., and Denver—and all three have embraced 21st century strategies. A few philanthropists have begun to shift their investment portfolios toward those strategies, and their colleagues in other foundations should do likewise. Embracing charter schools may be controversial, but when authorizers do their jobs, 21st century strategies produce superior results.

By offering significant funding for controversial initiatives, philanthropy can change the political equation substantially. The box on pp. 287–9 lists all the strategies I have just suggested, most of which philanthropists can help fund. The first six have particularly high leverage, but circumstances in each city and each district will be different, requiring different responses. The important thing is for foundations and other donors to listen to the data and invest in 21st century strategies.

What Can Parents Do?

Ultimately, big decisions about education reform are political, made by elected officials. Hence the most powerful thing anyone can do to influence those decisions is to turn out voters who will support the reforms I have just described. That's where the typical parent comes in. Parents of schoolchildren are part of a natural network that is rarely activated in political battles. When it is, it can be tremendously powerful. Even bringing 200 parents to a school board meeting can have a profound impact on those board members, who are accustomed to seeing 20 people in the audience.

There are many ways in which parents can make their voices heard. They can support and work for pro-charter, pro-reform candidates for the local school board or state legislature, or for ballot proposals and other change initiatives. They can get involved in larger organizations that already do such things, such as:

- 50CAN, the 50-State Campaign for Achievement Now, which works in about a dozen states
- Stand for Children, which has active offices in 11 states and 17 cities
- Education Reform Now, which has chapters in 11 states and the District of Columbia
- The Hispanic Council for Reform & Education Options
- Democrats for Education Reform, which has chapters in ten states and the District of Columbia

If none of these organizations have a chapter in your city or state, start one. Several of them provide training. 50CAN offers year-long fellowships

Potential 21st Century Strategies

For State Leaders

- Create a turnaround school district to hand failing schools to charter operators
- Take over a failing district and turn over failing schools to charter operators
- Create an independent state-local board to authorize certain failing schools, as Springfield and Massachusetts have
- Create a dedicated charter board to authorize charters in a city or region, as Congress did in D.C.
- Create a citywide education commission with power to open, close, replace, expand, or replicate district and charter schools, with power to override authorizers
- Remove barriers to 21st century models in state law and regulations
- Create financial incentives to support 21st century models, such as funding pools
- Allow districts greater flexibility by converting to "charter district" status
- Support comprehensive innovations such as Harlem Children's Zone
- Strengthen state charter laws and practices
- Make charter authorizers accountable for the performance of their schools
- Create politically independent, single-purpose charter authorizers
- Give grants to help charters flourish
- Extend teachers' pensions, insurance, and other benefits to charter teachers
- Adopt 21st century measurement and accountability systems (see chapter 13)
- Reform categorical funding streams, to create broader, more flexible funds
- Require districts to distribute 80 to 85 percent of their funds to schools to control
- Reform or eliminate teacher tenure laws

(continued)

- Eliminate barriers to teacher-run schools, and create incentives for teachers to create them
- Make it easier for talented people to change careers and begin teaching and running schools

For Mayors and City Councils

- Ask the state legislature to allow mayors to authorize charters
- Create new public authorities—real estate trusts—to handle school facilities in a politically neutral fashion
- Finance a pool to pay teachers whose schools are closed or replaced for a year, while they look for another teaching position
- Catalyze the formation of advocacy and support organizations like The Mind Trust and New Schools for New Orleans

For School Boards and Districts

- Pursue any of the four initiatives listed above for mayors and city councils
- Set up a separate, independent charter board, with no operating responsibilities, to authorize charters and/or innovation or pilot schools
- Shift to weighted student budgeting
- Create universal enrollment systems covering all traditional and charter schools
- Require a minimum percentage of low-income students in some or all schools, to integrate schools by income level (and often by race)
- Increase funding for schools with a healthy percentage of low-income children, to promote integration by income level
- Remove the monopoly from most internal services by allowing schools to purchase them elsewhere if they prefer

For Federal Leaders

- Meld categorical grant funds into broader grants
- Allow districts to combine certain categorical funding, below a set amount

(continued)

> - Reward states that strengthen their charter laws
> - Reward districts that create separate authorizing boards, use performance agreements to hold their schools accountable, replace failing schools, and give school leaders the power to control their budgets and hire, fire, and reward employees

with stipends, for intensive training, and Stand for Children offers Stand University for Parents, which is less intensive.

There are also a plethora of state and locally based reform organizations:

- Friends of Choice in Urban Schools (FOCUS), in D.C.
- A+ Colorado in Denver
- Student Success California
- The Memphis Lift
- Innovate Public Schools, in San Jose, CA
- Greater Oakland Public Schools
- The Georgia Center for Opportunity
- The Institute for Quality Education in Indiana
- The Children's Education Alliance of Missouri and Parents for Educational Progress
- The New Jersey School Choice and Education Reform Alliance
- Parents for Educational Freedom in North Carolina

If there is no such organization in your own area, create one. Build a network of other parents who support reform and educate them on the issues. Take them to outstanding schools, so they see the difference between real quality and their children's school. Then help them demand improvement or replacement by a better operator. Reach out to teachers who support the reform. Many teachers disagree with positions taken by their unions, and by enlisting them on your side you can level the playing field. To learn more about building a powerful network, read *Connecting to Change the World: Harnessing the Power of Networks for Social Impact*, by Peter Plastrik and Madeleine Taylor.

If you're involved in an existing organization that has an interest in better schools—a chamber of commerce, a community organization, even a neighborhood group—encourage the members to focus on these strategies. Hand them this book and others like it, and discuss what strategies might get the most traction in your locality or state. You can also influence the thinking of your school board members, administrators, city council members, and state legislators by giving them this book and others like it.

Once you belong to or have established an organization or network, use it to create events. Pro-charter marches in New York City brought together tens of thousands of parents and opened the eyes of many skeptics to the deep commitment that so many parents, of all races and backgrounds, have to charter schools. Bring large groups of parents to school board meetings where important reform issues are discussed, then follow up with phone calls, e-mail campaigns, op-eds, letters to the editor, and blogs to push board members to vote for the interests of children. In so many places, the teachers union is pushing them to vote for the interests of adults. Parents can be a powerful counterweight, particularly if they vote. So register as many pro-reform parents to vote as possible, help them understand the issues and candidates, and make sure they turn out on election day.

If you live in a place with no school board, pressure whatever body controls public education policy and operations—the mayor, a city council, an advisory board, or a charter authorizing board. When you get some traction, unite with parents in other parts of the state and bring the same kind of pressure to bear on the state legislature.

On another front, join the board of a charter school or network and help promote its success and expansion. If that's not possible, launch a charter school yourself!

If that's not your cup of tea, get involved in your school district. Many have committees and task forces on which residents sit, and some even include parents on search committees for new superintendents, principals, and teachers. When you're ready, run for school board or the state legislature. That's where decisions about school district governance are made, and the best way for activists to influence such bodies is from the inside. If it feels daunting, think of the many who have done this before you. The organizations listed earlier can put you in touch with some of them, who will no doubt be glad to share what they have learned.

The Political Battleground

Charter schools are like many education reforms: They have broad but shallow support among a majority of the population and intense but narrow opposition from teachers unions and their allies. This creates treacherous political ground to navigate.

First, the broad support: In polls, two thirds of the public consistently support charter schools, with less than 30 percent opposed. When the concept is explained, the support goes up to 73 percent. Support among Democrats has been stable at close to 60 percent for several years, and Republican support has averaged about 75 percent. In the 2016 *Education Next* poll, 61 percent of African Americans and 64 percent of Hispanics supported charters.

Among parents, support is even higher. A 2015 poll found that 72 percent of African American parents supported charter schools, and a 2016 poll found that 85 percent of Hispanic parents and 88 percent of low-income parents favored having a charter school in their community.

Now the bad news: The majority of Americans don't know what charter schools are. In a 2014 Phi Delta Kappa/Gallup poll, 48 percent of those surveyed thought charters were not public schools, 48 percent thought they were free to teach religion, 57 percent thought they could charge tuition, and 68 percent thought they could select students on the basis of ability. This helps explain why statewide ballot initiatives to increase the number of urban charters in Massachusetts and to create a statewide turnaround district in Georgia failed by large margins in November 2016—62 to 38 in Massachusetts, 60 to 40 in Georgia. In Massachusetts the teachers unions organized a year-long effort and spent more than $14 million to defeat the measure, telling voters that it would drain more than $400 million from traditional districts. (They neglected to say that the "drained" money would be used to educate the students who left the districts, nor that it would only affect a handful of urban districts that were already at the charter cap of 18 percent, nor that those districts would actually receive *more* money per pupil after they lost students to charters.) In Georgia the unions spent at least $4.7 million and told voters that private industry would come in and run the schools the new district took over—also untrue. Most people trust public school teachers and school boards, so when those two forces united in opposition and used the same distortions the unions were pushing, the outcome was a foregone conclusion.

But these defeats do not mean battles cannot be won on turf where people are more familiar with charters. Charter supporters won the day in New Orleans, D.C., Denver, and Indianapolis because charters produced superior results and charter parents rallied to their cause. Organizing charter parents goes a long way, as Success Academy's Eva Moskovitz and her allies have proven in New York City: They took thousands to Albany to protest Mayor de Blasio's attempt to put the cork back in the charter bottle. Even in Newark, all it took was turning charter parents out to vote to convince the new, anti-charter mayor, Ras Baraka, to support a "unity slate" with charter advocates for the advisory school board.

In such battles, most of the lessons from Denver's experience, on pp. 192–94, apply. Three further suggestions are drawn from experience in Newark and New Orleans:

- Register your supporters and convince them to vote
- When you win control of a system, pay attention to execution and deliver positive results
- Don't ignore the inevitable flaws in your new system; address them and fix them, as the RSD has done

The battle is fought on another level, however, where positive results don't help much: the level of unconscious assumptions. Most of us have been through public schools, and some of us have put children through public schools. We know what a public school system looks like—we have a mental paradigm firmly fixed in our minds. Most of us are not even conscious of this; we just assume, for instance, that a public school and its building are one and the same, or that only public employees teach in public schools. Although things are changing, many of us still assume a whole series of other things that don't have to be the case:

- Schools serve neighborhoods
- Schools last forever
- Schools operate from about 8 A.M. to 3 P.M., five days a week
- Schools and students take the summer off
- Once they prove themselves, teachers get lifetime jobs
- The longer teachers work, the more they get paid
- A teacher's role is to fill students with knowledge, to "instruct" them
- Elementary education involves one teacher teaching 20–30 children for nine months at a time
- Secondary education involves students rotating through a series of 45–60-minute classes taught by different teachers
- A student graduates by passing a certain number of courses taught that way

This 20th century paradigm has a very firm hold on most Americans' thoughts and opinions about schools. But *none* of it has to be true. And *most* of it is not true in New Orleans, D.C.'s charter sector, or many other cities' charter sectors. In fact, if you want to see how arbitrary it truly is, imagine if we treated restaurants the way we treat public schools:

- They would only be open certain hours for five days a week, eight and a half months a year
- We could only eat at the restaurant assigned to our neighborhood
- Restaurants would last forever, no matter how good or bad their food
- After the first two or three years, waiters would have jobs for life (unless they molested a customer—or worse)
- Waiters would be paid based on how many years they had worked, regardless of their performance
- Tipping would not be allowed
- Your local restaurant would be free, but if you didn't like it you'd have to pay to eat elsewhere
- The menu would be the same citywide—and pretty much the same nationwide
- There might be a few menu items you could choose—for dessert, perhaps—but most of the meals would be prescribed

No one would organize the restaurant industry this way, not even in a communist country. But that's exactly how we have organized public education for much of the last century. And a majority of Americans can't really imagine it any other way.

We don't organize preschools that way, nor higher education. Typically, states and cities that fund preschools use 21st century models: They contract with private providers, give parents choices, and try to measure school quality and close the worst schools. In higher education we have a mix of public and private providers, with enormous autonomy and choice. (We're not so good on the accountability side.) For job training, adult education, and human services, we usually contract with nonprofit organizations, just as we do with charter schools.

Opponents of charter schools have been very clever in choosing language that reflects the dominant paradigm. As noted in the introduction, they argue that "corporate reformers" want to "privatize" education. This is nonsense, but it resonates because of the public's fixed ideas about what constitutes a public school.

Reformers need to become as clever with their language as the charter haters are. We should stop talking about "portfolio strategies," a phrase that plays right into the hands of those who paint us as corporate reformers, and instead talk about "21st century systems" and "performance-based schools." We should feature the phrase "public school choice" regularly, because most parents value both public education and choices for their children. We should talk about "*public* charter schools," not just charter schools. And as Michelle

Rhee did when she launched her reform organization, Students First, we should emphasize putting students' interests ahead of adult interests.

Teachers unions are not terribly popular; almost half of Americans think unions have hurt the quality of public schools, far more than think the opposite. They are quite vulnerable to a counterattack, frankly. In truth, their mission is to feather their own nests at the expense of the children and the taxpayers, and reformers should say so. We should constantly remind the public that teachers unions are interest groups there to represent the interests of their members, period. For example, they work hard to create and defend teacher tenure, as well as seniority-based systems in which older teachers get to choose where they teach. The public doesn't realize that this means schools full of poor kids get inferior and inexperienced teachers and receive much less money per child than those full of middle-class kids. We should constantly point this out, to drive a wedge between the unions and their allies among minority and low-income communities.

Many teachers loathe their unions, and we should also exploit this. In many ways, teachers are the key to any statewide battle. We should appeal to younger teachers by changing seniority-based pay systems. We should appeal to all teachers by offering true *professional* status, including the opportunity for teachers to run schools and to lead other teachers. We should remind teachers that most charter schools *empower* them, while most traditional schools treat them like children. And we should organize charter teachers and parents as political forces, which lobby state legislatures just as often as teachers unions do.

For-profit charter schools have given the sector a black eye, over and over. They are not all bad, but too many have siphoned public dollars into private hands, at the expense of the children. Good authorizing is the key to cleaning up unethical charter behavior, and where effective authorizers are present, for-profit charters tend to close. As I said in the introduction, there are none left in New Orleans or Denver, and only three for-profit contractors in D.C. There is simply little profit to be had in inner-city schools. And if a school's education mission is second to the quest for profit, there should be no place for it in public education. Hence one trade-off worth making would be outlawing for-profit operators—if in exchange we get significant 21st century reforms.

The Charter-Lite Option

Leaders in some places find embracing charters to be politically impossible at the moment. Should they pursue the "charter-lite" options discussed in chapters 9 and 11?

If these options embody the seven C's, yes. But if not, no. As these chapters and appendix C make clear, "innovation schools" in most places have not outperformed traditional schools by much, and they have seriously under-performed charters. (In Memphis they have performed well, but at the expense of the traditional schools their principals and teachers left behind.) Denver's experience has been quite typical. So diverting energy away from charters into innovation schools would be a mistake in some places.

But Indianapolis, Springfield, and Denver are all experimenting with more promising approaches, which include nonprofit boards that oversee the inno-vation schools. Unfortunately, these boards in Indianapolis and Denver are not authorizers: They cannot open, close, replace, and replicate innovation schools. In both cities, the school board still plays this role, which at times conflicts with the interests of schools it operates and teachers it employs.

The most powerful charter-lite approach would involve an appointed board like the one Massachusetts and Springfield have created, with real authorizing power, independent of district control. Combine that with real accountabil-ity, choice, and the charter-like autonomy that Indianapolis gives its innova-tion network schools, and we might have something. Even if teachers in such schools were still district employees, when they brought political pressure to bear on the elected district board, the independent authorizing board might be able to ignore it, just as the appointed charter board in D.C. ignores pres-sure brought by city council members. (That would depend on how the autho-rizing board was appointed, for what terms, and how the politicians who appointed it behaved.) The authorizing board would also be free of distrac-tions caused by the task of operating schools. We have yet to see such a model, so we can't be sure it would work. But it could emerge.

The Achilles' heel of most charter-lite approaches is sustainability. People in bureaucracies tend to resent any special privileges given to those in "auton-omy zones," in all sectors of government. Education is no different. When the leaders who champion such efforts depart, as they always do, the bureaucracy usually reasserts its control as rapidly as possible. This is one reason why an independent authorizing board is so important: It can protect schools from the revenge of the bureaucracy.

The second way in which many charter-lite initiatives fall short is by not providing enough autonomy. Denver's innovation schools offer a classic example, as discussed in chapters 9 and 10.

A third common shortcoming is a failure to close or replace failing schools—to impose the kind of consequences that create real urgency among teachers and principals.

A fourth has to do with the challenge of redesigning schools to meet the needs of students who are difficult to educate. Those running schools in typi-cal innovation zones have shown less creativity and entrepreneurial drive than those running charter schools: They seldom rethink the basic school design. Again, Denver offers a good example.

The bottom line: Chartering (by any name) will usually produce significantly greater results than district-run "innovation" or "pilot" or "autonomous" schools. But if expansion of chartering is impossible, charter-lite models can outperform traditional districts. The more of the seven C's used to recode their DNA, the more effective such schools will be.

In Conclusion

A century ago, the creation of standardized, unified school systems with monopolies on free schooling had a dramatic impact on this country, helping us build the most powerful, innovative economy on earth. In the 21st century the emergence of a new model—decentralized, competitive, customer-driven, mission-driven, and performance-based, with steering separated from rowing— could have an equally profound effect. It could once again give us the best education system on the planet, driving huge economic and social gains. We are already seeing the impact in New Orleans, D.C., and Denver.

The impact would be far broader than improving education. It would help revive our cities, by giving middle-class families good urban schools, so they don't have to depart for the suburbs. We might even be able to foster greater integration of schools by income and race, which would help enormously in creating the understanding and trust we need in our multiracial, multicultural democracy. Indeed, these new systems are already beginning to play both roles in New Orleans, Denver, and Indianapolis.

Twenty-first century school systems would also help us reduce poverty. A study that followed 790 Baltimore first-graders for 25 years showed that most of those born into poor families—particularly African Americans in the inner city—remain poor as adults. To interrupt that pattern, we need dramatic change. Our school systems can't do it all. We also need universal access to preschool; interventions that start before birth by helping parents learn how to raise successful children; comprehensive efforts like the Harlem Children's Zone; investments in job training and lifelong learning; business- and job-creation strategies in poor communities; and more. But effective school systems can make an enormous difference. If we can make a dent in poverty, we will help everyone, not just the poor. Crime will go down, employment will go up, and the economy will grow faster.

"Since 1987," author Paul Tough reports, "when Pew started asking these questions, between 87 percent and 94 percent of respondents in every poll have agreed with the statement 'Our society should do what is necessary to make sure that everyone has an equal opportunity to succeed.'" There is no better strategy to make equal opportunity real than a 21st century school system.

THE PUBLIC WANTS an alternative to the bureaucratic education systems that are failing us, and the public usually gets what it wants, eventually. If the unions and their allies are successful in blocking the expansion of charters, however, there is an alternative path: vouchers parents can take to any school, public or private.

In 2012, Bobby Jindal, the Republican governor of Louisiana, pushed through a bill that offered vouchers to low- and moderate-income students in public schools rated C, D, or F by the state's accountability system. Half of the state's public school students qualified. In 2015, Nevada passed a bill allowing any parent whose child had been in public education for at least 100 days to take an Education Savings Account, or voucher. (A court later ruled that the law violated the state constitution.) In 2017, Arizona conservatives pushed a similar bill through their legislature; though it has a limit of 30,000 vouchers by 2022, that can easily be raised later. President Trump and his secretary of education, Betsy DeVos, are huge voucher supporters, as are most Republicans in Congress.

But vouchers have two big flaws, as I argued in the introduction. First, they offer no guarantee of academic success, because most private schools are not accountable to any public body and cannot be shut down. Second, vouchers create unequal opportunity. When limited to those who live in poverty, they enhance equal opportunity. But once half the state has access to them, it won't be long before everyone else demands them. At that point, those who can afford it will add their own money to the voucher and buy more expensive educations for their children, and the education market will stratify by income, like every other market. Most children will lose the chance to grow up with those from different social classes, races, and ethnic groups, and to learn that beneath their veneers, most humans are pretty much alike.

The risk is real, because vouchers are high on the Republican Party's agenda. If we fail to create effective public school systems, voucher bills will pass in state after state, and public systems will gradually give way to private schools. Twenty-first century systems offer a third way, neither public bureaucracy nor private market. They give us the healthy dynamics of decentralization, choice, and competition, but within a framework of equal opportunity and accountability for performance.

This is the future we must create, if we truly want to reinvent America's schools.

APPENDIX A: MEASURING SCHOOL PERFORMANCE IN NEW ORLEANS, WASHINGTON, D.C., AND DENVER

Louisiana's Charter School Performance Compact

In the RSD in New Orleans, school performance is measured using a state system called the Charter School Performance Compact. It has three elements: an academic performance rating, a financial performance rating, and an organizational performance rating. For schools that receive their charters from the state Board of Elementary and Secondary Education (BESE), as RSD charters do, the state Department of Education commissions an annual review of each school, which includes a school visit and an academic, financial, and organizational performance rating. If a school falls short, warnings are issued, and if it continues to fail, the school's charter can be revoked.

The academic rating uses the letter grades, from A to F, that all Louisiana schools receive. Unfortunately, they are based primarily on their students' test scores, and they include only current performance, not growth. All schools can earn 10 bonus points (on top of 150 possible points) for making significant improvement with those who are behind, but in spite of this adjustment, schools full of low-income and minority children rarely score well. If one simply measures test scores, schools full of middle-class kids look strong and schools full of poor kids look weak. The goal should be for all students to experience significant academic growth—a year or more of growth in a year's time—no matter where they start. Louisiana fails this test.

The narrow focus on test scores also discourages innovation. Documentary filmmaker John Merrow gives a good example: "When we were filming *Rebirth*, we learned of an aspiring charter school principal who was determined to open a performing arts school. He envisioned a vibrant building full of talented aspiring musicians, artists, dancers, and actors, all given the opportunity to develop their craft. However, once he realized that the charter review board cared only about test scores, he never even submitted an application." (For a full discussion of this issue, see chapter 13.)

For elementary schools, the Louisiana Department of Education's website explains, "100 percent of the school grade is based on student achievement on annual assessments in English language arts, math, science, and social studies. Schools may also earn [up to 10] points for significant improvement with students who are academically behind."

For middle schools (which cover grades seven and eight in Louisiana), "95 percent of the school grade is based on student achievement on annual assessments. Five percent of the school grade is based on credits earned through the end of students' 9th grade year." In other words, if middle school graduates do well in ninth grade, the school can earn up to 7.5 points extra, out of 150. As with elementary and high schools, they can earn up to 10 bonus points if students who are behind make significant progress.

For high schools, "Half of the school grade is based on student achievement on state assessments and the other half on graduation performance."

- 25 percent is based on student performance on the ACT or WorkKeys (an ACT assessment that measures skills employers value in the workplace)
- 25 percent is based on student performance on End-of-Course exams
- 25 percent is based on a "strength of diploma index," which rewards achievements such as passing Advanced Placement and International Baccalaureate exams
- 25 percent is based on the cohort graduation rate: the percentage of students who started 9th grade and graduated on time within four years

If schools score 100 or more points out of 150, they receive an A; 85 to 99.9, a B; 70 to 84.9, a C; 50 to 69.9, a D; and below 50, an F.

Like other states, Louisiana has adopted a more demanding annual test, aligned with the Common Core standards. As it made the transition, it chose to grade on a curve, to ensure that the distribution of A, B, C, D, and F schools, statewide, remained the same from 2012–13 through 2015–16. "For example, if 10 percent of schools earned an 'A' in 2012–2013, the top 10 percent of schools would earn an 'A' in 2013–2014, 2014–2015, and 2015–2016," its website explained. "Only after we have a new two-year baseline of accountability results in 2016 will BESE begin raising the bar toward our 2025 goal when an 'A' school will be a school where the majority of students are college- and career-ready."

The financial performance rating measures four indicators: (1) the school's fund balance, worth 30 of 100 points; (2) its audit findings, also worth 30 of

100 points; (3) its debt-to-asset ratio, worth 20 of 100 points; and (4) whether it has met state reporting deadlines, worth 20 of 100 points.

The organizational performance framework measures whether a school has met its legal and contractual obligations. There are seven areas of focus, which total 150 points:

1) Enrollment: a nondiscriminatory admissions process, overall enrollment numbers, percentages of at-risk students, re-enrollment rates, and transfer rates (20 points)
2) Facilities: meeting requirements regarding safety, public health, and the Americans with Disabilities Act and submitting an emergency operations plan annually (16 points)
3) Special education and at-risk student populations: whether the school evaluates students and identifies those who need special education, writes individual education plans for them, assesses their academic progress properly, enrolls at least as high a percentage of special education students as the district, retains them, and so on (38 points)
4) Governance: whether the school's board meets all requirements, follows all applicable laws and the Louisiana Code of Government Ethics, performs an annual ethics training, and the like (24 points)
5) Discipline: mostly suspension and expulsion rates and whether these disciplinary methods are conducted properly (16 points)
6) Health and safety: whether the school provides health services to students and follows bus safety protocols (8 pts)
7) Compliance and reporting: whether the school complies with all legal and contractual obligations and submits timely and accurate reports (28 points)

If schools meet or exceed expectations on the financial and organizational ratings and fulfill the terms of their charters, they are renewed based on their academic performance grades from their third year as a charter onward. Those earning A's can be renewed for six to ten years; B's for five to seven years; C's for four to six years; and D's for three years. Those receiving F's are normally not renewed, unless they are a "turnaround school"—a charter that took over a failing school—and have made an average of five or more points of improvement per year of their charter.

At the end of their second charter term or beyond, those with both D's *and* F's are not renewed unless they are a turnaround school and have made five or more points of improvement each year. There are exceptions: BESE can put failing schools on probation for one year, if its members choose to do so. And "alternative" charter schools that serve a unique population are judged only on whether they have met the student academic performance goals set out in their charters (in addition to the usual financial and organizational performance ratings).

For more information, see the *Louisiana Charter School Performance Compact (Types 2, 4, and 5 Charter Schools)*, published by the Louisiana Department of Education, at http://www.louisianabelieves.com/docs/default -source/school-choice/charter-performance-compact.pdf; and Bulletin 126, available at http://bese.louisiana.gov/documents-resources/policies-bulletins.

Washington, D.C.

The Public Charter School Board

When D.C.'s Charter Board, working with charter leaders, developed its Performance Management Frameworks (PMFs), the most contentious issue was how best to measure academic performance: how to capture both student achievement and growth. (See pp. 103–4.) There are different methods, and each has its strengths and weaknesses.

After much debate, the Charter Board chose the Colorado Growth Model, pioneered by Rich Wenning while he was at the Colorado Department of Education. As adopted in D.C., it compares each student's growth to a peer group of students who had similar test scores in the previous year. Next year, if the students perform the same as this peer group, they are at the 50th growth percentile. If they perform better, they are above 50; if worse, below 50. If they are at the 75th percentile, it means they performed as well as or better than 75 percent of their peer group. The staff then ranks each student at the school by their growth percentile, and the student in the exact middle gives the school its "median growth percentile." The Charter Board uses two years of data to calculate this, when it is available, to iron out year-to-year variability.

The Charter Board balances this measurement of growth with actual test scores, giving them equal weight for all but high schools. Both sectors in D.C. use the PARCC tests, which are aligned with Common Core standards. The board periodically adjusts the PMFs to make them more effective, to address problems the schools identify, and to gradually raise the bar.

As one example, here is the formula for grades four through eight in 2017, on a scale of zero to 100:

Student Progress: Academic Improvement Over Time—40 points:

- Growth in English language arts over time—20 points
- Growth in math over time—20 points

Student Achievement: Meeting or Exceeding Academic Standards—30 points

- English language arts: percentage of students approaching expectations for college and career readiness or above—9 points
- English language arts: percentage of students meeting or exceeding expectations—6 points
- Math: percentage of students approaching expectations or above—9 points
- Math: percentage of students meeting or exceeding expectations—6 points

Gateway: Outcomes in Subjects that Predict Future Educational Success—10 points

- Percentage of eighth-grade students who have attended for at least two full academic years and achieved a level 4 (meets expectations) or above on the PARCC math assessment

School Environment—20 points

- Attendance rates—10 points
- Re-enrollment rates (of those eligible to re-enroll)—10 points

The framework for elementary schools without pre-kindergarten was the same, except the "Gateway" indicator was the percentage of third-graders scoring level 4 (meets expectations) or above in reading.

High schoolers take the PARCC tests only once—in tenth grade—so their formula is a bit different. Student growth on that test accounts for only 15 percent of the total, compared with student achievement, which accounts for 25 percent. Gateway indicators are awarded 35 points, rather than 15, and they lean toward achievement:

- Four-year adjusted cohort graduation rate—3 points
- Five-year adjusted cohort graduation rate—4.5 points
- Percentage of 11th-graders scoring at least 80 on the PSAT test—7.5 points
- Percentage of 12th-graders scoring at least 800 on the SAT test—7.5 points
- Percentage of 12th-graders accepted to a full-time college or university—7.5 points

- College readiness: the rate of students passing Advanced Placement and/or International Baccalaureate exams, and/or the rate earning college credit by taking college-level courses through "dual enrollment"—5 points

"School Environment" is worth 25 points rather than 20; the five extra points are for the percentage of ninth-graders who have completed sufficient credits to be on track to graduate within four years. Schools can opt to add measures related to career and technical education, worth 1 percent each, which lower college readiness to 3 percent.

Generally, if a school's results on any indicator are at or above the 90th percentile for all charters of its type (preschool, elementary, middle, high, or adult school), it normally receives the maximum number of points possible. If they are at or below the 10th percentile, it receives no points. In between, it receives more points the higher its score.

If its point total reaches 65 to 100, the school is in tier one; if 35 to 64.9, tier two; and zero to 34.9, tier three.

The Charter Board created separate PMFs for early childhood education (schools with pre-K and up to third grade) and adult education. But if they are part of a larger school, preschool years are now included in the larger school's PMF. The early childhood indicators include attendance and an assessment of the quality of teachers' interaction with students, but they also allow schools to use a broad array of assessments of their own choice to measure math skills, literacy, and social and emotional growth.

The adult education framework includes:

- Student progress on adult basic education or English as a second language
- Student achievement: percentage of students earning a General Education Development (GED) degree or a state-recognized equivalent
- College and career readiness: the numbers of students who entered and retained employment or postsecondary education
- School environment: attendance and student retention
- And "mission-specific goals" unique to the particular school

Adult schools were assigned to tiers for the first time in November 2015.

"Alternative schools" have a mission of serving and enroll a high percentage of at-risk students, such as high-needs special education students, or those who have dropped out or are under court supervision. The Charter Board negotiates performance goals with each alternative school and judges its performance solely based on whether it achieves those goals.

The board also uses a Financial and Audit Review Framework to judge schools' financial performance and compliance with legal requirements. All three elements are considered during school reviews. Every five years, the Charter Board also conducts a qualitative assessment, using a model similar to the English inspection system (see pp. 264–5).

D.C. Public Schools (DCPS)

Accountability in DCPS is less focused on closing failing schools than on removing weak principals and teachers when schools are failing. The DCPS chancellor negotiates annual performance goals with each principal, which are used as part of their evaluations.

DCPS provides public scorecards for each school, but they do not add up to any rating; they are simply used to give comprehensive information about each school to parents and others. The scorecards include the following indicators for relevant schools (graduation rates are only relevant in high schools, for instance):

Student Performance
- Math: the percentage of students who score at each level on PARCC
- Reading: the percentage of students who score at each level on PARCC
- Four-year adjusted cohort graduation rate
- Five-year adjusted cohort graduation rate
- Advanced Placement performance: percentage of students passing AP exams

Student Progress
- Student growth in math and reading: median growth percentile
- First-time ninth grade completion: percentage of first-time ninth-grade students who earned enough credits to be on track for graduation in four years

Safe and Effective Schools
- Attendance: average percentage of students attending school daily
- Truancy rate: percentage of students with ten or more unexcused absences while still under the age at which school is compulsory
- Out-of-school suspensions: percentage of students who received at least one out-of-school suspension
- Long-term suspensions: percentage of students who received at least one suspension of 11 or more days
- Student safety: student ratings of safety and order at the school, from a survey, on a scale of zero to 100

- Student satisfaction: student ratings of satisfaction with the school, based on a survey, on a scale of zero to 100
- Student re-enrollment: percentage of students not in the school's highest grade who returned to school the following year
- Retention of effective teachers: percentage of teachers rated effective or highly effective who returned the following year

Unique School Indicators
- Here, schools include their own measures of success.

A Common Report Card for Parents

Parents in D.C. need a common set of school report cards, so they can judge all schools of each type (preschools, adult schools, career-tech schools, alternative schools, and more typical elementary, middle, and high schools) by the same criteria. The D.C. State Board of Education recently took the first step by approving a fairly rudimentary five-star rating system that will apply to both sectors (though neither will use it to make decisions about replacement, replication, and the like). For elementary and middle schools, it will give 30 percent of the weight to PARCC test scores (percent meeting or exceeding expectations), 40 percent to growth (median growth percentiles and growth to proficiency). Another 20 percent will reflect school climate measures such as attendance, truancy, re-enrollment rates, and ratings of pre-K offerings, if the school includes them. The remaining 10 percent will be split equally between gains in language development for English learners and how well-rounded the school curriculum is.

High schoolers only take PARCC exams once, and they have a choice between a variety of math classes, which makes it difficult to use PARCC to measure academic growth. The Office of the State Superintendent of Education (OSSE) says it intends to develop measures of academic growth in high school, but for now the formula will exclude growth. Half the weight will go to academic achievement, measured by PARCC scores, ACT scores, the percent taking Advanced Placement and International Baccalaureate tests, and the percent passing such tests. Another 20 percent will be based on graduation rates, a further 20 percent on the school climate measures noted above, and 10 percent split in the same way as for elementary and middle schools.

OSSE pledged to continue working to develop other useful measures, such as science assessments, assessments prior to third grade, and school climate surveys.

Denver's School Performance Framework

Since 2008, DPS has used a sophisticated School Performance Framework (SPF) to measure the quality of charter and traditional public schools. DPS has different SPF formulas for preschools, elementary schools, middle schools, high schools, and alternative schools. Most of them include reading, math, writing, and science scores. Over the years DPS has tweaked the formulas, and they underwent a major rewrite in 2016, in part because the state began using a new standardized test (PARCC) in 2015. (There are no SPF ratings for the school year 2014–15, because there is no scientific way to compare 2015 test scores to previous test scores.)

There are three important things to understand about the SPF. First, it is hopelessly complicated, with dozens of indicators and the possibility of earning various numbers of points for each one, depending upon performance. (If there were fewer than 16 students in the category being measured, the indicator is not even used, so different schools have different numbers of points they can earn.) It uses two years of data, but rather than averaging them, it uses a different matrix to combine the data for each indicator. The public doesn't understand what goes into the SPF, and it is far too complicated to serve as a useful performance dashboard for school leaders. DPS really needs two different instruments for two different purposes: a full SPF for use in making accountability decisions about intervention, closure, replacement, and replication, and a streamlined version to help parents make choices and school personnel track their progress and manage schools.

Second, all the points add up to a final score, and that number classifies the school into one of five performance categories, each of which is given a color. Most of the public understands these colors, though grades of A, B, C, D, and F would be clearer.

Third, the SPF relies far more heavily on students' academic growth than on their current proficiency levels. It is unfair to punish a school for low proficiency rates if most of its students arrived several years behind grade level, so growth is a fairer measure. Unfortunately, Denver overdid it. To measure growth, the state uses the Colorado Growth Model. This compares each student with their "academic peers": other students in the state who had similar test scores in the past one, two, or three years, depending upon what grade the student is in. A student scores at the 50th percentile if his or her academic peers make four months' progress in a year and the student does the same. If he makes six months' progress, he scores well above the 50th percentile— even though he has fallen further behind his grade level.

Schools are given a Median Growth Percentile (MGP) by calculating the

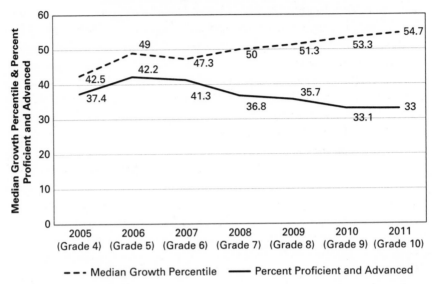

DPS Class of 2013: Improving Its Growth Scores While Falling Further Behind Grade Level

Figure A-1 Source: Alexander Ooms, "The Problem with Growth Scores," *Chalkbeat*, August 28, 2013. Used with permission of author.

growth percentile for each of their tested students and picking the median—the student exactly in the middle of the distribution. All of this means that a school can have a high MGP while its students are falling ever further behind grade-level proficiency. Since growth has accounted for roughly two thirds of a school's score in recent years, the problem is significant—as Figure A-1 demonstrates. By contrast, Washington, D.C., also uses the Colorado Growth Model, but it weights growth and proficiency more equally.

The other problem with the Colorado Growth Model is that it has a built-in tendency for schools to revert to the mean. If a school's students score well, they will be compared in the future to other high-scoring students. If they match those peers by scoring well again, the school's MGP will fall at the 50th percentile. Similarly, if a school's students perform poorly, they will be compared only to other low-scoring students, so it will be easier for them to score better next time. (Given this tendency, the fact that most DSST charters—whose students are roughly 80 percent minority and two thirds low-income—consistently score so high is truly remarkable.)

Over the years, DPS has adjusted the SPFs numerous times. In 2016–17, the SPFs for non-alternative K–12 schools consisted mostly of the following components, each given a different weight, though they differed a bit between elementary, middle, and high schools:

1. Student Progress Over Time (Growth), which in 2016–17 accounted for roughly two thirds of the score for elementary and middle schools and 60 percent for high schools. (For high schools, this number included the post-secondary readiness growth category listed for high school students below.) Schools were awarded zero to 12 points on each indicator, depending on how important the indicator was judged to be and how they performed. Indicators included:

- Median growth percentiles (MGPs) for literacy and math
- MGPs compared to schools with similar demographics
- MGPs for continuously enrolled students (elementary and middle schools only)
- MGPs for subgroups such as English-language learners, students who qualified for a free or reduced-price lunch, minorities, and students with disabilities
- MGPs on the ACCESS assessment for English-language learners
- Percentage of English-language learners on track toward proficiency on ACCESS
- Catch-up growth in early literacy, for students reading below grade level and significantly below grade level (elementary only)
- Catch-up growth: what percent of students moved up to a higher achievement level in literacy and math
- Keep-up growth: what percent of students remained at the two highest levels

2. Student Achievement (Status), which in 2016–17 accounted for 20 percent of an elementary or middle school's score and 30 percent of a high school's score. (The latter number includes the "postsecondary readiness" category cited below.) Indicators included:

- Percent meeting or exceeding "college- and career-ready" standards in literacy, math, and science
- Percent meeting or exceeding standards in literacy, math, and science, compared to schools with similar demographics
- Percent meeting or exceeding standards among English-language learners, those qualifying for a free or reduced-price lunch, students of color, and students with disabilities

- Percent meeting or exceeding standards among English-language learners, those qualifying for a free or reduced-price lunch, and students with disabilities compared to schools with similar demographics
- Percent reaching early literacy benchmarks in kindergarten and grades 1–3 (elementary only)

3. Parent and Student Engagement and Satisfaction, which in 2016–17 counted for roughly 10–13 percent of school scores. Indicators included:

- Attendance rates
- Results from student satisfaction surveys
- Availability of special education and enrichment offerings
- Percentage enrolled the entire year, compared to schools with similar demographics
- Enrollment change over the year (bonus points only; no points included in the denominator, the potential point total)
- Dropout rates (high schools only)
- Percent of parents with positive responses on survey
- Percent of parents who responded to the survey

4. Post-Secondary Readiness (Status), for high schools only (counted as part of the second category above). Indicators included:

- Graduation rates
- Graduation rates for English-language learners, students qualifying for a free or reduced price lunch, students of color, and students with disabilities
- On-track-to-graduation rate
- Performance on ACT tests (reading, math, English, and science)
- Performance on ACT tests for English-language learners, students qualifying for a free or reduced price lunch, students of color, and students with disabilities
- Enrollment in higher-level coursework such as Advanced Placement (AP) and International Baccalaureate (IB) classes
- Passing rates on AP and IB exams
- Passing rates in post-secondary readiness courses
- College remediation rates in math, reading, and writing
- College remediation rates compared to demographically similar schools in math, reading, and writing
- Percentage at benchmark on PSAT tests in reading, writing, and math

5. Improvement in college and career readiness, for high schools only (counted in the 60 percent weighting for growth noted in the first category above). Indicators included:

- Improvement in school graduation rates
- Improvements in performance on state and national assessments
- Changes in enrollment in AP and IB programs and college courses
- Changes in passing rates on AP and IB tests

In addition, indicators related to equity, which are already counted in the categories above, were pulled together to give each school an equity score, purely for informational purposes. The equity score was not included in a school's final rating, though there is discussion of creating a minimum equity score needed to qualify for the two highest ratings (blue and green) in the future. Indicators included:

- Growth in MGPs for students of color, English-language learners, those qualifying for a free or reduced-price lunch, and students with disabilities
- Growth in MGPs for students of color, English-language learners, and students with disabilities, compared to schools with similar demographics
- MGP on ACCESS assessment for English-language learners
- Percentage on track toward proficiency on ACCESS assessment for English-language learners
- Percent meeting or exceeding standards among English-language learners, those qualifying for a free or reduced-price lunch, and students of color
- Percent meeting or exceeding standards among English-language learners, those qualifying for a free or reduced-price lunch, students of color, and students with disabilities compared to schools with similar demographics
- Graduation rates for students of color, English-language learners, those qualifying for a free or reduced-price lunch, and students with disabilities

Once all points (other than the equity score) were added up, schools fell into five categories: "distinguished," or blue; "meets expectations," or green; "accredited on watch," or yellow; "accredited on priority watch," or orange; and "accredited on probation," or red.

Schools that fell in the bottom three categories received support, such as training, consultations on curriculum, help in using data to increase student achievement, and additional funding. In 2015–16, 35 schools shared almost $14 million, plus federal grant funds—a total of $1,647 more per student. The bottom two categories were also subject to interventions, from changes in academic programs or staff to schoolwide turnaround efforts, including closure and replacement.

Adjusting the SPF

In October 2014, more than a dozen organizations signed a letter to the Board of Education asking for changes in the SPF. Their biggest concern was its over-reliance on growth. The board responded by agreeing to shift from a three-to-one ratio of growth to status for elementary schools to a three-to-two ratio, and at middle schools to shift from three-to-one to two-to-one. But when faced with the PARCC exam results, it chose not to.

Even if it had, growth would be weighted too heavily. Consider a middle school that had a strong MGP, which accounted for two thirds of its SPF score, but a weak status score, which counted for only 20 percent. Overall, it would probably earn green status, even though its students were falling further behind grade level every year.

A second concern expressed in the letter was that the green category—"meets expectations"—was too broad, ranging from the 51st percentile through the 79th. A school just a bit above average was considered green, which meant everyone assumed it was performing fine. Yet the district's average was quite low in proficiency. As the group wrote, "Some green schools are on a strong path to proficiency while others are on a path to proficiency but will never get there. Students need to be in schools that actually produce learning—as measured by proficiency metrics." The board stuck with its ranges, however.

The group also argued that standards—as defined by "cut scores"—were too low. High schools could earn a maximum number of points for proficiency if only 20 percent of their students were proficient in math, 40 percent in writing, and 50 percent in reading, for example. "In setting the bar too low for schools," the group wrote, "the current rating system gives parents the wrong message, indicating that schools are high quality when, in fact, most students have little chance of meeting the state's standards." The board agreed to raise the standards, but when it got the first SPF scores after the PARCC exams in 2016, it did just the opposite.

Finally, the group asked that more weight be given in the SPF to narrowing achievement gaps between different income and racial groups, and the board agreed. DPS did a bit of this and also added the equity category, which does not count toward a school's ultimate score or rating.

The bottom line: DPS still has real work to do to create an SPF that truly reflects whether a school is getting its students on track for college or a career. It should weight growth and status more equally, raise standards, make the five performance bands more equal in their range, and create a simpler version that parents and school personnel can understand. When the people we depend upon to improve performance can't understand the yardstick by which they are measured, how can we expect it to motivate them?

Appendix B: What We Should Learn from Denver's Experience with Performance Pay

Denver's "ProComp" performance pay system, first passed and funded by voters in 2005, took effect in 2006. Incumbent teachers could opt in or continue with their old salary schedule, but all teachers hired after January 1, 2006, had to participate. The new system abandoned automatic salary increases for experience and graduate credit but offered potential raises and bonuses that could increase a teacher's annual pay by up to 20 percent. Teachers could earn them by:

- obtaining advanced degrees and certifications
- completing specialized professional development
- demonstrating proficient practice on a new evaluation system
- working at a hard-to-serve school or in a hard-to-staff position
- meeting classroom learning objectives
- exceeding student achievement expectations on state tests
- working in a school with distinguished achievement, and/or
- working in a school with high attendance and a high rate of growth

Unfortunately, Denver made two common mistakes. First, it used salary increases as the primary rewards rather than one-time bonuses. This makes performance pay systems very expensive, because any salary increase costs money for the rest of an employee's career, while a bonus raises costs for only one year. Salary increases also dilute the impact of performance incentives, compared to bonuses, because the reward lives on for years, regardless of future performance.

Second, Denver included incentives to participate in professional development courses and to get advanced degrees. They turned out to have no impact on student learning.

But many teachers loved ProComp, particularly because the new system imposed no ceiling on their incomes—they could continue earning salary increases for as long as they taught. "We learned that the incentives in late career to roll up your earnings were powerful but not productive," says Brad Jupp, the union leader who helped design it, then joined the DPS leadership. "And we needed to put more money at the front end of the career. This was a very painful learning for me, because it meant I had to burn a lot of bridges, but it was true. I watched friends stack up incentives as fast as they could, and they weren't becoming better teachers, they were getting more money. At the same time, we were getting high turnover in the early years."

So the district decided to renegotiate in 2008, when the contract expired. But the union resisted. In May 2008 it issued a vote of no confidence in Superintendent Bennet, and teachers called in sick to protest. There were rumors they might use job actions during the Democratic National Convention, held in August in Denver, if no contract had been signed. Eventually, both sides compromised.

ProComp version 2.0 shifted to more use of bonuses, and it eliminated all but two of the potential salary increases after a teacher's 14th year of service. "For a lot of teachers," says DCTA Executive Director Pam Shamburg, "that was a bait and switch."

Still, teachers hired since 2006 generally feel pretty good about ProComp, according to union leaders. Even veteran teachers are not nearly as negative about it as they are about school closures, teachers losing jobs, and charter schools.

But there is little evidence that ProComp has improved student performance. A 2010 evaluation by the University of Colorado at Boulder School of Education found that it seemed to have helped with teacher retention rates, particularly in hard-to-serve schools, but little else. A 2011 study by the University of Colorado in Denver found little impact on retention, teaching practices, or student achievement. And a 2014 study by Harvard's Strategic Data Project found that some incentives rewarded the most effective teachers, as measured by their students' median growth percentiles, but others did not.

The truth is, there is no one best way to compensate employees, just as there is no one best way to design or run a school. People are different, and students' needs are different. In the many district and charter schools I have visited across the country, I have found no consensus about performance pay. Some people like it and some don't. In Denver, many charters use performance pay, but they don't claim to have found the perfect system. They often tweak their systems over time, continually seeking to make them fairer and more effective in attracting and retaining the best teachers.

In contrast, when a large district bargains over performance pay with a teachers union, there is always pressure to water things down so that every employee gets something. "Every time we have a conversation about moving it to the next level, there's the usual, 'We want all steps for everybody,'" Board of Education member Happy Haines told me. "The union politics is, 'We represent everybody, we've got to do something for everybody.' Which is completely the opposite of what we think should happen. [We want to] invest where we know we're going to get the greatest return."

The lesson: To maximize performance, leave decisions about pay structures—and many other things—up to individual schools (or groups of schools that use the same educational model, such as charter networks).

Even Brad Jupp, an architect of ProComp, agrees. It's still too easy for teachers to boost their salaries by "buying graduate credit and degrees," he believes. That is not only expensive, it fails to reward excellence in the classroom. "Some compensation decisions might be better managed at the school level, just as they are at the firm level in the business world," he says. "I'm persuaded that the school as firm really matters. There's a lot of evidence we didn't get ProComp 100 percent right in its first two or three years, and that there is still room for improvement."

Rather than putting time and political capital into improving ProComp, however, DPS should accelerate the transition to charters and truly autonomous Innovation Zone schools. It should let them craft their own pay systems and give charters equal funding for performance pay, so they are no longer at a financial disadvantage. That is a far surer path toward higher performance than any district-wide pay system.

APPENDIX C: OTHER DISTRICTS PURSUING 21ST CENTURY STRATEGIES

Memphis

Background

Memphis is a poor city: 82 percent of its public school students are "economically disadvantaged," and 76 percent are African American. Eighteen percent missed at least 18 days of school a year in 2015–16, and 44,000 of 112,000 report a chronic health condition, such as asthma.

Until 2012, the school district was quite conventional: highly centralized, with control over school budgets, hiring, and curriculum firmly lodged at district headquarters, not in the hands of principals. Students were assigned to their neighborhood schools; they could choose another only if one of a handful of charter schools would take them, if space were available in another traditional school, or if they had high enough test scores to participate in a kind of magnet program, called Optional Schools.

Facing abysmal student performance and poor fiscal prospects due to a new state law, the school board decided in 2011 to dissolve itself into the surrounding Shelby County Schools (SCS). Board members thought the move would shore up the district's finances and improve its chances of integrating schools. Majorities of both the city's and county's residents (most of whom live in the city) voted for the change. Under state law, Shelby County Schools had no choice but to accept it, but the largely white suburbs would have none of it. Within a year all six suburban municipalities had seceded to form their own school districts—leaving Memphis schools back where they started.

By that time, however, the ground rules had changed. To compete for federal Race to the Top funds, Tennessee passed legislation in 2010 creating the Achievement School District, modeled after Louisiana's Recovery School District, and eliminating the state's cap on the number of charter schools. The combination helped it win $500 million over four years, as one of only two first-round winners.

The Achievement School District

The ASD recruited Chris Barbic from YES Prep Public Schools, a charter network he founded in Houston, to run the district. Barbic wanted to turn all the ASD schools over to charters, but leaders in the U.S. Department of Education, whose Race to the Top grant helped fund the ASD, insisted that he open schools in 2012, only a year after he arrived. So he reluctantly opened three schools run directly by the ASD that year and two the next year, which weighed ASD down with operational duties. When he resigned in late 2015, a year after suffering a heart attack, he still wanted to spin them off as a charter network. But as of late 2016 the move was only in the planning stages. Hence the ASD traveled the same path and learned the same lessons the RSD did in New Orleans, though with fewer direct-run schools.

Barbic recruited some of the nation's highest-performing charter networks to take over schools, including KIPP, Green Dot Public Schools, Achievement Schools, Aspire Public Schools, and Scholar Academies. But he also recruited local school leaders to create ten charter organizations.

Tennessee's legislation required that ASD schools remain neighborhood schools. Initially, they were prohibited from enrolling anyone from outside the school's zone, even if they had space. But in 2015 the ASD got the legislation amended to let schools fill open spots with students from other schools in the bottom 5 percent, after the neighborhood enrollment period, as long as they lived in poverty, tested below proficient in the previous year, or were children of ASD teachers and staff. Such students cannot exceed 25 percent of a school's population.

Most ASD charters had a rough start. Because they were in the bottom 5 percent on performance and most parents were not actively choosing them, operators faced a tougher challenge than in their other charter schools. As neighborhood schools, they suffered from high mobility and weak attendance: many students didn't enroll until school had been underway for several weeks, and more than a third moved in or out during the school year. (This compares to an average of 10 percent mobility in all charters in Tennessee.) Unfortunately, the state counted all test scores, regardless of when the students arrived.

A majority of ASD charters took over entire schools, rather than building a grade at a time, as most charter networks prefer. Few teachers chose to stay, since they would lose their seniority in SCS and have to work longer hours, so the charters started with a lot of novice teachers. And the ASD pressured them to minimize suspensions and expulsions. All these factors made it difficult to establish a school culture that reduced disruptive behavior, usually the first step in turning around a failing school.

ASD charters received the same per-pupil amount as their local districts, which averaged about $8,700. They didn't have to pay for their buildings, though unlike SCS schools they did pay for maintenance and utilities. Eighteen percent of their students had special needs, compared to 12 percent in SCS schools, but there was no extra money for those with severe needs. Traditional schools and charters authorized by SCS could turn to the district, which took advantage of economies of scale by bringing students with severe disabilities together in "cluster programs." ASD schools had no such help. Federal Individuals with Disabilities Education Act (IDEA) money helped a bit, but it fell far short of what the schools needed. One charter reported spending more than $1 million on special education but receiving only $66,000 a year.

A study published by the Tennessee Consortium on Research, Evaluation, and Development concluded that the high special education costs diverted resources from the schools' core academic operations. "One leader anticipated that these costs would require them to eliminate the extra academic time they provided in summer programs and Saturday school," it reported.

The ASD schools also ran into bureaucratic resistance from SCS and political resistance from teachers and communities that didn't want their schools replaced by charters. SCS changed enrollment boundaries on a few ASD schools, and in 2014 it suspended its policy of allowing some charters to phase in a grade at a time by keeping SCS principals and teachers in place to handle the grades that had not yet been taken over. Once that happened, students in those grades had to be bused to other schools, which stimulated vocal community opposition. This led both KIPP and YES Prep to withdraw from planned takeovers.

When the ASD takes a school, the district is not required to keep the teachers who are not retained. So just as in New Orleans, some African American teachers saw the reforms as a threat to their jobs. "Some view it as an attack on the African American middle class in Memphis," one black SCS principal told me, because the school system was a major employer. "A friend told me his parents always told them, 'If you get a job at Memphis City Schools, you'll be set for life.'"

"It got pretty loud" in the fall of 2014, says Barbic, "but it was mainly teachers. The community meetings that we held, it was really teachers who were the loudest and the noisiest. Unfortunately, there weren't a lot of parents there to begin with, but even the parents that were in the room were listening and were open."

By the ASD's third year, the political hostility to a perceived "white takeover" of black-run schools was widespread. "We had some elected officials who in the past were maybe not hugely supportive, but were at least quiet, who started to speak out against some of the stuff," Barbic recalls. In late 2015, the SCS Board voted to request a moratorium on the expansion of the ASD in Memphis.

The ASD charter operators soldiered on. To deal with high mobility and other challenges, they adapted. They introduced blended learning and small-group instruction based on where children were, so they could tailor classes to new arrivals and those far behind grade level. They raised philanthropic funds for students with severe disabilities and built their own capacity to educate them. They did home visits and other community outreach to build relationships, introduced wraparound services like health care, food banks, and financial literacy classes for parents, helped parents find jobs, and employed neighborhood men to do maintenance and lawn work. Some even bought and renovated abandoned homes and built new housing in their neighborhoods.

In their first year of existence, ASD charters struggled. But in their second and third years, as explained on pp. 213–14, they have scored in the top level for academic growth, on average. Overall, the ASD outpaced state growth over its first three years in science and math proficiency but not in reading. There it mirrored a statewide decline, which probably reflected changes made to align the state reading test more closely with Common Core standards. On surveys, 83 percent of parents indicated satisfaction with their ASD schools in 2015, 81 percent of students said they felt safe in their schools, and 83 percent of students said their schools had a positive culture—all gradual increases over time.

Meanwhile, the threat of takeover by the ASD lit a fire under Memphis's lowest performing schools. Schools in the bottom 5 percent that had not yet been taken over or put into SCS's Innovation Zone improved in recent years—not as rapidly as ASD schools in their second or third years, but as rapidly as the ASD average, including those in their first year. This has helped drive the statewide proficiency threshold for the bottom 5 percent in grades three through eight up from 16.7 percent in 2012 to 26 percent in 2015, a huge achievement.

The Innovation Zone

When Tennessee leaders decided to create the ASD, they wanted school districts "to have some skin in the turnaround game, so it wasn't just the ASD,"

Barbic explains. The legislation gave districts the ability to create innovation zones for their priority schools, with increased autonomy. The state pooled its federal School Improvement Grant money and asked districts to compete for it, based on their plans to create such zones.

As noted on p. 213, Shelby County Schools (SCS) recruited its strongest principals for the iZone, who recruited their strongest teachers. Memphis's innovation schools have performed well, but schools their principals and teachers left behind have suffered. Barbic notes that in other cities, where the ASD took over only two schools, innovation zones have not performed nearly as well as in Memphis. He believes that the ASD's aggressive takeovers in Memphis spurred SCS to make its zone a top priority. And SCS Superintendent Dorsey Hopson agrees: "I don't know if we hadn't had the intense focus and sense of urgency from the state, we wouldn't have been able to get those results."

There are also several question marks about the iZone's future. The first is financial: with a budget deficit forcing hundreds of layoffs, can the district maintain its level of investment in the iZone? The second is political: if the majority changes on the school board and/or the superintendent leaves, will their successors undermine the partial autonomy given to iZone schools? Within public bureaucracies, people resent special privileges given to any subset of institutions or people, so special zones like this are typically yanked back into the bureaucratic fold after a few years.

The third big question about the future of reform in Memphis is the relative paucity of parental choice, outside SCS's 45 charters. Parents and students who make choices tend to be more committed to their schools. And when no one is forced to attend a particular school, districts can encourage their schools to differentiate—to create models for different kinds of children with different interests and needs.

Other "Charter-Lite" Models

Boston Public Schools

Boston has several different autonomy models. In-district Horace Mann charters, "pilot schools," and "innovation schools" all have similar degrees of autonomy, while "turnaround schools" have some freedom from district policies but are largely managed by the district. Independent charters vastly outperform every other school model; "charter-lite" models have mixed results.

The first Horace Mann charters in Massachusetts were created in 1998, but they have not caught on: Charter founders have been more interested in creating independent charters, and the teachers union has opposed all charters. By 2016–17 there were only six "in-district," Horace Mann charters. The state board of education, the local school board, and the Boston Teachers Union must all approve their charters. Most teachers are union members and are on the union pay scale. Each school has a memorandum of understanding in which any waivers from collective bargaining agreements are outlined, which they submit to the state board along with their application. The schools' boards of trustees make many key decisions, as with independent charters, and the schools enjoy many of the autonomies that independent charters have: freedom to hire and fire teachers; to opt out of union seniority requirements during layoffs; to add teacher hours (with stipends); to change the schedule and calendar; to set the curriculum; to hire and fire the principal (with superintendent approval); and to establish their own professional development process for teachers. Admissions are through a state lottery system, although the charters set how many students they will admit.

There are 20 pilot schools in Boston. This initiative was launched in 1995 by Boston Public Schools and the Boston Teachers Union, to compete with charters—though after initial enthusiasm the union dragged its feet on new pilot schools for many years. Pilot schools can extend the school day or year—adding up to 95 teacher hours per year—and design their own curriculum and professional development. Each school negotiates its own labor agreement, to replace the district teachers' contract. But teachers remain on the district pay scale and retain their seniority and bumping rights during layoffs. School site councils, made up of the principal, teachers, parents, and high school students, make key decisions, including hiring the principal and teachers. They must use the district evaluation process to fire or reassign teachers, and the superintendent has to approve firing a principal.

Pilot school students show similar demographics to the district's, though only 21 percent are English-language learners, compared to nearly 30 percent districtwide. Perhaps this explains why a 2009 Boston Foundation study found that elementary pilot school students learned about three months more in English language arts than their counterparts in normal district schools but no more in math. In middle and high school, there was no statistically significant difference in learning between the two groups of schools.

The "innovation school" model was introduced in 2011. Each school operates under a memorandum of understanding with BPS and is governed by a school site council. Schools request specific autonomies in their innovation plans, which must be approved by the superintendent, school board, and teachers union. They operate under the district's collective bargaining agreement, unless the school includes waivers or modifications in the innovation plan. If a traditional school is converting to innovation status, its plan must be approved by two thirds of its teachers. If it is a new school, the plan must be negotiated with the teachers union. The only major flexibility that is off limits is the ability to fire the principal. There are only eight innovation schools (several of which are fairly new), but in 2015 and 2016 they performed better as a group than all but the two types of charter schools (see Figure A-2).

The turnaround model was created by the state in 2010 to address underperforming schools. There were 10 turnaround schools in Boston as of 2016–17. These schools have the least freedom from district policies of all the autonomy models, but they get increased support from the district. The school can select its principal, with the superintendent's approval, but the district manages teacher hiring. The school can reject teachers, reassigning them to the district pool, but it can only fire them through the district evaluation process. It is subject to the district collective bargaining agreement, but it can opt out of union seniority during layoffs and can pay stipends to staff for extra teaching time. BPS has replaced the principals at all turnaround schools and over 50 percent of the teachers at some. Others require staff to reapply for their positions, so only teachers who want to be part of the turnaround effort stay. The district sets the curriculum, but the schools can choose instructional materials and practices and control their timing. Budgetary freedom is limited, but schools control their professional development. Most schools that exit turnaround status move into another autonomous category, such as a pilot school.

In general, the more autonomy schools have, the higher their performance. In 2017 Harvard graduate students Molly Osborne and Jacob Taylor analyzed the performance of all charters and "charter-lite" models, compared to traditional public schools, on PARCC exams in 2015 and 2016. When they controlled for race, disability, and low income levels—to eliminate the impact of different demographics among different types of schools—independent charters performed best, followed by Horace Mann charters and innovation schools. Pilot schools and turnaround schools actually performed worse than traditional public schools in Boston. All results were statistically significant at a high level of confidence, and all were consistent with earlier analysis of 2013 test scores by The Boston Foundation.

The results are in Figure A-2:

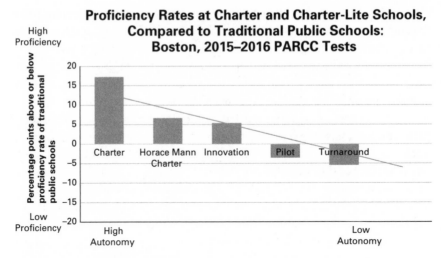

Figure A-2 Source: Molly Osborne and Jake Taylor, "Evaluating District-Run Autonomous Schools," Master's Thesis, Harvard Kennedy School, 2017.

Los Angeles Unified School District

Los Angeles has about 50 pilot schools (out of more than 1,000 total schools), which were modeled after Boston's and first launched in 2007–08. With autonomy over budgeting, staffing, curriculum, governance, and scheduling, these specialized, 400–500 student schools are considered the most flexible of the city's charter-lite models. Their teachers are district employees and are represented by the union, but they vote on an elect-to-work agreement that requires them to work longer hours and attend additional teacher training. An elected governing school council, made up of the principal and a combination of parents, teachers, staff, community members, and students, makes the governing decisions.

Most have performed well. In 2013, pilot schools gained an average of eight Academic Performance Index (API) points (on a scale of 0 to 1,000), while the district gained three and the state average fell by two points. The California Office of Reform Education (CORE), which measures school performance in Los Angeles and five other large districts, recently evaluated 714 Los Angeles public schools (excluding independent charters) and gave them a score from zero to 100 based on standardized test scores, graduation rates, attendance rates, suspension rates, and the performance of subgroups such as English learners. District schools averaged 60.27, while pilots averaged 64.02.

"Local initiative schools," launched in 2011, are similar but have not performed as well on CORE benchmarks. Some 25 "expanded school-based management schools" (ESBMM), which have more limited autonomy, serve mostly middle-class neighborhoods, and underperform district schools with comparable demographics.

In-district charters, which are converted traditional schools, also started with higher achieving students. They have produced greater academic gains than traditional district schools but less than independent charters. As one recent study concluded, "While conversion charters effectively maintained or widened differences in student performance vis-à-vis TPS [traditional public school] peers, start-ups [independent charters] held slight, yet at times significant, benefits after taking into account prior achievement and family background."

The final charter-lite model in Los Angeles was launched by former mayor Antonio Villaraigosa—once an organizer for the local teachers union. Later speaker of the State Assembly, Villaraigosa was elected mayor in 2005. He quickly sought the power to appoint the school board but was rebuffed. So in 2007 he ran a slate of candidates for the board, which won four of seven seats. He pushed them to sign a memorandum of understanding with a nonprofit organization he founded, the Mayor's Partnership for Los Angeles Schools, empowering it to take over some of the city's lowest-performing schools.

Like the new innovation zone in Denver, Villaraigosa's partnership has its own nonprofit board. By 2016 it oversaw 19 schools. They retained the district teachers union contract and their enrollment boundaries but had autonomy over their budgets and curriculum and some authority over staffing. When schools entered the partnership, by agreement between the nonprofit board and the district, the board could replace the principal and some of the teachers, who then went back to regular district schools. However, ultimate accountability remained with the district, which has consolidated two schools due to low enrollment but has not closed or replaced any based on performance—despite very low levels in some schools.

Using a "community schools" model involving wraparound support for students from a variety of nonprofit organizations, the partnership has successfully turned around some failing schools. It also runs Parent College, offered once a month to help parents become better advocates for their children's education, in which it says more than half of partnership families participate. In 2013 Partnership for Los Angeles Schools gained an average of 21 points on the API, more rapid improvement than any California district. Graduation rates have more than doubled, from 36 percent in 2008 to 77 percent in 2015.

Two other nonprofit partnership boards, LA's Promise and the Youth Policy Institute, also appear to be turning schools around effectively. LA's Promise's one middle and two high schools have averaged API gains of 37, 22.25, and 20.5 a year, respectively, and its two high schools have graduation rates of 79 and 80 percent. College acceptance rates have more than doubled over

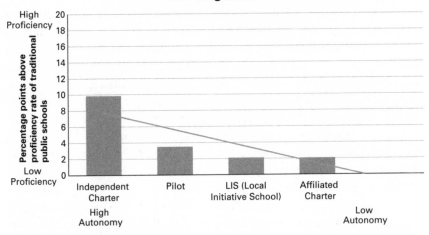

Proficiency Rates at Charter and Charter-Lite Schools, Compared to Traditional Public Schools: Los Angeles, 2015–2016

Figure A-3 Source: Molly Osborne and Jake Taylor, "Evaluating District-Run Autonomous Schools," Master's Thesis, Harvard Kennedy School, 2017.

four years in one high school, from 18 to 42 percent, and quadrupled in the other, from 9 to 37 percent.

In Osborne and Taylor's 2017 analysis of 2015 and 2016 test scores, there were not enough ESBMM schools or partnership schools to give statistically significant results. But the other charter-lite models showed slightly better results—again controlled for the race, disabilities, and income status of students—than traditional schools. Independent charters far outdistanced them, however, as Figure A-3 shows.

Two Steps Forward, One Step Back

Because urban school districts are highly political environments, the journey toward 21st century governance is rarely as linear as it has been in New Orleans, D.C., and Denver. Some cities have moved rapidly for a time, then slowed down or even experienced reversals.

Philadelphia

Philadelphia was an early pioneer, for instance, when the state took over the nearly bankrupt district in 2002. The state's five-person School Reform

Commission—three appointed by the governor and two by the mayor—adopted a "diverse provider" strategy and hired Paul Vallas, Chicago's former superintendent, to implement it. Vallas turned over management of 45 of the lowest performing elementary and middle schools to two universities and five charter management organizations, both nonprofit and for-profit. He restructured another 21 schools, giving them extra money and staff support. But all remained neighborhood schools, without parental choice or real competition for students and dollars, and the charters had far less autonomy than normal charter schools. Indeed, their principals and teachers remained district employees, still under their union contracts. (Not surprisingly, this didn't work very well.) Meanwhile, Vallas created 25 new small district high schools, contracted with private companies to open several alternative schools, and encouraged successful independent charters, such as Mastery Charter Schools, to expand and replicate. He considered all these school models part of his portfolio.

After Louisiana's Recovery School District lured Vallas away, in 2007, the commission hired former D.C. and San Francisco superintendent Arlene Ackerman, who had been hostile to charters in the past. For several years, the district quit authorizing independent charters. But in 2010 Ackerman launched a "renaissance schools" initiative, which turned low-performing schools into renaissance schools, operated by charters, or "promise academies," which remained district schools but could replace half their teachers. During the first year of this initiative, 2010–11, the city's portfolio of 355 schools had roughly 67 independent charters, 28 "partnership schools" with private managers (left over from Vallas's era), 17 alternative schools managed by outside organizations, 14 renaissance charter schools and promise academies, and 25 "vanguard schools"—high-performing schools that were given great autonomy, based on a performance agreement with district leaders. By 2015 there were 20 renaissance schools and 12 promise academies.

Not surprisingly, renaissance charters performed much better than either promise academies or the district as a whole. Independent charters performed even better, though they received only about 60 percent of the per-pupil funding district schools did.

Unfortunately, the district was too busy rowing—operating schools—to steer effectively. It did a poor job of holding charters and other models accountable for performance, rarely closing the failures. Nor did it keep a close eye on school finances: By 2010 some 18 charters were under federal investigation for financial irregularities. In 2016, with 32 percent of public school students in charters, the district finally released its first annual evaluation of all 72 charters.

By then a third wave of reform had begun. William Hite, who succeeded Ackerman, reorganized the district in 2015 into 13 learning networks of different kinds: a charter-lite "Innovative Schools Network," with seven district schools; a Turnaround Network, made up of the promise academies; an Opportunity Network, for alternative schools; an Autonomy Network, for high-performing schools; and so on.

New York City

New York City saw great progress under Mayor Michael Bloomberg, followed by political reversals under his successor. Bloomberg's chancellor, Joel Klein, expanded charter schools rapidly, gave them free space in district buildings, created hundreds of new small high schools, and handed significant new autonomies to all traditional schools. (For a compelling tale of this transformation, see Klein's book, *Lessons of Hope: How to Fix Our Schools*.) Performance improved steadily, but when Bill de Blasio succeeded Bloomberg in 2014, he tried to slam the brakes on charter expansion by ending the practice of sharing district buildings. Governor Andrew Cuomo and the state legislature thwarted him with new legislation, but the city's 21st century strategy is now history.

Chicago

Chicago experienced something similar. When Paul Vallas and Arne Duncan were superintendents, they embraced charter schools. When they hit a state-imposed cap on numbers, they let charters open multiple campuses or simply used outside operators to run "contract schools." In 2005–06 Duncan announced Renaissance 2010, which closed about 60 failing schools and opened almost 100 new schools, primarily on the near south side of the city, where low-performing schools were most concentrated. Every new school—even "performance schools" run by the district—had a five-year performance agreement, was measured by a standard set of metrics, including test scores, and had freedom over curriculum, budget, and length of school day and year. Charters and contract schools, the majority of the 100, also had freedom over staffing, school design, and most other matters.

By 2009–10, Chicago's 675 public schools included 71 charters, 18 alternative schools, 41 magnets, 15 contract schools, 15 "small" schools, eight "career academies," eight "achievement academies," eight selective enrollment high schools, 128 "autonomous management performance schools," 22 "innovation schools," 11 "diverse provider network schools," and 49 "recognition schools." Then fiscal crisis hit, after post-recession federal stimulus money dried up, and Mayor Rahm Emanuel decided in 2013 to close 47 schools, to save money. Past closures had triggered protests, so he promised that none of the empty buildings would be given to charters—effectively ending charter expansion.

Suddenly Chicago went from a portfolio strategy leader to a laggard, with only 15 percent of its students in charters. Then in late 2016, still in dire fiscal straits, Emanuel agreed to a new labor contract that limited growth in charter enrollment to just 1 percent over the three-year term.

Detroit

In Detroit a majority of public school students attend charters, and they learn more every year than similar district school students by about 50 days in reading and 65 days in math, according to CREDO. But as in Philadelphia and Cleveland, authorizing has been weak and failing schools are often allowed to survive. In Philadelphia the district is the only authorizer, but Michigan's law is the opposite: Detroit has a dozen authorizers, some of which do a poor job. The mayor and governor tried in 2015 and 2016 to create a commission with the power to close and replace failing schools in both sectors, as recommended by a citizens' task force, but Republican legislators and a majority of Michigan's charters opposed it. So Detroit hobbles on with some excellent charters, some average charters, and some mediocre charters, while the school district continues its two-decade-long death spiral.

Michigan Governor Rick Snyder created a version of Louisiana's RSD in 2011, the Educational Achievement Authority (EAA), to take over the lowest performing 5 percent of schools in the state. Because the legislature was not likely to pass a bill, he created it as a partnership between the Detroit Public Schools, then under a state-appointed emergency manager, and Eastern Michigan University, a charter authorizer. Something so difficult and controversial should never have been launched without a solid legislative and financial commitment. The EAA had shaky finances from the beginning, which made recruiting charters difficult. Its first chancellor decided the EAA should operate 12 of its 15 schools itself, then resigned after three years. The FBI and the U.S. Attorney's Office later opened a probe into an alleged vendor kickback scheme, and in early 2016 a former school principal pleaded guilty to bribery and money laundering. Soon afterward, state legislative leaders decided to kill the EAA, and Eastern Michigan University chose to withdraw from the partnership.

ENDNOTES

All quotations without endnotes are from interviews with the author.

INTRODUCTION

2   **When Paul R. Mort studied:** David B. Tyack and Larry Cuban, *Tinkering Toward Utopia: A Century of Public School Reform* (Cambridge, MA: Harvard University Press, 1995), p. 4.

2   **One in five families chooses:** There are about 50 million students in public schools (including charters) and about 5.3 million in private schools, according to the U.S. Department of Education. See G. Kena et al., "The Condition of Education 2015," NCES 2015-144 (Washington, DC: U.S. Department of Education, National Center for Education Statistics), http://nces.ed.gov/pubsearch. About 2.3 million students are homeschooled: See Brian D. Ray, "Research Facts on Homeschooling," National Home Education Research Institute, March 23, 2016, www.nheri.org/research/research-facts-on-homeschooling.html. According to the National Alliance for Public Charter Schools, "Estimated Charter Public School Enrollment, 2016–17" (Washington, D.C: National Alliance for Public Charter Schools, 2017), www.publiccharters .org/wp-content/uploads/2017/01/EER_Report_V5.pdf, there were 3.1 million children in charters schools by 2016–17. Thus, roughly 10.7 million children—more than 19 percent—are not in traditional public schools.

2   **17 percent fail to graduate on time:** Alyson Klein, "Graduation Rate Hits Record High of 83.2 Percent: Should Obama Take Credit?" *Education Week* (blog), October 17, 2016.

2   **Almost a quarter of those who apply to the U.S. Army:** Christina Theokas, *Shut Out of the Military: Today's High School Education Doesn't Mean You're Ready for Today's Army* (Washington, DC: Education Trust, December 2010), p. 3. Theokas reports that 23 percent of the nearly 350,000 high school graduates aged 17 to 20 who applied for entry into the Army between 2004 and 2009 and took the U.S. Army's Armed Forces Qualifications Test failed to achieve a qualifying score.

2   **more than a third of those who go on to college:** Mikhail Zinshteyn, "New Ways to Find Out Who Is Ready for College," *Higher Ed Beat*, March 8, 2016, www.ewa.org/ blog-higher-ed-beat-new-ways-find-out-who-ready-college?, reports that "42 percent of incoming college students are referred to remedial courses; the percentages are even higher for black, Latino, poor and community college students. Just one-tenth

of students who start college in remedial courses ever earn a degree a report by Complete College America calculated in 2014."

2   **half of college students never graduate:** William C. Symonds, Robert Schwartz, and Ronald F. Ferguson, "Pathways to Prosperity: Meeting the Challenge of Preparing Young Americans for the 21st Century" (Cambridge, MA:, Harvard University Graduate School of Education, 2011), https://dash.harvard.edu/bitstream/handle/1/4740480/Pathways_to_Prosperity_Feb2011-1.pdf?

2   **Only one in three rate their school culture positively:** Youth Truth Student Survey, "Learning from Student Voice: What Do Students Have to Say About School Culture?," December 2016, www.youthtruthsurvey.org/wp-content/uploads/2016/12/YouthTruth-Learning-from-Student-Voice-School-Culture.pdf (a survey of more than 80,000 students across 24 states in grades five through 12).

2   **Karen Fisher quote:** Karen Fisher, e-mail to author, June 2017.

2   **Among developed nations, the United States ranks 18th or worse:** Organization for Economic Cooperation and Development, "Education at a Glance 2015: OECD Indicators" (Paris: OECD Publishing, 2015), table A2.4, www.oecd.org/edu/education-at-a-glance-2015.htm. The United States probably ranks worse than 18th, because the OECD did not report results for Australia, Belgium, France, Germany, Iceland, the Netherlands, and the United Kingdom.

2   **in the bottom half in math, science, and reading proficiency:** *PISA 2015 Results (Volume I): Excellence and Equity in Education* (Paris: OECD Publishing, December 2016), www.oecd.org/education/pisa-2015-results-volume-i-9789264266490-en.htm. PISA is the OECD's Program for International Student Assessment.

3   **"The bad news is most state education systems":** Study Group on International Comparisons in Education, *No Time to Lose: How to Build a World-Class Education System State by State* (Denver, CO: National Conference of State Legislatures, August 2016), p. 3.

3   **urban superintendents last just three years on average:** According to research by the American Association of School Administrators. Cited in Brad Hughes, "NSBA, AASA Execs Worry About Board Member, Superintendent Turnover, Impact on Districts," National School Boards Association, March 22, 2015, www.nsba.org/newsroom/nsba-aasa-execs-worry-about-board-member-superintendent-turnover-impact-districts-0

5   **The district has improved faster than any other in the state—and no doubt in the nation:** See, for instance, Education Resource Strategies, *Denver Public Schools: Leveraging System Transformation to Improve Student Results* (N.p.: Education Resource Strategies, March 2017), p. 38. It shows that the RSD in New Orleans produced significantly greater gains per year in elementary school reading than any other district in ERS's database. ERS asserts that Denver had the second highest academic growth in the country, among districts with 25,000 or more students, from 2009–10 through 2012–13—a sample that apparently does not include New Orleans, perhaps because the RSD had fewer than 25,000 students during at least part of that time. But p. 38 shows significantly greater gains in New Orleans than in Denver in elementary school reading, and any other comparison of test score gains shows significantly faster improvement in New Orleans than in Denver. See also the work of Douglas Harris discussed and cited in chapter 3, which is summarized in Douglas N. Harris, "Good News for New Orleans," *Education Next* 15, no. 4 (Fall 2015).

5 **Number of charters in D.C.:** D.C. Public Charter School Board "Student Enrollment," 2016–17, http://www.dcpcsb.org/data/student-enrollment.

6 **By 2012 it had the highest:** Tom Boasberg, "Great Schools in Every Neighborhood," *My DPS* (blog), August 20, 2014, http://archive.constantcontact.com/fs151/1110617542386/archive/1118247564203.html.

6 **New Jersey followed New Orleans's lead in Camden:** For sources on Camden, Memphis, Indianapolis, Springfield, and three other states with RSDs, see chapter 11 and appendix C.

6 **And 30 large districts belong:** Paul Hill (Center on Reinventing Public Education), e-mail to author, February 2017.

6 **Stanford University's Center for Research on Educational Outcomes (CREDO):** Center for Research on Education Outcomes (henceforth cited as CREDO), "National Charter School Study, 2013" (Stanford, CA: Center for Research on Education Outcomes, 2013), p. 79, https://credo.stanford.edu/documents/NCSS%202013%20Final%20Draft.pdf.

6 **Urban students gain five months:** CREDO, "Urban Charter School Study: Report on 41 Regions, 2015" (Stanford, CA: Center for Research on Education Outcomes, 2015), p. 26, http://urbancharters.stanford.edu/download/Urban%20Charter%20School%20Study%20Report%20on%2041%20Regions.pdf.

6 **On five key characteristics:** Samuel Barrows, Paul E. Peterson, and Martin R. West, "What Do Parents Think of Their Children's Schools," *Education Next* 17, no. 2 (Spring 2017).

6 **In states where charter authorizers close:** CREDO, "National Charter School Study, 2013," and CREDO, "Urban Charter School Study: Report on 41 Regions, 2015."

7 **Some schools were created . . . needed on the farm:** Steven F. Wilson, *Learning on the Job* (Cambridge, MA: Harvard University Press, 2006), pp. 3–4.

7 **In 1843 Horace Mann . . . in the South and West:** Sarah Mondale and Sarah B. Patton, eds., *School: The Story of American Public Education* (Boston: Beacon Press, 2001), p. 11.

8 **As late as 1890, 71 percent:** Diane Ravitch and Maris A. Vinovskis, eds., *Learning from the Past: What History Teaches Us About School Reform* (Baltimore: Johns Hopkins University Press, 1995), p. 30.

8 **"Our schools are, in a sense, factories":** William Harris quoted in Nelson Smith, *An Accident of History: Breaking the District Monopoly on Public School Facilities* (Washington, DC: National Alliance of Public Charter Schools, 2012), p. 11.

8 **"The division of labor in the factory":** David Tyack, *The One Best System* (Cambridge, MA: Harvard University Press, 1964), pp. 28–29.

8 **At the time, political machines . . . battle cry:** Ibid., pp. 127–41.

9 **National Education Association . . . drive for uniformity:** Diane Ravitch, "The Search for Order and the Rejection of Conformity: Standards in American Education," in Ravitch and Vinovskis, *Learning from the Past*, p. 171.

9 **"In the 1890s there was . . . more than 2,600":** Tyack and Cuban, *Tinkering Toward Utopia*, p. 19.

9 **By the 1960s, New York City schools:** Ibid., p. 77.

9 **In 1950, Tyack tells us, roughly 90 percent:** Tyack, *The One Best System*, p. 278.

9 **Gallup began surveying the public on education:** Tyack and Cuban, *Tinkering Toward Utopia*, p. 32.

9   **"To succeed in improving the schooling of the dispossessed":** Tyack, *The One Best System*, p. 291.

10   **By 2014, a majority of public school students were minorities:** Kimberly Hefling and Jesse J. Holland, "White Students No Longer in the Majority: Rising Diversity Poses Challenges for Many Schools," *Boston Globe*, August 10, 2014.

10   **By 1989, a third of public school students . . . a majority were:** Southern Education Foundation, "A New Majority: Low Income Students Now a Majority In the Nation's Public Schools," January 2015, www.southerneducation.org/getattachment/4ac62e27 -5260-47a5-9d02-14896ec3a531/A-New-Majority-2015-Update-Low-Income-Students -Now.aspx.

11   **Turnout in school board elections:** Terry M. Moe, "The Union Label on the Ballot Box," *Education Next* 6, no. 3 (Summer 2006).

13   **Nationally, more than 70 percent of K–12 teachers:** According to National Center for Education Statistics, "Schools and Staffing Survey, 2011–12" (https://nces.ed.gov/ surveys/sass/), 73.8 percent of public school teachers reported that they were members of a teachers union or employee association similar to a union. This percentage was down from about 76 percent in 2007–8. Hence the figure by 2017–18 will probably be just above 70 percent. In that same 2011–12 survey, 50 percent of teachers said they were represented by a collective bargaining agreement, 8.4 percent by a "meet-and-confer," non-legally-binding agreement, and 1.4 percent by another type of agreement.

13   **only about 10 percent of those in charter schools:** For the current estimate for charter school unionization, from the Center on Education Reform, see Mel Leonor, "Teachers Unions Ramp Up Recruitment Efforts at Charter Schools," *Politico*, February 13, 2017. For information on Maryland, Kansas, Iowa, and Alaska, see also National Alliance for Public Charter Schools, "Measuring Up: A Tool for Comparing State Charter School Laws and Movements," www.publiccharters.org/get-the-facts/law-database/.

14   **now educate more than three million students:** National Alliance for Public Charter Schools, "Estimated Charter Public School Enrollment, 2016–17."

15   **less than 13 percent of charters:** National Alliance for Public Charter Schools, "Facts About Charters," www.publiccharters.org/get-the-facts/public-charter-schools/faqs/.

15   **There are none left in New Orleans or Denver:** New Orleans: e-mail from Leslie Jacobs, January 2017. Denver: telephone conversation with Van Schoales of A+ Colorado, January 2017. D.C.: email from Scott Pearson of D.C. Public Charter School Board, January 2017.

15   **At last count, in 2014, charters averaged only 72 percent:** Meagan Batdorff et al., *Charter School Funding: Inequity Expands* (Fayetteville: University of Arkansas, 2014), www.uaedreform.org/ charter-funding-inequity-expands.

16   **In truth, charters serve higher percentages of poor:** On poverty, see National Center for Education Statistics, "Characteristics of Traditional Public and Public Charter Schools," April 2016, https://nces.ed.gov/programs/coe/indicator_cla.asp. On race, "Over 56% of [charters'] students are Hispanic and African American, versus 39% in district schools," according to Bruno V. Manno and Chester E. Finn, Jr., "Progress Report on Charter Schools," *National Affairs* 24 (Summer 2015), www .nationalaffairs.com/publications/detail/a-progress-report-on-charter-schools.

CHAPTER I

21 **On September 8, 1900:** For information on the 1900 Galveston hurricane and its aftermath, see Bradley Robert Rice, *Progressive Cities: The Commission Government Movement in America, 1901–1920* (Austin: University of Texas Press, 1977); Eric Larson, *Isaac's Storm: A Man, a Time, and the Deadliest Hurricane in History* (New York: Random House, 2000); Mary G. Ramos, "Galveston's Response to the Hurricane of 1900," *Texas Almanac*, 1999, www.texasalmanac.com/topics/history/galves tons-response-hurricane-1900.

21 **By 2014, when the state switched:** 35 percent: John White and Adam Hawf, "A Playbook for a New Approach in New Orleans," in *20 Years: Transformative, Evidence-Based Ideas* (Bothell, WA: Center on Reinventing Public Education, 2014) pp. 32–37. 62 percent: Leslie Jacobs, "By the Numbers: Student and School Performance," *Educate Now.net*, Aug. 22, 2015, http://educatenow.net/2015/08/22/by-the-numbers -student-and-school-performance/.

21 **Schools in the RSD had improved:** See figure 3-1, p. 55.

22 **Before Katrina, 62 percent of students in New Orleans:** Leslie Jacobs, author interview, December 5, 2016; Louisiana Department of Education, "Expanding Opportunity: Louisiana Charter Schools Annual Report 2015–16" (Baton Rouge: Louisiana Department of Education, February 2016), www.louisianabelieves.com/docs/default -source/school-choice/2015-2016-charter-annual-report.pdf?sfvrsn=9.

22 **Graduation and college-going rates:** See endnotes on the same subject, pertaining to p. 54 of chapter 3.

22 **New Orleans has improved its schools faster than any other city:** See endnote on the same subject, pertaining to p. 5 of the introduction.

22 **one extraordinary and unlikely heroine:** Leslie Jacobs's background is from author interviews with her in March through September 2011, plus email communications in 2011 and 2015.

22 **It is hard to describe . . . clean audit finding:** On New Orleans schools before Katrina: Sarah Carr, *Hope Against Hope: Three Schools, One City, and the Struggle to Educate America's Children* (New York: Bloomsbury, 2013), p. 120; Cowen Institute for Public Education Initiatives (hereafter cited as Cowen Institute), *The State of Public Education in New Orleans: Five Years After Hurricane Katrina* (New Orleans: Cowen Institute for Public Education Initiatives, Tulane University, 2010); "Board games," *Gambit*, July 23, 2013, www.bestofneworleans.com/gambit/board-games/Content? oid=2228475; interviews with Leslie Jacobs, Anthony Amato, and others.

22 **the state itself ranked in the bottom five states:** National Center for Education Statistics, National Assessment of Education Progress (NAEP), "NAEP Data Explorer," https://nces.ed.gov/nationsreportcard/naepdata/dataset.aspx.

23 **A 2004 study showed:** "A Brief Overview of Public Education in New Orleans, 1995–2009" (New Orleans: New Schools for New Orleans, 2009).

24 **Between 1997 and 2005 . . . private school enrollment grew:** Ibid.

25 **Amato recounted an incident:** Dawn Ruth, "Anthony Amato Redux: Finding a New Perspective at International High School of New Orleans," *New Orleans Magazine*, October 2013.

25 **On another occasion . . . excused himself:** Interviews with Anthony Amato and Michael Cowan, August 2011.

25   **In 2003, a private investigator:** Douglas N. Harris, "Good News for New Orleans," *Education Next* 15, no. 4 (Fall 2015).

25   **When Amato announced:** Interview with Anthony Amato, August 2011.

25   **11 people were indicted:** Harris, "Good News for New Orleans."

25   **Amato stepped into a snake pit . . . renew his contract:** Interviews with Leslie Jacobs, March 2011, and Anthony Amato, August 2011, and personal communication from Jacobs, March 2017.

25   **at least 24 district leaders were indicted:** New Schools for New Orleans, "A Brief Overview of Public Education in New Orleans, 1995–2009."

26   **convicted of taking $140,000 in bribes:** Cindy Chang, "Orleans Parish School Board Is Fighting to Survive," *Times Picayune*, November 28, 2010.

26   **Mose Jefferson died in prison:** Frank Donze, "Betty Jefferson Gets 15 Months of Home Confinement, 5 Years Probation After Cooperating With Feds," *Times-Picayune*, August 31, 2011.

26   **Bill Jefferson . . . in federal prison:** Bruce Alpert, "William Jefferson Reports to Texas Prison to Begin 13-Year Sentence," *Times-Picayune*, May 4, 2012.

27   **54 of the state's 73 failing schools were in the city:** Nelson Smith, *The Louisiana Recovery School District: Lessons for the Buckeye State* (Washington, D.C.: Thomas Fordham Institute, January 2012), p. 4.

27   **In its first two years, the Recovery School District took control of five schools:** Jaime Sarrio, "Georgia Looks to New Orleans Model for Rescuing Schools," *Atlanta Journal-Constitution*, February 17, 2015.

27   **On September 15 it put all employees on unpaid disaster leave:** Supreme Court of Louisiana, ruling "*Eddy Oliver, Oscarlene Nixon and Mildred Goodwin v. Orleans Parish School Board* on Writ of Certiorari to the Court of Appeal, Fourth Circuit, Parish of Orleans, 2014-C-0329 Consolidated With 2014-C-0330," October 31, 2014, www.lasc.org/opinions/2014/14C0329cw14C0330.opn.pdf.

27   **Jacobs met with . . . charter schools, she said:** Interviews with Leslie Jacobs and Paul Pastorek, 2011.

27   **Democratic Governor Kathleen Blanco . . . collective bargaining in the RSD:** Ibid.

27   **the OPSB voted in December:** Supreme Court of Louisiana, "*Eddy Oliver.*"

28   **U.S. Department of Education had almost $30 million:** Interviews with Leslie Jacobs.

28   **She dipped into her own funds to help bankroll Sarah Usdin:** Interviews with Leslie Jacobs and Sarah Usdin, March 2011.

28   **TFA . . . brought about 70 teachers . . . 215 to 250 a year:** interview with Kira Orange-Jones, TFA executive director for Greater New Orleans Region, March 2011.

28   **the association recommended only six of 44 applicants:** Interview with Leslie Jacobs, March 2011.

28   **"When 17 RSD schools opened in mid-September 2006":** Leigh Dingerson, "Narrow and Unlovely," Rethinking Schools, Summer 2007, www.rethinkingschools.org/archive/21_04/narr214.shtml.

29   **Vallas had run . . . exactly that:** Interviews with Paul Vallas, 2011.

32   **They lengthened the school day . . . under state law:** Ibid.

32   **When Vallas first arrived:** Ibid.

32   **More than 90 percent . . ."camel's back":** Adam Nossiter, "A Tamer of Schools Has Plan in New Orleans," *New York Times*, September 24, 2007.

32   **Their average entrant was four years below grade level:** Vallas interviews, 2011.

33   **reducing from 127 to 87 school facilities:** "Lousiana's Turnaround Zone: Answering the Urgency of Now," Recovery School District, Jan. 2011, p. 6.

CHAPTER 2

34   **We created "a safe, intimate environment . . . but it was rare":** Jay Altman, TED talk, July 17, 2015, transcript provided by Altman to author.

35   **The teacher's union attacked them . . . private prep schools:** Interview with Jay Altman, March 2011.

35   **"People would say, 'What's your model?' ":** Orleans Public Education Network, *OPEN Public Education Awards 2015: Mr. Jay Altman & Dr. Anthony Recasner*, YouTube, www.youtube.com/watch?v=AjoQZDfZgnc.

37   **By then, Altman was looking for ways to squeeze:** On blended learning, author interviews with Jay Altman, March 2011 and Sept. 2013, and Sabrina Pence and her staff at Arthur Ashe Charter School, October 2013.

38   **By 2012–13 Arthur Ashe had earned a school performance score . . . B's and C's:** Louisiana Department of Education, "School Performance Scores," Louisiana Believes (website), www.louisianabelieves.com/resources/library/performance-scores.

39   **After a stint in Jefferson Parish . . . back in Algiers:** Ann Banks, "A Louisiana School Leader Answers the Call of Duty," *Edutopia*, September 23, 2009, www.edutopia.org/martin-behrman-charter-school-principal; interview with Rene Lewis-Carter, March 2011.

39   **a group of community leaders in Algiers had begun working:** Brian A. Riedlinger, testimony before U.S. Senate Subcommittee on Education and Early Childhood Development, *A Fresh Start for New Orleans' Children: Improving Education After Katrina*, Senate Hearing 109-626, 109th Congress, second session, July 14, 2006, www.gpo.gov/fdsys/pkg/CHRG-109shrg28864/html/CHRG-109shrg28864.htm.

39   **So along with more than 30 other principals:** Banks, "A Louisiana School Leader."

39   **She hired veteran teachers . . . free to learn:** Ibid.

40   **she implemented the Teacher Advancement Program:** Ibid.

40   **The next year, 98 percent . . . city's selective schools:** Louisiana Department of Education, "Data Center," Louisiana Believes (website), www.louisianabelieves.com/resources/library/test-results. Test scores for years before 2014, which were available online in the past, are now available from the department.

40   **In 2015 the state named Lewis-Carter middle school principal of the year:** Louisiana Department of Education, "Department Announces 2016 Teacher and Principal of the Year," July 11, 2015, www.louisianabelieves.com/newsroom/news-releases/2015/07/11/department-announces-2016-teacher-and-principal-of-the-year.

42   **They called the school New Orleans West:** Interview with Gary Robichaux, March 2011; Malcolm Gladwell, "Starting Over," *New Yorker*, August 24, 2015.

43   **In 2011 ReNEW also started an intensive . . . improvement every year:** Interview with Kevin Guittierrez, November 2016; Jessica Williams, "With Help of School Counseling, New Orleans Family Tackles Mental Disorders of Three Siblings," *The*

Lens, July 7, 2014, http://hechingerreport.org/help-school-counseling-new-orleans -family-tackles-mental-disorders-three-siblings/; Leah Fabel, "Hope Renewed," *One Day* (TFA alumni magazine), Spring 2014, pp. 38–41.

43 **By 2014 ReNEW had four schools . . . between 72 and 75:** For ReNEW school performance scores and grades, see Louisiana Department of Education, "Performance Scores," Louisiana Believes (website), www.louisianabelieves.com/resources/library/ performance-scores.

44 **the first school in the RSD to earn an A from the state:** Leslie Jacobs, e-mail, January, 2017.

44 **The charter network that took the most heat . . . not students or parents:** See, for example, Danielle Dreilinger, "Civil Rights Complaint Targets New Orleans Charter Group Collegiate Academies," *Times-Picayune*, April 15, 2014.

44 **"PR stunt" . . ."by a certain set of folks":** quoted in Andrew Vanacore, "Charter Schools Discipline Policy Under Fire," *New Orleans Advocate*, June 11, 2014.

45 **Ben Marcovitz was 28 . . . in New Orleans:** Sarah Carr, *Hope Against Hope: Three Schools, One City, and the Struggle to Educate America's Children* (New York: Bloomsbury, 2013), p. 49.

45 **In 2008 he opened the doors to 83 freshmen:** Noreen O'Donnell, "New Orleans' New Start: Charter School Becoming a Model for Transformation in Urban Schools," *The Daily*, November 26, 2011; see also Jackson Loo and Devon Puglia, directors, *Save Our Schools, Part 1*, YouTube, https://www.youtube.com/watch?v=FIDVgBobQOo.

45 **Five years later, when I visited:** interview with Allison Zimmer of Collegiate Academies, December 2013.

45 **Marcovitz and his teachers began . . . anything students needed:** Interviews with Allison Zimmer and visit to Sci Academy, December 2013; Carr, *Hope Against Hope*; O'Donnell, "New Orleans' New Start."

45 **Students very quickly "get a message":** O'Donnell, "New Orleans' New Start."

45 **"physically and emotionally scary place":** Carr, *Hope Against Hope*, p. 81.

45 **They typically had the highest self-reported suspension rates:** Meredith Simons, "The Student-Led Backlash Against New Orleans's Charter Schools," *Atlantic*, February 5, 2014; Kelsey Foster, "Carver Students, Parents Protest Schools' Discipline Policies at December Board Meeting," *The Lens*, December 31, 2013.

46 **During the first week of ninth . . . in seven states:** Carr, *Hope Against Hope*, p. 176.

46 **After the walkout Collegiate surveyed parents:** Dreilinger, "Civil Rights Complaint Targets New Orleans Charter Group Collegiate Academies."

46 **He set a goal of zero out-of-school suspensions . . . implemented its own:** Sarah Carr, "How Strict Is Too Strict," *Atlantic*, December 2014.

46 **In 2014–15, Collegiate's three schools expelled . . . on the same day:** Leslie Jacobs, "New Orleans' Expulsion Rate Below State Average," *Educate Now!.net*, July 29, 2015, http://educatenow.net/2015/07/; Richard Whitmire, "New Orleans Has Developed a New Normal in Education," *Real Clear Education*, May 29, 2015, www.realclearedu cation.com/articles/2015/05/29/new_orleans_has_developed_a_new_normal_in_ education_1199.html.

46 **Of the 83 in Sci Academy's first class . . . retention rates have risen:** Andrew Vanacore, "New Orleans Charter Schools Are Producing Success Stories," *Times Picayune*, May 27, 2012.

46   **Although 92 percent of its students:** O'Donnell, "New Orleans' New Start"; interview with Allison Zimmer of Collegiate Academies, December 2013.

46   **Sci Academy school performance grades:** Louisiana Department of Education, "School Performance Scores," Louisiana Believes (website), www.louisianabelieves.com/resources/library/performance-scores.

46   **Sci Academy students' ACT scores:** Sci Academy school report card, 2015–16, on Louisiana Department of Education website, Louisiana Believes, www.louisianabelieves.com/data/reportcards/2016/.

46   **highest of any nonselective school:** "Our Results," Collegiate Academies, http://collegiateacademies.thecanarycollective.com/page/82/results.

46   **Percentages of Sci Academy graduates going on to college:** 2012 and 2013: Nash Crews (Sci Academy), e-mail, January 2017. 2016: Sci Academy 2015–16 state report card, Louisiana Department of Education, Louisiana Believes (website), www.louisianabelieves.com/data/reportcards/2016/.

47   **Troy Simon column:** Troy Simon, "In Defense of Sci Academy and Other Charter Schools," *Times-Picayune*, April 17, 2014.

49   **Tony Amato returned to run:** Dawn Ruth, "Anthony Amato Redux," *New Orleans Magazine*, October 2013.

49   **In 2012, 35 children:** Sarah Carr, "Dreams Deferred," *Next City*, February 25, 2013, https://nextcity.org/features/view/dreams-deferred.

49   **A survey of more than 1,000 youths:** Institute of Women & Ethnic Studies, "Emotional Wellness and Exposure to Violence: Data from New Orleans Youth Age 11–15," 2015, http://iwesnola.org/resources/publications-articles/download-info/emotional-wellness-survey-report/.

49   **The NET Charter High School:** Jennifer Shaw, "New Orleans High School Turbocharges Restorative Justice," *Hechinger Report*, November 29, 2016.

49   **Crescent Leadership Academy:** Sally-Ann Roberts, "School That Takes On Struggling Students Has Had 14 Killed In 4 Years," Eyewitness News, WWL, May 16, 2016, www.wwltv.com/news/crime/taking-a-stand/school-that-takes-on-struggling-students-has-had-14-killed-in-4-years/196643174.

49   **Accelerated High School:** interviews with Gary Robichaux, December 2013 and February 2014; school visit, December 2013; Gary Robichaux emails.

50   **Blended learning grants:** Interview with Cate Swinburn (Educate Now!), December 8, 2016; Leslie Jacobs, "Personalized Learning Is Gaining Traction in New Orleans," *Educate Now!.net*, April 22, 2015, http://educatenow.net/2015/04/.

50   **KIPP Through College:** Danielle Dreilinger, "What Is KIPP Through College, and How Does It Work?" *Times-Picayune*, October 11, 2016.

50   **In 2016–17, only 8 percent of all public school students in the city were white:** Leslie Jacobs, "New Orleans by the Numbers: 2016 Enrollment," *Educate Now!.net*, December 4, 2016, http://educatenow.net/2016/12/04/new-orleans-by-the-numbers-2016-enrollment/.

51   **Homer A. Plessy Community School:** Eric Westervelt, "A New Orleans Charter School Marches To Its Own Tune," National Public Radio, October 13, 2014.

51   **Jay Altman quote:** Jay Altman, TED talk, New Orleans, July 17, 2015, transcript provided by Altman to author; also at www.youtube.com/watch?v=6xC-8JOdIiE.

51   **A study by Tulane University's Cowen Institute:** Kate Babineau, Dave Hand, and

Vincent Rossmeier, "No Longer Invisible: Opportunity Youth in New Orleans," October 2016, www.coweninstitute.com/wp-content/uploads/2016/10/OY-Data-Guide-2016-Revised-FINAL.pdf.

51   **Leslie Jacobs quote:** Leslie Jacobs, "The Promise of Career Prep," *Times-Picayune*, October 21, 2013.

52   **YouthForce NOLA:** Jennifer Larino, "Chase, Bloomberg Give $7.5 Million To Connect New Orleans Youth With Jobs," *Times-Picayune*, May 16, 2016; Leslie Jacobs, "YouthForce NOLA Poised to Provide Real-World Skills and Real-Life Success for New Orleans Students," *Educate Now!.net*, May 16, 2016, http://educatenow.net/2016/05/16/youthforce-nola-poised-to-provide-real-world-skills-and-real-life-suc cess-for-new-orleans-students/; interview with Cate Swinburn of Educate Now!, December 2016.

52   **Clark Preparatory High School performance scores:** Louisiana Department of Education, "School Performance Scores," Louisiana Believes (website), http://www .louisianabelieves.com/data/reportcards/.

52   **NOLA Tech at FirstLine's Clark High School:** Interview with Jay Altman, November 2016; Danielle Dreilinger, "Clark Prep Cuts Ninth Grade for 2016–17, Adds Vocational Options," *Times-Picayune*, April 6, 2016.

52   **Working group of FirstLine, YouthNOLA, RSD, and OPSB on career-tech:** Interviews with Jay Altman, November 2016, and Cate Swinburn (Educate Now!), December 2016.

52–3 **Rooted Charter School:** Dennis Arp, " 'Warrior Teacher' Jonathan Johnson '10 Leads a Revolution in Urban Education," *Chapman Magazine*, December 3, 2015, https:// blogs.chapman.edu/magazine/2015/12/03/warrior-teacher-jonathan-johnson-10-leads-a-revolution-in-urban-education/; Emmanuel Felton, "Do Black Students Really Need College to Get High Paying Jobs?" *Hechinger Report,* October 11, 2016; Jonathan Johnson e-mail, December 2016; Rooted School website, www.rooted school.org/academics/educational-model/, November 2016.

CHAPTER 3

54   **Before Katrina, 60 percent of New Orleans students . . . 13 percent did:** Neerav Kingsland, "Brown University vs. Science," *Relinquishment* (blog), December 22, 2015, https://relinquishment.org/2015/12/22/brown-university-vs-science/.

54   **Before Katrina, roughly half of public school students:** The high school graduation rate in 2005 was 56 percent, according to *A Brief Overview of Public Education in New Orleans 1995–2009* (New Orleans: New Schools for New Orleans, 2009), http:// newschoolsforneworleans.org/downloads/nsno_nolapubedfacts.pdf. But another 4.5 percent of students dropped out in grades seven and eight in 2004–5, according to Educate Now! ("Orleans Parish Public Schools Drop Outs: 2004–05 Compared to 2008–09, 2009–10 and 2010–11," http://educatenow.net/wp-content/uploads/2012/04/ Dropouts_Summary_All_Orleans_04-10.xls.pdf). Hence, about half of all students graduated at the time. Only 37 percent of graduates went on to college, according to Leslie Jacobs, "By the Numbers: Student and School Performance," *EducateNow!. net*, August 22, 2015, http://educatenow.net/2015/08/22/by-the-numbers-student-and

-school-performance-3/. This means less than 20 percent of all students went on to college.

54   **In 2015, 76 percent graduated:** Leslie Jacobs, "Reflection on 2015," *Educate Now!.net*, January 3, 2016, http://educatenow.net/2016/01/.

54   **In 2016, 64 percent of graduates entered college . . . :** Louisiana Department of Education, 2015–16 report card for "Orleans All" (Orleans Parish + RSD New Orleans Schools), Louisiana Believes (website), www.louisianabelieves.com/data/reportcards/2016/.

54   **In 2014–15, New Orleans high-schoolers performed:** Leslie Jacobs, "2015 EOC Results—New Orleans Ties the State!" *Educate Now!.net*, September 13, 2015, http://educatenow.net/2015/09/.

54   **Of all Louisiana high schools where three quarters . . . :** Leslie Jacobs, "Reflection on 2015."

54   **ACT scores in New Orleans compared to the state average:** Leslie Jacobs, "2015 ACT Scores: New Orleans Improves More than State," *Educate Now!.net*, July 16, 2015, http://educatenow.net/2015/07/16/2015-act-scores-new-orleans-improves-more-than-state/.

54–5 **CREDO study:** CREDO, "Urban Charter School Study: Report on 41 Regions 2015" (Stanford, CA: Center for Research on Education Outcomes, 2015).

55   **Percentage of students qualifying for a free or reduced-price lunch:** Cowen Institute, "NOLA by the Numbers: Free and Reduced-Price Lunch Eligibility, February 2014" (New Orleans: Cowen Institute, Tulane University, Feb. 2014), www.coweninstitute.com/wp-content/uploads/2014/04/NBTN-Enrollment-Feb14.pdf.

55   **Census data on poverty levels:** Andrew Vanacore, "Childhood Poverty in New Orleans Back at Pre-Katrina Levels," *New Orleans Advocate*, February 27, 2015.

55   **Changes in racial composition of New Orleans schools:** Leslie Jacobs, "New Orleans by the Numbers: 2016 Enrollment," *Educate Now!.net*, December 2016, http://educatenow.net/2016/12/04/new-orleans-by-the-numbers-2016-enrollment/#more-6724.

55   **RSD schools were more than 95 percent black during post-Katrina years:** Cowen Institute, "NOLA by the Numbers: School Enrollment and Demographics" (New Orleans: Cowen Institute, March 2011), p. 3, www.coweninstitute.com/wp-content/uploads/2011/03/NBTN-Enrollment-March-2011.pdf.

56   **African American scores on 2015 PARCC tests:** Neerav Kingsland, "Love It or Hate It, Common Core Is Giving Us Interesting Data About Black Student Achievement," *Relinquishment* (blog), April 10, 2016, https://relinquishment.org/2016/04/10/what-does-common-core-reveal-about-black-student-achievement/. New Orleans students used paper and pencil tests, and some evidence suggests that students who took the test online did not fare as well, on average.

56   **New Orleans' black students' ACT scores:** Leslie Jacobs, "Reflection on 2015."

56   **Black male graduation rates:** Danielle Dreilinger, "They're Off to College, and New Orleans Celebrates," *Times-Picayune*, May 8, 2015.

56   **college attendance rates have skyrocketed:** Ember Reichgott Junge, "21st Century Education Innovation and Breakthrough," *Zero Chance of Passage* (blog), July 17, 2015, http://myemail.constantcontact.com/21st-Century-Education-Weekly-Recap.html?soid=1109914538556&aid=TFLouGVB9zI. Reichgott-Junge writes, "Today, ten years after Hurricane Katrina, the system has gotten smaller, but the percentage of

students going to college has nearly tripled. Back then 700 of 3500 students went to college; last year it was 1400 students of 2650."

56   **New Orleans's graduation and college-going rates:** See endnotes for p. 54.

57   **30 percent of OPSB teachers who applied to the RSD:** Erik W. Robelen, "Desperately Seeking Educators," *Education Week*, February 21, 2007, www.edweek.org/ew/articles/2007/02/21/24orleans.h26.html.

57   **By 2015 African Americans still made up only 51 percent:** Leslie Jacobs, "By the Numbers: Who Is Leading Our Schools?" *Educate Now!.net*, August 9, 2015, http://educatenow.net/2015/08/09/by-the-numbers-who-is-leading-our-schools/; Danielle Dreilinger, "New Orleans' Katrina School Takeover to End, Legislature Decides," *Times Picayune*, May 5, 2016; Barrett and Harris, "Significant Changes in the New Orleans Teacher Workforce," Education Research Alliance, Tulane University, August 24, 2015, http://educationresearchalliancenola.org/files/publications/ERA-Policy-Brief-Changes-in-the-New-Orleans-Teacher-Workforce.pdf.

57   **71 percent of New Orleans public school teachers were black before Katrina:** Nathan Barrett and Douglas Harris, "Significant Changes in the New Orleans Teacher Workforce."

57   **In 2010 one activist said publicly:** Carr, *Hope Against Hope*, p. 4.

57–8   **a black woman spat in her face:** interview with Leslie Jacobs, September 2011.

58   **people called her "the white devil":** Interview with Michael Cowan (Common Good), March 2011.

58   **But by 2012–13 11.1 percent of students in RSD charters:** Leslie Jacobs, "Special Education—OPSB Not Serving Its Share," *Educate Now!.net*, May 21, 2013, http://educatenow.net/2013/05/21/special-education-opsb-not-serving-its-share/.

58   **2013 CREDO study:** CREDO, "Charter School Performance in Louisiana" (Stanford, CA: Center for Research on Education Outcomes, August 8, 2013), https://credo.stanford.edu/documents/la_report_2013_7_26_2013_final.pdf, p. 45.

58   **But by 2010 RSD schools received slightly less:** Leslie Jacobs, "The Money Myth," *Educate Now!.net*, May 16, 2011, http://educatenow.net/2011/05/16/the-money-myth/.

58   **Nationwide, traditional districts raise as much foundation money as charters do:** Meagan Batdorff et al., *Buckets of Water into the Ocean: Non-Public Revenue in Public Charter and Traditional Public Schools* (Fayetteville: University of Arkansas, Department of Education Reform, June 2015), www.uaedreform.org/non-public-revenue-in-public-charter-and-traditional-public-schools/.

59   **Michael Deshotels quote:** Michael Deshotels, "Education in Louisiana: A High Stakes Game for Adults," *Louisiana Educator* (blog), April 3, 2011, http://louisianaeducator.blogspot.com/2011_04_03_archive.html.

59   **Studies by Douglas Harris and his colleagues:** Douglas N. Harris, "Good News for New Orleans," *Education Next* 15, no. 4 (Fall 2015), http://educationnext.org/good-news-new-orleans-evidence-reform-student-achievement/.

59   **Study by Douglas Harris and colleagues on the "churn rate" in New Orleans:** Spiro Maroulis et al., "What Happened to Student Mobility After the New Orleans' Market-Based School Reforms?," Education Research Alliance, May 17, 2016, http://educationresearchalliancenola.org/files/publications/ERA-Policy-Brief-Mobility-Student-Performance-160512.pdf.

60 **Quotes from Douglas Harris:** Harris, "Good News for New Orleans."

60 **The black-white achievement gap in the United States:** Roland G. Fryer and Steven D. Levitt, "Falling Behind: New Evidence on the Black-White Achievement Gap," *Education Next*, Fall 2004, vol. 4, no. 4. One standard deviation is "roughly the difference in performance between the average 4th grader and the average 8th grader," according to the authors.

60 **Cowen Institute polls:** Cowen Institute, "K–12 Education Through the Public Eye: Parents' Perceptions of School Choice," Cowen Institute Research Brief, December 2011, www.coweninstitute.com/wp-content/uploads/2011/12/Public-Opinion-Poll-2011-Final1.pdf.

60 **April 2016 poll:** Kate Babineau, Dave Hand, and Vincent Rossmeier, "What Happens Next? Voters' Perceptions of K–12 Public Education in New Orleans," Cowen Institute, April 2016, www.coweninstitute.com/wp-content/uploads/2016/04/Cowen -Institute-2016-Poll-FINAL.pdf.

60 **March 2012 poll by Louisiana State University's Public Policy Research Lab:** Kirby Goidel and Michael Climek, "By the Numbers: Louisiana Survey Results Announced," Louisiana State University Public Policy Research Lab, June 7, 2012, http://pprllsu .com/wp-content/uploads/2015/12/LA-Survey-2012.pdf, p. 15.

63 **Several charter networks have created special programs . . .:** Leslie Jacobs, "Charter Schools Help Improve Special Education in New Orleans," *Times-Picayune*, December 26, 2014.

64 **By 2014, some 86 percent attended a school:** Douglas N. Harris and Matthew Larsen, "What Schools Do Families Want (And Why)? School Demand and Information Before and After the New Orleans Post-Katrina School Reforms," Education Research Alliance, January 2015; Anya Kamenetz, "A New Study Reveals Much About How Parents Really Choose Schools," National Public Radio, January 15, 2015.

64 **On a 2011 survey, 90 percent of parents agreed . . . in their choices":** Cowen Institute, "Key Findings of the 2011 Survey of Public School Parents," Cowen Institute, 2011, www.coweninstitute.com/wp-content/uploads/2011/12/Public-Opinion-Poll-2011-Final1.pdf.

64 **a 2015 analysis showed . . . higher performance scores:** Harris and Larsen, "What Schools Do Families Want (And Why)?"; Babineau, Hand, and Rossmeier, "What Happens Next?"; interview with Douglas Harris, May 2015.

64 **Paragraph on OneApp system:** Danielle Dreilinger, "Top New Orleans Public School Choices in OneApp Are Edna Karr, Baby Ben," *Times-Picayune*, April 23, 2014; Danielle Dreilinger, "OneApp Will List More New Orleans Pre-school Programs This Year," *Times-Picayune*, September 26, 2014; Arianna Prothero, "When Choice Doesn't Feel like a Choice," *Education Week*, August 19, https://neworleans.edweek. org/parents-struggle-with-school-choice-system/; Douglas N. Harris, Jon Valant, and Betheny Gross, "The New Orleans OneApp," *Education Next* 15, no. 4 (Fall 2015).

64 **The four selective schools will be allowed to remain selective:** interview with Leslie Jacobs, March 2017.

64 **EdNavigator:** Mareesa Nicosia, "Parents At Work: Has EdNavigator Fixed School Engagement by Making It A Job Benefit?" *The74million.org*, Jan. 24, 2017.

65 **Number of charter closures in New Orleans:** Danielle Dreilinger, "A First in 7 years: Low Scores Won't Close Any New Orleans Schools," *Times-Picayune*, December 23,

2015; Danielle Dreilinger, "BESE Pulls 2 New Orleans Charters, Extends 9 Others After Emotional Day," *Times-Picayune*, December 7, 2016; Marta Jewson, "Two New Orleans Charters Will Close Next Year. Students at One Will Get Special Treatment When Picking Their Next School," *The Lens*, November 22, 2016.

66   **The results were disappointing (of School Improvement Grants):** See Lisa Drago-set et al., *School Improvement Grants: Implementation and Effectiveness* (NCEE 2017-4013) (Washington, DC:, National Center for Education Evaluation and Regional Assistance, Institute of Education Sciences, U.S. Department of Education, January 2017), www.mathematica-mpr.com/our-publications-and-findings/publications/SIG-Implementation-and-Effectiveness. This study is not conclusive, but all the evidence in this study and elsewhere suggests that most schools chose the least radical option under the School Improvement Grants program, and the results were far less impressive than takeover of failing schools by charter management organizations has been in New Orleans, Denver, and other cities. For a useful discussion, see Neerav Kingsland, "A Weak SIG-nal: Subpart Research Design Means We Don't Really Know if SIG Worked," *Education Next*, January 24, 2017, http://educationnext.org/a-weak-sig-nal-subpar-research-design-means-we-dont-really-know-if-sig-worked/.

66   **A 2015 study of 50 cities by the Center on Reinventing Public Education:** Michael DeArmond et al., *Measuring Up: Educational Improvement and Opportunity in 50 Cities,* (Bothell, WA: Center on Reinventing Public Education, October 2015), p. 2, http://www.crpe.org/sites/default/files/measuringup_10.2015_0.pdf.

66   **They "likely either closed or were reconstituted":** Michael DeArmond and Patrick Denice, "More Than One Path Out of the Bottom," *The Lens* (online newsletter), Center on Reinventing Public Education, October 15, 2015, www.crpe.org/thelens/more-one-path-out-bottom.

66–7   **Douglas Harris's group study on effects of closure and replacement in New Orleans:** Whitney Bross, Douglas N. Harris, and Lihan Liu, "Extreme Measures: When and How School Closures and Charter Takeovers Benefit Students," Education Research Alliance, October 17, 2016, http://educationresearchalliancenola.org/files/publications/Education-Research-Alliance-New-Orleans-Policy-Brief-Closure-Takeover.pdf.

68   **An academic study published in 2016:** Andrew J. McEachin, Richard Osbourne Welsh, and Dominic James Brewer, "The Variation in Student Achievement and Behavior Within a Portfolio Management Model: Early Results from New Orleans," *Educational Evaluation and Policy Analysis* 38, no. 4 (December 2016): pp. 669–91.

69   **By 2011, more than 30 percent of the city's teachers:** Dana Brinson et al., *New Orleans–Style Education Reform: A Guide for Cities—Lessons Learned 2004–2010* (New Orleans: New Schools for New Orleans, January 2012), www.newschoolsforneworleans.org/guide/.

69   **Percentages of TFA members in New Orleans who were African American:** Kira Orange Jones (TFA Executive Director for the Greater New Orleans Region), e-mail, May 2016.

69   **Overall, 82 percent of public school students":** Jacobs, "New Orleans by the Numbers: 2016 Public School Enrollment."

69–70 **Percentages of African American, white, Hispanic, Asian, or Native American teachers:** Louisiana Department of Education. The percentages of white, Hispanic,

Asian, and Native American teachers are from 2014–15; the department has not yet made the 2015–16 numbers available.

70 **National survey of TFA teachers:** Morgaen L. Donaldson and Susan Moore Johnson, "TFA Teachers: How Long Do They Teach? Why Do They Leave?" *Phi Delta Kappan,* October 4, 2011, http://www.edweek.org/ew/articles/2011/10/04/kappan_donaldson.html.

70 **TFA corps members and alumni in New Orleans:** TFA Greater New Orleans–Louisiana Delta, "About Greater New Orleans–Louisiana," https://neworleans.teachforamerica.org.

71 **Peter Drucker quote:** Peter F. Drucker, *The Age of Discontinuities* (New York: Harper Torchbooks, 1978), p. 233.

72 **New policies governing expulsions and transfers:** Danielle Dreilinger, "Recovery School District Expulsions Down at Mid-Year, Orleans Schools Up, Officials Report," *Times-Picayune,* February 11, 2015; Thomas Toch, "The Big Easy's Grand Experiment," *U.S. News and World Report,* August 18, 2015; Jacobs, "Reflection on 2015."

72–3 **Youth Opportunities Center:** Patrick Sims and Debra Vaughan, *The State of Public Education in New Orleans: 2014 Report,* (New Orleans: Cowen Institute, Tulane University, 2014), www.speno2014.com/wp-content/uploads/2014/08/SPENO-Small.pdf, p. 25; Danielle Dreilinger, "In Move Toward Cooperation, New Orleans' Two School Systems Consider Agreement with Millions for Troubled Youth," *Times-Picayune,* March 13, 2014; Danielle Dreilinger, "New Orleans Public Schools Tackle Roots of Truancy In New Initiative," *Times-Picayune,* October 28, 2014.

73 **New fund dedicated to maintenance of school facilities:** Interview with Patrick Dobard (RSD superintendent), November 2016.

73–4 **Improvements in funding special education:** Jacobs, "Charter Schools Help Improve Special Education in New Orleans"; Adam Hawf, "Special Education Governance in New Orleans," *The Lens* (online newsletter), Center on Reinventing Public Education, March 30, 2015, www.crpe.org/thelens/special-education-governance-new-orleans; Beth Hawkins, "Once Largely Ignored, New Orleans Special Ed Students Find Meaning and Skills After High School," *The74million.org,* December 6, 2016; interview with and e-mails from Patrick Dobard, November–December 2016.

74 **Special education students' test scores:** State Superintendent John White, "Making a Pledge to Students and Families," *Times-Picayune,* September 7, 2011; Jacobs, "Charter Schools Help Improve Special Education in New Orleans"; Leslie Jacobs, "By the Numbers: Student and School Performance," *Educate Now!.net,* August 22, 2015, http://educatenow.net/2015/08/22/by-the-numbers-student-and-school-performance/.

74 **Special education students' graduation rates:** Jacobs, "Charter Schools Help Improve Special Education in New Orleans"; Adam Hawf, "Special Education Governance in New Orleans"; Danielle Dreilinger, "Graduation Rates and Other New Orleans Special Education Successes," *Times-Picayune,* May 26, 2015.

74 **Dobard believes is in the top 20 percent in the state:** Interview with RSD Superintendent Patrick Dobard, December 2016.

74 **the Southern Poverty Law Center wrote a letter:** "New Orleans Schools Must Ensure They Are Open to All Students," *Times-Picayune,* letter to the editor, January 14, 2015.

76 **Late that fall she invited . . . those fundamental principles:** Interview with Leslie Jacobs, December 2016; Educate Now!, "The Return Model: A New Approach to

Governance for Public Schools in New Orleans," 2016, www.coweninstitute.com/
wp-content/uploads/2011/06/Educate-Now-Return-Model-White-Paper.pdf.

76   **Karen Carter Peterson . . . introduced a bill:** "Act No. 91, Senate Bill No. 432,"
Louisiana State Legislature, 2016 Regular Session, www.legis.la.gov/legis/ViewDoc
ument.aspx?d=1003434.

77   **After Peterson's bill passed, the OPSB board unanimously approved:** Leslie
Jacobs, e-mail, January 2017.

77   **the reformers' principles, published in a statement:** "Forward New Orleans for
Public Schools," brochure, http://schools.forwardneworleans.com/wp-content/up
loads/2012/08/Forward_New-Orleans_School_brochure.pdf.

77   **charter schools can seek authorization from the state board . . . in New Orleans:**
State Superintendent John White, e-mail, December 2016.

77   **Ben Kleban argument and quote:** Ben Kleban, "Charter Schools CEO: Post-Katrina,
All Schools Should be Diverse by Design," *The Advocate*, September 10, 2015.

78   **83 percent of New Orleans's students are "economically disadvantaged":** Leslie
Jacobs, "New Orleans by the Numbers: Public School Enrollment," *Educate Now!.
net*, January 28, 2015, http://educatenow.net/2015/01/28/new-orleans-by-the-numbers
-public-school-enrollment/.

78   **Still, the four schools that participate in OneApp:** "Increasing the Diversity of
Public Schools in New Orleans," New Schools for New Orleans, July 28, 2016, www
.newschoolsforneworleans.org/school_diversity/.

78   **Local governments in the 1800s:** Bradley Robert Rice, *Progressive Cities: The Commission Government Movement in America, 1901–1920* (Austin: University of Texas
Press, 1977); Bradley R. Rice, "The Galveston Plan of City Government by Commission: The Birth of a Progressive Idea," *Southwestern Historical Quarterly* 78, no. 4
(April 1975): 365–408.

78   **Emergence of commission form of government in Galveston:** Ibid. (both sources).

78   **Galveston public works projects:** Mary G. Ramos, "Galveston's Response to the
Hurricane of 1900," *Texas Almanac*, 1999, www.texasalmanac.com/topics/history/
galvestons-response-hurricane-1900.

79   **The spread of the Galveston Plan:** Rice, *Progressive Cities*.

CHAPTER 4

83   **DCPS has more than 110 schools:** D.C. Public Schools, "DCPS at a Glance: Enrollment," "Schools" table, http://dcps.dc.gov/node/966292.

83   **65 independent charter organizations operate 118 schools:** "Student Enrollment,"
D.C. Public Charter School Board, 2017, www.dcpcsb.org/data/student-enrollment.

84   **Control Board review of D.C. Public Schools:** *Children in Crisis: A Report on the
Failure of D.C.'s Public Schools* (Washington, DC: District of Columbia Financial
Responsibility and Management Assistance Authority, November 12, 1996).

84   **Half of all students dropped out:** Ibid.

84   **Only 9 percent of ninth graders:** D.C. College Access Program et al., "Double the
Numbers for College Success: A Call to Action for the District of Columbia" (Washington, DC: 2006), www.newfuturesdc.org/wp-content/uploads/2009/03/double-
the-numbers.pdf, p. 4.

84   **Almost two thirds of teachers reported:** *Children in Crisis.*

84   **Kevin Chavous quotes:** Kevin Chavous, *Serving Our Children: Charter Schools and the Reform of American Public Education* (Sterling, VA: Capital Books, 2004), pp. 19–20.

84   **Payroll full of "ghosts," auditors unable to track money, and GAO report:** Jeffrey R. Henig et al., *The Color of School Reform: Race, Politics, and the Challenge of Urban Education* (Princeton: Princeton University Press, 1999), pp. 67–69.

84   **Nepotism was common:** Michelle Rhee, *Radical: Fighting to Put Students First* (New York: Harper, 2013), p. 111.

84   **Mayor Marion Barry steered contracts to supporters:** Henig et al, *Color of School Reform*, p. 126.

85   **Writing and passage of the bill and amendments:** Sara Mead, *Capital Campaign: Early Returns on District of Columbia Charter Schools* (Washington, DC: Progressive Policy Institute, October 2005), p. 7; interviews with Malcolm "Mike" Peabody, March and September 2015, and Ted Rebarber, October 2015.

88   **AppleTree operates six of its own charter preschools and partners with four other:** Jack McCarthy, e-mail, December 2016.

89   **KIPP had 16 schools in D.C. by 2017:** KIPP D.C. website, www.kippdc.org/.

89   **Initially, the new D.C. board of trustees:** Interview with Malcolm "Mike" Peabody, September 2015.

90   **2012 study on charter facilities:** Mary Levy, *Public Education Finance Reform in the District of Columbia: Uniformity, Equity, and Facilities* (Washington, DC: Friends of Choice in Public Education and D.C. Association of Chartered Public Schools, January 2012), http://dcacps.org/images/pdf/education_finance_reform.pdf, p. 20.

90   **Inadequate charter facilities:** According to FOCUS, "Equitable Funding and Services," www.focusdc.org/funding, "On average, the public charter schools can provide only 100 square feet per student, while DCPS students enjoy 140 square feet (elementary), 170 square feet (middle), or 190 square feet (high)." **Latin American Montessori Bilingual:** Interview with Cristina Encinas (principal), January 2015.

90   **Conversions of DCPS schools and resistance:** Josephine Baker, *The Evolution and Revolution of D.C. Charter Schools: A Transformation of Public Education in Washington, D.C.* (Washington, D.C., self-published, 2014), pp. 45–51; Nelson Smith, *An Accident of History: Breaking the District Monopoly on Public School Facilities* (Washington, DC: National Alliance of Public Charter Schools, July 2012), p. 11; interviews with Tom Nida and Josephine Baker, November 2014.

90   **Meanwhile, the city failed to provide nurses:** Interview with Nelson Smith, November 2014.

91   **Washington Teachers Union scandal:** Chavous, *Serving Our Children*, pp. 47–48; "D.C. Teachers' Union Plagued with Scandal," *Fox News*, January 17, 2003; Carol D. Leonnig, "Bullock Brazenly Recounts Embezzling," *Washington Post*, June 17, 2005 http://www.washingtonpost.com/wp-dyn/content/article/2005/06/16/AR2005061601538.html.

91   **Josephine Baker quote:** Josephine Baker, *Evolution and Revolution of D.C. Charter Schools*, p. 116.

91   **Catholic school conversions:** Ibid., pp. 51–52; interview with Tom Nida, November 2014.

92   **BOE charter oversight office scandal:** Bill Myers, "'Just Us Girls': The Charter Schools Saga," *Washington Examiner*, March 12, 2007; Carol D. Leonnig, "District's

Ex-Charter Schools Chief Admits Fraud," *Washington Post*, August 10, 2007; Keith L. Alexander, "35-Month Term in Schools Theft, and a Message," *Washington Post*, November 30, 2007.

93   **Charter Board closed an average of two schools a year:** Baker, *Evolution and Revolution of DC Charter Schools*, appendix D.

93   **But all schools encountering financial problems:** Interviews with Josephine Baker, February 2012 and November 2014.

CHAPTER 5

95   **DCPS enrollment numbers:** D.C. Public Charter School Board (henceforth cited as D.C. PCSB), "Historical Enrollment–Public Schools, Based on Charter and DCPS Enrollment, 1967 to the Present," https://data.dcpcsb.org/Enrollment-/Historial-Enrollment-Public-Schools/3db5-ujzr; D.C. PCSB, "Charter School Growth and Closures," www.dcpcsb.org/report/charter-school-growth-closures.

95   **NAEP scores in 2007:** Los Angeles was one point worse in reading in fourth and eighth grade, but according to NAEP, one point is not statistically significant. For the scores, see National Center for Education Statistics website, "NAEP Data Explorer," http://nces.ed.gov/nationsreportcard/naepdata/.

95   **Yet it spent more per child than almost every other big city:** Michelle Rhee, *Radical: Fighting to Put Students First* (New York: Harper, 2013), pp. 112, 135.

95   **Charters now educated almost 20,000 children:** D.C. PCSB, "Historical Enrollment—Public Schools."

95   **Josephine Baker quote:** Baker, *The Evolution and Revolution of DC Charter Schools: A Transformation of Public Education in Washington, D.C.* (Washington, D.C., self-published, 2014) pp. 15, 113.

95   **Effect of charter competition on D.C. Public Schools:** Interviews with Nelson Smith (former executive director of the Public School Charter Board and CEO of the National Alliance for Public Charter Schools), and former mayors Tony Williams and Vincent Gray, March 2015, and others.

95   **Fenty's decision to ask for control of DCPS and City Council vote:** Interview with Vincent Gray, March 2015.

96   **She convinced the City Council to convert her central office:** Rhee, *Radical*, p. 280.

96   **She closed 23 in her first year:** Ibid., p. 135, and Richard Whitmire, *The Bee Eater* (San Francisco: Jossey-Bass, 2011), p. 104.

96   **Protests against Rhee and Rhee quote:** Whitmire, *Bee Eater*, p. 93.

96   **By the time she left, in 2010, only half the principals:** Rhee, *Radical*, p. 137, and Whitmire, *Bee Eater*, pp. 131, 155.

96   **Only 8 percent of her eighth graders were proficient:** Whitmire, *Bee Eater*, p. 124.

96   **New IMPACT system:** Rhee, *Radical*, p. 152.

96   **"No schools superintendent anywhere in the country":** Whitmire, *Bee Eater*, p. 117.

96   **Rhee's contract offer and firings without union approval:** Ibid., p. 123; Education Consortium for Research and Evaluation, "Evaluation of the DC Public Education Reform Amendment Act (PERAA)" (Washington, DC: Office of the District of Columbia Auditor, July 15, 2013), www.dcauditor.org/sites/default/files/DCA132013.pdf, p. 10.

97   **The president of the teachers' union told his members:** Interview with Malcolm "Mike" Peabody, March 2015.

97   **The new teacher contract:** Rhee, *Radical*, pp. 164–6.

97   **Rhee's firing of teachers:** Whitmire, *Bee Eater*, pp. 127, 214, 239.

97   **DCPS had been "reconstituting" schools since the early 1990s:** Interview with Mary Levy, July 2016.

97   **Teachers options under reconstitutions:** Interview with Jason Kamras (DCPS chief of instructional practice), November 2014.

97   **In three and a half years, Rhee reconstituted 18 schools:** Peter Weber (deputy chancellor of DCPS), e-mail, June 2015.

97   **Meanwhile, Rhee increased foreign language:** Whitmire, *Bee Eater*, p. 236.

97   **Using funds provided by a universal preschool bill:** Tim Craig, "D.C. Mayoral Race: With Grit and Diplomacy, Gray Pushes Through Agenda," *Washington Post*, August 20, 2010.

97–8   **Rhee also began adopting . . . and professional development:** Education Consortium for Research and Evaluation, "Evaluation of the DC Public Education Reform Amendment Act (PERAA)."

98   **"The 50-year enrollment decline had ended":** Statistics from DCPS, "Historical Enrollment—Public Schools."

> 2006–7: 72,378 (charters 19,733; DCPS 52,645)
> 2007–8: 71,369 (charters 21,947; DCPS 49,422)
> 2008–9: 70,919 (charters 25,729; DCPS 45,190)
> 2009–10: 72,335 (charters 27,617; DCPS 44,718)
> 2010–11: 74,986 (charters 29,356; DCPS 45,630)

Hence, the increase in DCPS began in 2010–11, but was less than 1,000 that year. According to Office of the State Superintendent of Education's enrollment audit, DCPS had added just over 1,000 preschool seats between October 2007 and October 2010.

98   **2009 and 2011 NAEP scores:** National Center for Education Statistics, "NAEP Data Explorer," http://nces.ed.gov/nationsreportcard/naepdata/.

98   **Whitmire on anti-Rhee sentiment in 2010:** Whitmire, *Bee Eater*, pp. 128, 220.

98   **Vince Gray positions in 2010 election, and on charter funding:** Interview with former mayor Vince Gray, March 2015.

99   **2010 election results:** Whitmire, *Bee Eater*, p. 196.

99   **Quote from Mayor-Elect Gray:** Quoted in Kristin Capps, "Meet the New Boss, Same As the Old Boss," *NBC Washington*, October 13, 2010.

99   **Relationship between Michelle Rhee and Kaya Henderson:** Whitmire, *Bea Eater*, pp. 87–89; Gary Tischler, "Kaya Henderson Up Close," *The Georgetowner*, March 9, 2011, www.georgetowner.com/articles/2011/mar/09/kaya-henderson-close/.

99   **Henderson continued using IMPACT to terminate about 100 teachers a year:** Interview with Kaya Henderson, January 2015; National Research Council, *An Evaluation of the Public Schools of the District of Columbia: Reform in a Changing Landscape* (Washington, DC: National Academies Press, 2015), www.nap.edu/catalog.php?record_id=21743, pp. 4–20 and table 4-5.

100   **Description of IMPACT:** Interview with Jason Kamras, November 2014; e-mails from Michelle Hudacsko (DCPS deputy chief, IMPACT), December 2016.

100   **Teacher earnings in DCPS:** Michelle Hudacsko, December 2016 e-mail; Jason Kamras, *DCPS Teacher Effectiveness Update* (Washington, DC: D.C. Public Schools, October 30, 2014); Ryan Schuette, "Does It Pay to Pay Teachers $100,000? " *nprEd*, November 19, 2015, www.npr.org/sections/ed/2015/11/19/455378792/does-it-pay-to-pay-teachers-100-000; Nithya Joseph and Nancy Waymack, *Smart Money: What Teachers Make, How Long It Takes and What It Buys Them* (Washington, DC: National Council on Teacher Quality, December 2014), www.nctq.org/dmsView/Smart_Money. According to Joseph and Waymack's appendix C, teacher pay in D.C. is far higher than in other cities, and in the average district it takes teachers 24 years to reach their maximum pay.

100   **Those rated "ineffective" once, "minimally effective" two years:** Kamras, *DCPS Teacher Effectiveness Update*, pp. 4–5; Michelle Hudacsko, e-mail, December 2016.

100   **Wycoff and Dee studies:** Thomas Dee and James Wyckoff, "Incentives, Selection, and Teacher Performance: Evidence from IMPACT," NBER Working Paper No. 19529 (Cambridge, MA: National Bureau of Economic Research, October 2013), in *Journal of Policy Analysis and Management* 34, no. 2, pp. 267–97; Melinda Adnot et al., "Teacher Turnover, Teacher Quality, and Student Achievement in DCPS," NBER Working Paper No. 21922 (Cambridge, MA: National Bureau for Economic Research, January 2016).

101   **25 percent annual turnover in principals:** Jonetta Rose Barras, "When Will DCPS Stop Sending Principals Through a Revolving Door?" *Washington Post*, May 21, 2014.

101   **Jason Kamras quote:** Quoted in Jay Matthews, "Learning Lessons of the Past, D.C. Overhauls Teacher Evaluations. Will It Work?" *Washington Post*, February 21, 2016.

101   **Henderson's strategies to recruit and develop principals:** Ibid.; interview with Kaya Henderson, January 2015.

101–2   **60 schools had adopted the model by 2016–17:** Jason Kamras, e-mail, December 2016.

102   **New approach to teacher evaluation and teacher leaders:** Matthews, "Learning Lessons of the Past"; Emma Brown, "D.C. Public Schools, Closely Watched for Its Reform Efforts, Is Overhauling Teacher Evaluation and Training," *Washington Post*, February 10, 2016; DCPS Office of Instructional Practice, *LEAP Team Design Guide* (Washington, DC: DCPS, February 2016).

102   **Reconstituting nine more schools:** Michelle Lerner, DCPS press secretary, e-mail, March 2017.

102   **Lengthening school days and years:** Ibid.

102   **by 2011 DCPS was the most expensive large district in the country:** Megan Batdorff et al., "Charter School Funding: Inequity Expands" (Fayetteville: University of Arkansas, Department of Education Reform, April 2014), www.uaedreform.org/charter-funding-inequity-expands.

CHAPTER 6

104   **Public Charter School Board approach to accountability under Scott Pearson:** Interview with Scott Pearson, November 2014, and subsequent e-mails.

105   **Those succeeding with some grade levels but not others:** Jeffrey Cohen, Alex Doty, and Florian Schalliol, *Transforming Public Education in the Nation's Capital: An*

In-Depth Look into a High-Quality Charter School Authorizer (Washington, D.C., FSG, 2014), pp. 38–41.

105   **Average of five school closures per year:** For list of charter school openings and clos-ings, see D.C. PCSB website, "Closed Charter Schools," http://www.dcpcsb.org/sites/default/files/Closed%20Public%20Charter%20Schools.pdf.

105   **A third of charters were closed over first 20 years:** D.C. PCSB, "Charter School Growth and Closures," www.dcpcsb.org/report/charter-school-growth-closures. Another seven charter schools were approved but never opened, according to Josephine Baker, *The Evolution and Revolution of D.C Charter Schools: A Transformation of Public Education in Washington, D.C.* (Washington, D.C., self-published, 2014), Appendix.

105   **In Pearson's first four years, it approved only 13 of 41:** Megan Walsh (PCSB staff), e-mail, August 2015.

105   **Percentage of students enrolled in tier 1 and tier 3 schools:** D.C. PCSB, "School Quality Reports," www.dcpcsb.org/report/school-quality-reports-pmf; Natalie Wex-ler, "Five Things You Should Know About What Happened This Year in DC Educa-tion," *Greatergreaterwashington.org*, December 31, 2014.

106   **Briya Public Charter School:** Briya website, http://briya.org; Emily Leayman, "New D.C. Campus Coming for Charter That Caters to 'The Whole Family in One Place,'" *Education Watchdog.org*, May 10, 2016.

106   **National Alliance for Public Charter Schools reports on health of charter move-ment:** Louann Bierlein Palmer and Todd Ziebarth, *The Health of the Charter Public School Movement: A State-by-State Analysis* (Washington, DC: National Alliance for Public Charter Schools, March 2016), www.publiccharters.org/publications/health-charter-public-school-movement-state-by-state-analysis/; Louann Bierlein Palmer and Todd Ziebarth, *Health of the Public Charter School Movement: A State-By-State Analysis* (Washington, DC: NAPCS, September 2014, www.publiccharters.org/pub lications/charter-movement-2014/.

107   **Data on midyear withdrawals, suspensions, expulsions, and special education enrollment:** Emily Leayman, "New D.C. Charter School Data Refutes Myths on Discipline, Diversity," *Education Watchdog.org*, December 19, 2016; Ella Krivitch-enko (PCSB staff), email; May 2017.

107   **Pearson also convinced the city council to double the board's budget:** Interview with Scott Pearson, November 2014.

107   **Financial scandals among charters:** See, for example, Emma Brown, "D.C. Officials Allege Improper Diversion of Charter Funds," *Washington Post*, June 2, 2014; Michael Allison Chandler, "Judge Orders D.C. Charter to Stop Payments to Com-pany Founded by School Leaders," *Washington Post*, October 27, 2014.

107   **In 2016, Pearson finally convinced the city council:** Emily Leayman, "D.C. Council Approves Charter School Transparency Measure," *Education Watchdog.org*, June 7, 2016.

108   **Information on FOCUS:** Interviews with former executive director Robert Cane, November 2014 and January 2015; see also https://focusdc.org.

108   **Information on New Schools Venture Fund:** Interviews with The Venture Fund's Maura Morino, November 2014 and October 2016; quote is from Education Forward DC website, http://edforwarddc.org.

109   **Information on Charter Board Partners:** Interview with Carrie Irvin, January 2015.

109   **Information on Flamboyan Foundation:** Interview with Kristin Ehrgood, April 2015; Flamboyan website, http://flamboyanfoundation.org.

109   **Instead, the keys are "a parent holding":** Flamboyan Foundation, "Setting the Stage: The Family Engagement Field," June 9, 2011, http://flamboyanfoundation.org/wp/wp-content/uploads/2011/06/Setting-the-stage-4-28-11.pdf.

109   **One study found "that teachers who reached out to parents":** Lela Spielberg, "Successful Family Engagement in the Classroom: What Teachers Need to Know and Be Able to Do to Engage Families in Raising Student Achievement," Flamboyan Foundation and Harvard Family Research Project, March 2011, http://flamboyanfoundation .org/wp/wp-content/uploads/2011/06/FINE-Flamboyan_Article-March-2011.pdf. The paper cited the following study: Westat & Policy Studies Associates, *The Longitudinal Evaluation of School Change and Performance (LESCP) in Title I Schools* (Washington, DC: U.S. Department of Education, 2001), http://www2.ed.gov/offices/ OUS/PES/esed/lescp_highlights.html.

110   **"By 2017, Flamboyan . . . in the city":** Kristin Ehrgood, e-mail, December 2016.

111   **D.C. Common Core Collaborative and Capital Teaching Residency:** Interview with Jennifer Niles, November 2014.

111   **"Kaya Henderson gives the Capital Teaching Residency credit":** Henderson credited the Capital Teaching Residency with inspiring her in a hearing before the Education Committee of the D.C. City Council, on June 22, 2015.

112   **DCPS has agreed to take over two schools:** The two were Hospitality High and one of the Community Academy Public Charter Schools.

112   **DCPS Academy for Construction and Design at Cardoza High School:** Daniel J. Sernovitz, "Academy For Construction and Design to Uproot from Its Long-Time Home at Cardozo," *Washington Business Journal*, May 14, 2015; IDEA Public Charter School website, "Academy of Construction & Design," www.ideapcs.org/apps/pages/ACAD.

CHAPTER 7

113   **Enrollment data in D.C.:** Different sources have slightly different data for 2006–7, hence the 82 to 85 percent range. I relied primarily on data from the Office of the State Superintendent of Education, which had 85 percent. See Office of the State Superintendent of Education (henceforth cited as OSSE), "OSSE Quality Schools Project: Phase One," table C-6, http://osse.dc.gov/sites/default/files/dc/sites/osse/pub lication/attachments/Planning%20for%20Quality%20Schools_Appendix_C_1.2.4._ Demand_Data_final_feb_2008.pdf. For 2015–16 data, see OSSE, "District of Columbia 2015–2016 Equity Report" (Washington, DC: OSSE, December 2016), http://osse. dc.gov/sites/default/files/dc/sites/osse/publication/attachments/2015_Equity_Report_ Citywide_District%20of%20Columbia.pdf. There is some overlap in data such as this between whites and Hispanics, because some Hispanics are also identified as white.

113   **Demographic data on the two systems:** D.C. PCSB, "2015–2016 DC School Equity Reports, Public Charter Schools" (Washington, DC: Public Charter School Board, December 2016), www.dcpcsb.org/sites/default/files/report/2016_Equity_Reports_ Charter_Trends_.pdf; Sara Mead, "Clinton's Baseless Charter School Claim," *U.S. News and World Report*, November 24, 2015.

113   **Reading scores by race on 2014 standardized tests:** OSSE, "2014 District of Columbia Comprehensive Assessment System Results (DC CAS)," July 31, 2014, https://osse.dc.gov/sites/default/files/dc/sites/osse/publication/attachments/2014%20DC%20CAS%20Result%20July%2031%202014 . . . FINAL_.pdf, p. 16.

113   **Difference in total spending per pupil between DCPS and charters:** This funding disparity came from five main sources. First, D.C. and the federal government fund pensions for DCPS teachers but not charter teachers, unless they have come from a DCPS school and the charter contributes to the pension fund. The amounts have varied year to year, but in 2015, according to the veteran fiscal analyst Mary Levy, DCPS spent $837 per pupil on pensions.

Second, D.C. launched a major capital investment drive to rebuild and renovate DCPS schools in 2008. Since then, it has spent an average of about $7,400 per student each year on DCPS schools, while charters have received about $3,000 per student annually in facilities funding. (See The Finance Project and Augenblick, Palaich and Associates, *Cost of Student Achievement: Report of the DC Education Adequacy Study: Final Report* (Washington, DC: The Finance Project, prepared for the D.C. deputy mayor of education, December 20, 2013), p. 82, Table 4.5 for figures on annual capital spending on DCPS schools.)

Third, other DC agencies have spent money on DCPS schools—for maintenance, security, health services, and other services—that did not always go to charter schools. A 2012 study estimated the difference at $40 million to $60 million a year between 2008 and 2012. (Mary Levy, *Public Education Finance Reform in the District of Columbia: Uniformity, Equity, and Facilities* (Washington, DC: Friends of Choice in Urban Schools and D.C. Association of Chartered Public Schools, 2012), p. 13, http://dcacps.org/images/pdf/education_finance_reform.pdf.) This number has been coming down as the city has equalized spending in several categories, but according to Levy, it amounted to $858 per student in fiscal year 2015.

Fourth, DCPS schools have been funded based on projected enrollments, while charters have been funded based on current-year enrollment audits in October; Levy estimated the annual difference at $41 per student. (According to Deputy Mayor for Education Niles, the city is transitioning to a system that will fund both sectors on the same basis.)

Fifth, the city council has occasionally made supplemental appropriations to DCPS but not to charters.

Levy estimated the total difference in annual funding at $5800 per student in fiscal 2014. In 2016, FOCUS estimated the total difference at $6,558 per student per year. ("City Budget Fails to Adequately Fund Public Charter School Facilities," press release, May 18, 2016, http://focusdc.org/sites/focusdc.org/files/Press%20Release-May18-Facilities%20Allowance.pdf.)

114   **Definition of "at-risk" students in D.C.:** Abigail Smith (then deputy mayor for education), "Clarification Regarding the 'At-Risk for Academic Failure' Weight in the Uniform per Student Funding Formula," Office of the Deputy Mayor for Education, October 6, 2014, http://osse.dc.gov/publication/risk-academic-failure-guidance. The percentage who qualify for a free or reduced-price lunch is no longer an accurate measure of income, because since 2012–13, D.C. has used the Department of Agriculture's

"community eligibility" option to give *all* students a free lunch in schools with more than 40 percent "at-risk" students.

114 **Percentages of at-risk students in DCPS and charters:** OSSE, "Overview," http://osse.dc.gov/sites/default/files/dc/sites/osse/publication/attachments/SY%202015-16%20School-by-School%20Enrollment%20Audit%20Data%20%28Updated%29.pdf.

114 **In 2014–15—not counting alternative schools—some two dozen DCPS schools:** Ginger Moored, "Can School Lotteries Make Schools More Diverse?" D.C. Office of Revenue Analysis, October 7, 2015, http://districtmeasured.com/2015/10/07/can-school-lotteries-make-schools-more-diverse/.

114 **Charters also expel more students than DCPS:** D.C. PCSB, "Attendance and Truancy Report SY 2015–16," September 27, 2016, www.dcpcsb.org/sites/default/files/report/DC%20PCSB%20SY%202015-16%20Truancy%20Report.pdf.

114 **Most DCPS schools accept students midyear:** Interview with Jeff Noel, then assistant superintendent of data, accountability, and research at OSSE, January 2015.

114 **2015 Mobility Study by OSSE:** Division of Data, Accountability, and Research, "Mid-Year Student Movement in DC," (OSSE, July 2015).

114 **Most of these had *not* been expelled:** According to OSSE, 134 students were expelled by both sectors in 2014–15, and 99 the following school year. Most were in charter schools. See Alejandra Matos, "Suspensions and Expulsions in D.C. Schools Decrease, but Racial Disparities Persist," *Washington Post*, February 2, 2017.

114 **The city is encouraging schools to retain students:** Deputy Mayor for Education Jennifer Niles, e-mail, December 2016.

115 **From 2007–8 through 2010–11, CREDO found:** CREDO, "National Charter School Study 2013" (Stanford, CA: Center for Research on Education Outcomes, 2013), http://credo.stanford.edu/documents/NCSS%202013%20Final%20Draft.pdf, p. 52.

115 **CREDO 2015 study:** CREDO, "Urban Charter School Study: Report on 41 Regions, 2015" (Stanford, CA: Center for Research on Education Outcomes, 2015), http://urbancharters.stanford.edu/download/Urban%20Charter%20School%20Study%20Report%20on%2041%20Regions.pdf, p. 20.

115 **the impact was more than double:** CREDO, "Urban Charter School Impact in Washington D.C." (Stanford, CA: Center for Research on Education Outcomes, March 2015), http://urbancharters.stanford.edu/states.php, slide 11.

115 **Another independent study:** Office of the Deputy Mayor for Education, TEMBO, and Raise DC, *District of Columbia Graduation Pathways Project Summary* (Washington, DC: Office of the Deputy Mayor for Education, September 2014), http://docplayer.net/10420204-District-of-columbia-graduation-pathways-project-summary.html, pp. 26–27.

115 **Before 2007, only an estimated 9 percent:** D.C. College Access Program et al., *Double the Numbers for College Success: A Call to Action for the District of Columbia* (Washington, DC: 2006), www.newfuturesdc.org/wp-content/uploads/2009/03/double-the-numbers.pdf.

115 **College persistence rates are improving, according to OSSE:** Interview with Jeff Noel (then assistant superintendent of data, accountability, and research at OSSE), June 2015.

115 **4-year high school graduation rates:** Division of Data, Assessments, and Research, "DC 2016 Adjusted Cohort 4-Year Graduation Rate (9th Grade Class Entering for the First Time in 2012–13 School Year)," OSSE, http://osse.dc.gov/sites/default/files/

dc/sites/osse/publication/attachments/Adjusted%20Cohort%20Graduation%20
Rate%20Overview%202015-16.pdf.

115   **5-year high school graduation rates:** OSSE, "DC 2014 4-year & 2015 5-year Adjusted
Cohort Graduation Rates, by School (2010–11 School Year 9 Grade Cohort)," http://
osse.dc.gov/sites/default/files/dc/sites/osse/publication/attachments/Graduationby
School_2014ACGR_5yr%20%282%29.pdf.

116   **Among black and low-income students:** OSSE, "DC 2015 4-year Adjusted Cohort
Graduation Rates, by Subgroup," http://osse.dc.gov/sites/default/files/dc/sites/osse/
publication/attachments/Adjusted%20Cohort%20Graduation%20Rate%20by%20
Subgroup%202014-15.pdf.

116   **Given that almost seven of every ten black males:** Melissa S. Kearney et al., *Ten
Economic Facts About Crime and Incarceration in the United States* (Washington,
DC: Hamilton Project and Brookings Institution, May 2014), www.brookings.edu/
research/reports/2014/05/10-crime-facts.

116   **In 2016, 97.2 percent of charter graduates:** Scott Pearson (D.C. PCSB executive
director), e-mail, December 2016.

116   **College enrollment data:** Mikayla Lytton (PCSB manager for finance, analysis, and
strategy), e-mail, July, 2015.

116   **Attendance data is problematic as well:** Jeff Noel (then assistant superintendent of
data, accountability, and research at OSSE), e-mail, June, 2015.

116   **Reported attendance rates:** D.C. PCSB, "DC Public Charter School Board Attendance and Truancy Report SY 2015–16," September 27, 2016, www.dcpcsb.org/sites/
default/files/report/DC%20PCSB%20SY%202015-16%20Truancy%20Report.pdf;
D.C. Public Schools, "Annual Truancy Report," August 2016, http://dcps.dc.gov/
sites/default/zfiles/dc/sites/dcps/publication/attachments/DCPS%20Annual%20
Attendance%20Report_SY1516_FINAL.pdf.

116   **In recent years, charters have grown by 2,000 to 3,000:** OSSE, "SY 2015–16 General
Education Final Enrollment," February 2016, https://osse.dc.gov/sites/default/files/
dc/sites/osse/publication/attachments/EA%20Final%20Enrollment%20PPT%20
2%2029%202016.pdf. **In 2016–17:** OSSE, "Public School Enrollment in the District of
Columbia Increases for Eighth Consecutive Year," March 6, 2017, https://osse.dc.gov/
release/public-school-enrollment-district-columbia-increases-eighth-consecutive
-year.

116   **Waiting lists in 2016:** D.C. Public Charter School Board, "Demand for a Quality DC
Public Charter School Continues to Grow in Washington, D.C.," www.dcpcsb.org/
blog/demand-quality-dc-public-charter-school-continues-grow-washington-dc;
Michelle Lerner, DCPS press secretary, email, March 2017. These numbers do not
count the same child twice if they are on more than one school waiting list.

116   **OSSE has tightened test protocols and monitoring:** Interview with Jeff Noel, January 2015.

117   **DC CAS test scores:** OSSE, "2014 District of Columbia Comprehensive Assessment
System Results (DC CAS)," July 31, 2014, http://osse.dc.gov/sites/default/files/dc/sites/
osse/publication/attachments/2014%20DC%20CAS%20Result%20July%2031%20
2014 . . . FINAL_.pdf.

117   **Wards 5, 7, and 8, are D.C.'s poorest:** National Research Council, *An Evaluation of
the Public Schools of the District of Columbia* (Washington, DC: National Academies

Press, 2015), https://www.nap.edu/catalog/21743/an-evaluation-of-the-public-schools
-of-the-district-of-columbia, table 2-3 and 2-4, p. 30.

117   **PARCC test results:** FOCUS, "2016 DC PARCC Results by Sector," https://focusdc.org/
parcc. Among Hispanics, DCPS had roughly one percentage point more students
score in these top two categories in math, but six points fewer in English language arts.

117   **In high school, five charters outperformed:** FOCUS, "D.C. Public Charter Schools
Continue Improvement Trend," press release, August 30, 2016, https://focusdc.org/
sites/focusdc.org/files/FOCUS%20Press%20Release%20Final.pdf.

117   **All six schools that earned "Bold Performance Awards":** Josh Boots, "Students Are
Beating the Odds at EmpowerK12 'Bold Performance' Schools," EmpowerK12, September 9, 2016, https://empowerk12.wordpress.com/2016/09/09/2016-empowerk12
-bold-performance-schools/.

117   **NAEP scores: In 2013 and 2015, the two sectors combined:** National Center for
Education Statistics, "NAEP Data Explorer," http://nces.ed.gov/nationsreportcard/
naepdata/.

117   **two recent analyses found that a quarter to a third:** Kevin Lang and Ginger
Moored, "The Role of Demographics in NAEP and PARCC Scores," *District, Measured* (Posts from the District of Columbia's Office of Revenue), November 5, 2015,
https://districtmeasured.com/2015/11/; Kristin Blagg and Matthew Chingos, "Gentrification Isn't the Only Reason DC's Test Scores Are Rising," Greater Greater Washington website, May 25, 2016, https://ggwash.org/view/41822/gentrification-isnt-the
-only-reason-dcs-test-scores-are-rising.

117   **Rankings of DCPS on NAEP:** D.C. Public Schools (henceforth cited as DCPS),
"DC Public Schools Continues Momentum as the Fastest Improving Urban School
District in the Country," October 28, 2015, http://dcps.dc.gov/release/dc-public
-schools-continues-momentum-fastest-improving-urban-school-district-country.
These rankings are done using average NAEP scores.

117   **Charters have performed far better among African American:** National Center for
Education Statistics, "NAEP Data Explorer," http://nces.ed.gov/nationsreportcard/
naepdata/. Data on low-income students is less accurate for the last two tests, because
in 2012–13 D.C. began using the Department of Agriculture's "community eligibility" option to declare that all students in schools with more than 40 percent "at-risk"
students would receive free lunch. Data on special-education students is also considered unreliable, according to Jeff Noel, former OSSE assistant superintendent of
data, accountability and research.

117   **White students in DCPS score higher than whites:** National Center for Education
Statistics, "NAEP Data Explorer", http://nces.ed.gov/nationsreportcard/naepdata/.

124   **Ward 8 DCPS middle and high schools:** FOCUS, "2016 DC PARCC Results by
School," https://focusdc.org/2016-dc-parcc-results-school.

124   **the largest in the history of the test:** DCPS, "DC Public Schools Continues Momentum as the Fastest Improving Urban School District in the Country."

124   **Indeed, a 2014 Washington Post poll:** Natalie Wexler, "Can DCPS Stem the Middle
School Exodus? " Greater Greater Washington website, May 27, 2015, https://ggwash
.org/view/38272/can-dcps-stem-the-middle-school-exodus.

129   **Kaya Henderson quote:** Quoted in Michael Alison Chandler, "At-Risk Funds Will Follow Students; Chancellor Will Have Say in Spending," *Washington Post*, March 4, 2015.

129   **Henderson also required that all high schools offer:** Jay Matthews, "'AP Lite' for Poor, Urban Kids Is a Pipe Dream That Ignores School Realities," *Washington Post,* November 15, 2015; Natalie Wexler, "DCPS Is Expanding AP Classes, but at Some Schools Everyone Fails the Test," Greater Greater Washington website, September 29, 2015, https://ggwash.org/view/39409/dcps-is-expanding-ap-classes-but-at-some-schools-everyone-fails-the-test.

129–30 **Most DCPS principals have not had the option:** Perry Stein, "For Thousands of D.C. Students, School Starts Early with New, Year-Round Schedule," *Washington Post,* August 7, 2016.

131   **Patrick Pope quote:** Quoted in Natalie Wexler, "To Keep Its Best Principals, DCPS Needs to Give Them More Autonomy," Greater Greater Washington website, July 13, 2015, http://greatergreaterwashington.org/post/27348/to-keep-its-best-principals-dcps-needs-to-give-them-more-autonomy/.

132   **Vincent Gray quote:** Quoted in Jason Russell, "Former D.C. Mayor: Competition Works for Schools," *Washington Examiner,* October 15, 2015.

132   **Rhee closed about 25 schools because their buildings:** Data from DCPS Deputy Chancellor Peter Weber, e-mail, June 2015.

132   **CREDO studies show that:** CREDO, "National Charter School Study 2013"; CREDO, "Urban Charter School Study, 2015."

133   **Indeed, by 2015–16, 18 open schools:** DCPS, "2015–16 MFP Annual Supplement, Appendix A: DCPS Facility Data and Utilization Plans" (Washington, DC: District of Columbia Public Schools, 2016), http://dme.dc.gov/sites/default/files/dc/sites/dme/publication/attachments/Copy%20of%20DCPS%20Enrollment%20and%20Utilization%2003%2004%2016%20Final.pdf.

133   **Diversity of school types in DCPS:** For school profiles see DCPS website, "Find a School," http://profiles.dcps.dc.gov; *DCPS Parent Handbook* (Washington, DC: District of Columbia Public Schools, April 2016), http://dcps.dc.gov/sites/default/files/dc/sites/dcps/publication/attachments/DCPS%20Parent%20Handbook_ENG-FINAL.pdf, appendix.

133   **Students at all of its high schools could apply:** DCPS, "Participate in Dual Enrollment," http://dcps.dc.gov/service/participate-dual-enrollment.

134   **The charter sector creates four or five new schools every year:** Data from D.C. PCSB website, "DC Charter Growth and Closures," https://data.dcpcsb.org/Schools-/DC-Charter-Growth-And-Closures/f9ru-s5re.

134   **Washington Leadership Academy:** Richard Whitmire, "A D.C. Charter Wins $10M to Invent Virtual Reality Programs That Will Change High School—All of Them," *The74milion.org,* September 14, 2016; Emma Brown, "D.C. Charter School Wins $10 Million Prize To Redesign High School," *Washington Post,* September 14, 2016.

136   **public school enrollment climbed 25 percent:** On 2006–7 enrollment see D.C. PCSB, "Historical Enrollment–Public Schools," https://data.dcpcsb.org/Enrollment-/Historial-Enrollment-Public-Schools/3db5-ujzr. On 2016–17 enrollment see OSSE, "Public School Enrollment in the District of Columbia Increases for Eighth Consecutive Year."

136   **Having the nation's most robust preschool program:** Former mayor Vince Gray, written communication, March 2015; W. S. Barnet et al., *The State of Preschool 2014: State Preschool Yearbook* (New Brunswick, NJ: National Institute for Early

Education Research, 2015), http://nieer.org/wp-content/uploads/2016/05/Yearbook_2015_rev1.pdf.

136   **2016 PARCC proficiency levels:** OSSE, "2016 DC PARCC Results," August 30, 2016, http://osse.dc.gov/sites/default/files/dc/sites/osse/publication/attachments/2016%20OSSE%20PARCC%20Presentation.pdf, p. 26. These scores are averages of scores in math and English language arts.

136   **Andy Smarick recommendations:** Andy Smarick, "Laying the Foundation for the Next Decade of D.C. Reform," *Flypaper*, March 10, 2016, https://edexcellence.net/articles/laying-the-foundation-for-the-next-decade-of-dc-reform.

137   **In 2015–16, five DCPS buildings sat empty:** D.C. PCSB, "Three Benefits of Public Charter Schools Using Vacant School DCPS Buildings," March 30, 2016, www.dcpcsb.org/blog/three-benefits-public-charter-schools-using-vacant-school-buildings.

137   **DCPS wanted to keep all the empty buildings:** Mark Lerner, "DCPS Chancellor Henderson Wants to Keep School Buildings Under Her Control," *Washington Examiner*, May 4, 2015.

137   **Mayor Muriel Bowser announced in February 2017:** "Should D.C. Let Charter Schools Give an Edge to Children Who Live Nearby?," editorial, *Washington Post*, February 3, 2017.

CHAPTER 8

141   **Between 2005 and 2015 it closed or replaced 48 schools:** Melanie Asmar, "Denver Public Schools Approves New Policy for Closing Struggling Schools, but Questions Remain," *Chalkbeat*, December 17, 2015.

141   **opened more than 70, the majority charters:** interview with Tom Boasberg, DPS superintendent, October 2014.

141   **Collaboration Compact:** Denver Public Schools (henceforth cited as DPS), "District-Charter Collaboration Compact," 2010, http://portfolio.dpsk12.org/wp-content/uploads/2015/07/DPSDistrictCharterCollaborationCompact.pdf.

141   **Numbers of charter and innovation schools in 2016–17:** Matthew Lanz (data analyst for the senior director of portfolio management, DPS), e-mail, January, 2017.

141   **Percentages of students in charters and innovation schools in 2016–17:** Brian Eschbacher (DPS director of planning and enrollment), e-mail, January 2017.

142   **But the strategy produced steady results:** Tom Boasberg, "Celebrating Strong Progress, Focusing on Growth Gaps," Denver Public Schools, September 23, 2016, www.dpsk12.org/celebrating-strong-progress-focusing-on-growth-gaps/.

142   **It is the number one destination for the millennial generation:** John Hanc, "Denver's Appeal to Millennials? Jobs, Mountains and, Yes, Weed," *New York Times*, July 20, 2016.

142   **one of the nation's top ten cities for business start-ups:** Jeremy Quittner, "The 25 Hottest Cities for Startups," *Fortune*, August 25, 2016.

142   **a smaller percentage of residents are overweight:** "Denver—the City," HomeToDenver website, www.hometodenver.com/stats_denver.htm, citing a 1996 federal report.

142   **Percentages of population for each race:** U.S. Census Bureau, "QuickFacts, Denver County, Colorado," www.census.gov/quickfacts/table/PST045215/08031.

142   **Percentage of college graduates:** U.S. Census Bureau, "American FactFinder," http://factfinder.census.gov/faces/tableservices/jsf/pages/productview.xhtml?src=bkmk.

142   **Enrollment increased 25 percent between 2007 and 2015:** DPS, *Adopted Budget Book, Fiscal Year 2014–2015* (Denver: Denver Public Schools, 2014), http://finan cialservices.dpsk12.org/wp-content/uploads/2014/07/DPS-Adopted-Budget-Book -FY2014-15.pdf, pp. 7, 12.

142   **Colorado ranked 42nd in the nation in state spending per pupil:** Susana Cordova, "Separating Fact from Myth in School Funding," *OurDPS Weekly* (blog), February 26, 2016.

142   **DPS revenue was $2,000 to $2,500 less per student:** Tom Boasberg, "A Deeply Committed Group of Educators," *OurDPS Weekly* (blog), August 5, 2016, http:// myemail.constantcontact.com/Our-DPS-Weekly—A-Deeply-Committed-Group-of-Educators.html?soid=1110617542386&aid=2S4MYKXM85c; Jenny Brundin, "In Colorado, School Funding Lags Despite Booming Economy," Colorado Public Radio, April 29, 2016, www.cpr.org/news/story/colorado-school-funding-lags-despite-boom ing-economy#sthash.VRJpzIrP.dpuf.

142   **still below 2009-10:** Erik Johnson (DPS executive director for finance), e-mail, March 2016.

143   **Percentages of poor students and English language learners:** DPS, "Facts and Figures: DPS by the Numbers, 2017," http://communications.dpsk12.org/facts.html.

143   **94 percent of low-income students are minorities:** DPS, "The Denver Plan" (Denver: Denver Public Schools, August 2014), www.dpsk12.org/denverplan/.

143   **Percentage of students who are Hispanic, white, and African American:** DPS, "Facts and Figures: DPS by the Numbers, 2017."

143   **Student numbers in 2005:** Burt Hubbard and Nancy Mitchell, "Leaving to Learn: A Seven Day Special Report," report undertaken in partnership with the Piton Foundation, *Rocky Mountain News*, April 16–22, 2007.

143   **Pension crisis:** Sam Sperry, "Portfolio Reform in Denver: A Mile High and Climbing," Center on Reinventing Public Education, March 2012; Paul T. Hill, Christine Campbell, and Betheny Gross, *Strife and Progress: Portfolio Strategies for Managing Urban Districts* (Washington, DC: Brookings Institution Press, 2013), pp. 52–55.

143   **Mayor John Hickenlooper urged his 40-year-old chief of staff:** Interview with Governor John Hickenlooper, May 2016.

143   **He was reconstituting 13 elementary and middle schools:** Sperry, *Portfolio Reform in Denver*, pp. 6–7.

143   **Number of charters and students in 2004-5:** Colorado Department of Education, "The State of Charter Schools in Colorado 2004–05," January 2006, p. 26.

143   **half performed below the district average:** Interview with Bruce Hoyt (DPS board member from 2003 through 2011), January 2016.

143   **Greenberg quote about Bennet's opposition to charters:** David Ethan Greenberg, "Bennet's Perplexing Silence On Charters," *EdNews Colorado*, May 8, 2009.

143   **The Denver Plan, 2005:** Sperry, *Portfolio Reform in Denver*, p. 11.

144   **Manual High School troubles:** Ibid., p. 4.

145   **And the teachers' union complained that teachers:** Allison Sherry, "Teachers Ask Board to Slow Down Reforms," *Denver Post*, November 16, 2006.

145   ***Rocky Mountain News* series:** Hubbard and Mitchell, "Leaving to Learn."

145   **"It is hard to admit," they wrote:** Quoted in Hill, Campbell, and Gross, *Strife and Progress*, pp. 52–53.

146   **They told Bennet that superintendents did not survive:** Van Schoales (CEO of A+ Colorado), e-mail, December 2015.

146   **So Bennet pared the plan down to eight school closures:** Hill, Campbell, and Gross, *Strife and Progress*, p. 53.

146   **A month later the board adopted a New School Development Plan . . . Office of New Schools:** Judy Bray and Alex Medler, *Denver's Public Schools: Reforms, Challenges, and the Future* (Denver: Colorado Children's Campaign, A+ Denver, and Metro Organizations for People, June 2009), pp. 27, 28.

146   **modeled at least in part on what New York City:** Interview with Van Schoales, October 2014.

147   **Metro Organizations for People had picked up on this:** Interview with Michael Kromrey (Colorado Together, formerly Metro Organizations for People), May 2016.

147   **By 2015 about 56 percent of operating money followed the student:** Kate Kotaska (deputy chief financial officer at DPS), e-mail, November 2014. See also Katie Furtick, *Annual Privatization Report 2014: Education* (Los Angeles: Reason Foundation, April 2014), http://reason.org/news/show/apr-2014-education, p. 2.

150   **As early as late 2005 they had developed a draft "balanced scorecard":** Bray and Medler, "Denver's Public Schools," p. 28.

151   **charter schools quickly dominated the top ten lists:** DPS, "District-Charter Collaboration Compact," December 2010, http://portfolio.dpsk12.org/wp-content/up loads/2015/07/DPSDistrictCharterCollaborationCompact.pdf, p. 1.

151   **Greenberg quote:** Greenberg, "Bennet's Perplexing Silence on Charters."

151   **Eight more DSST schools, on four campuses:** Interview with Bill Kurtz, December 2015.

152   **Boasberg quote:** Quoted in Sarah Yatsko, "Hiring District Leaders from the Charter Sector: A Conversation with Superintendents Tom Boasberg and Duncan Klussmann," Center on Reinventing Public Education, August 27, 2015, www.crpe.org/thelens/hiring -district-leaders-charter-sector-conversation-superintendents-tom-boasberg-and -duncan.

153   **Nate Easley becoming board president:** Interviews with Nate Easley, November 2014 and December 2015.

153   **The next March, Jiminez introduced a resolution:** Jeremy P. Meyer, "DPS Board Member Denies His Proposal Was a Moratorium on New Schools," *Denver Post*, March 19, 2010.

155   **Senate Bill 191:** Interviews with State Senator Michael Johnston, December 2015 and January 2016.

155   **DPS "improperly applied the law to unfairly":** Kerrie Dallman (president of the Colorado Education Association), "Lawsuit Against SB 191 Seeks to Save Good Teachers," *Denver Post*, February 1, 2014.

156   **Boasberg called that "a civil rights travesty":** Quoted in Melanie Asmar, "Denver Public Schools Is Getting Rid of Good Teachers, Says Rep Behind Here-And-Gone Bill," *Westword*, April 9 2014, www.westword.com/news/denver-public-schools-is -getting-rid-of-good-teachers-says-rep-behind-here-and-gone-bill-5873837.

156   **District-Charter Collaboration Compact:** DPS, "District-Charter Collaboration Compact," December 2010.

157   **By 2013, 78 percent of them were in DPS facilities:** Interview with Alyssa White-head-Bust (then DPS chief academic and innovation officer), October 2014.

157   **The compact also led charters to create more centers:** Tom Boasberg, "Choice—For All Our Families," *OurDPS Weekly* (blog), January 27, 2017, www.dpsk12.org/choice-for-all-our-families/.

157   **In 2010–11, they closed 25 percent of charters:** Adam Hawf and Neerav Kingsland, "Achieving Equity in Denver Public Schools," PowerPoint presentation prepared for Denver Public Schools, June 10, 2015, slides 82–83.

157   **And since 2010, they have opened five to six:** DPS, "Charter Schools of DPS," http://portfolio.dpsk12.org/our-schools/charter-schools/charter-schools-of-denver-public-schools/. There were 38 on the list created over seven years, beginning with 2010–11 (which does not include any that were created and later closed).

157   **With a plethora of magnet schools, DPS had more than 60:** Jeremy C. Fox, "Denver's Unified School Enrollments May Offer Boston a Lesson," *Boston Globe*, January 25, 2016.

157   **DPS schools were creaming:** Institute for Innovation in Public School Choice, *An Assessment of Enrollment and Choice in Denver Public Schools* (Denver: Denver Enrollment Study Group, May, 2010).

158   **Surveys conducted by the Center on Reinventing Public Education:** Betheny Gross, Michael DeArmond, and Patrick Denice, *Common Enrollment, Parents, and School Choice: Early Evidence from Denver and New Orleans* (Bothell, WA: Center on Reinventing Public Education, May 2015).

158   **It has clearly increased equity:** Marcus A. Winters, "Guest Commentary: Simplifying Access to Charter Schools," *Denver Post*, December 29, 2015.

158   **As one local parent wrote on a blog:** Fox, "Denver's Unified School Enrollments May Offer Boston a Lesson."

158   **During the system's first three years, 95 percent:** DPS, "Nearly 10 Percent Jump in SchoolChoice Participation Shows Increasing Demand for High-Quality DPS Schools," March 16, 2015, http://communications.dpsk12.org/announcement.html?id=1227.

158   **roughly three quarters received their top choice:** Betheny Gross and Patrick Denice, *An Evaluation of Denver's SchoolChoice Process, 2012–2014: Is the School Enrollment System Working for Families?* report prepared for the SchoolChoice Transparency Committee at A+ Denver (Bothell, WA: Center on Reinventing Public Education, January 2015), pp. 12–13.

158   **Generally, higher quality schools were in greater demand:** Ibid., p. 16. As the Center on Reinventing Public Education study put it, "The most requested schools in the city are often the highest rated. Indeed, the demand for quality has grown over time, particularly when comparing 2014 to 2012."

158   **To their credit, Boasberg and his staff:** Yatsko, "Hiring District Leaders from the Charter Sector."

158   **By 2015, 84 percent of teachers rated their principals "effective":** Tom Boasberg, "Teachers' Ratings of Principals Show Strong Advances," *My DPS* (blog), January 23, 2015; Susana Cordova, "Graduation Rates Continue to Rise, Our Students Soar," *OurDPS Weekly* (blog), January 25, 2016.

159   **2011 School Board election:** Sperry, *Portfolio Reform in Denver*, p. 39; Charlie Brennan, "One Last DPS Election Fundraiser," *EdNews Colorado*, December 7, 2011, www

.aplusdenver.org/_blog/Local_and_National_News/post/One_last_DPS_election _fundraiser/.

160   **2015 School Board election, including quote:** Eric Gorski, "In Denver School Board Race, a Telling Divide over What Defines a 'Neighborhood School,'" *Chalkbeat*, October 29, 2015, http://co.chalkbeat.org/2015/10/29/in-denver-school-board-race-a -telling-divide-over-what-defines-a-neighborhood-school/

CHAPTER 9

161   **Improvements in dropout and graduation rates:** Tom Boasberg, "Lots More Caps and Gowns," *OurDPS Weekly* (blog), January 20, 2017; DPS, "On-Time Graduation and On-Time Completion Rates Continue to Increase," www.dpsk12.org/wp-content/ uploads/GradCompRate_summarypresentation.pdf.

161   **Through 2014, the percentage of students scoring:** A+ Denver, "Start with the Facts: Denver Public Schools Progress Report," September 2014, www.aplusdenver .org/_docs/SWTF-Final1.pdf.

161   **2015 and 2016 PARCC results:** A+ Colorado, "Denver Public Schools Progress Report: Big Gains, Big Gaps, Big Ideas," April 2016, http://apluscolorado.org/reports/ denver-public-schools-progress-report-big-gains-big-gaps-big-ideas/; A+ Colorado, "The Outliers: The State of Colorado School Districts 2016," February 2017, http:// apluscolorado.org/wp-content/uploads/2017/02/FINAL-Outliers-PRINT.pdf; information from Lisa Berdie (A+ Colorado), e-mail, January 2017.

163   **In 2005, DPS trailed statewide averages:** Tom Boasberg, "Progress, but Opportunity Gaps Remain," *OurDPS Weekly* (blog), September 2, 2016, www.dpsk12.org/ progress-but-opportunity-gaps-remain/.

163   **DPS progress on advanced placement:** Susana Cordova, "Celebrating Our Students' Bright Futures with College Signing Day," *Our DPS Weekly* (blog), April 29, 2016, http://thecommons.dpsk12.org/site/default.aspx?PageType=3&DomainID=4&Modu leInstanceID=15&ViewID=BC3F6802-A1E9-49B0-94F1-; A+ Colorado, "Denver Public Schools Progress Report: Big Gains, Big Gaps, Big Ideas," p. 11; Susana Cordova, "DPS Named College Board AP District of the Year," *Our DPS Weekly* (blog), March 11, 20162016 http://thecommons.dpsk12.org/site/default.aspx?PageType=3&Domain ID=4&ModuleInstanceID=15&ViewID=BC3F6802-A1E9-49B0-94F1-0522ABC8691 B&RenderLoc=0&FlexDataID=7&PageID=1.

163   **DPS progress on ACT scores:** Denver and Colorado scores: Colorado Department of Education, www.cde.state.co.us/assessment/coact. National scores: ACT, "2015 ACT National and State Scores," www.act.org/newsroom/data/2015/states.html; ACT, "The ACT Profile Report—National, Graduating Class 2016," 2016, www.act.org/content/ dam/act/unsecured/documents/P_99_999999_N_S_N00_ACT-GCPR_National.pdf.

164   **College enrollment rates in DPS vs. Colorado:** A+ Denver, "DPS Progress Report: Big Gains, Big Gaps, Big Ideas," p. 13.

164   **one in seven low-income students:** Paul Hill, presentation at Center on Reinventing Public Education conference in Memphis, January 2015.

164   **Improvement in college remediation rate:** Colorado Department of Higher Education, "District at a Glance," http://highered.colorado.gov/Data/DistrictHSSummary .aspx.

164　**An analysis done by the Donnell-Kay Foundation:** Alexander Ooms, *Beyond Averages: School Quality in Denver Public Schools* (Denver: Donnell-Kay Foundation, 2014), http://files.eric.ed.gov/fulltext/ED558119.pdf, p. 11.

164　**Widening achievement gaps in DPS:** A+ Denver, "Start With the Facts 2014;" Van Schoales (CEO of A+ Colorado), e-mail, January 2016.

165　**They also accounted for three quarters of DPS enrollment growth:** Brian Eschbacher (DPS director of planning and enrollment), e-mail, January 2017.

165　**Alexander Ooms quote:** Ooms, *Beyond Averages*, p. 20.

165　**Six of the top eight schools were charters:** Department of Accountability, Research, and Evaluation, "School Performance Framework 2013–2014: SPF Rating and Indicator Summary Report," DPS, 2014, http://spf.dpsk12.org/documents/current/05SPF %20-%20Rating%20and%20Indicator%20Summary%20%28Traditional%29.pdf.

165　**in academic growth all of the top 12 secondary schools were charters:** Eric Gorski, "Latest Scores Are Big Test for Growing Denver Charter School Network," *Denver Post*, August 15, 2014.

165　**Charters had 13 percent more African American students:** A+ Denver, "Start with the Facts 2014."

165　**37 percent:** Brian Eschbacher, DPS, e-mail, March 2016. **60 percent:** Betheny Gross and Patrick Denice, *An Evaluation of Denver's SchoolChoice Process, 2012–2014: Is the School Enrollment System Working for Families?*, report prepared for the School-Choice Transparency Committee at A+ Denver (Bothell, WA: Center on Reinventing Public Education, January 2015), table 1.

165　**But in 2016, five of the six top scoring high schools:** Jenny Brundin, "The 2016 Grades Are In for Denver Public Schools," Colorado Public Radio, October 28, 2016.

165　**And 15 of the 19 secondary schools:** Chris Gibbons, "Performance Matters: A Look at the DPS School Performance Framework," Strive Preparatory Schools, October 27, 2016, www.striveprep.org/blog/thought-leadership/performance-matters-look-dps -school-performance-framework/.

166　**Study by economists at the Massachusetts Institute of Technology and Duke University:** Atila Abdulkadiroğlu et al., "Research Design Meets Market Design: Using Centralized Assignment for Impact Evaluation," NBER Working Paper No. 21705, National Bureau of Economic Research, November 2015, p. 25.

166　**The gains in math were the equivalent:** Roland G. Fryer and Steven D. Levitt, "Falling Behind: New Evidence on the Black-White Achievement Gap," *Education Next* 4, no. 4 (Fall 2004), estimate the gap between white and black students in the U.S. at 1 standard deviation. This is "roughly the difference in performance between the average 4th grader and the average 8th grader," according to the authors. The gap found by the MIT-Duke study was a bit more than .4 standard deviations in math, .1 in reading, and .3 in writing. The paper's authors communicated by e-mail that they considered this the most appropriate way to illustrate the scale of these standard deviations.

166　**charters backfill empty seats at a slightly lower rate:** Hawf and Kingsland, "Achieving Equity in Denver Public Schools," PowerPoint presentation prepared for Denver Public Schools, June 10, 2015, slide 39.

166　**charters get 19 percent less money per student:** Megan Batdorff et al., *Charter School Funding: Inequity Expands* (Fayetteville: University of Arkansas, Department of Education Reform, April 2014), www.uaedreform.org/ charter-funding-inequity-expands, p. 82.

166 **ProComp bonuses average $7,396 for a second-year teacher:** Hawf and Kingsland, "Achieving Equity in Denver Public Schools," slide 72.

166 **Data on percentages of low-income, ELL, and special education students:** Ibid., slides 4–26.

166 **Center on Reinventing Public Education study:** Marcus A. Winters, *Understanding the Charter School Special Education Gap: Evidence from Denver, Colorado* (Bothell, WA: Center on Reinventing Public Education, June 2014), www.crpe.org/sites/default/files/CRPE_Specialed_Denver_Report.pdf, p. 4.

166 **Expulsion rates:** Hawf and Kingsland, "Achieving Equity in Denver Public Schools," slides 33–36, 40–41.

166 **2015 CREDO study:** CREDO, "Urban Charter Schools Impact in Colorado" (Stanford, Ca.: CREDO, 2015), slide 27, http://urbancharters.stanford.edu/states.php slide 27.

166 **Scatterplot analysis of test scores and percentages of low-income students:** This analysis is based on 2015 PARCC and ACT data. For the full analysis and the scatterplots—which would not reproduce well in black and white—see David Osborne, *A 21st Century School System in the Mile-High City* (Washington, DC: Progressive Policy Institute, May 2016), www.progressivepolicy.org/issues/education/21st-century -school-system-mile-high-city/, figures 8–12.

168 **Although more than two thirds of its students are low-income:** According to DSST Public Schools, "DSST By the Numbers," www.dsstpublicschools.org/dsst -numbers, the figure is 69 percent.

168 **Data on DSST college enrollments and remediation:** From DSST, e-mail, December and January 2017.

168 **"By comparison, 42 percent of all students":** D. Shapiro et al., *Completing College: A National View of Student Attainment Rates—Fall 2009 Cohort* (Signature Report No. 10) (Herndon, VA: National Student Clearinghouse Research Center, November 2015), https://nscresearchcenter.org/signaturereport10/#Sig10-Results-3. This study reports that in 2009, 1,111,368 students started at public two-year colleges, and 15 percent, 166,705 students, earned four-year degrees within six years (see figure 19). (The report did not include data about students who started at private two-year institutions.) In 2009, 2,911,898 started at four-year public and private institutions, and 52.9 percent of them, 1,540,394 students, completed a four-year degree within six years (see figure 5). Doing the math, total completers = 1,707,099, total starters = 4,023,266, and the percentage of completers = 42.4 percent.

168 **9 percent of low-income students:** Margaret Cahalan and Laura Perna, *Indicators of Higher Education Equity in the United States: 45 Year Trend Report, 2015 Revised Edition* (N.p.: Pell Institute for the Study of Opportunity in Higher Education and Penn Ahead-Alliance for Higher Education and Democracy, 2015), www.pellinstitute.org/downloads/publications-Indicators_of_Higher_Education_Equity_in_the_US_45_ Year_Trend_Report.pdf.

171 **Roughly 40 percent of students:** Interview with Christine Nelson (DSST chief of staff), October 2014; **lower than DPS-operated high schools:** Brian Eschbacher (DPS director of planning and enrollment), e-mail, March 2017.

174   **Career ladder and pay scale at DSST:** Interviews with DSST staff, October 2014; update by Ashley Wiegner (director of DSST's Teacher Career Pathway work), e-mail, March 2017.

174   **DPS annual funding of charter schools per student:** Interview with Erik Johnson (DPS budget director), March 2016.

174   **Information about teacher retention and survey:** Interview with Pete Fishman (DSST fellow from Harvard University), October 2014; Christine Nelson (DSST chief of staff), e-mail, March 2016.

174–5   **Data on 2016 growth and SPF scores:** DSST Director of Data Steve Coit, e-mail, January 2017. Growth scores are median growth percentiles.

175   **DSST ACT scores:** A+ Colorado, "The Outliers: The State of Colorado School Districts 2016," p. 26.

175   **In 2014 its low-income 10th-graders had:** Nicholas Garcia, "After Unusual Accomplishment, Denver Charter Network Opens Third High School," *Chalkbeat*, August 25, 2014.

175   **DSST outperforms Colorado public high schools:** Data from the Colorado Department of Education.

175   ***Chalkbeat* quote:** "Five Issues to Watch as Denver Public Schools Students Return to the Classroom," *Chalkbeat*, August 24, 2015.

175   **Despite the success of individual innovation schools:** Susan Connors et al., *Innovation Schools in DPS: Year Three of an Evaluation Study* (Denver: University of Colorado, School of Education and Human Development, Evaluation Center, October, 2013); Abdulkadiroğlu et al., "Research Design Meets Market Design," p. 25; Osborne, *A 21st Century School System in the Mile-High City*, pp. 18–22. In addition, Kelly Kovacic, then DPS's executive director of portfolio management, acknowledged to me in December 2015 that innovation schools had not bent the curve on performance.

175   **The bar was a bit lower for innovation schools:** December 2015 interview with Kelly Kovacic.

176   **Denver Green School material:** Interviews at the school, October 2014.

177   **Denver Green School 2016 SPF scores:** DPS, *Great Schools Enrollment Guide, Elementary 2017–18* (Denver: Denver Public Schools, 2016), http://schoolchoice.dpsk12. org/wp-content/uploads/2016/11/DPS_EnrollmentGuide1718_ElementaryEnglish_ Web.pdf; DPS, *Great Schools Enrollment Guide, Middle and High 2017–18* (Denver: Denver Public Schools, 2016), http://schoolchoice.dpsk12.org/wp-content/uploads/ 2016/11/DPS_EnrollmentGuide1718_SecondaryEnglish_Web.pdf.

177   **Grant Beacon Middle School demographics:** DPS, "Stoplight Summary Scorecard: School Performance Framework 2013–14, Grant Beacon Middle School," http://spf. dpsk12.org/documents/current/405%20-%20Stoplight%20Scorecard.pdf.

177   **Grant Beacon Middle School material:** Interviews at the school, December 2015.

178   **Grant Beacon 2016 PARCC scores compared to Strive Prep and DSST:** Colorado Department of Education, "2016 CMAS ELA and Math District and School Summary for release-v3," www.cde.state.co.us/assessment (download).

181   **"There's an incredible value for schools":** Quoted in Melanie Asmar, "In Denver, Four Schools Want to Push the Boundaries of Innovation," *Chalkbeat*, February 24, 2016.

182   **"Whenever someone pushed for more school autonomy":** Barbara O'Brien, remarks at "Reinventing America's Schools: Lessons from the Denver Experience," a conference sponsored by the Progressive Policy Institute in Denver, May 3–4, 2016.

182   **What Luminary Learning Network schools have done with $425 per student:** Interview with Frank Coyne (Denver Green School), December 2016,

CHAPTER 10

184   **The Imaginarium:** Interview with Alyssa Whitehead-Bust (then DPS chief of innovation and reform), October 2014; Tom VanderArk, "Elected Board Urges Innovation in Denver," *Getting Smart*, August 13, 2015, http://gettingsmart.com/2015/08/elected-board-urges-innovation-in-denver/.

184   **Test scores and evaluations suggest the investment is paying off:** Sheridan Green, Caroline Ponce, and Diana Mangels, "Denver Preschool Program: Report on Child Outcomes, 2013–14 School Year" (Denver: Clayton Early Learning Institute, 2014), www.dpp.org/results-and-research/our-results.

184   **By 2016, only about a third of students:** Tom Boasberg, "Progress, but Opportunity Gaps Remain," *OurDPS Weekly* (blog), September 2, 2016, www.dpsk12.org/progress-but-opportunity-gaps-remain/.

185   **A recent study by the Center on Reinventing Public Education:** Michael DeArmond et al., *Measuring Up: Educational Improvement and Opportunity in 50 Cities* (Bothell, WA: Center on Reinventing Public Education, October 2015), www.crpe.org/publications/measuring-educational-improvement-and-opportunity-50-cities, p. 2.

185   **Schools on probation still open in 2015:** Adam Hawf and Neerav Kingsland, "Achieving Equity in Denver Public Schools," PowerPoint presentation prepared for Denver Public Schools, June 10, 2015, slide 86.

185   **Alexander Ooms quote:** Alexander Ooms, *Beyond Averages: School Quality in Denver Public Schools* (Denver: Donnell-Kay Foundation, 2014), http://files.eric.ed.gov/fulltext/ED558119.pdf, pp. 12, 14.

186   **This approach, pioneered 30 years ago by Edmonton, Alberta:** For a description of what Edmonton did, see William Ouchi, *Making Schools Work* (New York: Simon & Schuster, 2008). For more on how this approach works, see David Osborne and Peter Plastrik, *The Reinventor's Fieldbook: Tools for Transforming Your Government* (San Francisco: Jossey-Bass, 2000), chapter 4, available as chapter 8 at Reinventing Government (website), http://reinventgov.com/wp-content/uploads/2014/02/09.0Enterp riseManagement.pdf.

187   **Mary Seawell says she never appreciated the role:** Seawell explained this at "Reinventing America's Schools: Lessons from the Denver Experience," a conference sponsored by the Progressive Policy Institute in Denver, May 3–4, 2016.

188   **Over the past decade, DPS has reduced:** Rebecca Klein, "Denver Is Leading the Way in Dismantling the School-to-Prison Pipeline. Here's How," *Huffington Post*, July 15, 2015.

188   **Bruce Randolph School open letter to Boasberg:** Julie Poppen, "Discipline Concerns Flare in Denver Schools," *Chalkbeat*, May 14, 2013.

188   **In March, 2015, the union conducted a survey of teachers:** Jenny Brundin, "Denver Teachers Union Survey Puts Spotlight on Student Discipline Issues," Colorado Public Radio, March 22, 2015.

189   **Letter from a resigning teacher:** Ibid.

189   **Greg Ahrnsbrak on DPS discipline committee and continued problems:** Interview with Greg Ahrnsbrak, February 2016, and e-mail update, December 2016.

189   **Newark experience with "One Newark" plan:** Dale Russakoff, *The Prize: Who's In Charge of America's Schools?* (Boston: Houghton Mifflin Harcourt, 2015). Anderson announced One Newark in June 2013; she was asked to resign in June 2015.

190   **By 2016, Denver had the most school choice:** Grover J. Whitehurst, *Education Choice and Competition Index 2016* (Washington, DC: Brookings Institution, Center on Children and Families, March 2017). Priscilla Wohlstetter, Dara Zeehandelaar, and David Griffith, *America's Best (and Worst) Cities for School Choice* (New York: Columbia University Teachers College, Thomas B. Fordham Institute, December 2015), ranked Denver third best for school choice, after New Orleans and Washington, D.C.

190   **Polls showed strong support for public school choice:** Tom Boasberg, "More Families Exercising Choice; More Entrusting DPS for Students' Education," *Our DPS Weekly* (blog), March 13, 2015, link at www.facebook.com/permalink.php?id=44144 5425004&story_fbid=10155249111290005; Peter Huidekoper Jr., "Another View on School Choice in Denver," *Another View*, no. 134, August 13, 2015, http://apluscolorado .org/blog/another-view-school-choice-denver/.

190   **Data on participation in SchoolChoice enrollment process:** Betheny Gross and Patrick Denice, *An Evaluation of Denver's SchoolChoice Process, 2012–2014: Is the School Enrollment System Working for Families?*, report prepared for the SchoolChoice Transparency Committee at A+ Denver (Bothell, WA: Center on Reinventing Public Education, January 2015).

190   **DPS has established 11 multi-school "shared enrollment zones":** Brian Eschbacher (DPS director of planning and enrollment), e-mail, March 2017. According to Eschbacher, DPS will probably double that number over the next two to three years.

190   **These zones covered less than a third of the city:** Hawf and Kingsland, "Achieving Equity in Denver Public Schools," slide 50.

190   **Only five zone bus systems provide fairly full access:** Brian Eschbacher, March 2017 e-mail.

190   **By 2015–16, close to one in five kids:** Based on 2015–16 School Performance Framework scores, there were 42 "intensive-support" and "strategic-support" schools in 2016, with roughly 17,000 students, or about 19 percent of the total in DPS. In 2016, the 25 intensive-support schools had 89 percent students receiving subsidized meals, 93 percent minority students; 12 percent of students were proficient in math and 14 percent were proficient in ELA. The 17 strategic-support schools had 82 percent of their students receiving subsidized meals, 89 percent were minorities, and 12 and 18 percent scored proficient in math and ELA, respectively. Average proficiencies in the district were 32 percent and 43 percent. The data come from Denver Public Schools, "Focus on Achievement: Great Schools in Every Neighborhood," November 3, 2016, www.boarddocs.com/co/dpsk12/Board.nsf/files/AFCSJ7703E87/$file/11-3-16%20 BOE%20FOA%20-%20Great%20Schools%20SPF%20%20TSF%20-%20Final.pdf. Enrollment data is from the Colorado Department of Education, "2015–16 Pupil Membership by School and Grade," www.cde.state.co.us/cdereval/2015-16-pupil membership-byschoolgrade-pdf/.

191   **Those who were not poor were 6.5 to eight times:** DeArmond et al., *Measuring Up*, pp. 26–29.

191   **How average teacher salaries lead to lower spending on poor students:** See, for instance, Marguerite Roza, "Many a Slip 'Tween Cup and Lip: District Fiscal Practices

and Their Effect on School Spending," report prepared for the Aspen Institute Congressional Program, "The Challenge of Education Reform: Standards, Accountability, Resources and Policy," February 22–27, 2005, http://crpe.org/sites/default/files/pub_sfrp_district_feb05_0.pdf.

191   **Denver is no exception:** 14 percent of teachers in the lowest performing quintile of schools are novices, and the schools' two-year teacher attrition rate is 54 percent. In the highest-performing quintile of schools, 6 percent are novices and the two-year attrition rate is 33 percent. *Denver Public Schools: Leveraging System Transformation to Improve Student Results* (N.p.: Education Resource Strategies, March 2017), p. 33, https://www.documentcloud.org/documents/3518089-Denver2020-for-DPS-Mgmt-Review.html.

CHAPTER 11

200   **Ballard expanded the number of charters from 16 to 39:** Interview with Brandon Brown (former head of Mayor Ballard's charter office), April 2016.

200   **By 2016 the mayor authorized 35 schools on 40 campuses:** Office of Education Innovation, "Mayor-Sponsored Charter Schools," http://oei.indy.gov/mayor-sponsored-charter-schools/. For enrollment data for these schools see Indiana Department of Education, "Indianapolis Public Schools (5385)," http://compass.doe.in.gov/dashboard/overview.aspx?type=corp&id=5385.

200   **Indiana Charter School Board charters in Indianapolis:** Indiana Charter School Board, "ICSB Charter Schools," www.in.gov/icsb/2448.htm. The board plans to open four more charters in Indianapolis in the fall of 2017.

200   **Ball State University charters in Indianapolis:** Ball State University, "Charter Schools Authorized by Ball State University," http://cms.bsu.edu/academics/collegesanddepartments/teachers/schools/charter/charterschool/charterschools.

200   **The Mind Trust's role in Indianapolis:** Mind Trust, "The City of Indianapolis: Quality, Innovation, and Autonomy," report prepared for "Reinventing America's Schools: Lessons from the Denver Experience," a Progressive Policy Institute conference in Denver, May 3–4, 2016.

200   **The mayor's office's track record as an authorizer:** Interviews with Ahmed Young (director of Mayor Hogsett's Office of Education Innovation), Brandon Brown (former director of the office under Mayor Ballard), Scott Bess (head of school at Purdue Polytechnic Institute), and others, April 2016.

200   **Comparison of demographics at mayoral charter schools and IPS schools:** Indiana Department of Education website, "Find School and Corporation Reports," www.doe.in.gov/accountability/find-school-and-corporation-data-reports. In 2015 both IPS and charter schools had about 79 percent students of color. Eighty-one percent of charter students qualified for subsidized meals, compared to 71 percent in IPS. Thirteen percent of students in charters were classified as special education students, compared to 17.5 percent in IPS. And 11.6 percent were English language learners, compared to 14.7 in IPS.

201   **Mayoral charters have received roughly $4200 per student less than IPS schools:** Brandon Brown interview, April 2016.

201   **Performance comparisons between mayoral charters and IPS schools:** For data on test scores and median growth percentiles, see Mayor's Office of Innovation in Education,

"OEI Results Deck," PowerPoint presentation. In 2015 the percentages achieving proficiency at mayoral charters were 11.2 points higher in ELA and 8.4 points higher in math, according to Mind Trust, "The City of Indianapolis: Quality, Innovation, and Autonomy." For graduation rates: Ahmed Young via email, April 2017; and Chelsea Schneider, "IPS Sees Big Gains in Graduation Rate," *Indianapolis Star*, January 12, 2017.

201　**Mayoral charters showing more rapid improvement than IPS schools:** Mayor's Office of Innovation in Education, "OEI Results Deck."

201　**CREDO studies:** CREDO, "Charter School Performance in Indiana" (Stanford, CA: Center for Research on Educational Outcomes, December 2012), pp. 15, 35, https://credo.stanford.edu/pdfs/IN_2012_FINAL_20121213_no_watermark.pdf; CREDO, "Urban Charter School Study: Report on 41 Regions, 2015" (Stanford, CA: Center for Research on Educational Outcomes, 2015), https://urbancharters.stanford.edu/download/Urban%20Charter%20School%20Study%20Report%20on%2041%20Regions.pdf; see in particular CREDO, "Urban Charter Schools Impact in Indiana" (Stanford, CA: Center for Research on Educational Outcomes, March 2015), http://urbancharters.stanford.edu/states.php, slide 11.

201　**David Harris views:** Interview with David Harris, December 2015. **David Harris quote:** Harris, "Let Mayors Authorize Charter Schools," *Real Clear Policy*, December 22, 2014.

202　**44 percent of IPS schools were still rated D or F:** David Harris, e-mail, December 2016.

202　**IPS enrollment 50 years ago and in 2016:** Arianna Prothero, "Indianapolis Superintendent Enlists Charters as Allies to Improve City's Schools," *Education Week*, February 24, 2016, http://leaders.edweek.org/profile/lewis-ferebee-superintendent-charter-district-partnerships/.

202　**Within its geographic boundaries . . . schools for adults:** Mind Trust, e-mail, September 2016. According to this data, shown below, about a third of public school students who lived within IPS's boundaries attended a charter school in 2015–16, or 36 percent if you include adults attending six charter Excel Centers. These numbers do not include students who lived within IPS's boundaries and attended an online, virtual charter school.

	2015–16 Including Adult High School	2015–16 Excluding Adult HS
Innovation network schools		
without a charter	571	571
with a charter	864	864
Independent charter schools	13,869	11,530
State takeover schools	1,623	1,623
Indianapolis Public Schools	29,012	29,012
Total	45,939	43,600

202　**Numbers receiving vouchers in Indianapolis:** Jason Weeby, Kelly Robson, and George Mu, *The U.S. Education Innovation Index: Prototype and Report* (Washington,

DC: Bellwether Education Partners, September 2016), http://bellwethereducation
.org/sites/default/files/Bellwether_USEIIndex_Final.pdf, p. 42.

202   **The Mind Trust's 150-page report:** Public Impact, *Creating Opportunity Schools: A Bold Plan to Transform Indianapolis Public Schools* (Indianapolis: Mind Trust, December 2011), www.themindtrust.org/wp-content/uploads/2016/02/opp-schools-full-report.pdf.

204   **Innovation network schools bill:** Article 25.5. Innovation Network Schools, 118th General Assembly, 2nd session, 2014, House Enrolled Act No. 1321, http://iga.in.gov/ static-documents/6/c/a/b/6cabcd52/HB1321.06.ENRH.pdf.

205   **Four types of innovation network schools:** Interviews with Mary Ann Sullivan (school board president), and Aleesia Johnson (IPS innovation officer), April 2016.

205   **Union response to innovation network schools:** Prothero, "Indianapolis Superintendent Enlists Charters as Allies to Improve City's Schools"; interviews with David Harris, December 2015, Aleesia Johnson and Brandon Brown, April 2016; Aleesia Johnson e-mail, December 2016.

206   **Francis Scott Key Elementary School 103 . . . $10,000:** Eric Weddle, "Investing for the Long Haul on the Far Eastside," WFYI, June 29, 2016, https://wfyinews.atavist .com/chasingthedream#chapter-1141664.

206   **The school had one of the most transient . . . state exams:** Adam Wren, "The Mind Trust Is . . . (A) Revolutionizing the City Schools (B) Swaying Elections (C) Enabling Gentrification D) All of the Above," *Indianapolis Monthly*, September 2016, http://www .indianapolismonthly.com/news-opinion/the-mind-trusts-long-road-to-school -revolution/, p. 178.

207   **"We cannot waste a year of a child's life":** Quoted in Ibid.

207   **IREAD scores doubled:** Dylan Peers McCoy, "Reading Scores Jump at Some Indianapolis Public Schools, While Others Flounder," *Chalkbeat*, July 6, 2016.

207   **Glick investments:** Glick Philanthropies, "Far Eastside Success Initiative: Update to the IPS Board of School Commissioners," September 27, 2016, www.boarddocs.com/ in/indps/Board.nsf/files/AE7S8F716F13/$file/Far%20Eastside%20Success%20Initia tive%20Update%20-%20September%202016.pdf.

209   **Enrollment increases at innovation network schools:** 17 percent, in Weddle, "Investing for the Long Haul on the Far Eastside," pp. 178–79; 15 percent, in data provided by Phalen Leadership Academies, November 2016. **Global Prep Academy:** Mariama Carson, e-mail, November 2016. **Kindezi Academy:** Data from school administrator, November 2016.

209   **As of 2016–17, more than 10 percent of IPS students:** Dylan Peers McCoy, "Indianapolis Public Schools Adds Schools to 'Innovation' Program, Reshaping District," *Chalkbeat*, March 17, 2016.

209   **IPS has weeded out 56 percent of its failing schools:** Interview with Lewis Ferebee, April 2016.

210   **In the first year, Ferebee chose six of the eight schools:** Dylan Peers McCoy, "IPS Picks Six Schools to Try Out More Freedom for Principals," *Chalkbeat*, February 8, 2016.

212   **The ASD has turned some 26 failing Memphis schools over to charter operators:** Interview with Margo Roen (Achievement School District, chief of strategy and portfolio management), March 2017.

212   **By 2016, ASD schools in Memphis educated about 12,000 students:** Margot Roen, e-mail, October 2016.

212   **They will stay in the ASD for at least ten years:** Juli Kim, Tim Field, and Elaine Hargrave, *The Achievement School District: Lessons from Tennessee* (Chapel Hill, NC: Public Impact and New Orleans,/LA: New Schools for New Orleans, 2015), http://achievementschooldistrict.org/wp-content/uploads/2015/11/The-Achievement-School-District-Lessons-from-Tennessee-UPDATE.pdf.

212   **69 of the 85 priority schools were in Memphis:** Chris Barbic, "If We Work Together, Our Priority Schools Will Shine," *The Tennessean*, September 14, 2014.

212   **CREDO study:** CREDO, "Urban Charter School Study: Report on 41 Regions, 2015."

212   **Graduation rates:** *Shelby County Charter Schools: 2016 Annual Report* (Memphis: Shelby County Schools, 2016), www.scsk12.org/calendar/files/2016/2016-Charter-Report.pdf.

212   **District-charter compact and advisory committee:** Micaela Watts, "School Board Vote Commits Shelby County's District and Charter Sectors to Trying to Collaborate," *Chalkbeat*, January 26, 2016; Shelby County School Board, "District/Charter/Multi-Operator Compact for Quality Schools," January 2016.

213   **ASD schools' TVAAS scores, 2015:** John Buntin, "Assessing the Nation's Most Ambitious Education Reforms in Memphis, Tennessee," *Governing*, September 2015.

213   **The Innovation Zone:** John Buntin, "Changing a Culture Inside and Out of School," *Governing,* January 2015; Marta Aldrich, "Latest IZone Expansion Will Leave Few Memphis Priority Schools to Improve on Their Own," *Chalkbeat*, December 16, 2015.

213   **But once a teacher was hired and had tenure:** Jaclyn Zubrzycki, "Remaking Memphis: Charters, Choice, and Experimentation," *Education Week*, October 9, 2013.

213   **There were other limits on autonomy:** Christine Campbell and Libuse Binder, *In Depth Portfolio Assessment: Shelby County Schools—Memphis, TN* (Bothell, WA: Center on Reinventing Public Education, 2014), www.crpe.org/publications/depth-portfolio-assessment-shelby-county-schools-memphis-tn.

213   **For their first two years they showed faster academic growth:** Malika Anderson, "Stay the Course with Achievement School District," *The Tennessean*, February 11, 2016.

214   **Seven iZone schools had improved enough:** Erin McIntyre, "Memphis 'Innovation Zone' Schools See Turnaround Success," *Education Dive*, May 11, 2016, www.educationdive.com/news/memphis-innovation-zone-schools-see-turnaround-success/417615/.

214   **Four of seven elementary schools and five of seven middle schools:** Buntin, "Changing a Culture Inside and Out of School."

214   **John Buntin quote:** Ibid.

214   **31 Memphis schools had been taken over by the ASD:** Margo Roen, interview, March 2017. **21 had been moved into the iZone:** McIntyre, "Memphis 'Innovation Zone' Schools See Turnaround Success." **13 priority schools had been closed or consolidated:** Laura Faith Kebede, "Here's What Happened to the Original 69 Priority Schools in Memphis," *Chalkbeat*, June 6, 2016.

214   **Center on Reinventing Public Education study:** Michael DeArmond et al., *Measuring Up: Educational Improvement and Opportunity in 50 Cities* (Bothell, WA: Center on Reinventing Public Education, October 2015), www.crpe.org/publications/measuring-educational-improvement-and-opportunity-50-cities, p. 2.

214   **Camden population and poverty:** "New Census Statistics Paint Grim Picture of Camden," *Philly.com*, September 2, 2012, www.philly.com/philly/blogs/camden_ flow/170812236.html#vbY2w0149Vf8hg0w.99.

214   **Camden college degrees and crime rates:** Naomi Nix, "Jersey Roar: Schools Make a Comeback in Camden, the Nation's Most Distressed City," *The74million.org*, July 11, 2016.

214   **Camden school performance before state takeover:** Ibid.

215   **If carried through, Rouhanifard's plan would put:** The Renaissance schools would have more than 9,000 students, and there were already nine other charter schools in the city, with 4,490 students. See Meir Rinde, "Some Improvement Seen in Camden Schools: Blip or New Beginning?" *NJ Spotlight*, August 19, 2016

215   **It was hard to argue with him:** National Alliance for Public Charter Schools (henceforth cited as NAPCS), *A Growing Movement: America's Largest Charter Public School Communities and Their Impact on Student Outcomes, 11th Annual Edition* (Washington, DC: National Alliance for Public Charter Schools, November 2016), p. 4.

215   **By 2016, surveys showed students felt safer:** Allison Steele, "For 3rd Straight Year, More Camden Kids Are Graduating from High School," *Philadelphia Inquirer*, December 11, 2016.

215   **Proficiency rates in English . . . Mastery Renaissance schools:** George E. Norcross III, "Working Together Has Saved Camden's Schools," *Newark Star Ledger*, April 13, 2017.

215   **Russakoff book:** Dale Russakoff, *The Prize: Who's in Charge of America's Schools* (Boston: Houghton Mifflin Harcourt, 2015). See also Juli Kim et al., *Early Lessons From Newark's Experience With Charter Schools* (Menlo Park, CA: Startup: Education, 2015), http://publicimpact.com/web/wp-content/uploads/2015/08/Early_Les sons_from-Newarks_Experience_With_Charter_Schools-Public_Impact.pdf.

215   **Mayor Baraka backed "unity slates":** Tom Moran, "In Newark, Booming Charter Schools Flex New Political Muscle," *Newark Star Ledger*, April 25, 2016; "Newark Public Schools elections (2017)," *Ballotpedia*, http://ballotpedia.org/Newark_public _schools_elections_(2017).

215   **By then, 30 percent of Newark's public school:** NAPCS, *A Growing Movement*.

215   **CREDO study:** CREDO, "Urban Charter School Study: Report on 41 Regions, 2015."

215   **Proficiency data from Cleveland:** National Center for Education Statistics, "NAEP Data Explorer," http://nces.ed.gov/nationsreportcard/naepdata/.

216   **Among Ohio districts, Cleveland ranked 608th:** Center on Reinventing Public Education (henceforth cited as CRPE), "Cleveland, OH: District-Charter Improvement on a Countdown Clock," Center on Reinventing Public Education, November 25, 2014, www.crpe.org/research/district-charter-collaboration/cleveland-oh-district -charter-improvement-countdown-clock.

216   **Performance of charter schools in Cleveland:** See CREDO, "Urban Charter Schools Impact in Ohio" (Stanford, CA: Center for Research on Educational Outcomes, March 2015), http://urbancharters.stanford.edu/states.php.

216   **Quote from Eric Gordon:** Eric Gordon, "State of the Schools Address," Cleveland Metropolitan School District, September 14, 2016, www.clevelandmetroschools.org/ cms/lib05/OH01915844/Centricity/Domain/2632/State%20Of%20The%20Schools %20Address%20-%202016.pdf.

216   **Information on the Cleveland Plan:** Daniela Doyle, Christen Holly, and Bryan C. Hassel, *Is Détente Possible? District-Charter School Relations in Four Cities* (Washington, DC: Public Impact and Fordham Institute, November 2015), https://www.charterschoolcenter.org/sites/default/files/files/field_publication_attachment/is_detente_possible_report_final.pdf, pp. 52–59; Terry Ryan, "Ohio's Big Cities Are Rapidly Becoming National School Reform Leaders," *Ohio Gadfly Daily*, June 3, 2013, www.edexcellence.net/commentary/education-gadfly-daily/ohio-gadfly-daily/2013/ohios-big-cities-are-rapidly-becoming-national-school-reform-leaders.html.

217   **Three years later, reformers finally got a state law passed:** Patrick O'Donnell, "Poor-Performing Charter Schools Aren't Finding Second Chances After Ohio's Charter Reform," *Cleveland Plain Dealer*, June 17, 2016.

217   **After it passed, seven charter schools in Cleveland closed:** E-mail from Stephanie Klupinski (Cleveland Municipal School District), December 2016.

217   **Enrollment is rising for the first time in decades:** Cleveland Metropolitan School District, "Cleveland Schools Progress," www.clevelandmetroschools.org/cms/lib05/OH01915844/Centricity/Domain/1321/ReportCardInfographics-3-OL.pdf.

217   **The five-year rate reached 74 percent in 2016:** Ohio Department of Education, "2015–2016 Report Card for Cleveland Municipal School District," http://reportcard.education.ohio.gov/Pages/District-Report.aspx?DistrictIRN=043786.

217   **Improving academic growth and NAEP scores in Cleveland:** CMSD News Bureau, "CEO named Urban Educator of the Year," press release, October 10, 2016, www.clevelandmetroschools.org/site/default.aspx?PageType=3&DomainID=1425&ModuleInstanceID=5629&ViewID=047E6BE3-6D87-4130-8424-D8E4E9ED6C2A&RenderLoc=0&FlexDataID=13380&PageID=3632.

217–8 **Information on Pembroke Pines charter schools:** Pembroke Pines Charter Schools website, https://www.pinescharter.net; Brian Ballou, "Pines Charter School System Rebounds From Funding Woes," *Sun Sentinel*, June 6, 2016.

218   **Hall County School District information:** Hall County School District website, https://www.hallco.org/boe/site/. **"personalized education pathways":** Superintendent Will Schofield, "Who Are We?," Hall County Schools, www.hallco.org/boe/site/who-we-are/.

218   **Numbers of different school types in Hall County:** Chris Kardish, "Why Is One of America's Most Charter-Heavy School Districts in Suburban Georgia?," *Governing*, December 18, 2013.

218   **Network of portfolio districts and those with compacts:** CRPE, "Portfolio Strategy," www.crpe.org/research/portfolio-strategy/network; CRPE, "District-Charter Collaboration," www.crpe.org/research/district-charter-collaboration/cities.

218   **Boston's charter schools are the strongest in the country:** CREDO, "Urban Charter School Study: Report on 41 Regions, 2015"; James A. Peyser, "Boston and the Charter School Cap," *Education Next*, September 10, 2013.

219   **Los Angeles:** For a good history of LAUSD's attempts to decentralize, and their failure, see Charles Taylor Kerchner et al., *Learning from L.A.: Institutional Change in American Public Education* (Cambridge, MA: Harvard Education Press, 2008).

219   **CREDO study on Los Angeles:** CREDO, "Charter School Performance in Los Angeles" (Stanford, CA: Center for Research on Educational Outcomes, February 2014), https://credo.stanford.edu/pdfs/Los_Angeles_report_2014_FINAL_001.pdf.

376 NOTES TO PAGES 219–226

219   **In addition, 75 percent of students at charters complete:** California Charter Schools Association, "Charter School Data—LAUSD," 2015, www.ccsa.org/2015LAUSD_ Charters_FactSheet_Fall_2015_.pdf.

219   **Lawrence, Massachusetts:** For a good overview of reforms in Lawrence, see Education Resource Strategies and Center for Collaborative Education, *The Path Forward: School Autonomy and Its Implications for the Future of Boston's Public Schools* (Boston: Boston Foundation and Boston Public Schools, June 2014), p. 24, and the district website, www.lawrence.k12.ma.us/about-lps/key-facts. **Replacing principals and teachers:** Scott Lehigh, "Mitchell Chester's Drive for Better Schools," *Boston Globe*, September 25, 2014. **Data on performance:** Eric Schnurer, *The Springfield Empowerment Zone Partnership* (Washington, DC: Progressive Policy Institute, January 2017), www.progressivepolicy.org/issues/education/springfield-empowerment-zone-part nership/, pp. 6–8. **Graduation rate data:** "Massachusetts Takes On a Failing School District," *New York Times*, editorial, June 17, 2015; Massachusetts Department of Education, "School and District Profiles," http://profiles.doe.mass.edu/grad/grad_ report.aspx?orgcode=01490000&orgtypecode=5.

219   **Information on Springfield, Massachusetts:** Schnurer, "Springfield Empowerment Zone Partnership;" Chris Gabrieli, chairman of The SEZP board, email, May 2017.

220   **Tulsa, Oklahoma:** Memo prepared by Tulsa Public Schools for "Reinventing America's Schools: Lessons from the Denver Experience," a conference sponsored by the Progressive Policy Institute in Denver, May 3–4, 2016.

220   **San Antonio:** Interviews with Superintendent Pedro Martinez and Legislative Coordinator Seth Rau, March 2017.

220   **Shakespeare quote:** William Shakespeare, *A Midsummer Night's Dream*, Act 1, scene 1.

CHAPTER I 2

223   **Quotation from Henig et al:** Jeffrey R. Henig et al., *The Color of School Reform: Race, Politics, and the Challenge of Urban Education* (Princeton: Princeton University Press, 1999), pp. 12, 64.

223   **Gene Maeroff quote:** Gene I. Maeroff, *Reforming a School System, Reviving a City: The Promise of Say Yes to Education in Syracuse* (New York: Palgrave Macmillan, 2013).

224   **Kerchner et al. book:** Charles Taylor Kerchner et al., *Learning from L.A.: Institutional Change in American Public Education* (Cambridge, MA.: Harvard Education Press, 2008).

224   **My past books on transforming public bureaucracies:** David Osborne and Peter Hutchinson, *The Price of Government* (New York: Basic Books, 2004); David Osborne and Peter Plastrik, *The Reinventor's Fieldbook: Tools for Transforming Your Government* (San Francisco: Jossey-Bass, 2000); David Osborne and Peter Plastrik, *Banishing Bureaucracy* (Reading, MA: Addison-Wesley, 1997); David Osborne and Ted Gaebler, *Reinventing Government* (Reading, MA: Addison-Wesley, 1992).

225   **Amanda Ripley quote:** Amanda Ripley, *The Smartest Kids in the World* (New York: Simon & Schuster, 2013), p. 133.

226   **Quote from Martin West and Ludger Woessman:** Quoted in Charles L. Glenn Jr., "School Choice and Accountability: Finding the Right Balance," *Choice Words,*

February 5, 2014, https://edexcellence.net/commentary/education-gadfly-daily/choice-words/school-choice-and-accountability-finding-the-right.

226 **Quote from "one American observer" on Dutch schools:** Sarah Butrymowicz, "A Country Where Teachers Have a Voice," *TheAtlantic.com*, January 15 2015. See also "What Can We Learn from the Dutch? Can Reformist and Teacher Agendas Co-Exist?" *Ed in the Apple* (blog), January 20, 2015, https://mets2006.wordpress.com/2015/01/20/what-can-we-learn-from-the-dutch-can-reformist-and-teacher-agendas-co-exist/.

226 **In the United Kingdom, then Prime Minister David Cameron:** Campbell Brown, "Education Reform: Why America Needs a David Cameron," *Daily Beast*, October 16, 2015.

226–7 **Cathy Mincberg quote:** Cathy Mincberg, "School Boards Must Narrow Their Focus," *Education Week*, June 7, 2016, p. 26.

227 **Charter Board in D.C. has 38 employees . . . has 902:** Scott Pearson (executive director of the Public Charter School Board), email, January 2017; Michelle Lerner, DCPS press secretary, email, March 2017.

229 **Quote from CREDO's first national study:** CREDO, "Multiple Choice: Charter School Performance in 16 States" (Stanford, CA: Center for Research on Education Outcomes, 2009), p. 4. CREDO has not returned to this question, but its director told me it plans to in 2017 or 2018.

229 **Massachusetts, New Jersey, D.C., and New Orleans among highest-performing charter sectors:** CREDO, "National Charter School Study 2013 (Stanford, CA: Center for Research on Educational Outcomes, 2013); CREDO, "Urban Charter School Study: Report on 41 Regions, 2015" (Stanford, CA: Center for Research on Educational Outcomes, 2015).

230 **"Where state charter legislation":** CREDO, "Multiple Choice."

231 **Removing a tenured teacher for performance:** David Griffith and Victoria McDougald, *Undue Process: Why Bad Teachers in Twenty-Five Diverse Districts Rarely Get Fired* (Washington, DC: Thomas B. Fordham Institute, December 2016), https://edexcellence.net/publications/undue-process, p. 10; Mark Harris, "Vergara Plaintiffs Conclude Case, with Two Views on Laws' Impact," *LA School Report*, February 19, 2014, http://laschoolreport.com/vergara-plaintiffs-conclude-case-with-two-views-on-laws-impact/.

231 **Al Shanker quote:** Al Shanker, speech at the first anniversary of the Saturn School in Saint Paul, May 1991, quoted in Ted Kolderie, *Creating the Capacity for Change* (St. Paul: Education Evolving, 2004), p. 14.

232 **But as study after study shows, most such efforts fail:** See endnote in chapter 3 for p. 66, "The results were disappointing." See also Michael Hansen and Kilchan Choi, "Chronically Low-performing Schools and Turnaround: Evidence from Three States," National Center for Analysis of Longitudinal Data in Education Research Working Paper No. 60, August 2012, www.caldercenter.org/sites/default/files/wp-60.pdf. Its abstract says, "In Florida, we identified approximately 15% of chronically low-performing elementary and 14% of chronically low-performing middle schools as turnarounds in at least one subject. Similar rates were observed in North Carolina—13% and 16%, respectively; and even higher in Texas—29% and 31%, respectively." The criterion for a turnaround was improving the number of students reaching

proficiency in math or reading by at least five percentile points for at least three of the five years in question, while sustaining median growth percentiles of at least 65 percent.

232 **In state after state, less than 1 percent of teachers:** Matthew A. Kraft and Allison F. Gilmour, "Revisiting the Widget Effect: Teacher Evaluation Reforms and the Distribution of Teacher Effectiveness," Brown University Working Paper, February 2016, http://scholar.harvard.edu/files/mkraft/files/kraft_gilmour_2016_revisiting_the_ widget_effect_wp.pdf.

232 **Neerav Kingsland quote:** Neerav Kingsland, "What Happens at Higher Rates: Charter School Closure or Teacher Termination?" *Relinquishment* (blog), March 6, 2016, https://relinquishment.org/2016/03/06/what-happens-at-higher-rates-charter -school-closure-or-teacher-termination/.

233 **MetLife survey of teachers:** MetLife, *The MetLife Survey of the American Teacher: Challenges for School Leadership* (New York: MetLife, Inc., February 2013), www .metlife.com/assets/cao/foundation/MetLife-Teacher-Survey-2012.pdf, p. 45.

233 **Thomas Arnett quote:** Thomas Arnett, "When Do Teacher Evaluations Constrain Teacher Effectiveness?" Clayton Christensen Institute, August 15, 2014, www.chris tenseninstitute.org/blog/when-do-teacher-evaluations-constrain-teacher-effective ness/.

234 **Ted Kolderie quote:** Ted Kolderie, *Innovation-Based Systemic Reform: How to Get Beyond Traditional School* (St. Paul: Education Evolving, April 2010), www.education evolving.org/files/Innovation-Based-Systemic-Reform.pdf.

234 **Howard Gardner's multiple intelligences:** Howard Gardner, *Frames of Mind: The Theory of Multiple Intelligences* (New York: Basic Books, 1983), pp. 9–10.

234 **Ball Aptitude Battery:** "Ball Foundation, What the Tests Measure," www.ballfoun dation.org/tests-measure/.

237 **Quote from the Center on Reinventing Public Education:** Ashley Jochim, "Lessons from the Trenches on Making School Choice Work," Brookings website, *Brown Center Chalkboard* (blog), August 12, 2015, www.brookings.edu/blog/brown-center-chalk board/2015/08/12/lessons-from-the-trenches-on-making-school-choice-work/.

238 **As economists have long explained:** For an example, see Hans B. Thorelli, "Philosophies of Consumer Information Programs," in *Advances in Consumer Research*, edited by William D. Perrault Jr., volume 4 (Atlanta: Association for Consumer Research, 1977), pp. 282–87.

238 **In New Orleans, mobility between schools actually decreased:** Spiro Maroulis et al., "The Push and Pull of School Performance: Evidence from Student Mobility in New Orleans," Education Research Alliance, Tulane University, May 17, 2016, http:// educationresearchalliancenola.org/files/publications/Push-Pull-Working-Paper -20160516.pdf.

238 **Research has shown that low-income children benefit:** For a good review of the research, see Richard Kahlenberg, ed., *The Future of School Integration: Socioeconomic Diversity as an Education Reform Strategy* (New York: Century Foundation, 2007).

239 **Quote from TNTP:** *Shortchanged: The Hidden Costs of Lockstep Teacher Pay* (N.p.: TNTP, 2014), introduction, https://tntp.org/assets/documents/TNTP_Shortchanged _2014.pdf.

239–40 **Fordham Institute study and quote:** Griffith and McDougald, *Undue Process*, p. 10.

240 **In New York City, the United Federation of Teachers contract:** Joel Klein, *Lessons of Hope: How to Fix Our Schools* (New York: HarperCollins, 2014), pp. 194–95.

240 **Even in the model district of Union City:** David L. Kirp, *Improbable Scholars* (New York: Oxford University Press, 2013), pp. 91, 93, 154, 184.

240 **KIPP procurement story from Newark:** Julie O'Connor, "Beating Newark's Odds, KIPP Charter Network Is Poised to Expand," *Newark Star-Ledger*, May 9, 2015.

240 **On surveys, most teachers with more than 20 years:** Steve Farkas, Jean Johnson, and Ann Duffett, *Stand by Me: What Teachers Really Think About Unions, Merit Pay, and Other Professional Matters* (New York: Public Agenda, 2003), www.publicagenda .org/files/stand_by_me.pdf, p. 43.

241 **Those children get the most inexperienced:** See Marguerite Roza, "Many a Slip 'Tween Cup and Lip: District Fiscal Practices and Their Effect on School Spending," report prepared for the Aspen Institute Congressional Program; "The Challenge of Education Reform: Standards, Accountability, Resources and Policy," February 22–27, 2005, http://crpe.org/sites/default/files/pub_sfrp_district_feb05_0.pdf; Dan Goldhaber, Lesley Lavery, and Roddy Theorbald, "Uneven Playing Field? Assessing the Teacher Quality Gap Between Advantaged and Disadvantaged Students," *Educational Researcher*, June 2015, http://journals.sagepub.com/doi/abs/10.3102/0013189X15592622; Sarah Almy and Christina Theokas, "Not Prepared for Class: High-Poverty Schools Continue to Have Fewer In-Field Teachers," Education Trust, November 2010, http:// edtrust.org/wp-content/uploads/2013/10/Not-Prepared-for-Class.pdf.

241 **2012 MetLife Survey of the American Teacher:** MetLife, "MetLife Survey of the American Teacher," p. 23.

241 **Michael Petrilli and Amber Northern quote:** Michael J. Petrilli and Amber M. Northern, "Teacher Leadership: Yet Another Charter School Innovation?" *Flypaper*, November 25, 2014, https://edexcellence.net/articles/teacher-leadership-yet-another -charter-school-innovation.

242 **Gallup has found that teachers are the least likely:** Gallup, "State of America's Schools: The Path to Winning Again in Education," 2014, www.gallup.com/services/ 178709/state-america-schools-report.aspx.

242 **Quote from anonymous teacher:** Valerie Straus, "Teacher: What I Wish Everyone Knew About Working in Some High-Needs Schools," *Washington Post*, April 25, 2015.

242 **Richard Ingersoll quote:** Quoted in Liz Riggs, "Why Do Teachers Quit?" *Atlantic. com*, October 18, 2013.

242 **Creating a more supportive, professional environment:** See, for instance, Matthew A. Kraft and John P. Papay, "Can Professional Environments in Schools Promote Teacher Development? Explaining Heterogeneity in Returns to Teaching Experience," *Educational Evaluation and Policy Analysis* 36, no. 4 (December 2014).

242 **There are about 110 public schools in the U.S. run by teacher partnerships:** Lars Esdal (Education Evolving), e-mail, January 2017.

243 **Education Evolving poll in 2014:** Education Evolving, "Teacher-Powered Schools: Generating Lasting Impact Through Common Sense Innovation," Education Evolving, May 2014, www.teacherpowered.org/files/Teacher-Powered-Schools-Whitepaper .pdf, pp. 5–6.

243   **Information about the Minnesota Guild:** Molly Koppes (Minnesota Guild), e-mail, January 2017.

243   **The culture strategy:** For more on public sector cultures and how to reshape them, see David Osborne and Peter Plastrik, *Banishing Bureaucracy*, chapter 8, and *The Reinventor's Fieldbook*, chapters 13–15. Both are available, as chapters 20–23, at Reinventing Government (website), http://reinventgov.com/books/books-online/.

243   **Robin Lake at CRPE cites:** Robin J. Lake, ed., *Hope, Fears & Reality: A Balanced Look at American Charter Schools in 2009* (Bothell, WA: Center on Reinventing Public Education, January 2010), pp. 27–28. Lake cites Katherine Merseth et al., *Inside Urban Charter Schools* (Cambridge, MA: Harvard Education Press, 2009).

244   **Gordon MacInnes quote:** Gordon MacInnes, *In Plain Sight: Simple, Difficult Lessons from New Jersey's Effort to Close the Achievement Gap* (New York: Century Foundation Press, 2009), p. 63.

244   **I believe this is because young children:** Studies find that intrinsic motivation declines over the years in traditional schools, according to Don Berg, *Every Parent's Dilemma* (Bloomington, IN: Trafford, 2014), p. 20. Berg cites 11 studies that come to this conclusion.

244   **Carrie Leana quote:** Carrie R. Leana, "The Missing Link in School Reform," *Stanford Social Innovation Review* 9, no. 4 (Fall 2011), https://ssir.org/articles/entry/the_missing_link_in_school_reform.

245   **Careful studies show three things:** For a good review of the literature, see Scott Alexander, "Teachers: Much More Than You Wanted to Know," *Slate Star Codex* (blog), May 9, 2016, http://slatestarcodex.com/2016/05/19/teachers-much-more-than-you-wanted-to-know/.

245   **Frederick Hess quote:** Frederick Hess, *Education Unbound* (Alexandria, VA: Association for Supervision & Curriculum Development, 2010), p. 95.

245   **Almost two thirds of education schools fail:** Motoko Rich, "As Apprentices in Classroom, Teachers Learn What Works," *New York Times*, October 10, 2014. **National Council on Teacher Quality study:** Julie Geenberg, Kate Walsh, and Arthur McKee, *Teacher Prep Review 2014 Report: A Review of the Nation's Teacher Pereparation Programs* (Washington, DC: National Council on Teacher Quality, June 2014), www.nctq.org/dmsStage/Teacher_Prep_Review_2014_Report.

245   **Peter Hutchinson quote:** Peter Hutchinson, e-mail, January 2017.

245   **even in recent decades, their days were given over to:** Steven F. Wilson, *Learning on the Job* (Cambridge, MA: Harvard University Press, 2006), pp. 101, 250. Wilson cites Paul T. Hill, Gail E. Foster, and Tamar Gendler, *High Schools with Character* (Santa Monica, CA: RAND Corporation, 1990), and National Association of Secondary School Principals, "Priorities and Barriers in High School Leadership: A Survey of Principals," press release, November 13, 2001.

246   **Relay now trains more than 2,400 teachers and principals each year:** Relay Graduate School of Education website, www.relay.edu.

247   **Al Shanker quote:** Albert Shanker, "Letting Schools Compete," *Northeast-Midwest Economic Review*, November 13, 1989, pp. 4–8.

247   **And even with less real choice, they can use other tools:** See Osborne and Plastrik, *The Reinventor's Fieldbook*, chapter 9, available as chapter 15 at Reinventing Government (website), http://reinventgov.com/books/books-online/.

CHAPTER 13

251   **Instead, districts or authorizers should hold alternative schools:** We must be careful, however, that districts and authorizers don't label too many schools "alternative" and dump their worst students in them, to make the rest of the district look good. According to Leslie Jacobs, one city in Louisiana has done this, putting one of every four high school students in alternative schools. State departments of education should take a close look at any district or authorizer that has more than 5 percent of its students in alternative schools. For one examination of the practice, see Heather Vogell and Hannah Fresques, " 'Alternative' Education: Using Charter Schools to Hide Dropouts and Game the System," *USA Today* and *ProPublica*, February 21, 2017, www.propublica.org/article/alternative-education-using-charter-schools-hide-dropouts-and-game-system.

252   **University Preparatory Academies:** Interviews and e-mail correspondence with Doug Ross over many years.

252   **Other Big Picture schools had similar experiences:** Scott Bess, a founder of the Indianapolis Metropolitan High School, recounted similar experiences in an interview in April 2016.

255   **Center for American Progress study:** Carmel Martin, Scott Sargrad, and Samantha Batel, *Making the Grade: A 50-State Analysis of School Accountability Systems* (Washington, DC: Center for American Progress, May 2016), p. 15. The authors write: "Together, academic achievement and student growth make up a combined average of 91 percent of elementary and middle school ratings—with a minimum of 71 percent and maximum of 100 percent—and an average of 63 percent of high school ratings—with a minimum of 40 percent and a maximum of 100 percent." This does not include AP, SAT, and ACT college readiness tests, which add perhaps an average of 10 percent to high school ratings, according to the report (pp. 24–26).

256   **Number of states testing writing, science, and social sciences:** Ibid., p. 9.

256   **Donald Campbell quote:** Donald T. Campbell, "Assessing the Impact of Planned Social Change," Occasional Paper Series, No. 8, Dartmouth College Public Affairs Center, December 1976, http://journals.sfu.ca/jmde/index.php/jmde_1/article/view/297/292.

256   **Quote from Union City teacher:** David L. Kirp, *Improbable Scholars* (New York: Oxford University Press, 2013), pp. 173–74.

257   **Mission High School:** Kristina Rizga, *Mission High* (New York: Nation Books, 2015).

257   **Some studies find a correlation between good test scores:** See, for instance, the debate between Michael Petrilli and Jay Greene in *Flypaper*, May 2016. You can find all six links at https://edexcellence.net/articles/test-score-gains-predict-long-term-outcomes-so-we-shouldnt-be-too-shy-about-using-them.

257   **Quotes from Education Sector:** Anne Hyslop and Bill Tucker, "Ready by Design: A College and Career Agenda for California" (Washington, DC: Education Sector, 2012), http://educationpolicy.air.org/sites/default/files/publications/ReadybyDesign-RELEASED.pdf.

257   **Quote from "one superintendent":** Quoted in Ted Kolderie, *Creating the Capacity for Change* (St. Paul: Education Evolving, 2004), p. 67.

258   **Most experts believe the Common Core tests move:** Mikhail Zinshteyn, "Should the U.S. Make Standardized Tests Harder?" *TheAtlantic.com*, November 24, 2014.

258   **EdVisions schools' test scores:** Charles Taylor Kerchner, "Can Teachers Run Their Own Schools? Tales from the Islands of Teacher Cooperatives," Claremont Graduate University, October 2010, http://charlestkerchner.com/cr/uploadImages/Teacher_run_case.pdf.

258   **Quote from Governor Rudy Perpich:** Quoted in Kolderie, *Creating the Capacity for Change*, p. 129.

259   **2015 Gallup and Phi Delta Kappa survey:** "The 47th Annual PDK/Gallup Poll of the Public's Attitudes Toward the Public Schools—Testing Doesn't Measure Up for Americans, A Special Supplement to *Kappan* Magazine," *Phi Delta Kappan*, September 2015, http://pdkpoll2015.pdkintl.org/wp-content/uploads/2015/10/pdkpoll47_2015.pdf.

259–60 **Description of ESSA's requirements:** Martin, Sargrad, and Batel, "Making the Grade."

260   **But the majority of states still give greater weight:** Ibid., pp. 13–16; Morgan S. Polikoff et al., "The Waive of the Future: School Accountability in the Waiver Era," *Educational Researcher* 43, no. 1 (January–February 2014), www.aera.net/Newsroom/Recent-AERA-Research/The-Waive-of-the-Future-School-Accountability-in-the-Waiver-Era.

260   **There are many different ways to measure student growth:** For a description of the alternatives, see Lyria Boast and Tim Field, *Quality School Ratings: Trends in Evaluating School Academic Quality* (Washington, DC: National Alliance for Public Charter Schools, 2013), www.publiccharters.org/wp-content/uploads/2014/01/Quality-Ratings-Report_20131010T114517.pdf.

261   **Letter to Secretary King by 40 experts:** Morgan Polikoff et al., "A Letter to the U.S. Department of Education," *On Education Research*, July 22, 2016, https://morganpolikoff.com/2016/07/12/a-letter-to-the-u-s-department-of-education/.

261   **In addition, some states use growth models:** Michael J. Petrilli et al., *High Stakes for High Achievers: An Analysis of State Accountability Systems in the Age of ESSA* (Washington, DC: Fordham Institute, August 31, 2016), https://edexcellence.net/publications/high-stakes-for-high-achievers, p. 16.

261   **There are a surprising number of the latter:** A 2016 national study by the Institute for Education Policy found that 20 to 40 percent of elementary and middle school students perform at least one grade level above their grade in reading, and 11 to 30 percent do so in math. See Matthew C. Makel et al., "How Can So Many Students Be Invisible: Large Percentages of American Students Perform Above Grade Level" Johns Hopkins University, Institute for Education Policy, August 16, 2016, http://edpolicy.education.jhu.edu/wordpress/?p=153.

261–2 **Fordham Institute quote:** Petrilli et al., *High Stakes for High Achievers*, p. 4.

262   **Eight states already used this kind of index:** Michael Petrilli, "Two Changes to the Department of Education's ESSA Implementation Rule," *Flypaper*, August 1, 2016, https://edexcellence.net/articles/two-changes-to-the-department-of-educations-essa-implementation-rule.

262   **Just four states have praiseworthy systems:** Petrilli et al., *High Stakes for High Achievers*, p. 8.

262   **Some states have included five-year, six-year:** Martin, Sargrad, and Batel, *Making the Grade*, p. 22.

262   **An estimated 42 percent of those who enroll:** Mikhail Zinshteyn, "New Ways to Find Out Who Is Ready for College," *Higher Ed Beat*, March 8, 2016, www.ewa.org/blog -higher-ed-beat/new-ways-find-out-who-ready-college?utm_source=salsa&utm_ medium=email&utm_campaign=newsletter. He writes: "Nationally, 42 percent of incoming college students are referred to remedial courses; the percentages are even higher for black, Latino, poor and community college students. Just one tenth of students who start college in remedial courses ever earn a degree a report by Complete College America calculated in 2014."

262   **"Distinguished achievement" programs in Texas:** See Texas Education Agency, "Questions and Answers on the Distinguished Achievement Program," http://tea.texas .gov/WorkArea/linkit.aspx?LinkIdentifier=id&ItemID=2147487536&libID=2147487534.

262   **"Regents diplomas with advanced designation with honors":** See New York State Department of Education, "Diploma/Credential Requirements," www.p12.nysed. gov/specialed/diploma-credentials.html.

262   **Some of them award points in their performance indexes:** Martin, Sargrad, and Batel, *Making the Grade*, p. 25; Boast and Field, *Quality School Ratings*, p. 15.

262–3 **Florida, Indiana, Louisiana, Maryland, New Mexico:** Boast and Field, *Quality School Ratings*, p. 15.

263   **Hence many charter authorizers and a few states include:** Ibid., p. 15; Martin, Sargrad, and Batel, *Making the Grade*, p. 24.

263   **In addition, Denver measures the percentage:** Boast and Field, *Quality School Ratings*, pp. 16.

264   **A majority of states now track the wages:** According to the National Skills Coalition: Sophie Quinton, "Using Data to Connect Degrees to Dollars," *eCampusNews*, August 10, 2016, http://www.ecampusnews.com/curriculum/data-degrees-dollars/.

264–5 **English and Scottish qualitative evaluations of schools:** See Craig D. Jerald, "On Her Majesty's School Inspection Service," *Education Sector*, 2012, http://education policy.air.org/sites/default/files/publications/UKInspections-RELEASED.pdf.

264   **New York City, Denver, and Charlotte-Mecklenburg:** For more on New York City, Charlotte-Mecklenberg, and Massachusetts, see Linda Darling-Hammond et al., *Pathways to New Accountability Through the Every Student Succeeds Act* (Palo Alto, CA: Learning Policy Institute, 2016), http://learningpolicyinstitute.org/our-work/ publications-resources/pathways-new-accountability-every-student-succeeds-act, pp. 31–33; Chad Aldeman, *Grading Schools: How States Should Define "School Quality" Under the Every Student Succeeds Act* (Washington, DC: Bellwether Education Partners, October 2016), p. 24.

265   **The effectiveness of the English inspection system:** Aldeman, *Grading Schools*, p. 27; Rebecca Allen and Simon Burgess, "How Should We Treat Under-Performing Schools? A Regression Discontinuity Analysis of School Inspections in England," Working Paper No. 12/287, Centre for Market and Public Organisation, March 2012, www.bristol.ac.uk/media-library/sites/cmpo/migrated/documents/wp287.pdf; Iftikhar Hussain, "Subjective Performance Evaluation in the Public Sector: Evidence from School Inspections," *Journal of Human Resources* 50, no. 1 (2015): pp. 189–221, http://jhr.uwpress.org/content/50/1/189.abstract.

266   **For instance, geometry students at Spaulding High School:** Shaina Cavazos, "Building Better Student Assessments," *Educated Reporter*, June 23, 2016, www.ewa

.org/blog-educated-reporter/building-better-student-assessments?utm_source=
salsa&utm_medium=email&utm_campaign=newsletter.

266   **Deeper learning assessments are common in other:** David T. Conley and Linda
Darling-Hammond, *Creating Systems of Assessment for Deeper Learning* (Stanford, CA:
Stanford Center for Opportunity Policy in Education, 2013), https://edpolicy.stan
ford.edu/sites/default/files/publications/creating-systems-assessment-deeper-learning
_0.pdf; Zinshteyn, "Should the U.S. Make Standardized Tests Harder?"

266   **The Council of Chief State School Officers' Innovation Lab Network:** CCSSO website, www.ccsso.org/Resources/Programs/Balanced_Systems_of_Assessment_and_
Aligned_Accountability.html.

266–7   **New York Performance Standards consortium:** "Educating for the 21st Century:
Data Report on the New York Performance Standards Consortium," New York Performance Standards Consortium, n.d., http://performanceassessment.org/articles/
DataReport_NY_PSC.pdf; Gail Robinson, "NYC Schools That Skip Standardized
Tests Have Higher Graduation Rates," *Hechinger Report*, October 30, 2015, http://
hechingerreport.org/nyc-schools-that-skip-standardized-tests-have-higher-gradu
ation-rates/.

267   **Other nations, including the Netherlands, Singapore:** Conley and Darling-
Hammond, *Creating Systems of Assessment for Deeper Learning*, pp. 10–13.

267   **Starting in 2010, the Bill and Melinda Gates Foundation funded research:** MET
(Measures of Effective Teaching) Project, *Ensuring Fair and Reliable Measures of
Effective Teaching: Illuminating Findings from the MET Project's Three-Year Study*
(Seattle: Bill and Melinda Gates Foundation, January 2013), http://k12education
.gatesfoundation.org/wp-content/uploads/2015/05/MET_Ensuring_Fair_and_Reliable
_Measures_Practitioner_Brief.pdf.

267   **a decade of research by Professor Ronald Ferguson at Harvard University:** Rob
Ramsdell (Tripod Education Partners), e-mail, July 2016.

267   **Results from Gates Foundation funded surveys:** MET Project, *Ensuring Fair and
Reliable Measures of Effective Teaching*, pp. 11–13; interview with Rob Ramsdell (Tripod Education Partners), July 2016.

267   **At least 100 districts and a thousand schools . . . character skills:** Rob Ramsdell,
July 2016 interview.

269   **Quotes from Gabrieli, Ansel, and Krachman paper:** Chris Gabrieli, Dana Ansel,
and Sara Bartolino Krachman, "Ready to Be Counted: The Research Case for Education Policy Action on Non-Cognitive Skills, Version 1.0," Transforming Education,
December 2015, static1.squarespace.com/static/55bb6b62e4b00dce923f1666/t/5665e1
c30e4c114d99b28889/1449517507245/ReadytoBeCounted_Release.pdf.

269   **A 2013 national teacher survey found:** Ibid.

269   **Summit Public Schools:** For more, see David Osborne, *Schools of the Future: California's Summit Public Schools* (Washington, DC: Progressive Policy Institute, January 2016), www.progressivepolicy.org/slider/schools-of-the-future-californias-sum
mit-public-schools/.

270   **Quote from Ted Dintersmith and Tony Wagner:** "America Desperately Needs To
Redefine 'College and Career Ready,'" *Market Watch*, August 8, 2016, www.market-
watch.com/story/america-desperately-needs-to-redefine-college-and-career
-ready-2016-08-05.

270–1 **CORE Districts' School Quality Improvement Index**: CORE Districts, "School Quality Improvement System History," http://coredistricts.org/school-quality-im provement-system-waiver/.

271 **According to Harvard Professor Martin West**: Martin West, "Should Non-Cognitive Skills Be Included in School Accountability Systems? Preliminary Evidence from California's CORE Districts," *Evidence Speaks Reports* 1, no. 13 (March 17, 2016), www .brookings.edu/wp-content/uploads/2016/07/EvidenceSpeaksWest031716.pdf.

271 **Already NAEP and PISA are adding measurements**: Jonathan E. Martin, "We Should Measure Students' Noncognitive Skills," *Education Week*, July 27, 2016.

271 **Collaborative for Academic, Social, and Emotional Learning initiative**: Evie Blad, "Social-Emotional Learning: States Collaborate to Craft Standards, Policies" *Education Week*, August 1, 2016.

274–5 **Letter from Torlakson and Kirst**: Letter to Meredith Miller, U.S. Department of Education, August 1, 2016, Docket ID: ED-2016-OESE-0032, www.cde.ca.gov/re/es/ regletter1.asp.

275 **Chad Aldeman quote**: Chad Aldeman, "Summative Ratings Are All Around Us. Why Are We Afraid of Them in K–12 Education?" *Education Next*, August 9, 2016, http://educationnext.org/summative-ratings-are-all-around-us-why-are-we-afraid -of-them-in-k-12-education/.

275 **Utah, New York City, and Philadelphia have all done this**: Boast and Field, *Quality School Ratings*, p. 21.

276 **parents have indicated their strong preference for brief reports**: On reporting results, see A-Plus Communications, "What the Public Wants to Know" (Arlington, VA: A-Plus Communications, 1999), p. 9. (A-Plus Communications is now KSA-Plus Communications, www.ksaplus.com/about-us.html.)

277 **In Massachusetts, charter schools must meet**: See Massachusetts Office of Charter Schools and School Redesign, "Charter School Performance Criteria, Version 3.3" Massachusetts Department of Elementary and Secondary Education, June 2016, www .doe.mass.edu/charter/acct.html?section=criteria.

277 **CREDO data on Massachusetts**: CREDO, "National Charter School Study 2013," (Stanford, CA: Center for Research on Education Outcomes, 2013).

CHAPTER 14

278 **As Ashley Jochim of Center on Reinventing Public Education has written**: Ashley Jochim, *Measures of Last Resort: Assessing Strategies for State-Initiated Turnarounds* (Bothell, WA: Center on Reinventing Public Education, Nov. 2016), https://crpe.org/ publications/measures-last-resort, p. 1.

279 **Already, 25 states have the authority**: Ibid., p. 10.

279 **Charter pioneer Ted Kolderie has suggested**: Ted Kolderie, *The Split-Screen Strategy: Improvement + Innovation* (Edina, MN: Beaver's Pond Press, 2014), pp. 37–38.

279 **as the Center on Reinventing Public Education has recommended**: Jordan Posamentier, Robin Lake, and Paul Hill, *How States Can Promote Local Innovation, Options, and Problem-Solving in Public Education* (Bothell, WA.: Center on Reinventing Public Education, April 2017), http://www.crpe.org/publications/states-promote -local-innovation?platform=hootsuite.

280   **Finally, states could support innovations such as:** For more on the Harlem Children's Zone, see Paul Tough, *Whatever It Takes* (Boston: Houghton Mifflin Harcourt, 2008); for more on Promise Neighborhoods, see the Promise Neighborhoods Institute website, www.promiseneighborhoodsinstitute.org/.

281   **Grants from state of Florida:** Arianna Prothero, "Often Foes, Some Districts and Charters Forge Partnerships," *Education Week*, October 15, 2014.

282   **A decade ago all 50 states . . . district schools:** Frederick Hess, *Education Unbound* (Alexandria, VA: Association for Supervision & Curriculum Development, 2010), pp. 50–51.

282–3   **Public real estate trusts to manage facilities:** For more, see Michael DeArmond, "Getting Out of the Facilities Business: A Public School Real Estate Trust," in *Making School Reform Work*, edited by Paul T. Hill and James Harvey (Washington, DC: Brookings Institution Press, 2004).

284   **David Riemer suggestions:** David Riemer, e-mail, 2016. For more of Riemer's views, see his website, "Putting Government In Its Place," www.govinplace.org/. The specific section on education is at www.govinplace.org/economic_security/the_way_forward_on_education.php.

284–5   **"Enterprise" or "entrepreneurial" management of internal services:** See David Osborne and Peter Plastrik, *The Reinventor's Fieldbook: Tools for Reinventing Your Government* (San Francisco: Jossey-Bass, 2000), chapter 4, http://reinventgov.com/wp-content/uploads/2014/02/09.0EnterpriseManagement.pdf, as chapter 8.

285   **A few of them have figured out:** It is impossible to prove which large cities with high poverty rates are the fastest improving in the country, but the evidence points toward these three. Re. New Orleans, see endnote to p. 5, in the introduction, and endnotes to pp. 54–6 in chapter 3. Re. Washington, D.C.: It is the fastest improving state on NAEP exams, and DCPS is the fastest improving of the 21 TUDA districts that participate in NAEP. Re. Denver: According to the Stanford Education Data Archive assembled by the Center for Education Policy Analysis at Stanford University (https://cepa.stanford.edu/seda/overview), Denver Public Schools had the second highest academic growth from grade 3 to 8 of any district in the country with more than 25,000 students between 2009–10 and 2012–13 (a sample that did not include the RSD in New Orleans), and the highest of any district with more than 50 percent of students qualifying for subsidized meals. See Education Resource Strategies, *Denver Public Schools: Leveraging System Transformation to Improve Student Results* (N.p.: Education Resource Strategies, March 2017), p. 11.

290–1   **In polls, two thirds of the public consistently support charter schools:** Paul E. Peterson et al., "Ten-year Trends in Public Opinion From the EdNext Poll," *Education Next* 17, no. 1 (Winter 2017). **less than 30 percent opposed:** Michael B. Henderson, Martin R. West, and Paul E. Peterson, "The 2015 EdNext Poll on School Reform," *Education Next* 16, no. 1 (Winter 2016).

291   **When the concept is explained, the support goes up to 73 percent:** Center for Education Reform, "America's Attitudes Towards Education Reform: Executive Summary 2013," www.edreform.com/wp-content/uploads/2014/06/AMERICA%E2%80%99S-ATTITUDES-TOWARDS-EDUCATION-REFORM_Exec-Summary-2013.pdf. In the PDK/Gallup 2014 survey the figure was 70 percent: William J. Bushaw

and Valerie J. Calderon, "Try It Again, Uncle Sam: PDK/Gallup Poll of the Public's Attitudes Toward the Public Schools," *Phi Delta Kappan* 96, no. 1 (September, 2014), pp. 18–19, http://pdkintl.org/noindex/PDK_Poll_46.pdf.

291   **Support among Democrats has been stable:** Peterson et al., "Ten-year Trends in Public Opinion from the EdNext Poll."

291   **Among parents, support is even higher . . . their community:** Charles Barone and Marianne Lombardo, "A Democratic Guide to Public Charter Schools," Education Reform Now, October 2016, https://edreformnow.org/wp-content/uploads/2016/10/A-Democratic-Guide-to-Public-Charter-Schools.final_.10.19.16.pdf, p. 12. The 2015 poll was by TV One and RolandSMartin.com. The 2016 poll was by the National Alliance for Public Charters Schools.

291   **In a 2014 Phi Delta Kappa/Gallup poll:** Bushaw and Calderon, "Try It Again, Uncle Sam."

291   **In Massachusetts the teachers unions organized:** Mark Keierleber, "Poll Results Diverge as $38M Campaign Over Massachusetts Charter Cap Hits Ballot Tuesday," *The74million.org*, November 6, 2016.

291   **In Georgia the unions spent at least $4.7 million:** Ty Tagami, "What Stopped the Opportunity Schools Measure, and What Comes Next?" *Atlanta Journal-Constitution*, November 9, 2016.

291   **Most people trust public school teachers:** William J. Bushaw and Shane J. Lopez, "Which Way Do We Go? The 45th Annual PDK/Gallup Poll of the Public's Attitudes Toward the Public Schools," *Phi Delta Kappan* 95, no. 1 (September 2013); http://pdkintl.org/noindex/2013_PDKGallup.pdf; Stu Silberman, "In Teachers We Trust—But How Much?" *Education Week*, September 17, 2013.

294   **Teachers' unions are not terribly popular:** Alexandra Rice, "Poll: Americans Trust Teachers, Split on Teachers Unions," *Education Week*, August 17, 2011; Policy Analysis for California Education, "California Voters Reject Tenure, Layoff Rules for Public School Teachers," June 26, 2014, www.edpolicyinca.org/projects/calif-voters-reject-tenure-layoff-rules-public-school-teachers.

294   **There are no for-profit charters left in New Orleans or Denver:** See endnote for p. 15: "There are none left in New Orleans or Denver."

296   **A study that followed 790 Baltimore first-graders:** Karl K. Alexander, Doris Entwisle, and Linda Olson, *The Long Shadow: Family Background, Disadvantaged Urban Youth, and the Transition to Adulthood* (New York: Russell Sage Foundation, 2014).

296–7 **Quote from Paul Tough:** Tough, *How Children Succeed*, p. 186. The last time Pew asked this question, in 2012, 86 percent agreed. See Pew Research Center for the People and the Press, *Trends in American Values: 1987–2012, Partisan Polarization Surges in Bush, Obama Years* (Washington, D.C.: Pew Research Center for the People and the Press, June 4, 2012).

APPENDIX A

299   **John Merrow quote:** John Merrow, "Deciphering School in New Orleans, Post-Katrina," *The Merrow Report*, Aug. 11, 2015, http://themerrowreport.com/2015/08/11/deciphering-schooling-in-new-orleans-post-katrina/.

300   **Quotes and description of Louisiana performance framework:** Louisiana Department of Education, "School Letter Grades," Louisiana Believes (website), www.louisianabelieves.com/assessment/school-letter-grades.

300   **Like other states, Louisiana . . . career ready":** "Louisiana's Transition To Higher Expectations," Louisiana Believes (website), www.louisianabelieves.com/data/report cards/2016/.

302–4   **Information on D.C.'s charter performance management frameworks:** D.C. Public Charter School Board, *2015–16 Performance Management Framework Policy & Technical Guide* (Washington D.C.: Public Charter School Board, February 2016), http://www.dcpcsb.org/sites/default/files/Vote—2015-16%20PMF_Policy%20%20Tech_March%20Meeting%20Final%20Clean%20Copy.pdf.

305–6   **Information on DCPS scorecards:** Office of Data and Strategy, *School Year 2014–15 Scorecard User Guide* (Washington, D.C.: D.C. Public Schools, 2015), http://profiles.dcps.dc.gov/pdf/ScorecardUserGuideSY14-15_draft_forwebsite.pdf; and the DCPS "School Profiles" website, http://profiles.dcps.dc.gov. At this writing, this is the most recent guide available on the DCPS website.

306   **A Common Report Card for Parents:** For details on the new report card, see Office of the State Superintendent of Education, *District of Columbia Revised State Template for the Consolidated State Plan* (Washington D.C.: OSSE, March 17, 2017), http://sboe.dc.gov/sites/default/files/dc/sites/sboe/page_content/attachments/OSSE%20ESSA%320State%20Plan_%20March%2017%202017%20Final.pdf.

307–12   **Description of DPS School Performance Framework for 2016–17:** Denver Public Schools, "School Performance Framework," http://spf.dpsk12.org/en/. The weightings cited here are from the 2016 version of the SPF. They have changed substantially over the years, putting more and more weight on growth.

312   **In 2015–16, 35 schools shared almost $14 million:** Melanie Asmar, "Your Guide to Understanding Denver Public Schools' Color-Coded School Rating System," *Chalkbeat,* October 27, 2016, http://www.chalkbeat.org/posts/co/2016/10/27/your-guide-to-understanding-denver-public-schools-color-coded-school-rating-system/.

312   **In October 2014, more than a dozen organizations:** "Release: Local Education Groups Call On DPS School Board for Action on SPF," *A+ Denver News,* October 21, 2014, http://www.aplusdenver.org/_blog/A_Plus_Denver_News/post/release-local-education-groups-call-on-dps-school-board-for-action-on-spf/.

312   **The board responded by agreeing to shift:** Interview with Grant Guyer, DPS executive director of accountability, research and evaluation, December 2015.

312–3   **Finally, the group asked . . . and the board agreed:** "Update on Denver's SPF Changes," *A+ Denver News,* April 20, 2015, at http://www.aplusdenver.org/_blog/A_Plus_Denver_News/post/update-on-denvers-spf-changes/.

APPENDIX B

315–6   **2006 and 2008 versions of ProComp:** For comparisons of ProComp 1.0 and 2.0, see Denver Public Schools, "Welcome to Teacher ProComp," http://denverprocomp.dpsk12.org/about/significant_changes.

315   **They turned out to have no impact on student learning:** Diane Proctor, et al., *Making a Difference in Education Reform: ProComp External Evaluation Report 2006–2010*

(Denver: University of Colorado at Denver, October 2011), p. xv, http://www.the-evaluation-center.org/wp-content/uploads/2011/04/Final-ProComp-Report-Oct-14-2011-Making-a-Difference-in-Education-Reform-ProComp-External-Evaluation-Report.pdf.

316 **ProComp version 2.0 shifted to more use of bonuses:** Denver Public Schools and Denver Classroom Teachers Association, "ProComp," 2014, http://static.dpsk12.org/gems/newprocomp/DPS.ProcompWebFINAL.pdf. Version 2.0 continued to award salary increases for an entire career for advanced degrees, licenses, or certificates and for meeting student learning objectives. Before the 14-year limit was reached, it awarded salary increases for satisfactory evaluations and for professional development units (the latter became bonuses after 14 years). It provided bonuses for working in "high needs schools" and in "hard-to-staff" roles, for those whose students' test score growth exceeded expectations, and for teachers in top performing schools and high growth schools, based on the SPF. (Five of the bonuses were for $2481 each.) Finally, it provided up to $4,000 over a career in tuition and student loan reimbursement.

316 **Still, teachers hired since 2006 generally feel . . . charter schools:** Interviews with Kerrie Dallman, president of the Colorado Education Association, and Pam Shamburg, executive director of the Denver Classroom Teachers Association, November 2014.

316 **2010 evaluation by the University of Colorado at Boulder:** Edward W. Wiley, Eleanor R. Spindler, and Amy N. Subert, *Denver ProComp: An Outcomes Evaluation of Denver's Alternative Teacher Compensation System* (Boulder: University of Colorado at Boulder, School of Education, 2010), http://static.dpsk12.org/gems/newprocomp/ProCompOutcomesEvaluationApril2010final.pdf.

316 **2011 study by the University of Colorado in Denver:** Proctor, et al., *Making a Difference in Education Reform.*

316 **2014 study by Harvard's Strategic Data Project:** Strategic Data Project, *SDP Human Capital Diagnostic: Denver Public Schools* (Cambridge, MA: Center for Education Policy Research at Harvard University, November 2014), http://cepr.harvard.edu/publications/sdp-human-capital-diagnostic-denver-public-schools.

APPENDIX C

319 **Memphis is a poor city:** Shelby County Schools, "Shelby County Schools by the Numbers 2016–17," http://www.scsk12.org/about/.

319 **Eighteen percent missed at least 18 days of school:** Caroline Bauman, "How Do You Fight Chronic Absenteeism? Put a Nurse in Every School," *Chalkbeat*, October 5, 2016, http://www.chalkbeat.org/posts/tn/2016/10/05/how-do-you-fight-chronic-absenteeism-put-a-nurse-in-every-school/#.V_ZO8jKZPm1. **Total public school enrollment in Memphis in 2014–15:** State Report Card on Shelby County Schools 2015–16, https://www.tn.gov/education/topic/report-card.

319 **Until 2012, the school district was quite conventional:** Christine Campbell and Libuse Binder, *In-Depth Portfolio Assessment: Shelby County Schools, Memphis, TN* (Bothell, WA: Center on Reinventing Public Education, June 2014), http://www.crpe.org/sites/default/files/CRPEMemphisPortfolioAssessment.pdf.

320 **Barbic wanted to turn all the ASD schools . . . as a charter network:** Interview with Chris Barbic, January 2015.

320 **Tennessee's legislation required . . . of a school's population:** Juli Kim, Tim Field, and Elaine Hargrave, *The Achievement School District: Lessons from Tennessee* (Chapel Hill, NC: Public Impact and New Orleans: New Schools for New Orleans, 2015), http://achievementschooldistrict.org/wp-content/uploads/2015/11/The-Achievement-School-District-Lessons-from-Tennessee-UPDATE.pdf, p. 17.

320 **Most ASD charters had a rough start . . . students arrived:** Diane Massell, Joshua L. Glazer, and Matthew Malone, *"This Is the Big Leagues:" Charter-Led Turnaround in a Non-Charter World* (Nashville: Tennessee Consortium on Research, Evaluation & Development, Vanderbilt University's Peabody College, June 2016), pp. 16–17, https://www.researchgate.net/publication/305210374_THIS_IS_THE_BIG_LEAGUES_CHARTER-LED_TURNAROUND_IN_A_NON-CHARTER_WORLD.

321 **A majority of ASD charters took over entire schools:** Kim, Field, and Hargrave, *The Achievement School District: Lessons from Tennessee*, pp. 17–18.

321 **Few teachers chose to stay . . . a failing school:** Massell, Glazer, and Malone, *"This Is the Big Leagues."*

321 **ASD charters received the same per-pupil amount:** Chris Barbic, via email, October 2016.

321 **Eighteen percent of their students had special needs:** Kim, Field, and Hargrave, *The Achievement School District: Lessons from Tennessee*, p. 23.

321 **ASD schools had little extra money or help for children with severe disabilities:** Interview with Derwin Sisnett, CEO of Gestalt Community Schools, a charter operator, January 2015; and Massell, Glazer, and Malone, *"This is the Big Leagues,"* pp. 16–17.

321 **Study by Tennessee Consortium on Research, Evaluation, and Development:** Massell, Glazer, and Malone, *"This is the Big Leagues,"* pp. 16–17.

321 **The ASD schools also ran into . . . planned takeovers:** Ibid. pp. 18–21.

321 **When the ASD takes a school:** Interview with Chris Barbic, January 2015.

322 **In late 2015, the SCS Board voted:** Micaela Watts, "School Board Vote Commits Shelby County's District And Charter Sectors To Trying To Collaborate," *Chalkbeat,* January 26, 2016.

322 **The ASD charters operators soldiered on . . . in their neighborhoods:** Massell, Glazer, and Malone, *"This is the Big Leagues,"* pp. 22–27.

322 **Academic growth in ASD schools:** Achievement School District, "Building the Possible: Year Three Results," http://achievementschooldistrict.org/wp-content/uploads/2015/07/ASD-3rd-Year-Results-Presentation.pdf. Over its first three years, the percentage of students reaching proficiency in the ASD increased 10.7 points in math, compared to 8.4 statewide, and 10 points in science, compared to four statewide, but it declined 4.3 points in reading, compared to 1.5 statewide, according to the ASD. Since less than a quarter of ASD students have reached proficiency, however, this statistic tells us much less than the academic growth numbers.

322 **Survey data on ASD schools:** Ibid.

322 **Schools in the bottom 5 percent . . . a huge achievement:** Malika Anderson, "Fighting for Every Student's Right to a Great Education," ASD email, February 5, 2016; and Kim, Field, and Hargrave; *The Achievement School District: Lessons from Tennessee*, p. 8.

323 **Quote from Superintendent Dorsey Hopson:** Quoted in Achievement School District, "Building the Possible: Year Three Results."

323 **The first is financial:** Micaela Watts and Laura Faith Kebede, "Building on Innovation Zone Successes, Shelby County Schools to Launch Separate 'Empowerment Zone,' " *Chalkbeat*, April 19, 2016, http://www.chalkbeat.org/posts/tn/2016/04/19/ building-on-innovation-zone-successes-shelby-county-schools-to-launch-separate -empowerment-zone/

324 **By 2016–17 there were only six "in-district," Horace Mann charters:** Boston Public Schools (website), "School Types," http://www.bostonpublicschools.org/Page/941.

324 **Basic description of Horace Mann charters:** Dan French, Karen Hawley Miles, and Linda Nathan, *The Path Forward: School Autonomy and Its Implications for the Future of Boston's Public Schools* (Boston: The Boston Foundation and Boston Public Schools, June 2014), http://www.bostonpublicschools.org/cms/lib07/MA01906464/Centricity/ Domain/238/BPS_Report_2014_6-2-14.pdf.

324 **Basic description of pilot schools:** Ibid., and Molly Osborne and Jake Taylor, "Evaluating District Run Autonomous Schools," Master's Thesis, Harvard Kennedy School, 2017.

324 **2009 Boston Foundation study:** Atila Abdulkadiroglu, et al., *Informing the Debate: Comparing Boston's Charter, Pilot, and Traditional Schools* (Boston: The Boston Foundation, January 2009), http://www.tbf.org/impact/objectives-and-strategies/strategies/ ~/media/TBFOrg/Files/Reports/InformingTheDebate_Final.pdf.

324–5 **Basic description of innovation schools:** Massachusetts Department of Elementary and Secondary Education (website), "Comparison of Innovation Schools, Pilot Schools, Horace Mann Charter Schools, and Commonwealth Charter Schools— Updated April 2016," http://www.doe.mass.edu/redesign/innovation/Autonomous Comparison.docx.

325 **The only major flexibility that is off limits:** French, Hawley Miles, and Nathan, *The Path Forward*.

325 **Basic description of turnaround schools:** Ibid., and Osborne and Taylor "Evaluating District Run Autonomous Schools."

325 **BPS has replaced the principals at all turnaround schools:** "Turnaround Spotlight: Boston Public Schools," *Innovate Public Schools*, November 11, 2014, http://innovate-schools.org/effective-education-policies/turnaround-spotlight-boston-public -schools/.

325 **Earlier analysis of 2013 test scores by The Boston Foundation:** Ted McEnroe, *Taking Stock: Five Years of Structural Change in Boston's Public Schools* (Boston: The Boston Foundation, January 2014), http://www.bostonindicators.org/~/media/Files/ IndicatorsReports/Reports/Indicator%20Reports/Taking%20Stock.pdf.

326 **More than 1,000 schools in Los Angeles:** Los Angeles Unified School District (website; henceforth cited as LAUSD), "About the Los Angeles Unified School District," http://achieve.lausd.net/about; this includes 187 independent charter schools, as of 2017.

326 **Basic information about pilot schools:** Yana Gracile, "After Surge in LAUSD Autonomy Schools, Growth Has Slowed," *LA School Report*, August 5, 2014, http:// laschoolreport.com/after-early-surge-lausd-autonomy-school-growth-slowing/; and Office of Intensive Support & Intervention, "Los Angeles Pilot Schools Manual 2014–2015," LAUSD, June 2, 2014, http://pilotschools.lausd.net/LA%20Pilot%20Manual _2014-15_draft_6_2_14_TOC.pdf.

326   **Pilot schools considered the most flexible of charter-lite models in L.A.:** Gracile, "After Surge in LAUSD Autonomy Schools, Growth Has Slowed," *LA School Report.*

326   **In 2013, pilot schools gained an average of eight:** LAUSD, "LAUSD Ranks Near Top in 2013 API for Urban Districts in California," August 29, 2013, http://home.lausd.net/apps/news/article/323414.

326   **District schools averaged 60.27:** Craig Clough, "New Data Reveal Best and Worst of LAUSD Schools," *LA School Report,* Apr. 11, 2016, http://laschoolreport.com/new-data-reveal-best-and-worst-of-lausd-schools/. Average of pilot school scores computed from CORE data at http://coredistricts.org/indexreports/.

326–7 **Performance of Local Initiative and ESBMM schools:** Using CORE data from 2016, the average score for 17 Local Initiative schools was 58.38, and for ESBMM schools 55.33, both below the average of 60.27 for all district schools. Calculated from CORE data, http://coredistricts.org/indexreports/.

327   **Quote from one recent study comparing independent and in-district charters:** Hyo Jeong Shin, Bruce Fuller, and Luke Dauter, *Differing Effects from Diverse Charter Schools—Uneven Student Selection and Achievement Growth in Los Angeles* (Berkeley, CA: Institute of Human Development, University of California, December 2015), https://gse.berkeley.edu/sites/default/files/docs/FINAL%20Berkeley%20L.A.%20Charter%20Report%20-%20December%202015.pdf.

327   **Basic information about Mayor's Partnership for Los Angeles Schools:** Partnership for Los Angeles Schools (website), "Our Schools," http://partnershipla.org/Our_schools; Tom Vander Ark, "Partnership for LA Schools Making Progress," *Getting Smart,* January 7, 2014, http://gettingsmart.com/2014/01/partnership-la-schools-making-progress/; Partnership for Los Angeles Schools (website), "Parent College," July 21, 2016, http://partnershipla.org/Our_Approach/Parent_College.

327   **In 2013 Partnership schools gained an average of 21:** LAUSD, "LAUSD Ranks Near Top in 2013 API for Urban Districts in California."

327   **Graduation rates have more than doubled:** Partnership for Los Angeles Schools, "Graduation Rate for Partnership for LA Schools More Than Doubles to 77%," December 17, 2015, http://partnershipla.org/news/view/2015-12-graduation-rate-for-partnership-for-la-schools-more.

327–8 **Information on L.A.'s Promise schools:** LA's Promise (website), "LA's Promise," http://www.laspromise.org/assets/lap_presskit_1216.pdf.

328–9 **Information on reform in Philadelphia between 2002 and 2010:** Katrina E. Bulkley, Jolley Bruce Christman, and Eva Gold, "One Step Back, Two Steps Forward," in *Between Public and Private: Politics, Governance, and the New Portfolio Models for Urban School Reform,* ed. Katrina E. Bulkley, Jeffrey R. Henig, and Henry M. Levin (Cambridge, MA.: Harvard Education Press, 2010); and Brian Gill, Ron Zimmer, Jolley Christman, and Suzanne Blanc, *State Takeover, School Restructuring, Private Management, and Student Achievement in Philadelphia* (Santa Monica, CA: Rand Corporation, 2007).

329   **Numbers of different types of Philadelphia public schools in 2010–11:** Bulkley, Christman, and Gold, "One Step Back, Two Steps Forward."

329   **By 2015 there were 20 Renaissance Schools and 12 Promise Academies:** Paul Brennan, "Education Week-in-Review: Charter Schools Need More Space and More Freedom," *Watchdog.org,* May 29, 2015, http://watchdog.org/221697/week-review-charter/.

329   **Not surprisingly, Renaissance charters performed much better:** Tonya Wolford, Kati Stratos, and Adrienne Reitano, *Renaissance Schools Initiative Progress Report: 2010–2011 through 2012–2013* (Philadelphia: The School District of Philadelphia, December 2013), http://webgui.phila.k12.pa.us/uploads/TM/8_/TM8_61FkJvho5xIy LNSS9w/Renaissance_Report_Dec_2013.pdf.

329   **Independent charters performed even better:** According to CREDO, their students gained about 43 days of learning a year in both math and reading every year from 2006–07 through 2012–13, compared to demographically similar children in district schools with similar past test scores: Center for Research on Education Outcomes (henceforth cited as CREDO), "Urban Charter School Study: Report on 41 Regions, 2015" (Stanford, CA: Center for Research on Education Outcomes, 2015). **By their fourth year in a charter, the impact was almost three times greater:** CREDO, "Urban Charter Schools Impact in Pennsylvania" (Stanford, CA: Center for Research on Education Outcomes, March 2015), http://urbancharters.stanford.edu/states.php, slide 11.

329   **Charters receive only 60 percent of district school funding:** Rep. Mike Turzai, "SRC Must Expand Number of Phila. Charters Now," *Philadelphia Inquirer*, Feb. 3, 2015.

329   **It did a poor job of holding charters . . . financial irregularities:** Bulkley, Christman, and Gold, "One Step Back, Two Steps Forward."

329   **In 2016, with 32 percent of public school students in charters:** National Alliance for Public Charter Schools, *A Growing Movement: America's Largest Charter Public School Communities and Their Impact on Outcomes, Eleventh Annual Edition* (Washington, D.C.: National Alliance for Public Charter Schools, November 2016), http://www.publiccharters.org/wp-content/uploads/2016/11/CharterSchoolEnrollment ShareReport2016.pdf.

329   **the district finally released its first annual evaluation:** Wilford Shamlin III, "Charter School Evaluation Report Applauded," *Philadelphia Tribune*, April 26, 2016, http://www.phillytrib.com/news/charter-school-evaluation-report-applauded/article_2870 64cf-9552-5c7b-887b-f351c9d1afa8.html.

329–30 **William Hite's reorganization:** Solomon Leach, "Philly Schools Expand Learning Networks," *Philadelphia Inquirer and Daily News*, July 9, 2015, http://www.philly .com/philly/education/20150709_Philly_schools_expand_learning_networks.html.

330   **Background on Chicago reforms before 2010:** David Menefee-Libey, "Neoliberal School Reform in Chicago? Renaissance 2010, Portfolios of Schools, and Diverse Providers," in *Between Public and Private*, ed. Bulkley, Henig, and Levin.

331   **15 percent of students in charters:** National Alliance for Public Charter Schools, *A Growing Movement*, 2016.

331   **Then in late 2016, still in dire fiscal straits:** Mel Leonor, "Teachers Unions Ramp Up Recruitment Efforts at Charter Schools," *Politico*, February 13, 2017, http://www .politico.com/story/2017/02/teachers-unions-ramp-up-recruitment-efforts-at-charter -schools-234958.

331   **Performance of charter schools in Detroit:** CREDO, "Urban Charter School Study: Report on 41 Regions 2015."

331   **Michigan Governor Rick Snyder created . . . after three years:** Nelson Smith, *Redefining the School District in Michigan* (Washington, D.C.: Thomas B. Fordham Institute, October 2014).

331   **Former school principal pleaded guilty:** Matt Barnum, " 'A National Disgrace':
Explaining the Past, Present, and Future of Detroit Public Schools," *The74million.org*,
January 28, 2016, https://www.the74million.org/article/a-national-disgrace-explaining
-the-past-present-and-future-of-detroit-public-schools; and Corey Mitchell, "In
Michigan, a Move to Fix Detroit's Schools Muddied by Probe," *Education Week*, Nov.
4, 2015, http://www.edweek.org/ew/articles/2015/11/04/corruption-probe-muddies
-efforts-to-fix-detroits.html.

331   **Soon afterward, state legislative leaders:** Ryan Stanton, "EMU Terminates Involvement with EAA, Ends Agreement with Detroit Schools," *MLive*, February 5, 2016,
http://www.mlive.com/news/ann-arbor/index.ssf/2016/02/emu_decides_to_termi
nate_invol.html.

Index

A Note on the Author

David Osborne is the author or coauthor of five other nonfiction books: *Laboratories of Democracy*, *Reinventing Government* (a *New York Times* bestseller), *Banishing Bureaucracy*, *The Reinventor's Fieldbook*, and *The Price of Government*. He is also the author of a historical novel, *The Coming*, published in February 2017. Over the years his work has appeared in dozens of publications, including the *Atlantic*, the *New York Times Magazine*, the *Washington Post*, *Mother Jones*, *Harper's*, *U.S. News & World Report*, *Governing*, *Education Week*, and *Education Next*. In past decades he has served as an advisor or consultant to Vice President Al Gore, to help run the National Performance Review, as well as countless governors, mayors, city managers, superintendents, and foreign leaders. He is currently a senior fellow at the Progressive Policy Institute, where he directs a project on Reinventing America's Schools. He lives in Gloucester, Massachusetts.